I0821304

OUR INDIAN SUMMER
IN THE FAR WEST

THE CHARLES M. RUSSELL CENTER SERIES ON
ART AND PHOTOGRAPHY OF THE AMERICAN WEST
B. Byron Price, General Editor

Our Indian Summer

In the Far West

OUR INDIAN SUMMER IN THE FAR WEST

AN AUTUMN TOUR OF FIFTEEN THOUSAND MILES IN KANSAS, TEXAS, NEW MEXICO, COLORADO, AND THE INDIAN TERRITORY

BY S. NUGENT TOWNSHEND
("ST. KAMES" OF "THE FIELD")

ILLUSTRATED BY J. G. HYDE

Edited by Alex Hunt *and* Kristin Loyd

UNIVERSITY OF OKLAHOMA PRESS : NORMAN

This book is published with the generous assistance of the Nita Stewart Haley Memorial Library and J. Evetts Haley History Center, Midland, Texas, and the Wallace C. Thompson Endowment Fund, University of Oklahoma Foundation.

The following images appear uncaptioned on the pages noted:

Page ii: Cover from the original printing of Townshend and Hyde, *Our Indian Summer in the Far West*, 1880. The blue buckram is the most commonly found color, though bindings with reddish-brown and green colors exist as well.

Page 21: Title page from the original printing of Townshend and Hyde, *Our Indian Summer in the Far West*, 1880.

LIBRARY OF CONGRESS CATALOGING-IN-PUBLICATION DATA

Names: Townshend, S. Nugent (Samuel Nugent), 1844–1910. | Hyde, J. G. (John George) | Hunt, Alex. | Loyd, Kristin.

Title: Our Indian summer in the far West : an autumn tour of fifteen Thousand miles in Kansas, Texas, New Mexico, Colorado, and the Indian Territory/ by S. Nugent Townshend ("St. Karnes" of "The Field") ; illustrated by J. G. Hyde ; edited by Alex Hunt and Kristin Loyd.

Description: Norman : University of Oklahoma Press, 2016. | Originally published: London : Charles Whittingham, 1880. | Includes Bibliographical references and index.

Identifiers: LCCN 2015033014 | ISBN 978-0-8061-8702-0 (hardcover : alkaline paper)

Subjects: LCSH: Townshend, S. Nugent (Samuel Nugent), 1844–1910—Travel—West (U.S.) | Hyde, J. G. (John George)—Travel—West (U.S.) | British—Travel—West (U.S.)—History—19th century. | West (U.S.)—Description and travel.

Classification: LCC F594 .T75 2016 | DDC 917.804—dc23

LC record available at http://lccn.loc.gov/2015033014

Our Indian Summer in the Far West: An Autumn Tour of Fifteen Thousand Miles in Kansas, Texas, New Mexico, Colorado, and the Indian Territory is Volume 25 in The Charles M. Russell Center Series on Art and Photography of the American West.

The paper in this book meets the guidelines for permanence and durability of the Committee on Production Guidelines for Book Longevity of the Council on Library Resources, Inc. ∞

Copyright © 2016 by the University of Oklahoma Press, Norman, Publishing Division of the University. Manufactured in China.

All rights reserved. No part of this publication may be reproduced, stored in a retrieval system, or transmitted, in any form or by any means, electronic, mechanical, photocopying, recording, or otherwise—except as permitted under Section 107 or 108 of the United States Copyright Act—without the prior written permission of the University of Oklahoma Press. To request permission to reproduce selections from this book, write to Permissions, University of Oklahoma Press, 2800 Venture Drive, Norman, OK 73069, or email rights.oupress@ou.edu.

1 2 3 4 5 6 7 8 9 10

TO

John George Adair, ESQ.,

Rathdair, Monasterevin,

These pages and photographs we inscribe; a gentleman whose enterprise, extensive experience, intimate knowledge, and wise forethought have induced him, though already a large proprietor in Ireland, to become one of the most important landowners in the northern portion of the state of Texas.

CONTENTS

CONTENTS

ILLUSTRATIONS

FIGURES

MAP

ACKNOWLEDGMENTS

We were assisted by a great many individuals who shared their expertise and skill or who gave support. These include Bill Green, Amy Von Lintel, Bonnie Roos, Bill Hunt, B. Byron Price, and Bob Spude. At the Haley Library, whose original copy of Townshend and Hyde's book was crucial to our work, thanks go to Pat McDaniel, Glenna Gifford, Cathy Smith, and Nancy Jordan. Unless otherwise noted, all images from the original book that are reproduced in this volume are provided courtesy of the Haley Memorial Library and History Center, Midland, Texas. Of the many special collection and rare book librarians who answered queries and assisted with images, we are especially indebted to Sidnye Johnson from West Texas A&M University's Cornette Library, and Cindy Wallace at the Amarillo Public Library. Warren Stricker and Millie Vanover at the Panhandle-Plains Historical Museum Research Center were also crucial. We would also like to thank our supportive WTAMU administrators Stephen Severn, Jessica Mallard, and Wade Shaffer. Joe Bill Sherrod was also instrumental. Finally, not least, great thanks are due to the keen eyes and research skills of WTAMU students Aaron Howland, Hillarie Easley-McPherson, Maureen Hubbart, Dollie Lookingbill, and Dylan Atkins.

OUR INDIAN SUMMER
IN THE FAR WEST

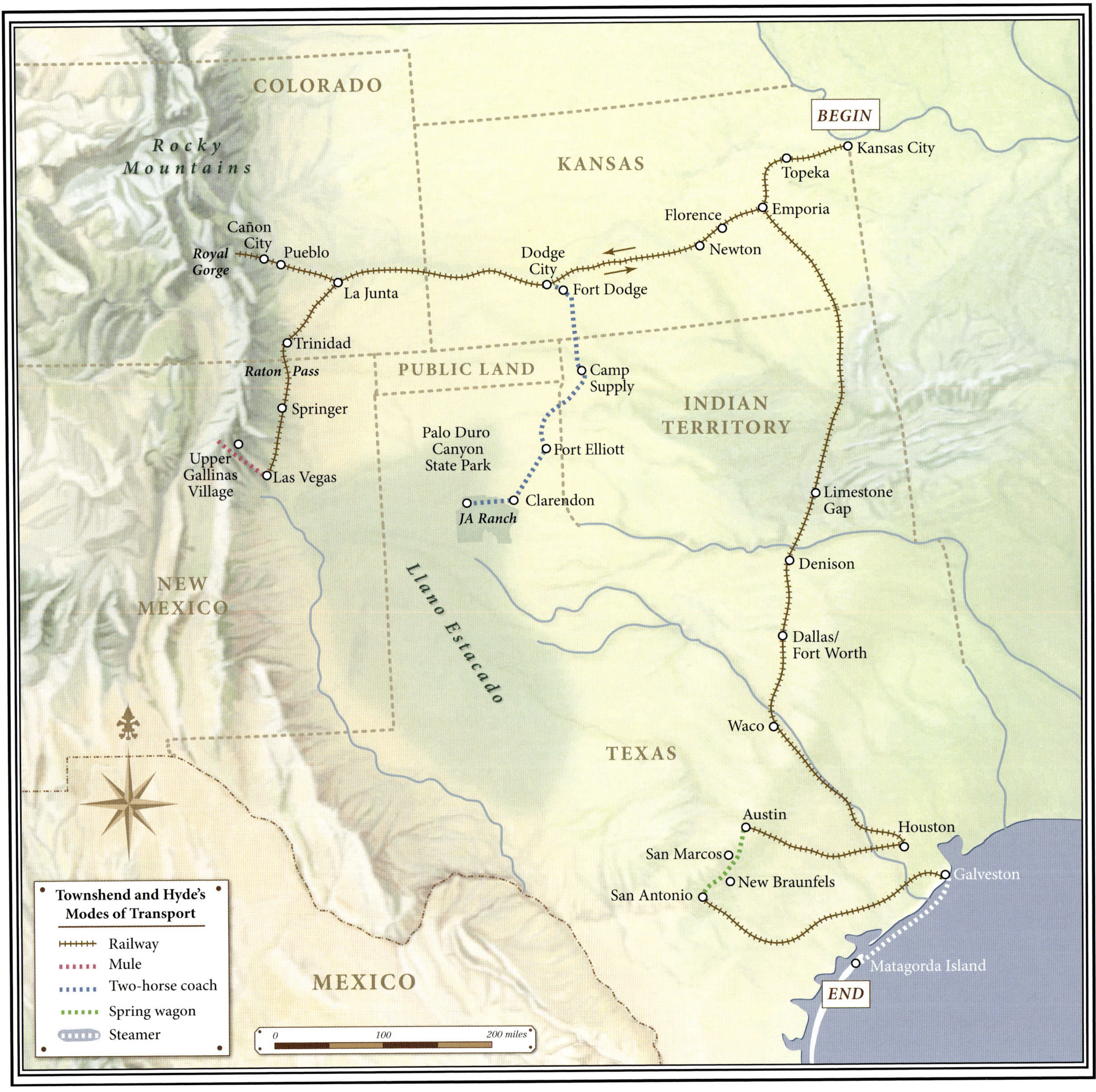

Samuel Nugent Townshend and John George Hyde's routes and modes of transport. Map by Gerry Krieg. Copyright © 2016 by the University of Oklahoma Press.

INTRODUCTION

British Empire and the American West

Alex Hunt

Samuel Nugent Townshend and John George Hyde were hardly intrepid explorers. By 1879, travel in the American West was more uncomfortable than dangerous, but indomitable Victorians that they were, the men faced such difficulties head on. Because it was almost impossible to find a hotel with a bath, they carried along from England a portable bathtub made of India rubber. Their possession of such a convenience, more than a minor colorful detail from the narrative, says much of their world, their place in it, and their approach to it. Rubber trees, native to South America, were a closely guarded commodity. Eventually, however, seeds smuggled out of Brazil were successfully planted at Kew Gardens in London and thence exported for commercial production to India and other British colonial holdings. The portable bathtub would have been a fairly new commodity in a complex world of international business by the time Townshend and Hyde carried it across the Atlantic to the dusty American West. Their possession of such a tub is testimony to the fact that they had the funds to spend, the will to make comfort a priority, and the confidence that there would always be a man to carry their bags.

Townshend and Hyde begin their adventure in London, where, bemoaning the English weather, they impulsively decide to seek a pleasant Indian summer on a tour of the American West in 1879. They take the midnight Pullman train to Liverpool, where they depart on *The Queen*, an American steamship of the National Line, which, after a stop at Queenstown (now Cobh, Northern Ireland), sails for New York City. After seeing sights and paying visits in the city, the pair departs for Niagara Falls for what had long been a standard aesthetic experience of the American tour. The train journey continues through Philadelphia, Pittsburgh, and Chicago to Kansas City. After crossing the Missouri River, they arrive in the "new state of Kansas," the beginning of the western lands and opportunities central to their interest. Their narrative slows as several chapters detail western Kansas farming operations. They proceed to Colorado, where they discuss further agricultural opportunities. In the Rocky Mountain region they pay more attention to scenery and sport, for they have brought their shotguns as well as the camera. From Colorado they turn south and cross the Raton Pass into New Mexico. After a bear hunt near Santa Fe, they turn eastward again, traveling back by train to Dodge City. From there they travel by stagecoach south into Oklahoma or "Indian Territory" and then into the Texas Panhandle, where they visit Fort Elliott and the JA Ranch. Here they meet the famed ranger and rancher Charles Goodnight on the vast holding bankrolled by Townshend's relative, the Irish financier John George Adair. From this remote country the only route to the "civilized" parts of Texas requires backtracking to Fort Dodge and continuing by train to Denison, Texas. The pair tours through Dallas and other Texas cities including San Antonio, where they find a prosperous community of English gentlemen. From San Antonio they proceed to Galveston

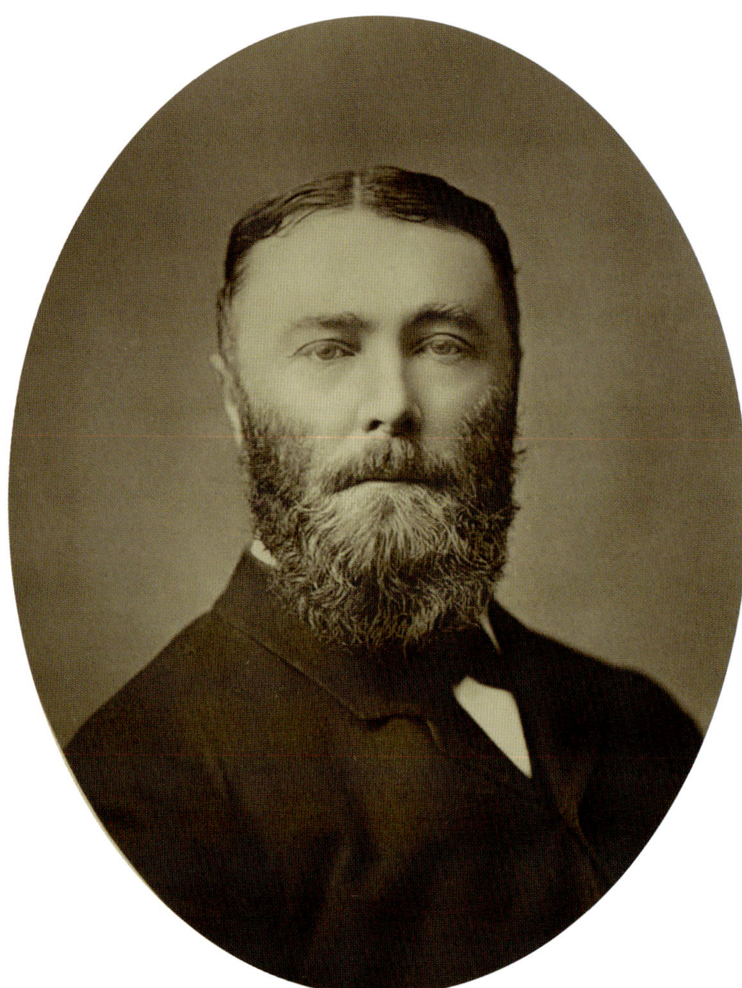

Samuel Nugent Townshend, membership photograph for the Royal Geographical Society, 1882. (Used with permission of the Royal Geographical Society, London, England)

to hunt fowl. They finally take trains back to New York and sail home on the steamer *City of Richmond*. While they are vague on the precise dates along the way of their Indian summer tour, the two depart Liverpool on September 24, 1879, and return to England in December; their book is under production at Chiswick Press quickly thereafter.

The published account of this trip, *Our Indian Summer in the Far West*, is an important and curious artifact. With a narrative of forty-seven thousand words written by Samuel Nugent Townshend, correspondent for the London periodical *The Field*, and sixty-two hand-mounted photographs taken by John George Hyde, the product is an amusing travelogue related in lively style. But its inclusion of facts and statistics relevant to western lands remind us that it is also an extended investment advertisement by men who were business associates as well as friends. Furthermore, the photographic documentation places the volume as one of very few books of photography depicting the American West at this early period. Thus, this example of what is termed a "photographic book"[1] provides us a revealing window into a transatlantic American West that merits our attention, for it is heretofore little known. The volume is exceedingly rare.[2] Published by Charles Whittingham/Chiswick Press of London in 1880, only 250 copies were produced.[3] Today, some thirty libraries hold a copy of *Our Indian Summer*. The British Library has no copy; the U.S. Library of Congress copy is lost.

The book's London publication in 1880 places it amid an active period of British investment in land and other enterprises in the American Great Plains and Mountain West. While a diverting narrative, its primary purpose was to encourage investment in farming, ranching, mining, and railroad-building in the West. Townshend states his goal is to make information available to would-be immigrants. That is, Townshend intends to provide information on the expense of establishing a farm in Kansas, for example, so that his readers could then pass on information to members of "the humbler classes," who "would naturally look for advice" to their social betters (40). Significantly, Townshend emphasizes the nature of their tour as relatively spontaneous and easy. The crossing is eleven days over and eight back, and train travel makes the great West available. The subtext is that an energetic Englishman, one perhaps looking in on his business arrangements, could make a rather quick trip of it.[4]

Other scholars have noted British investment in the American West, but few have closely examined the intersection between adventure and investment so well demonstrated by Townshend's text. Lee Olson's *Marmalade and Whiskey* (1993) includes a chapter on the British in Texas, including Adair and Alfred Rowe, and a discussion of the importance of British investment and Scottish financiers.[5] Robert Athearn's *Westward the Briton* (1953) describes the English in Colorado, drawing upon Townshend's book on that state (discussed later). Athearn reminds us that Colorado Springs was once familiarly known as "L'il Lunnon" for its colony of British.[6] Lawrence Woods's *British Gentlemen in the Wild West* (1989) demonstrates a remarkable affinity between the code of the Victorian gentleman and what we might recognize as the code of western masculinity and heroism.[7] Most recently, Peter Pagnamenta's *Prairie Fever* (2012) traces different phases of British adventuring and investing in the American West.

Much British capital preceded Townshend and Hyde into the American West, an economic trend that paused during the Civil War and was energetically renewed with postbellum railroad development and the new business of cattle driving. English investors put a great deal of capital into Iowa and then on to Kansas, where they created agricultural colonies at Runnymede and Victoria. The Earl of Dunraven infamously purchased Estes Park and what would eventually become Rocky Mountain National Park as a "private paradise."[8] British travel and investment was rampant throughout the prairie and mountain West. Though scholars have long documented this trend, the significance of British presence, influence, and capital seldom penetrates the powerful myth of the rugged individual frontiersman. That is, we Americans tend to favor the heroic cattleman, like Charles Goodnight, over the capitalist who bankrolled him, like John George Adair.

The present volume contributes a primary document to the historians of capitalism, for our travelers make their visit at a moment when transatlantic finance was big business and at a period in which British empire and investment were closely entwined. Townshend and Hyde document a scene of transition, what W. G. Kerr terms "the American credit frontier."[9] Vast territories became available for enclosure and privatization, and the "openings" of these western lands required capital for development. These transitions were great opportunities for those who possessed capital or could extend credit—greater opportunity, perhaps, for the venture capitalist than the yeoman farmer finding his homestead. The investment in railroad building was of course a primary aspect of this historical moment, transportation and shipping being crucial to land development and resource exploitation. Townshend is not merely noting his itinerary, therefore, when he reports what railway lines he travels. He is providing investors strategic information. Adair, we learn, had invested with William Henry Blackmore—a noted British financier and collector of western American ethnography—in railroads.

When Townshend and Hyde entered Kansas heading for Pueblo, Colorado, in the autumn of 1879, they rode on the Atchison, Topeka, and Santa Fe (ATSF) Railroad. They also rode into a significant period of expansion and competition in western railroad development. Western railroad history is complex, characterized by disputes and contention at every level, and full of figures, great and infamous, like Jay Gould and Collis P. Huntington. Federal and state subsidies and charters, along with capital raised through stocks and bonds, awarded by the federal government, funded the first transcontinental line, completed when the Union Pacific met the Central Pacific at Promontory Summit, Utah, in 1869.[10] The subsequent Panic of 1873, largely caused by the crash of overcapitalized railway companies, meant a major slowdown in railroad construction. However, the ATSF, financed mostly by Boston investors, was sustained during this difficult period by a combination of state subsidies and federal land grants, steady economic growth of the region through providing rail access to trail drivers bringing Texas cattle north to market, and new settlements of immigrant German-Russian wheat farmers in Kansas.[11]

The notorious Jay Gould, whom Townshend mentions

unfavorably, had a complex role in the story of the ATSF. When economic prosperity returned in the later 1870s and early 1880s, Gould sought to take advantage of the mania to build new transcontinental railroads and acquired control of the Missouri Pacific, the Texas Pacific, and the Denver and Rio Grande (DRG) Railroads, in direct competition with the ATSF. The DRG, organized in Denver in 1870, had slowly built south to Pueblo, Colorado, when it came into competition with the ATSF's plans to build west to tap the new mining boom camp of Leadville as well as south across Raton Pass into New Mexico.[12] When Townshend and Hyde passed through Colorado, in October 1879, the two railroad companies were locked in an armed confrontation in the Royal Gorge of the Arkansas River, where narrow canyon walls dictated that only one rail line could be built west toward Leadville. The ATSF averted a railroad war when it acquired a favorable lease of the DRG in 1879, only to have the stock manipulator Jay Gould step in with a sweeter deal, and, as Townshend points out, acquire the DRG outright (a later Supreme Court decision gave the line to the DRG). Townshend's comments, casting Gould as unscrupulous villain, reveal that Adair had invested in the DRG but had sold his shares during Gould's maneuverings and legal battles.

Townshend casts no aspersions on the ATSF, which gave Townshend and Hyde preferential treatment, including their own sight-seeing train to carry them through the Royal Gorge and back. The ATSF also won the battle for Raton Pass, beating the DRG track layers, and in 1879–80 was busily laying track south, a line followed by our travelers. Townshend later wrote promotional literature for the line, which completed the second transcontinental railroad when it joined the Southern Pacific at Deming, New Mexico, in 1881. Remaining independent and strong, the ATSF continued to expand in the West and completed its own transcontinental line between Chicago and the Pacific Coast at San Francisco and Los Angeles by 1888.[13] Gould's transcontinental dreams were completed by his son George, who early in the twentieth century completed a Saint Louis to San Francisco transcontinental route via the Gould system—the Missouri Pacific, which went from Saint Louis to a link with Denver and Rio Grande at Pueblo, Colorado, then to Salt Lake City via the DRG, and finally via Western Pacific from Utah to the San Francisco Bay.

Still, Townshend and John George Adair seem more interested in investment in agriculture and ranching than in railroads, and it was ranching that particularly excited the interests of the British investor class at this moment. A number of British periodicals published articles that extolled ranching investment opportunities out west, including *Lippincott's*, the *Fortnightly Review*, and not least, Townshend's employer, a leading sporting magazine for British gentlemen, *The Field*. Townshend began writing for *The Field* in 1876, the year before Adair and Goodnight forged their partnership, so he was early on the case. In fact, his writings preceded most of the other magazine stories that endorsed British investment. W. B. Grohman's "Cattle Ranches in the Far West," published in 1880 in the *Fortnightly Review*, cites the British Royal Commission with which Townshend was associated but favors more northern and northwestern climes to Texas.[14] In an 1882 article George Rex Buckman credits the English for popularizing western cattle business for Americans:

> It was the English who first sought out the new land, and Americans learned of cattle-raising on the Colorado plains through correspondence in magazines and newspapers from across the water. Then began the exodus of young collegians and professional men from the overcrowded East; and, as a consequence, the new West is largely peopled to-day with the sons of families in which learning and culture have long been hereditary.[15]

Buckman's claim goes to a ridiculous extreme, but it illustrates the degree of enthusiasm that some British felt toward the American West and cattle business.

Townshend and Hyde's book devotes the most time to Kansas and Texas, with somewhat less emphasis on Colorado and New Mexico. Townshend was familiar with Kansas from earlier trips and provides a great deal of information about prices for land and agricultural expenses and profits. As for Colorado, perhaps because he had already produced a book on agriculture and other prospects of that state, he chiefly discusses railroads, mining, and sport. New Mexico, too, a brief foray, is primarily devoted to a sporting adventure, with some mention of mining prospects. Description of Texas comprises the greatest attention in the book, and in many ways it is the panhandle of Texas that seems a target of the narrative.

Notably, Townshend and Hyde dedicate their book to the Scots-Irish financier John George Adair, recognized as a leading western ranch investor and partner of Charles Goodnight in the JA Ranch of Texas. In addition to paying homage to Adair's savvy investment in the American West, both currying favor and capitalizing on his reputation, Townshend here acknowledges a family relation: Townshend is a distant cousin to Adair's mother, Elizabeth Trench.[16] In 1879 the travelers paid a visit to the JA Ranch, where they met Charles Goodnight and praised Adair's perspicacity.

John George Adair is generally credited as prescient in his investment in Texas land and cattle, and, indeed, his profitable partnership with Charles Goodnight led a rush of British investment in Texas and the West. Peter Pagnamenta calls Adair "the inspiration for many Britons" and the individual "who showed them what was possible."[17] The Adairs' friends and associates, all well-connected, spread investor interest in western cattle ranching. One noteworthy individual, who accompanied the Adairs to the JA Ranch in 1878, was Englishman Morten Frewen, who was inspired to imitate Adair's efforts in Wyoming.[18] In 1882, a big year, Henry Grierson of the Capitol Land and Cattle Company, which would finance the Chicago-based XIT, returned to London to report, "I fully endorse the generally received opinion among cattle owners that the Panhandle is geographically the best situation in America for cattle raising." He predicted vast profits.[19] The XIT was subsequently bankrolled by the British syndicate from 1885 to 1909. Townshend and Hyde's book was part of this encouragement and advertisement. And its enticing photographs, as John Miller Morris has suggested, brought further British investment and sped regional development of the Texas Panhandle.[20] The Texas Panhandle then became the primary focus of Townshend's narrative both because of the relationship between Townshend and Adair and because this region was the "rawest" of the frontier, only lately opened. At Fort Elliott and the JA Ranch, the men found themselves at the furthest remove from their world of verdant English estates and the cosmopolitan capital of London. The region captured the imagination of both the writer and the photographer.

Here, too, Townshend and Hyde are preceded by a great many of their countrymen. In fact the Texas Panhandle has a colorful history of British adventurers and financiers. Among the earliest was Walter James "Frank" Collinson. Collinson came from Yorkshire, England, and landed in Galveston, Texas, in 1872. From 1874 to 1877, Collinson was hunting buffalo in the Texas Panhandle. He subsequently cowboyed and ranched in New Mexico and the Big Bend country of Texas, later lived for years in Clarendon in the panhandle, and died in El Paso in 1943. A noteworthy writer, Collinson authored numerous magazine articles based on his frontier life. An edited collection of these writings, *Life in the Saddle*, is a classic of western Americana. Also early in the panhandle were the Cator brothers. James Hamilton Cator and Arthur J. L. "Bob" Cator came to the United States from England in 1871. They came to Kansas to farm but soon turned toward commercial buffalo hunting. They moved to Texas in 1873 and camped along the North Palo Duro Creek. After the buffalo were hunted out, they tried their hand at ranching and started a store, naming it Zulu Stockade because they found it "as wild as the Zululand region of Africa"—a place they had no experience of save through periodicals and letters from England. Like Collinson, the Cators stayed on in the West, bringing family and wives from England, and are credited as founders of Hartley County.[21] By some reckonings they stand as the earliest settlers of the panhandle.

Other British contributors to panhandle history were more in the vein of John George and Cornelia Adair, who invested in ranches or were involved in thier management. Charles Goodnight assisted Alfred Rowe in establishing the RO Ranch. Rowe's greatest claim to fame is not his ranching but his death on the *Titanic*'s fateful voyage. Scotsman Murdo Mackenzie came as a manager for the Prairie Cattle Company to Trinidad, Colorado, before becoming head in 1890 of the Matador Ranch in Texas, which had been purchased by Scots investors. Montague K. Brown came from London to manage the White Deer Land Company in 1903, leaving a significant impact on the community of Pampa, Texas. Brown became a U.S. citizen and a business leader and developer. Overall, in 1885, some two-thirds of Texas Panhandle ranches, including the XIT, JA, Rocking Chair, RO, LX, Spur, and T-Anchor, were owned or controlled, founded or incorporated by U.K. (English and Scots) investment companies. It is difficult to offer exact figures, but over a three-year period, ending in 1882, $15.5 million of English and Scottish capital were invested, or—conservatively—$364 million today.[22] From 1875 to 1900, English and Scottish investors put $34 million into western American ranching, perhaps $900 million today.[23] Many syndicates involved members of the aristocracy who were featured prominently on boards of directors. On the scene, British adventurers were typically second sons, remittance men, sent to the American West to broaden family investment but also to be, one hoped, gainfully engaged in business in healthy western climes. Townshend and Hyde's 1880 book must be credited as influential in this British interest in the Texas Panhandle in particular.

Samuel Nugent Townshend, Esq., J.P. (1844–1910), was not a remittance man, nor did he seem to have ambitions to found or manage a ranch. But he was keen about western American investment and himself invested in land around Topeka, Kansas, which he listed as one of his domiciles. Townshend was landed gentry, a member of the peerage, an Irish landlord, and justice of the peace appointed in 1867. Educated at Queen's University in Belfast, he inherited his family's farms in county Cork, Saint Kames Island, Skibbereen.[24] He also owned land in several other parishes in Cork. Like a great many Irish landlords, Townshend preferred to be absent, seemingly put off by the tiresome troubles of the Irish, and in the 1890s had addresses in Kew and London.[25] His distaste of the Irish question is evident from Townshend's letters to the editor of the *Times.* One published on May 22, 1882, discusses the difficulty of gaining arrears from tenant farmers. He concludes, in part, "Personally, so much of my income is now derived from abroad that I do not care much what becomes of my little Irish property. If it were to be sacrificed to patriotism, I should not regret it; but few of us in Ireland, however, think that there is any patriotism involved; rather do we suspect that our interests are being sacrificed to ill-disguised Communism." Another published on April 27, 1897, defends the Royal Irish Constabulary as a sort of paramilitary police that should serve as a model for other colonial holdings.

While Townshend might have pursued business opportunities in India, Australia, Africa, or any number of British colonies, he clearly developed a taste for the United States. This developed to some degree by happenstance, as opportunity followed inclination. In his own words, from his book *Colorado*, Townshend describes his involvement with the West:

> Having spent the summer of 1876 at the Centennial Exhibition, Philadelphia, I accepted an official invitation to become a member of an international press party to visit the Western States of North America, dipping far out of the regular route into the Ex-Confederate States, so as to see the best parts of the reclaimed, but only partially settled lands of that region. . . . We all pursued slightly different objects, mine being agriculture, stock-feeding, scenery, and shooting.[26]

His official purpose as appointee of the British Commission to this international delegation was to investigate and publicize western American agricultural prospects.[27] Fulfilling this charge, Townshend took up the pen, writing under the nom de plume "St. Kames" as correspondent for *The Field* magazine.

Writing the "Notes from America" column of *The Field*'s "Travel and Colonization" pages between 1878 and 1881 gave Townshend opportunity to range widely in subjects like hunting and mining. As St. Kames, Townshend writes colorfully of the United States in a manner to be appreciated by his audience. In describing the railroad up La Veta Pass in Colorado, he remarks that "an English engineer would be knighted for half the achievement. 9310 feet of altitude is reached at the Divide station; 4500 feet is ascended in a run of fourteen miles. The enterprise is largely English."[28] Traveling through central Texas in summer of 1878, he comments, along the bank of the Nueces,

> I have heard this part of Texas compared to Ireland. Well, if all the Irish furze bushes were Acacia algarobia or mesquite, if the Irish hedge brier were a thornless white-flowering vine, if the Irish bogrush clumps were cactus, if the Irish thermometer were pushed up thirty degrees permanently, and all the Fenians were transformed into mosquitoes, with the leaders or head-centres rattlesnakes, then Ireland would indeed be very like South-Western Texas; but until such changes are effected the parallel between the countries fails totally to strike the perhaps obtuse.[29]

It is difficult to be sure whether Townshend here prefers Texas to Ireland, but his position on Fenians is unambiguous.

A number of citations to Townshend's work in Reginald Aldridge's *Life on a Ranch*, published in London in 1884, shows direct evidence of Townshend's influence. In 1877 Aldridge, describing himself as unemployed and without prospects during a time of depression, came across Townshend's work: "There had been during that year several letters in the 'Field,' from a correspondent signing himself 'St. Kames,' written from Kansas and Colorado, in the United States of America. The letters, I thought, presented a decidedly favourable view of those regions, and I finally made up my mind to go over there."[30] Aldridge wound up involved in cattle and land business in Kansas, Colorado, and into the Texas Panhandle. In concluding his short book, he provides encouragement to his countrymen and expresses satisfaction at following St. Kames's path.

Townshend's columns provided the material for his other books. First was *Colorado: Its Agriculture, Stockfeeding, Scenery, and Shooting*, published by *The Field* in London and New York in 1879. At the same time, Townshend published letters to London newspapers including the *Times* and the *Economist* on the subject of American agricultural and land investment. In 1881, Townshend published his third book, more a pamphlet, exhaustively titled *The New Southern Route from San Francisco, through Southern California, Arizona, New Mexico, Colorado and Kansas to New York and the Atlantic Seaboard, through St. Louis, Chicago, or Canada*, which was further described on its title page as "written specially for Australian and New Zealand Travel." This pamphlet was, like *Colorado*, drawn largely from Townshend's articles in *The Field* and its Chicago publication seems to have been bankrolled by the railroad company to market travel to British settlers of the South Pacific interested in American tourism.

Keeping a London address, Townshend was well-known in the Southsea yachting community as a member of the Royal Yacht Squadron and the Royal Albert Yacht Club and led an active social life. His 1882 membership form for the Royal Geographical Society (RGS) lists addresses in London, Cork, and Topeka, Kansas. (The RGS Reading Room holds a copy of *Our Indian Summer* inscribed, "To the Royal Geographical Society from the author, May 28 1883."[31]) Townshend's American experience led to further business opportunities, many unsuccessful, including, for example, an advertisement in the *Times* of March 28, 1885, for "Raymond's American Excursions," offering a fifty-nine-day tour through the American West by "S. Nugent Townshend, English Agent for the Atchison, Topeka and Santa Fe Railroad, and European Agent for Raymond's American Excursions" of London. Other notices, in these cases bankruptcies listing Townshend as chairman or board member, include the Josz Metallochrome Printing Company Limited (1891), the New Australian Goldfields Limited (1894), and Jersey Lily Gold Mines Limited of Arizona (1899).[32] These are evidence of Townshend's ambition and his connections in international business, however unsuccessful.

John George Hyde (1838–1902) kept a lower profile in London. A member of the London Stock Exchange at least from 1874 to 1892, Hyde was a descendent of a family much connected with the East India Company, a monopoly disbanded in 1874. In his role as broker, Hyde was connected with businesses including the Universal Telegram Company of London,[33] the North British Water-Gas

Syndicate,[34] and Zout Kom Nitrates Incorporated of Cape Town, South Africa.[35] Interestingly, years after his American tour, Hyde pursued several opportunities involving Townshend. In the American Stove and Furnace Company of Boston, brokered by Hyde and Sons, Townshend is listed as a member of the board of directors.[36] And Townshend is listed as manager of the English branch of the Equitable Mortgage Company of New York, also brokered by Hyde and Sons.[37]

As a member of the Amateur Photographic Association (APA) (1861–1905), Hyde clearly had a passion for photography. Several of his photos, pastoral scenes of Hever Castle in Kent and of the ruins of Sherkin Abbey on an island off Cork, can be found in the group's yearbook albums of the late 1860s. One, "Cottage Near Cookham," featuring a woman walking on the lawn between a lake and a picturesque cottage, apparently won an APA prize in 1869.[38] The APA, founded in 1861, was an upper-class affair oriented toward the aesthetic appreciation of photographs rather than technical matters. However, to be an amateur photographer at this period meant far more involvement than the term implies for our own era, including chemical and darkroom skills—in other words, an amateur was often a skilled and committed practitioner having the developed sensibilities of a connoisseur.[39]

According to correspondence in the Chiswick Press papers at the British Library, it was Hyde who financed publication of *Our Indian Summer* and saw it through the printing process. The fine volume was printed by Chiswick Press, Charles Whittingham, publisher, a firm of long and distinguished standing. Founded by Charles Whittingham in 1811, Chiswick was first known for producing affordable book editions. When the press was later headed by Whittingham's nephew, also named Charles Whittingham, Chiswick entered into many contracts with William Pickering and so became known for producing high-quality literary editions including Shakespeare's plays. Whittingham the younger died in 1874, but the press continued under the Chiswick imprint until 1960.[40] As a contract print job, Townshend and Hyde's book was a distinguished, beautifully produced volume.

The book is bound in blue-colored modern buckram, string bound, and embossed in gold decoration and lettering. The cover has an ornate framing design, gold and black, with a leaf motif at the corners. Between the titles "Our Indian Summer" and "In The Far West," all in gold, is a detailed image of a camping scene, a tent pitched among trees against a cloudy sky and a body of water with a canoe floating in the background. Rifles stand against the trunk of a tree, a pot boils over the fire, and, significantly, a box camera on a tripod stands ready to record the scene (see *frontis*, this volume). The book's pages are gilded, and on the inside title page the main title and place of publication appear in red ink. The title page includes a floral motif that is echoed in the design of the decorative initial beginning each chapter. Hyde's photographs, albumen prints, are mounted, glued or "tipped" in by hand, throughout the book and primarily at the beginning and ends of chapters, on heavier stock paper with ornate intaglio printed borders and captions. The book is quarto size, while the photographic prints are approximately four by six inches.

On February 24, 1880, less than two months after their return, Hyde received an estimate from Chiswick Press for the book's publication. The estimate for what was then titled "American Tour" specifies 250 copies. By June 19, Chiswick had done its work and thanked Hyde for payment received, in the amount of £80.6.6., a bit more than £6,500 today. The books were packaged and sent to Teddington, presumably where the photographic mounting and binding was completed. Of this lengthy and expensive process, presumably more costly than the book printing itself, no record remains. Interestingly, some number of books includes J. G. Hyde in the place of the first author as well as illustrator, both on the book's spine and its title page. These copies are correspondingly rare. Hyde probably wished to represent himself more prominently on books that he intended to give to friends or potential investors he particularly wished to impress.[41] Many of the existing volumes include inscriptions, some to recognizably prominent members of the British aristocracy, including Lady Beecher.[42] While no record of the volume's distribution could be located, it seems likely that some of the copies were presented and others sold by subscription.[43]

While the production quality of *Our Indian Summer* sets it apart from other British travel writing, it nevertheless participates in this tradition that has become a significant field of literary study. Simply surveying travel narratives of the United States by British Victorians is daunting. Many adventurers out west wrote narratives, including Robert Louis Stevenson, who rode the rails to California in 1879 and published *Across the Plains* in 1895. One noteworthy author and distinguished personage, Col. Frederick Trench Townshend, was Samuel Nugent's fourth cousin.[44] Between military posts, Trench Townshend wrote two books of American travels. In *Ten Thousand Miles of Travel, Sport, and Adventure*, published in 1869, the colonel described his journey from the East Coast to California, punctuated with adventurous buffalo hunts on the plains, and then his return home via the Panama Isthmus. Isabella Bird published *A Lady's Life in the Rocky Mountains* in 1879. Based on letters written to her sister in Scotland, it has remained a classic work of British western Americana. T. S. Hudson's *A Scamper through America; or, 15,000 Miles of Ocean and Continent* was published in 1882. This narrative took journal form and detailed local color in exciting fashion, including outlaws of the Southwest. While not all such narratives demonstrate Townshend's eye for business investment and immigration opportunity, they otherwise share many predictable traits with Townshend's narrative: descriptions of western landscapes, interests in what might loosely be called ethnography, relations of adventurous hunts and explorations, discussions of class relations, and numerous observations on the absence of the many conveniences of British life and domestic travel.

Townshend's narrative, particularly at the outset, has a sophomoric quality of British school boys on a lark—though Townshend was thirty-five and Hyde forty-one at the time of their trip. For example, the voyage from England to New York is entirely silly, as a clique of travelers form "The Moonlight Club" and enjoy citizenship in "The Antient [*sic*] and Honourable Society of Whisky Corks." American girls provide flirtatious fun and "intimate friendship" (25). Upon arrival Townshend complains of U.S. customs that "we were informed that we were being made test cases of, but what the nature of the test was, except perhaps to test our tempers, we could not discover" (29). The use of first-person plural throughout the narrative enhances this clubby quality.

Yet as their journey began in earnest, particularly when the travelers got as far as Kansas, in the third chapter, the pace slows and the tone becomes more serious. Here, Townshend announces, "sport, and to study the progress of the settler out West, were now our only objects" (39). At this point Townshend, apologizing for a tiresome turn, provides information such as the expenses required for an immigrant to purchase land in Kansas, including materials for building, seed, and equipment. He also repeats, in some detail, the "rain follows the plow" thesis, a commonly believed idea at this time, which posited that plowing up land for farming would change the atmospheric conditions and produce more rainfall. It is difficult to quantify the significance of British investment in the United States during this period, but it was vast. In particular, investment in land and railroads meant big money that was driving American development west. Townshend and Hyde's book shows us a particular example of how this phenomenon worked, and what ideas motivated it.

At this time American Anglophilia at the glory of Victorian achievement competed with nativist and Anglophobic legislation aimed at limiting foreign control of U.S. land in the West. The "second colonization of America"[45] by the British beginning in the late 1870s incited fears among Americans not only because they felt threatened by foreign ownership of vast quantities of land but also out of fears that British gentry were importing their practices of tenant farming from Ireland.[46] Such fear escalated after an 1884 federal Land Office study concluded, in exaggerated and inaccurate fashion, that foreign nobility owned twenty-one million acres of U.S. land. Many attempts at legislation that would limit such ownership met with no real success, and difficult economic turns eventually made such laws beside the point.[47] At the same time, however, Americans, then as now, demonstrated a fascination with British nobility.

British feelings about Americans were similarly ambivalent. British aristocracy had long frowned upon Americans as political and social upstarts, and British travelers complained routinely about the lack of "deference" for those of social standing.[48] However, great travelers and adventurers that they were, the English loved to experience the American West and clearly saw it increasingly less as a playground and more a place of economic opportunity. Townshend—in full awareness of his British aristocratic audience—describes the American movement of Manifest Destiny as yet another chapter of British Empire:

> The words "United States" have a very mixed meaning to most untravelled Englishmen. The name to most of us means an immense friendly Power—a Power sprung from ourselves and of which we are proud; a Power which, when it fully fills up and develops the American continent, will assuredly take up the spread of civilization, and of the Anglo-Saxon race, at perhaps the point where our senility as an empire may force us to leave off, and consign to the offspring of England the perfection of the glorious task—the emancipation of the world from thralldom and tyranny—laboured for by its parent for many a century, and carried out regardless of either blood or treasure. (40)

While many Americans would have bridled at such a claim, Townshend's vision lends both a nationalistic and a moral justification to British investment, which here takes on dimensions of "the work" of British colonization, which is never just profit but motivated by "an idea at the back of it" as Joseph Conrad famously wrote.[49] To the late Victorian, the justification of British power in the world was that it enlightened, liberated, and civilized those dark places on the map. While the Texas Panhandle in 1875 was quite different from South Africa, these were linked in the imaginations of men like the Cators, who named the "Zulu Stockade," and Townshend. Nor was this only a British perspective. Americans of a certain class, and with certain visions of national destiny, welcomed such comparisons with the British.

In thinking of such implicit kinships and shared imperialist ideology, we might usefully remember a relationship between two writers, one British, one American—Rudyard Kipling and Owen Wister. Kipling was known as the British chronicler of the empire, writing *Kim* and *The Jungle Book*, championing the beneficent power of British civilization. Wister admired Kipling, and the two later became friends. But, earlier on, when Owen Wister sat down to write *The Virginian*, the novel that would prove to be the seminal literary Western, he said that it was his goal to become the American Kipling, to write of the American West as Kipling wrote of India.[50] And there are parallels in their thinking about imperialism within their writings. Kipling published a poem in *McClure's Magazine* in 1899 called "The White Man's Burden: The United States and the Philippine Islands," in which he enjoined Americans to fulfill their responsibility to colonize and civilize the savage parts of the globe. The American, writes Kipling, in implicit agreement with Townshend, must grow up and accept his place, alongside the British, in exercising the duty of the white race to civilize the rest.[51]

In Wister's essay "The Evolution of the Cow-Puncher," published in 1895, he traces some similar ideas. He describes two men sitting opposite one another engaged in mutual contempt. One is a British peer, a wealthy member of the aristocracy. The other is a wealthy American on tour in England, but one whose "trans-Missouri" roots are evident, a western American made good, not far removed from his frontier formation. Wister describes them as dog and cat in their instinctive antipathy. Yet, he maintains, both are Anglo-Saxons, and just as the frontiersman can advance himself to wealth and social standing, so could the English peer mount a horse and quickly relearn cruder ways. In short, argues Wister, these men are of the same blood but rest at different points of social evolution.[52] This parable opens the way for Wister's white supremacist screed in which he maintains that Anglo-Saxons are solely responsible for the greatness of America, a situation he finds still evident in the cattle country of the American West, where the cowboy is the latest manifestation of the conquering Anglo, the knight of Camelot. This, indeed, is the racial and racist theory that underlies much of his great novel, *The Virginian*, published seven years later and much praised by his friend Teddy Roosevelt.

Ideas of power, race, and destiny shared by Kipling and Wister characterize a transatlantic late-Victorian cultural attitude prefigured in Townshend and Hyde's efforts. In short, Townshend's writing evinces particular ideas of race and power that link British and American identities and interests in the late nineteenth century. So too did the activities of John George Adair, who in an infamous episode evicted his tenant farmers in order to build a better hunting park on his land in Donegal, Ireland, before marrying an American heiress and traveling west to form a great cattle ranch in Texas. Although America was no longer a British colony, to the British aristocracy America, and particularly the emergent American West, was a landscape of grand financial adventure, an economic frontier.

Townshend's thoughts on colonialism and race, particularly on the treatment of indigenous peoples and racial mixing, are distasteful to the contemporary reader but, again, are instructive in understanding Victorian colonial attitudes, attitudes often shared by both British and Euro-American commentators during this era. Despite traveling through places of significant Native American history and presence, Townshend has not much to say apart from a disquisition on British Canadian versus American Indian policy. Even in Indian Territory (which would be consolidated with Oklahoma in 1907), he never reports seeing an indigenous person. In chapter 11, nevertheless, he asserts that American Indian policy, while seemingly more liberal in its granting of sovereign rights, actually does Indians a disservice because treaty rights are continually disregarded after the fact. British Canadian policy, conversely, while seeming harsh, ultimately serves Indians by making no false promises regarding indigenous rights. After all, "savages, according to modern practice, really have no rights, whether guaranteed by treaty, or otherwise, which civilized Powers respect." In the end, "the rule of an autocratic empire best suits the savage or semi-savage all the world over." In an era that saw much debate as to the cultural or evolutionary fate of Native Americans, Townshend's position has some nuance as he declares U.S. Indian policy to blame for indigenous decline: "The red man must eventually disappear off the face of the United States, before a civilization that is too liberal to coerce him into its ways, yet too illiberal to permit him to live in any other."

Townshend's brief portrayal of Hispanic people in New Mexico is far more descriptive than his policy-level discussion of American Indians, yet, if possible, far more racist and dismissive. In addition to providing a hundred lines of a satirical racist poem written by an unnamed U.S. Army officer, Townshend offers his own assessment of this people. He does spare a kind word for "the one redeeming feature of the Mexican race, its girl, who becomes often a faithful, good wife, and *always* an excellent mother" (79). Otherwise, he views "Mexicans" as immoral, lazy, and in general a people retrogressive to the development of civilization. Implicit though discernible in Townshend's treatment are a nationalistic contempt for a history of Spanish colonialism and a British blueblood distaste for racial mixing.

If Townshend's sense of the progress of civilization is from a contemporary standpoint hopelessly racist, in other ways *Our Indian Summer* demonstrates a late nineteenth-century sense of onrushing modernity and technological progress more familiar to us. If steamships and railroads are of primary importance here, so too is the changing technology of photography. Consideration of Hyde's photographs within the book opens up other insights and dimensions of inquiry. The narrative reports that the men carry "Wratten and Wainwright's instantaneous plates" (24). Of these they must be conservative, as it is not possible yet to obtain these plates in the United States (40). Townshend and Hyde make a bold claim in the narrative: "This instantaneous photography is a beautiful and wonderful thing, and we present to our readers—we believe, for the first time—a photograph of the actual performance of a ship in a gale of wind, everything of this sort we have before seen being merely a photograph of a painting, and much more striking and effective than truthfully real" (28). The desire for instantaneity among photographers, both professional and amateur, was acute at the time, making this claim an important aspect of the book's appeal.

Hyde's equipment was a dry-plate negative technology using instantaneous film. The glass plates were carried along "securely packed with felt round their cases, and then put into a large tin box" for the journey (24). Townshend, after all not the photographer, does not relate much of the photographic work but does make mention of one occasion: "From here we faced the clear-sighted little camera—the *lens* of which had gazed unmoved upon so many beautiful scenes in the Holy Land—toward Fisher's Peak, and taking off his veil gave him a three seconds' glimpse of it—about three times as long as we generally permitted him to stare with his big eye at anything or anyone" (83). The hint that Hyde had traveled to the Holy Land to take photographs is intriguing, and we get a sense of exposure times. Such plates, just invented, would have been a great deal easier to transport and use under difficult circumstances of travel. Along the way, in convenient places, Townshend and Hyde produced negatives from their film, and the description is helpful for understanding the technology. Here, they find a convenient refuge on Raton Pass:

> As evening began to approach it became necessary to develop the last six plates we had taken in Colorado, and put new ones in the slides ready for New Mexico the next day, so to a dug-out we repaired, and as this residence had no window, it appeared only necessary to hang our rugs and coats inside the door, and across the hearth, to ensure perfect darkness. But once shut in, various pencil-rays of light appeared through cracks in the mud walls, and the nautical expression "caulking" is the only way to describe our efforts to cure these defects in our required dark-room. At last, a newspaper here, a cushion there, our portable bath in another place, and planks stood on end everywhere, rendered our laboratory perfect. Miners' gunpowder-cans contained all the water we wanted, and the expiration of two hours and a half saw our six plates turned out beauties; ready for printing. This time would appear great to professionals; but in an extempore dark-room, a miner's hovel where water has to be fetched from a distant well, and one tumbles from time to time over picks and boots, dishes, and powder-cans—everything general disposed to go wrong—and one has to not only develop six plates , but open the plate boxes, and put six new ones into the slide-cases, the time consumed here was not greater than that occupied in most other camping-places. Our first picture in Northern New Mexico, Otero Station, with the special train on which we travelled, and of Mr. Moore, the paymaster of the line, shows that no light got at our plates before use, as the little shop's inscription, "Tienda Mas Barata de Otero"—"The store of most cheapness in Otero"—can easily be read in this picture. (83)

One can understand from Townshend's comments that not only the developing work but also the loading and unloading of the camera must be accomplished in a darkroom. Moreover, the use of the word "laboratory" emphasizes the technical skill still necessary for producing quality photographs in the field. While much less onerous than the wet-plate technology that preceded their dry plates, it is important to understand that we are yet a long way from the snapshot capabilities of the Kodak.

The Chiswick Press produced frames and captions for Hyde's photos, which were elsewhere individually printed and glued in. The photographs in the book are albumen prints. This term refers to the process by which photographic negatives can be transferred from the negative on the plate and chemically affixed to paper, thus becoming commercially available, such as in book publication. In the end, contact prints would have been made from these plates via direct exposure to sunlight.[53] As Martha Sandweiss has noted of using such images in books, this was an arduous and time-consuming process, each print taking as much as half an hour—not including the time and labor of actually mounting over fifteen thousand prints.[54] Townshend and Hyde's book is therefore noteworthy as an artistic and historical rarity, for as Sandweiss notes, "few photographically illustrated books about the trans-Mississippi West appeared in the nineteenth century. A recent bibliography lists only sixty-seven titles that meet the criteria of having at least thirty-two pages and more than two original mounted photographs."[55] Of these, many are government or corporate undertakings,[56] making Townshend and Hyde's that much more unique.

Hyde's photography in *Our Indian Summer* demonstrates his

commitment to aesthetics of the picturesque and the tradition of British and American travel art and photography. It is true that Hyde's purpose is on the one hand documentary, working with Townshend's narrative to produce a sense of the American West as poised at a moment between untamed wilderness and overdevelopment—in other words, a moment ripe for ready investors. On the other hand, as one sees early on in the Niagara sequence, Hyde has learned well the lessons imparted by the Amateur Photographic Association, producing images that emphasize the beauty of landscapes both dramatic and mundane within the tradition epitomized in the work of English photographer Roger Fenton.[57] Hyde does not seek artistic effect for its own sake, perhaps, but does deliberately frame and compose shots in a balanced manner that draws the eye in and allows the viewer to appreciate depth and scale in each scene—more often than not, a landscape signifies a particular place or experience. "Niagara, American Falls, New York State" (30) places leafy trees in the foreground in a manner that seems to demonstrate the influence of Japanese prints. The following shots of American and Horseshoe Falls emphasize the use of instantaneous film in capturing the falling water with impressive sharpness. More than the others, the photos of Niagara Falls seem conventional, as these views have long been a set-piece of European tourists. It is possible that Hyde considered Niagara a desirable location to test his technology and hone his skills for the trip ahead. As mentioned above, Townshend notes that the plates are unavailable in the United States, and they must conserve and ration them for their trip. There are five images of Niagara, but no photos of the journey between Niagara and Whitewater, Kansas. Certainly this choice reinforces the purpose of the book in furthering British investment in the West.

While it is clear from remarks in the narrative that Townshend and Hyde are well-pleased with the improved technology of instantaneous film and dry plates, Hyde's object is the capturing of the scene itself more than the production of photographic art. Hyde's images seek to draw viewers into the scene, where they can imagine themselves in these American places, as with "Vista on the Whitewater" (41), where along the lushly forested bank can be seen a man—seemingly Hyde himself. Yet Hyde's images break with picturesque tradition to the degree that they include the suggestion of labor within the landscape. This is evident in "Corn-Shelling" (45), which similarly invites the viewer through formal composition. The frame balances the bags of corn on the right with the wall of a structure on the left, while diagonally positioned wagon tongues draw the eye from the lower left corner toward the men working. Overall, Hyde's images, particularly those taken in the developing country of Kansas, Colorado, New Mexico, and the Texas Panhandle, recall something of the effect of the chroniclers of the post–Civil War West like Alexander Gardner, Timothy O'Sullivan, William Henry Jackson, and Carleton Watkins. These topographic photographers often joined government or railroad surveys and documented the grand landscapes of the American West and the transcontinental movement of Americans with both grandeur and realism but also for practical and economic ends including investment potential, not unlike Hyde and Townshend.[58] While Hyde's images cannot be judged equal in quality or moment to the work of such professionals, the accomplishment not nearly so significant in photographic history, the goal seems comparable and the result similarly valuable as a document of western places at a transitional moment.[59] Martha Sandweiss argues that such American photographers' works provide a pervasive sense of national futurity or "western destiny."[60] Townshend and Hyde's pro American spirit and excitement about the nation as a site of investment, and thus its future success, lends Hyde's images, again, a comparable sense of good things happening and greater things coming.

The desire to capture this opportune moment, of a wilderness just-tamed and still open for the timely and shrewd investor or immigrant, is evident in the image "Farm of Dietrich Claassen, Kansas, Distant View, Showing Prairie" (50). This photograph, presented in an oval border, shows a field in the foreground and farmhouse and buildings, including windmill, on the horizon against a Kansas sky that fills two-thirds of the image. The sense of safety and orderly domesticity seems an island in a vastness of space that awaits more sturdy pioneers as Claassen. Another instance, though a very different subject, are the photos of troops at Fort Elliott in the Texas Panhandle. In particular, "23rd Infantry, Fort Elliot, Pan Handle of Texas" (113) gives the sense of order and control as a row of troops stand in parade rest, clean white gloves glowing, before newly constructed fort buildings set against the stark open plains. (It bears mention, here, that another Fort Elliott photo, "A Scouting Party, Fort Elliot" (114), documents a troop of African American soldiers whose presence is an important aspect of the region's military history.) Such scenes lend confidence to the potential investor, providing a counter to images—still powerful in popular consciousness—of a West characterized by wilderness, rampaging Indians, lawlessness.

While Colorado and New Mexico comprise little space in Townshend's narrative, the mountain views inspire a larger proportion of photos. The views of the Arkansas Canyon, which Townshend and Hyde enjoyed as invited guests of the railroad on a "special" train side trip, are among the more dramatic landscape views. One example is a bridge that Townshend describes in some detail as a great engineering feat, "A. T. and S. F. R. R. Bridge, Grand Cañon of the Arkansas, Colorado" (64), which is also the most difficult to fathom in terms of photographic perspective, given the severe pitch of the canyon. There are also a good many images taken during the unsuccessful bear hunt on which the two were invited in Gallinas Canyon west of Las Vegas, New Mexico. These are punctuated with architectural photos of bridges and hotels along with shots of railroad tracks and trains. More than simply informative to would-be tourists, these images again highlight a sense of the progress of civilization in a still wide-open land of financial opportunity. The photo of the hotel still under construction, "A. T. and S. F. R. R. Hotel, Los Vegos [*sic*], New Mexico" (94), has this sense of the rapidly developing frontier about it. The photographer doesn't bother depicting the New Mexicans whom Townshend disparages so heavily, though there are a number of human subjects, identified in the narrative.

Despite Hyde's emphasis on the documentary and the picturesque in his photographs, several noteworthy exceptions hearken toward a more modern, highly self-conscious, artistic attempt. One example, "View in Grand Cañon of the Arkansas" (66), is particularly striking. The image presents a landscape composed in three overlapping Vs—first a forked tree, then the canyon walls making a turn in the foreground, and then further off canyon walls on the horizon. Though a "found" scene, the composition is distinctive and geometrically self-conscious enough to suggest Hyde's artistic attempt. Another striking image is a railroad scene later in North Texas, "Bridge, Red River. M. K. and T. R. R." (145). While it is unclear whether the train is moving or at rest, the cars are caught between a grid of crisscrossed diagonals of steel girders and cable, providing a feeling of speed and modern technology overcoming nature (quite literally) in the form of the broad-flowing Red River below.

Significantly, as Michael R. Grauer has documented, Hyde's are not only the first photographs but also the "first graphic images" of the JA Ranch, the prototypical ranch of the Texas Panhandle.[61] While—strangely—Hyde photographed neither cowboys nor cattle, which Townshend does praise (129–32), he did capture an image of one of Goodnight's bison, an ecologically and historically important remnant of the southern plains herds (128).[62] The photos also depict Charles Goodnight, at that time forty-three years of age, on the JA Ranch ("Log Hut on Turkey Creek, Pan Handle, Texas" [135]). As Townshend explains, the main house on the ranch is still under construction, as seen in a well-composed image, "A Lonely Home in Texas (Grande Vista)" (127). In the main house's storeroom, Townshend and Hyde "spent a few hours developing our negatives" (129). That the first images of the JA Ranch were photographs produced via instantaneous film and new dry-plate technology, and were developed on-site at the ranch, is consistent with the ranch's status as a modern enterprise. After all, it was the first ranch in the newly opened Texas Panhandle, established in 1876, the first partnership in the region with British capital (Adair), and often praised for its modern scientific breeding operation and early adoption of barbed wire.

We might go on to say a great deal here about notable features of Townshend's text and interesting features of Hyde's photographs, for they merit our curiosity and examination in various ways. It is, however, the complementary combination of the narrative and the photography that makes the book really noteworthy. The dual elements have a reciprocal relationship, as neither on its own would quite carry the work. While the narrative relates more of the journey than the photos alone can, the photos clearly act as the writer's structuring device as each photo is a signpost of the journey, its route, conveyances, people met, and of course landscape. On the other hand, the narrative provides gloss of the photographs—far more than the captions do—and interpretation. For the most part, the narrative and photographs seem perfectly in synch. Townshend's dismissive attitude about Americans Indians and Hispanics, for example, is matched by the definite lack of any ethnographic-type photography. Interestingly, there is one "Mexican" named in the narrative. A man named Frank is "lent," along with two horses, to Townshend and Hyde by a fellow Englishman, A. B. Legard, as a helper and perhaps a guide from Fort Elliott south to the JA Ranch. Yet after being initially identified as "a Mexican servant" (119), Townshend makes nothing more of the man's race. He appears in one of Hyde's images, "The Surprise (on M'Clellen Creek, Indian Territory)" (123), as an indistinguishable figure but for Townshend's description (122).

The example of Frank makes the point that Townshend's narrative, which touches upon virtually every photograph as it proceeds, adds information that would be lost had we only the image and its caption. Figures like Charles Barnes "Barnsey" Austin and Charles Goodnight are identified in the narrative with specific reference to position in the photograph in a way that complements the caption immeasurably. Similarly, places referred to imprecisely or erroneously in the captions (which seem to have been written by a third party with no great regard for spelling) are more precisely located in Townshend's narrative, as in the case of "Cotton Press" (149), which we know from Townshend was located near Denison, Texas. Conversely, and at the same time, photographs provide the writer detail and visual anchoring, acting in mnemonic fashion for Townshend's narrative.

Also noteworthy are moments at which text and photo struggle together to make meaning clear for the reader/viewer, as in the case of a railroad bridge in the Arkansas Canyon that the men find a marvel of construction. Townshend notes that the photograph, "A. T. and S. F. R. R. Bridge, Grand Cañon of the Arkansas, Colorado" (64), is insufficient:

> The walls of the cañon here are so perpendicular, and the Arkansas so fully takes up all the space between them, that a long bridge is necessary. It will be seen that one side—the outer one of the structure—is held up by two girders of unequal length, arranged like a roof, the apex of which just comes over the outer edge of the bridge—the inner edge of it resting on a ledge of rock. Without sunlight it is impossible to give a really good photographic representation of this unique piece of talented engineering, but the subject is too remarkable to permit any sense of false pride in our art, forbidding us to present what our critics may safely call a rather inferior picture. (65)

We might add that Townshend's description, too, falls short of its mark in this case, and that together text and image cooperate and struggle to help the book's interlocutor understand the grand scenery and human endeavor at which the men marvel.

On the subject of geography, land, and scenery, text and image also impart much that could not have been intentional. It is worth saying that Townshend and Hyde's book offers value to environmental historians of the plains and mountain West. From their reports of logging on New Mexican land grants, the prevalence of cattle along the Arkansas River, the presence of mesquite and other plants, and the relative presence or absence of wildlife, like black bears on the JA Ranch, the Townshend's narrative and Hyde's photographs offer much detail to the discerning reader.

Finally, the importance and interest of this volume are its reminders of the interconnections between American and British history and specifically the prominent role of British investment in the development of the American West. Moreover, in intriguing fashion, this volume reminds us that the development of the West, so powerfully iconic in its cowboy image, so powerful as an image of American-ness, was to some degree and from a British perspective a part of the empire—not the cattle empire of a Charles Goodnight, but the British Empire by imaginative and economic extension. While this Anglo-American economic experiment came to an abrupt end after bad winters, drought and an ever-crowding range took its toll, it is nevertheless possible to understand the American West from 1876 to 1890—the very heart of the cowboy era—as enabled by Victorian British colonial imagination at play on the range.

Consider a final example, suggestive in its geographical scope. Dick Walsh, a native of Dublin, Ireland, was friend of Cornelia Adair's son by her first marriage, Jack Ritchie, who then resided in England. Walsh came to the JA Ranch in 1885. By now, J. G. Adair had died, and his widow Cornelia had taken his place in partnering with Charles Goodnight, though they dissolved this arrangement in 1887. Walsh began at the lowliest post to learn the business and worked his way up to management, becoming the foreman in 1892. Walsh was known for his graceful management of nesters who had set up on the ranch, buying them out or swapping parcels on favorable terms for land outside the range. Walsh is also credited with bringing the ranch's herds to a very high quality of breeding, winning top honors at international livestock shows in Chicago and Saint Louis. At around this time, Jack Ritchie left to fight in the British Army in the second Boer War; a significant number of horses were purchased in Texas, and in the panhandle, for use by the British army in this conflict.[63] After resigning in 1910, Walsh traveled with Murdo Mackenzie, the Scotsman who had managed the Matador Ranch in Texas, to examine ranching opportunities in Brazil, where Mackenzie indeed relocated to manage the Brazil Land and Cattle Company in 1912. In the meantime, in 1910, Walsh moved on to Rhodesia as ranch manager for the British South Africa Company, where he "introduced modern cattle ranching methods."[64] Walsh evidently succumbed to the tsetse fly and died in Rhodesia in 1921.[65] This career and its geographical scope, from Ireland to England to Texas and the American West, and to South America and Africa, demonstrate the global reach and powerful influence of the British (cattle) empire of the late Victorian and modern era.

Townshend and Hyde's *Our Indian Summer in the Far West* depicts an "old West" that is decidedly a modern West, a West surprisingly cosmopolitan even as it remains sparsely settled and culturally crude—the sort of place to which one has to bring his own bathtub. This photographic book, more than the sum of its parts, is itself an artifact of this modernity and cosmopolitanism, of a Victorian American West. The recovery and republication of this volume, in its present form, makes available an important primary document of this brief but pivotal historical moment. While Townshend and Hyde were on the one hand not major figures in this moment, their accomplishment is noteworthy in its particular aspects and for its status as a document of an international cultural phenomenon. They described and photographed for the first time rare scenes of frontier America, met business leaders and western pioneers, and praised the American spirit of the era. As men of their times, they reveal frankly the attitudes and beliefs concerning the future of civilization, including the uglier face of white supremacy, and in their facts and figures show us something of how the project of civilization, for both good and ill, got done.

A NOTE ON EDITORIAL PRACTICES

In writing footnotes to Townshend's text and Hyde's photographs, our primary goal was to be of help to readers in making sense of the book. In most cases, this meant providing historical and factual information. Sometimes, it meant offering interpretative remarks that clarify or inform without, we hope, becoming overly didactic. We avoided the temptation to overanalyze Townshend's many literary quotations, which are often inexact, as if inserted as the author recalled them from memory. Townshend names many individuals whom the travelers met. When we could not positively identify such individuals, we offered no note in preference to speculation. In addition, we preserved Townshend's idiosyncrasies of spelling and punctuation.

NOTES

1. May Castleberry defines photographic books as "bound and printed publications distinguished by original contributions of photographic images, whether they have been printed in runs of a few copies or in larger trade editions numbering in the thousands. Such books encompass albums with printed title pages and tipped in original photographs, as well as the more familiar publications with photographs reproduced by gravure, offset lithography, or other printing techniques." Castleberry, introduction to *Perpetual Mirage*, 16.

2. Some bibliographical sources do catalog the book. See *Travels in the New South: A Bibliography*, vol. 1, *The Postwar South, 1865–1900: An Era of Reconstruction and Readjustment*, ed. Thomas D. Clark (Norman: University of Oklahoma Press, 1962), 117–18; Jeff C. Dykes, *Western High Spots: A Preeminent Book Collector and Historian Presents Bibliographic Profiles of Published Western Americana* (Flagstaff, Ariz.: Northland Press, 1977), 58–61, 71–72. See also David Margolis, *To Delight the Eye: Original Photographic Book Illustrations of the American West* (DeGolyer Library, Southern Methodist University, 1994), 60–63; Ada B. Nisbet, *British Comment on the United States: A Chronological Bibliography, 1832–1899* (Oakland: University of California Press, 2001), 277, 283, 288. Nisbet captures all three of Townshend's books, *Colorado, Our Indian Summer*, and *The New Southern Route from San Francisco*.

3. This and much other detailed information about the volume was gained through examination of the Chiswick Press Papers held at the British National Library.

4. Pagnamenta discusses the acceleration of British activity that came with faster travel (*Prairie Fever*, 155). Townshend and Hyde's narrative emphasizes the speed and relative ease of travel not only to promote railroad investment but to encourage British investment.

5. Olson, *Marmalade and Whiskey*, 85, 94–95.

6. Athearn, *Westward the Briton*, 50.

7. Woods, *British Gentlemen*, 29–39.

8. Pagnamenta, *Prairie Fever*, 167.

9. Kerr, *Scottish Capital*.

10. Riegel, *Story of the Western Railroads*, 90–91.

11. White, *Railroaded*, 77–78; Bryant, "Entering the Global Economy," 219–20; Riegel, *Story of the Western Railroads*, 117–18.

12. Riegel, *Story of the Western Railroads*, 161–62.

13. Riegel, *Story of the Western Railroads*, 187; Bryant, "Entering the Global Economy," 219.

14. Grohman, "Cattle Ranches," 438.

15. Buckman, "Ranches and Rancheros of the Far West," 434–35.

16. John Townsend, personal communication, June 6, 2012. John Townsend is cocreator of the Townsend (Townshend) genealogy site, http://www.astro.wisc.edu/~townsend/tree/home.php.

17. Pagnamenta, *Prairie Fever*, 232.

18. This is detailed in Woods, *British Gentlemen*, 55.

19. Quoted in Sheffy, "British Capital and the Cattle Business," 29.

20. Morris, "When Corporations Rule the Llano Estacado," 58–59. Morris emphasizes the book's influence on luring British investment and further suggests that the book may have cultivated Victorian interest in buffalo conservation.

21. Anderson, "Cator, James Hamilton."

22. Jackson, "British Interests," 160.

23. White, *Railroaded*, 472–73.

24. Samuel Nugent Townshend contributed a sketch ("Townsends, Townshends, or Townesendes of Whitehall," 233–39) of his family lineage in Cork (dating back to his great-grandfather's Dragoon military action in the mid-eighteenth century) in R. B. Townshend's *An Officer of the Long Parliament*.

25. See "The Townsend (Townshend) Family Records," http://www.astro.wisc.edu/~townsend/tree/record.php?ref=432.

26. Townshend, *Colorado*, 1.

17. "Mr. Nugent Townshend," obituary, *Times*, December 19, 1910, 13.

28. Townshend, *The Field*, January 12, 1878, 31.

29. Ibid., October 5, 1878, 432.

30. Aldridge, *Life on a Ranch*, 4.

31. Personal communication, Royal Geographic Society, September 4, 2013.

32. See the *London Gazette* of November 20, 1891, February 4, 1898, and February 24, 1899, respectively.

33. Prospectus offered in the *Times*, Thursday, March 27, 1873, 13.

34. Prospectus offered in the *Times*, Saturday, May 4, 1889, 4.

35. Prospectus offered in the *Times*, Saturday, January 26, 1889, n.p.

36. Prospectus offered in the *Times*, Tuesday, October 7, 1890, 14.

37. Prospectus offered in the *Times*, Thursday, February 9, 1888.

38. Thanks to Miriam Katz, Research Associate, Department of Photography, J. Paul Getty Museum, personal communication, June 18, 2013. See also http://special.lib.gla.ac.uk/manuscripts/search/detail_p.cfm?NID=25654&AID=&CID=74175.

39. Von Lintel, "Camera to Crayon," 67.

40. Ing, "Charles Whittingham," 1–2.

41. Some mysteries about this volume persist. First, Chiswick papers indicate that of the 250 copies produced, 50 were to have "extra red in title." However, of copies examined and libraries queried, all title pages have the same use of red ink—"Our Indian Summer in the Far West" and "London" being in red. It is possible that 200 of the books were cheaply bound, and the extant copies in libraries are the presentation copies, well bound between boards, that have survived. Second, as mentioned above, several copies held by libraries have an important difference. J. G. Hyde is presented on the title page and book spine as first author as well as "illustrator" of the volume. These copies are distinctly a minority; one is held at Texas A&M Library, another at History Colorado. While the publication date is the same (1880), Chiswick Press records make no mention of this discrepant version being produced. Third, Chiswick Press records indicate that the published material was to be sent to Teddington (at

that time, a sleepy village south of London). Presumably, some aspect of the book's production—binding, printing of photographs, and/or mounting of photographs took place at Teddington. However, our research could not turn up evidence of the book's production at Teddington or indeed of its circulation once production was complete. Certainly it is clear from inscriptions in the copies to be found at libraries that many copies were presented rather than sold in a bookshop. Fourth, concerning photographs, although the authoritative guides (DeGolyer, *To Delight the Eye*; Dykes, *Western High Spots*) indicate that Townshend and Hyde's book has 60 images, and Chiswick Press records confirm 60 mounts per book, in fact there are discrepancies between copies. The Haley Library copy (59 images), the Amarillo Public Library copy (59 images), and the DeGolyer Library (60 images) are all slightly different from one another by two or three images. We have demonstrated the existence of 62 distinct images, all included in this reprint. As a final note, survey of libraries has uncovered some variety in color of the original bindings. A few are in brown/maroon and even one in green, though blue is predominant.

42. This is the Princeton Library copy.

43. Martha A. Sandweiss, personal communication, November 13, 2013. "Sometimes these elaborate books were produced on a subscription basis, sometimes not. In the case of a promotional project like this one, one imagines it might have been a mixed financial venture."

44. See "The Townsend (Townshend) Family Records," http://www.astro.wisc.edu/~townsend/tree/home.php.

45. Pagnamenta, *Prairie Fever*, 194.

46. Ibid., 268.

47. Ibid., 179.

48. Ibid., 19.

49. Conrad, *Heart of Darkness*, 7.

50. Payne, *Owen Wister*, 122–23.

51. Kipling, "White Man's Burden," 290–91.

52. Wister, "Evolution of the Cow-Puncher," 603–604.

53. Martha A. Sandweiss, personal communication, November 13, 2013.

54. Sandweiss, *Print the Legend*, 278.

55. Ibid., 278.

56. Sandweiss, "Dry Light," 24.

57. Clarke, *Photograph*, 55–57.

58. Orvell, *American Photography*, 49–51.

59. See Newhall, *History of Photography*, 94–105.

60. Sandweiss, *Print the Legend*, 157.

61. Grauer, "Graphic Images," 13–14.

62. The JA Ranch would be photographed more extensively in the early 1900s by the cowboy photographer Erwin E. Smith. See Price, *Imagining the Open Range*.

63. Hendrix, *If I Can Do It Horseback*, 106.

64. Burton, *History of the JA Ranch*, 109–10.

65. This link to the *Breeder's Gazette* of 1921 includes both an article about Richard Walsh's ranching activities in Rhodesia (November 17, 1921, 697–98) and a joint obituary of Richard Walsh and Cornelia Adair (October 6, 1921, 491), http://books.google.com/books?id=bJE5AQAAMAAJ&pg=PA697&lpg=PA697&dq=dick+walsh+ranch+rhodesia&source=bl&ots=ByLtnJJU1J&sig=TtqPSpcmbqn4400kYYfqxz528xw&hl=en&sa=X&ei=NZOvUvS_AanP2wX-xoDACQ&ved=0CCkQ6AEwAA#v=onepage&q=dick%20walsh%20ranch%20rhodesia&f=false.

OUR INDIAN SUMMER

IN THE FAR WEST.

AN AUTUMN TOUR OF FIFTEEN THOUSAND MILES IN
KANSAS, TEXAS, NEW MEXICO, COLORADO,
AND THE INDIAN TERRITORY.

BY S. NUGENT TOWNSHEND
("ST. KAMES" OF "THE FIELD").

ILLUSTRATED BY J. G. HYDE.

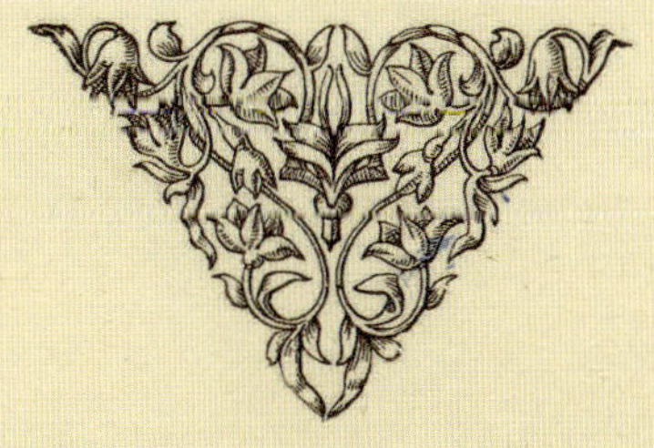

LONDON:
PRINTED BY CHARLES WHITTINGHAM.
1880.

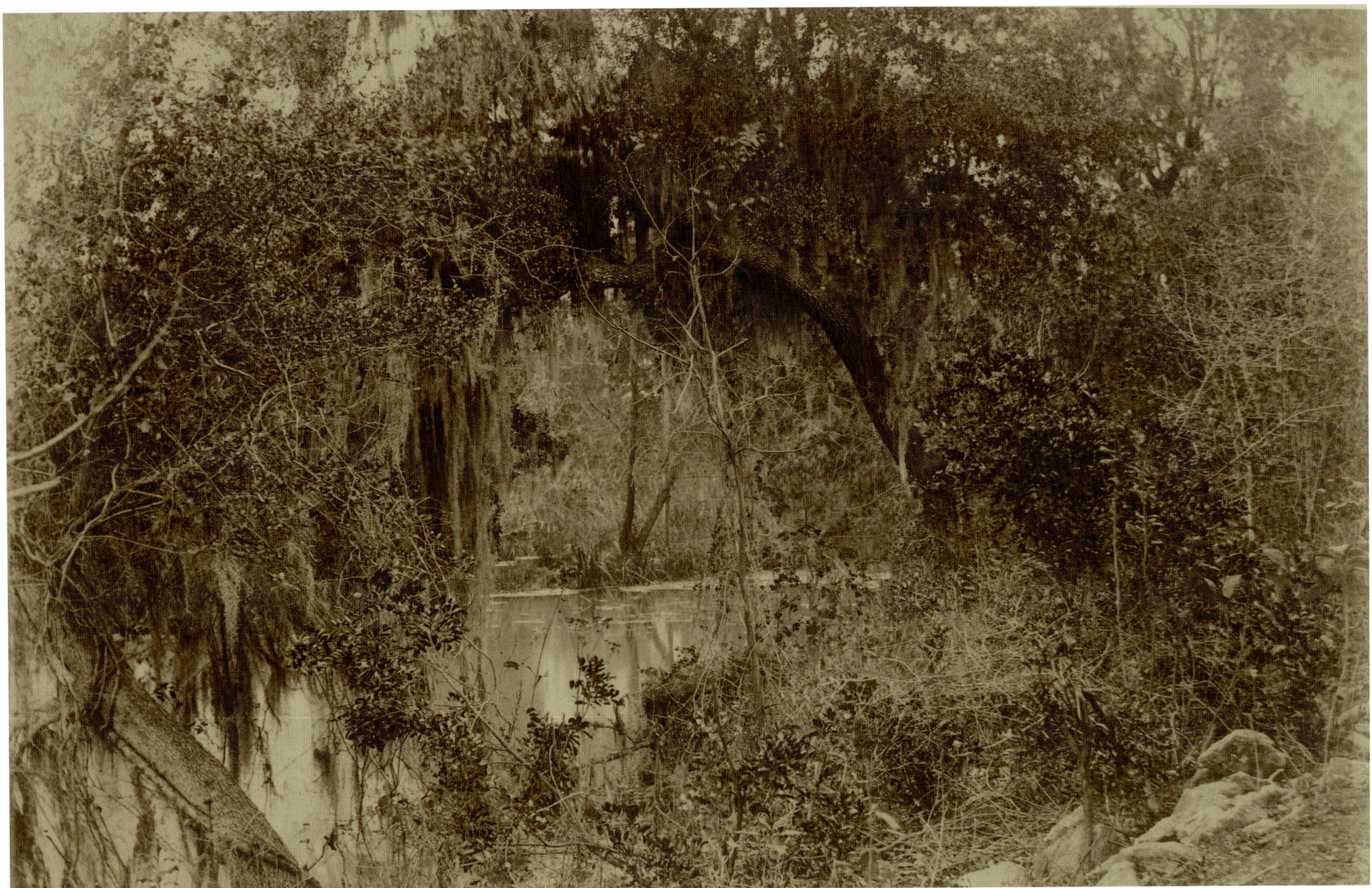

Source of the San Antonio River, Texas.

Taken on the estate of George W. Brackenridge, called "Head of the River." This photo takes pride of place perhaps because Townshend professed to find this the prettiest place in Texas. He perhaps also wished to honor Brackenridge as the Texas banker most friendly to British investors. The photo demonstrates Hyde's artistic skill at framing a natural scene by the features of the setting, the horizontal lines drawing the viewer into the scene.

CHAPTER I

Our Start from London—Our Programme and Outfit—Life at Sea in Bad Weather—The Moonlight Club and Ancient Society of Whisky Corks—American Girls—"The Spoon"—Emigrants to Texas—Instantaneous Photography—Arrival in New York.

"'Thicker than water' in one rill,
Through centuries of story,
Our Saxon blood has flow'd, and still
We share with you its good and ill,
The shadow and the glory."
Whittier, *To Englishmen*

When summer has waned, and the stormy equinox shatters the short-lived beauty of England's summer, then chilly Boreas howls in undisputed sway over the Atlantic, and rudely challenges all comers to a very rough-and-tumble conflict with him and his sequents, Neptune's maddened, angry, roaring, watery mountains.

But with a purpose not to be thwarted, we decided to recall a couple of months of glorious sunshine, blue skies, and air free from damp and depression.

The word "Italy" is uttered at once by the Meteorologic Sybarite.[1] "But why not the Gulf of Mexico?" inquires M.S. No. 2. "The United States?" mildly remonstrates No. 1. "Oh nonsense! The climate there is worse than ours; and where are the historic associations so dear to everyone above the status of a mere globe trotter to be found?" But Meteorologic Sybarite No. 2 is not to be daunted. "We will have the entire beautiful Indian summer over there," he exclaims; "we will defy both Neptune and Boreas in one of the great transatlantic steamships. We will reach Niagara when no two leaves are of the same hue. We will strike Lake Michigan, that great inland sea, when for weeks not a ripple disturbs its vast surface of pellucid depths. On our Westward journey, we will overthrow many a prairie grouse and quail; study the progress of the new settlers in Kansas; follow the Arkansas up through a wonderful cañon to its mountain-home in the eternally snow-clad 'Rockies.' And then, as winter sets in, we will move down the New Mexico and South Pacific Railroad; hunt up turkeys and bears in the valleys of the Gyamas or Gallinas, and do the same in the Pan Handle of Texas.[2] Then we will away southward through the Lone Star State; shape our course for San Antonio de Bexar, and onward to the much-sung

Epigraph: John Greenleaf Whittier (1807–92) is an American poet, journalist, and abolitionist. Popular in his day in both the United States and England, Whittier is associated with the Fireside Poets of New England. He is regarded as a great humanitarian and, as a Quaker, a religious poet. "To Englishmen" (1862) laments English sympathy with the South during the ongoing American Civil War, stressing Anglo-American kinship and England's own colonial abolition acts. Townshend's choice of epigraph emphasizes the kinship, with a nod toward both "the shadow and the glory" of colonial enterprises.

1. An ironic title meaning one who takes pleasure in fine weather.

2. The "valleys of the Gyamas or Gallinas" refers to the canyon of the Gallinas River that flows out of the New Mexico Rockies southeastward through the town of Las Vegas, New Mexico, which our travelers visit.

shores of the Gulf of Mexico, where summer ever reigns, and where the wild fowl of the North considerately come down each winter to attract thither the sybaritic sportsman."

"We will write a book of our travels?" suggests M.S. No. 1. "Yes, and be classified as mendacious emigration agents," sneered M.S. No. 2.[3] "But why not photograph everything?" retorted M.S. No. 1. "A photograph has this pull over an emigration agent, that it can't tell lies."

"Consider yourself embraced by me for the suggestion," apologized the second Meteorologic Sybarite. "Settle up all your private business without delay, for the next National boat from Liverpool bears us to the bosom of—first, Neptune, and then, Uncle Sam."

So it was arranged. Our guns, a Greener and a Reilly, No. 12 central fire, were subjected to the closest scrutiny, and looked as if they could do all the work we wanted.[4] Our portable india-rubber bath was water-tight. Some bottles of Collis Browne's Chlorodyne, Lamplough's Pyretic Saline, and Eno's Fruit Salt were our medical stores.[5] A stout leather case, holding two half-gallon bottles sewn in felt, was our cellaret. Wratten and Wainwright's instantaneous plates for our photographs were also securely packed with felt round their cases, and then put into a large tin box.[6] Letters of credit on the San Antonio National Bank of Texas were procured from Messrs. Henry S. King and Co., the Cornhill bankers,[7] and then we said good-bye to Old England for a time, and taking the Midland midnight Pullman train, soon found ourselves on board that fine steady old sea-boat "The Queen," of the National Line,[8] and leaving Liverpool on September 24th, called off Queenstown for more passengers next day.

"How often, O how often,
We had wish'd that the ebbing tide
Would bear us away on its bosom
O'er the ocean, wild and wide."[9]

Now our wish was granted, and the weather for the first week was wild enough to please even a stormy petrel.

We were old sailors and took everything as it came; and it came

3. Another ironic comment, this one refers to the business of attracting English and other emigrants to the United States with the promise of cheap land and lucrative agricultural and other opportunities. The remark invites consideration of Townshend's own efforts as American correspondent for *The Field* magazine. Townshend may refer to recent (1870s) British ventures in American agricultural colonies such as that of George Grant's Victoria, Kansas; Thomas Hughes's Rugby, Tennessee; or William and Frederick Close's Le Mars, Iowa. Pagnamenta, *Prairie Fever*, 177–220.

4. Townshend and Hyde brought no rifles (perhaps because they did not expect to find buffalo to hunt), but they did bring shotguns, anticipating bird hunting. Greener refers to a shotgun produced by the W. W. Greener firearm manufacturing firm of Birmingham. Reilly refers to E. M. Reilly gun makers of London. Wieland, *Vintage British Shotguns*.

5. Chlorodyne was a patent medicine developed by J. Collis Browne, a British army surgeon in India, marketed for cholera and other ills, consisting primarily of laudanum (Parssinen, *Secret Passions, Secret Remedies*). Described as an effervescent that revitalized the blood and marketed especially for jungle travel and travel to hot climates, particularly Australia, Lamplough's Pyretic Saline targeted headaches, bilious fevers, and other complaints (Leach, *Ship Captain's Medical Guide*). Eno's Fruit Salt, primarily sodium bicarbonate, was marketed as a laxative and was a popular remedy for indigestion (American Medical Association, *Nostrums and Quackery*).

6. See the volume editors' introduction for more information about Wratten and Wainright and the photographic technology employed by John George Hyde.

7. Still a financial district in London, Cornhill ward was home to Smith Elder & Co., East India agents, shippers, and bankers since 1816. In 1868 Henry Samuel King took over Smith Elder's banking and India agency work becoming Henry S King & Co. "Henry S King & Co," *British Banking History Society*, accessed March 28, 2015, www.banking-history.co.uk/king.html.

8. S.S. *The Queen* was a steamship known for its Liverpool to New York runs during the 1870s and 1880s. She sailed from her launching in 1865 until she was scrapped in 1896. The National Line was an American company that advertised departures from its dock in New York to Liverpool and London every Saturday morning and to London direct every Wednesday. A crossing might take as long as seven days. "National Line Steamships, S.S. *The Queen*, 4471 tons [back]," *Boston Public Library*, accessed March 28, 2015, https://www.flickr.com/photos/boston_public_library/8270438266/in/photostream/; "S/S The Queen, National Line," *Norway-Heritage*, accessed March 28, 1015, www.norwayheritage.com/p_ship.asp?sh=thequ.

9. From "The Bridge" in *The Belfry of Bruges and Other Poems* (1845) by American poet Henry Wadsworth Longfellow (1807–82). Longfellow was much beloved in his day by American and British readers. "The Bridge" describes the speaker's feelings as he stands upon a bridge over a river flowing out to sea and reflects upon the longing to escape from his cares. The West Boston Bridge, constructed in 1739 and crossing the Charles River, is the setting of this poem. It has since been replaced and is today called the Longfellow Bridge in honor of Longfellow's poem. Townshend's quotation emphasizes the romantic sentiment of escapism.

in the form of continued head winds, for only a few hours were we under canvas, the wind persistently hanging a few points north or south of west, and the consequence was a twelve-day passage. The good ship rolled unceasingly, and pitched in a determined but dignified manner; the advantage of this, however, at sea is very manifest, the young ladies requiring such an immense amount of assistance and holding up. This soon changes acquaintance into intimate friendship, and on very long and rough voyages even Cupid has been known to govern the scene. The nights were much finer than the days as a rule, and soon a knot of us formed a Moonlight Club, usually termed the M.C.

Then a time-honoured institution—a branch of the Antient[10] and Honourable Society of Whisky Corks, under warrant from the Grand Bung of Canada—existed on board "The Queen." Of the sacred emblem of this society, the "Whangdoodle,"[11] we heard a great deal, and the G.C. or Grand Cork well supported the hospitality of the lodge. Often just before lights were put out would the Moonlight Club, whispering soft nothings to each other, hear the musical voices of the Corks singing their parting anthem, the first verse of which ran—

"We pity the noodle
Who slights our Whangdoodle,
For over the stern to the fishes goes he.
Round files he shall gnaw,
By our great Grand Bung's law,
As he's kick'd round the vessel by our own G.C."

A ship is a little world, and the captain is a jolly king of it, if he likes; and if he doesn't, about all he can do is to have the lights put out very punctually. Society in a transatlantic steamer resolves itself into circles more or less exclusive in a few days. No one ventures near the M.C.'s when they hold their meetings on deck, the Lodge of Whisky Corks was jealously guarded, and when all the ladies had selected their beaux for the trip, outsiders had to fall back, and take to quoits or whist, poker or the smoking-room, as best suited their forlorn condition.

All our girls were American, bright as bees, sharp as needles, great fun, and well able to take care of themselves. After the manner of their race, they disliked much walking, and rather disapproved of spooning until after dinner—then, look out.

"Rock'd in the cradle of the deep,"[12]

and rocked tremendously too, with a confiding little arm holding tight to yours, with bright eyes looking furtively at you, and wondering why the Britisher does not say more, with the clear moonlight above, and the long-troubled, moonlit, phosphorescent track of the propeller extending miles apparently away behind us, we lean over the taffrail. How any male member of the M.C. escaped his fair American cousin is more than we can account for.

Our great study of human nature was, however, a fellow-passenger who was known as "the Spoon," and who had never been to sea before.

"A life on the ocean wave!
The man who wrote it was green,
A ship he had ne'er been on,
And the sea he had never seen,"[13]

10. An archaic form of "ancient." *Oxford English Dictionary Online,* s.v. "ancient, adj. and n. 1," accessed March 21, 2015, www.oed.com.

11. While the Whangdoodle has an American literary and folkloric sense as a sort of fabulous beast, it is here referenced in its more general sense, as in "thingamajig," to refer to an object without a convenient or ready name. *Oxford English Dictionary Online,* s.v. "whangdoodle | whang-doodle, n.," accessed March 21, 2015, www.oed.com.

12. Lyric from a popular American song of the same title composed by Emma Hart Willard and Joseph Philip Knight in 1840 and subsequently republished in commercially available sheet music. The song has a distinctly more Christian sentiment than Townshend's reference here would suggest. Stedman, *American Anthology.*

13. "A Life on the Ocean Wave" (1838) is the title of a poem by Epes Sargent. The poem was set to music by Henry Russell and enjoyed popularity in the United States and Britain. The verse that Townshend here quotes, however, is recognizable only by the initial line; the lyrics of the Sargent song are distinctly more heroic, suggesting perhaps that Townshend is quoting from a contemporary send-up of the original. Stedman, *American Anthology.*

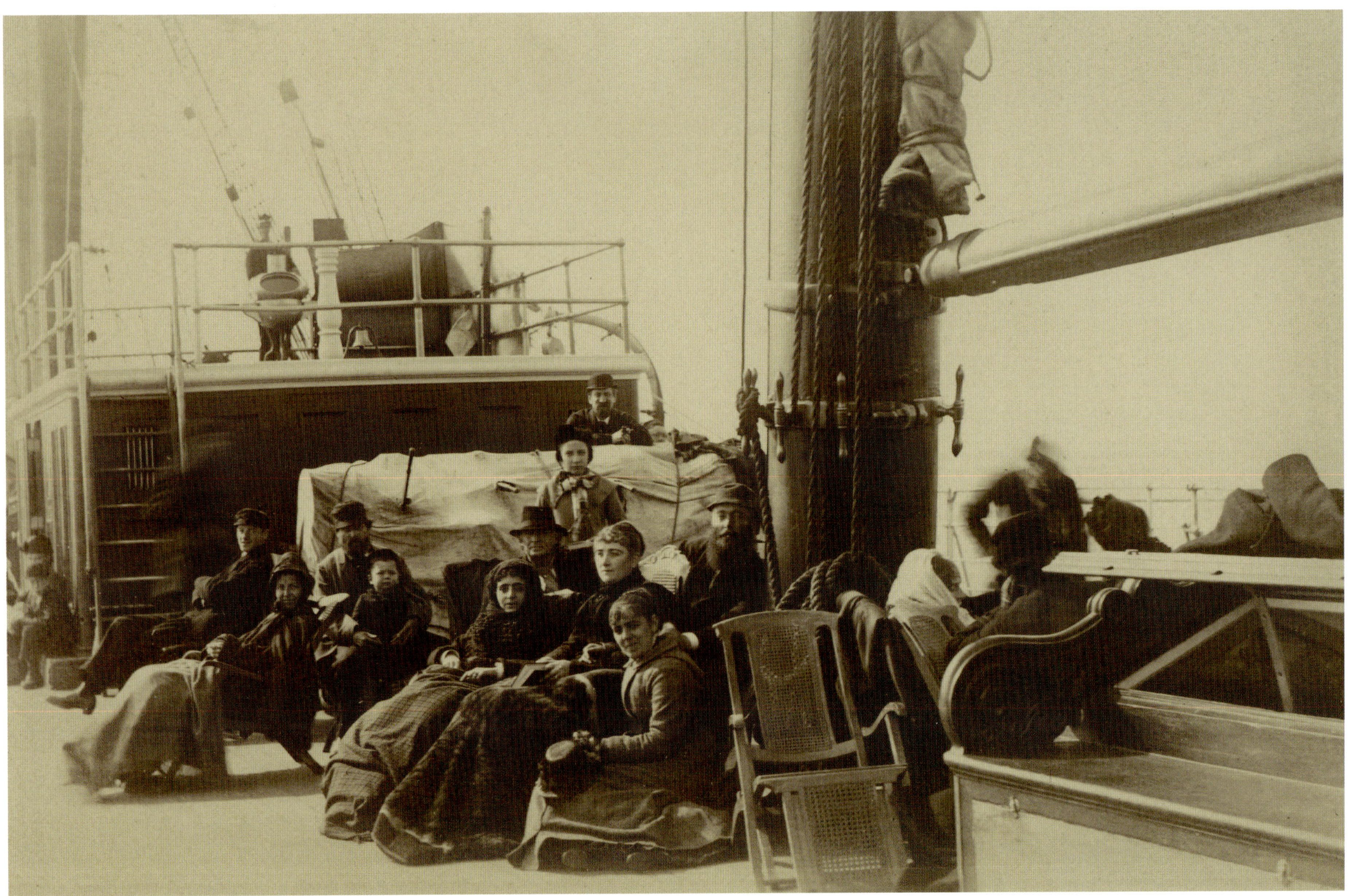

On Board the S.S. "Queen." (The Moonlight Club.) The man reclining against the mast among the women passengers appears to be Townshend. The empty rocking chair in the foreground, possibly intended for photographer Hyde, is also inviting of the viewer. A sailor at the rail above seems to stand guard over the domestic scene.

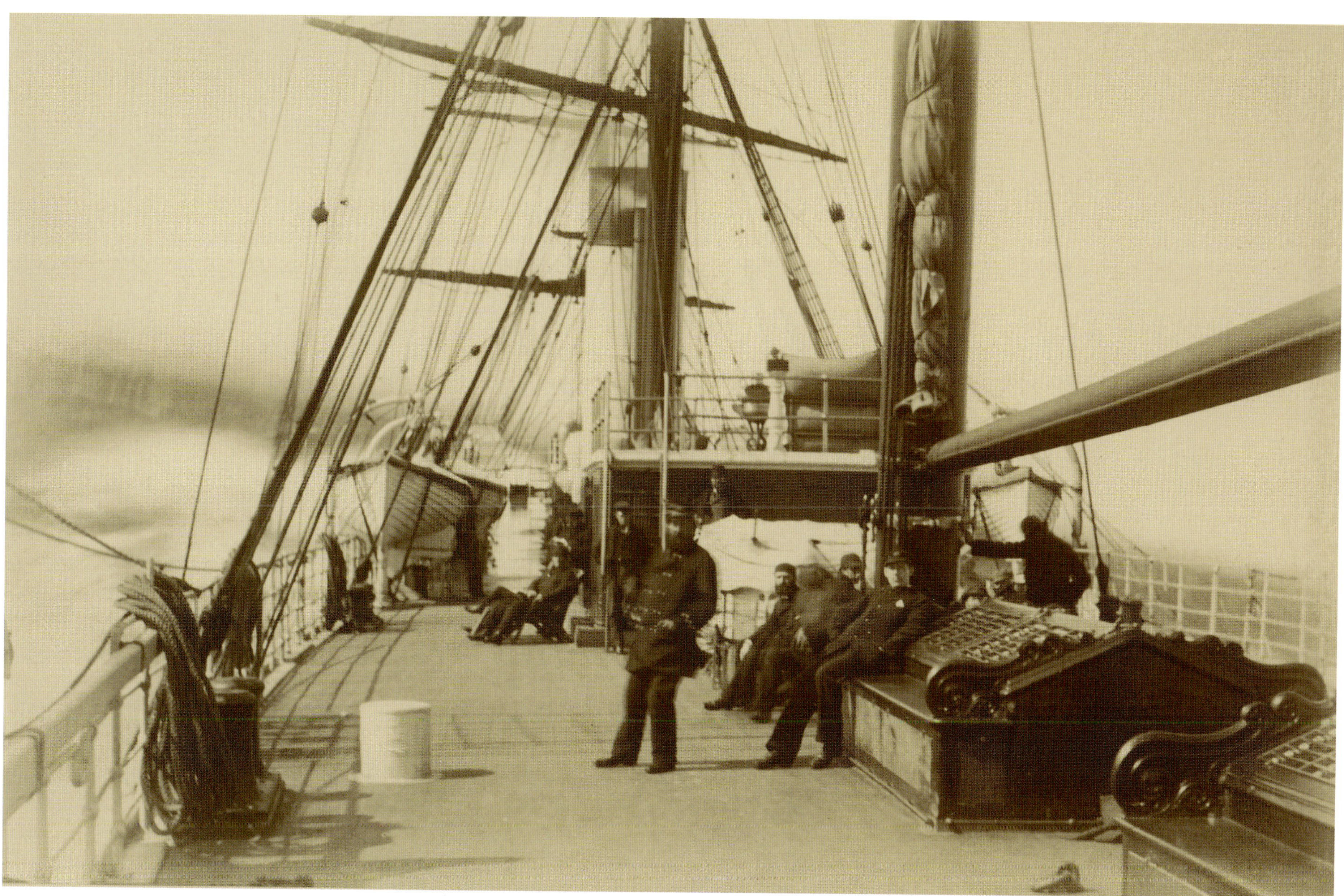

The S.S. "Queen." (A Gale of Wind—Mid-Ocean.)
This photo holds a place of pride for Townshend and Hyde with their instantaneous film, as they speculate that it may be the first photograph to capture the action of a storm at sea.

exactly describes him. When he came on board at Liverpool he told us he so hoped to experience a gale of wind at sea, and when we got our first baptism of salt water off the Fastnett Rock, as—

> "The startled waves leap over it, the storm
> Smites it with all the scourges of the rain,
> And steadily against its solid form
> Press the great shoulders of the hurricane,"[14]

he clapped his hands, and exclaimed, "Grand! we shall have a gale now." To which an old salt angrily replied, "Yes, my stormy petrel, and when we get it you will cry like a child with fear."

Subsequently when the gale increased the same salt remarked, "I calculate, stranger, you are the Jonah of this ship, and if it gets worse you will have to go overboard." The poor Spoon was terribly frightened, and also sick very soon afterwards.

There were some emigrants for Southern Texas on board. We cannot help thinking that English farmers are foolish in going to any spot where the crops they understand cannot be grown, when the splendid, fertile plains of Kansas, Nebraska, and Northern Texas are so much more suited to their acquirements, tastes, and constitutions.[15]

However, let us not anticipate our experience of the great West, but still plough our watery way onward, over

> "The depths of that mysterious deep,
> Where every life is but a beauteous wave
> That breaks one moment into consciousness,
> Then backward shudders to its watery grave."[16]

We photograph the M.C. and we photograph the ship as she pitches heavily into a sea. This instantaneous photography is a beautiful and wonderful thing, and we present to our readers—we believe, for the first time—a photograph of the actual performance of a ship in a gale of wind, everything of this sort we have before seen being merely a photograph of a painting, and much more striking and effective than truthfully real. The Antient and Honourable Society of Whisky Corks in uniform would not make nearly so pretty a picture as the Moonlight Club, but we would have presented the Corks to our readers also, if the Grand Bung had not strictly enjoined that no Cork uniform was to be worn outside of lodge, and the lodge was too closely guarded to permit the camera to peep inside it.

A northerly wind on the Newfoundland banks blows away the all but perpetual fog that makes the mariner avoid as far as possible the British possessions in approaching North America, and we reel off at 300 miles per day the latter end of our voyage, attended by a large shoal of whales and porpoises, and in lovely sunny warm weather. The beautiful, graceful, and large pilot boats we met some hundreds of miles east of New York; and on October 6th we steamed up to that city, and had more or less pathetic farewells to take of the darling American girls who had made the voyage so pleasant to us. We promised never to forget them, and they intimated that they might remember us for "quite a time," if they met with no more agreeable friends.

14. From "The Lighthouse" in *The Seaside and the Fireside* (1850) by Henry Wadsworth Longfellow. In the poem, Longfellow praises the lighthouse as it stands against the fierce and dangerous sea, which Townshend's chosen lines emphasize.

15. Townshend's comments here remind us of the dire agricultural situation in Britain at this time and of Townshend's own decided preference for the prairies, as evidenced in his writings for *The Field* and his connections in Kansas.

16. From "Two Voices" in *Songs of the Year and Other Poems by "Charlton"* (1875) by Charlotte Pendleton. Now, it is rather an obscure book of poetry published by a Cincinnati press, Robert Clarke and Company. However, Pendleton published some poems in *Lippincott's Magazine,* where Townshend may have come across her work. "Two Voices" is an ocean-side contemplation of mortality.

CHAPTER II

New York—Its Custom House—The Civil Service—Cab Fares—Newspapers—Millionaires and Flirts—Run to Niagara on the New York Central Railroad—The American "Dead-Beat"—The Newsboy—Niagara Falls, and the Extortion threat—Our First Photographs in the United States.

"I've heard there is a famous land
For public spirit known,
Whose patriots love its interests
Much better than their own."

Hood

The autumnal equinox was with the Atlantic Ocean now all behind, and a thermometer at 74° in the shade met us in New York, on October 6th. A stranger's impressions of the largest transatlantic city, are, at starting, rarely peculiarly agreeable. The Custom House is the first annoyance, and woe betide the sportsman who carries more than one gun. For two dreary days we were tramping about that institution, making the acquaintance of every officer connected with it, in order to get our guns released, which they eventually were. We were informed that we were being made test cases of, but what the nature of the test was, except perhaps to test our tempers, we could not discover.

It is a great misfortune that the Customs and other civil services of the United States are not permanent, and a class of people who make their particular business a life-long study, are not employed by Government, instead of its picking up every four years, at random, employés who are for some time necessarily more or less incompetent, or whose over-zeal to perform duties they do not understand, defeats their own laudable purposes. The tremendous duty upon almost everything foreign, would tax the best Custom House staff in the world to its fullest capacity, and the New York appraisers and examining officers appear to lose their heads altogether under the strain consequent on the arrival of a transatlantic steamship.

The next annoyance one meets with is the two-dollar-and-a-half hack fare, from the wharf to the hotel. The licensed city conveyances are not allowed to enter the steamships' premises, and you have no remedy against an unlicensed or unnumbered hack for extortion. We cannot help thinking that this is more the fault of the Liverpool Steamer Companies than it is of our transatlantic cousins. However, once the Custom House and the hack has been removed from one's mind, everything is good and pleasant in New York. Nothing could be more sumptuous and splendid than the Metropolitan Hotel, on Broadway, and the charge, including everything but a bath, which is fifty cents (or two shillings), is only three dollars per diem.[1]

Epigraph: From Thomas Hood's "A Plain Direction" in *The Poetical Works of Thomas Hood* (1861). Thomas Hood (1799–1845) was an English social protest poet whose work addresses social ills such as sweated labor and unemployment. This text imagines the utopia that Britain could be and asks how to arrive there only to be met repeatedly with the incomprehensible answer: "Straight down the Crooked Lane, / And all round the Square." Townshend excerpts lines 81–84 and applies them to the United States.

1. Operating from 1852 until 1895, the five-story brownstone was praised for its lavish appointments, fine food, and amenities including a theater and concert hall. Situated on

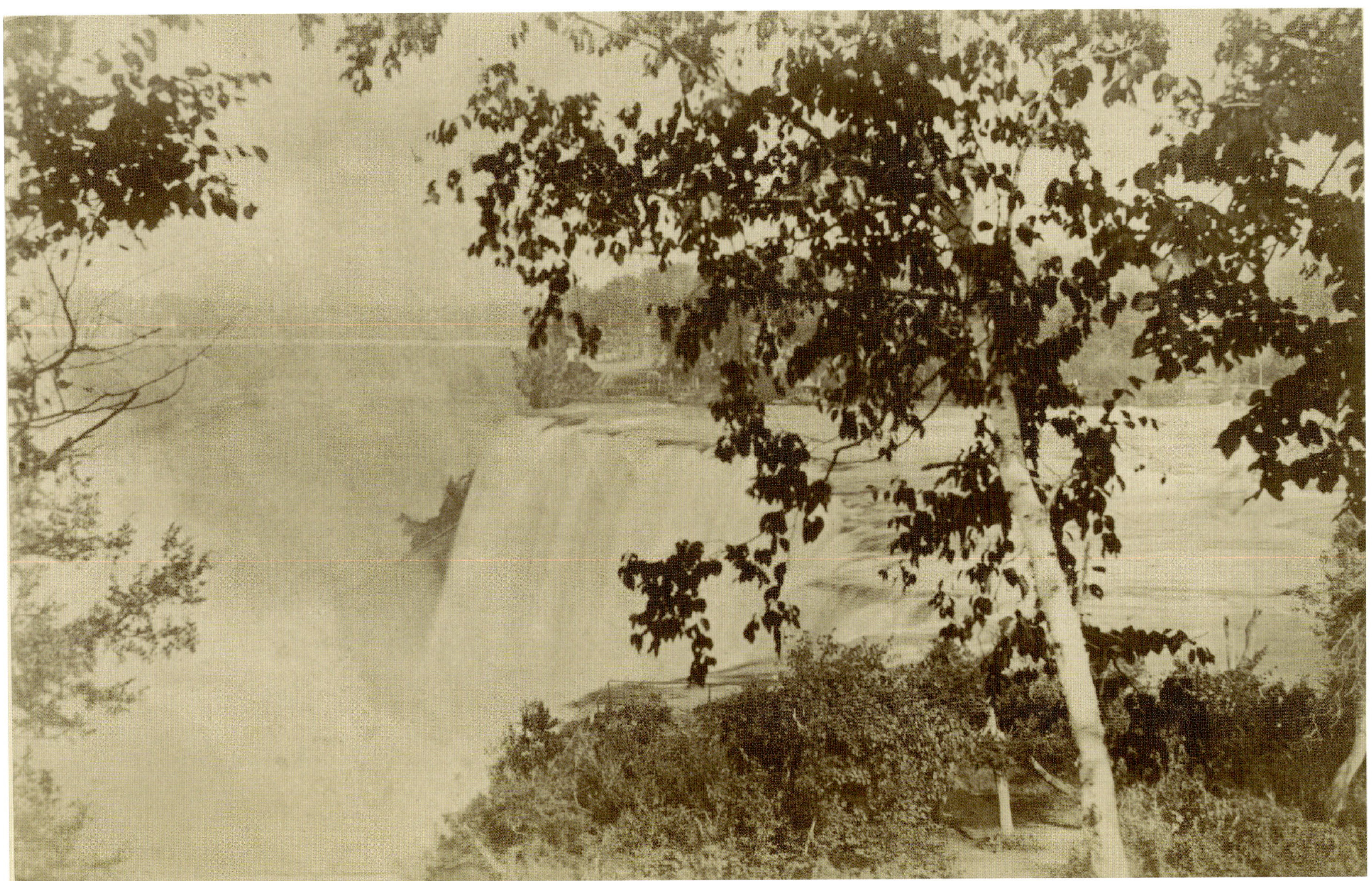

Niagara. American Falls, New York State.
Townshend describes the perspective as "from the head of the elevator mill race." The suspension bridge over the river is visible at the left.

The Equitable Life Office, the enormous business houses of the Tiffanys and the representatives of the late A. T. Stewart, are the most noteworthy buildings to be seen in the city.[2] The genial, chatty editorial rooms of "The World," and "Forest and Stream," and of the Orange Judd Publishing Company, are intellectual treats to those favoured few who have the *entrée*.[3]

One of the originators of the Atlantic cable, that jolly old millionaire Moses Taylor, may be seen daily at the National City Bank, of which he is chairman. He puts bread into a thousand mouths every day. The cares of business sit easily upon the good old gentleman, and his genial smile and winning welcome to those foreigners who have the good luck to bring letters of introduction to him, make one feel quite at home on the spot, and regret that there are not millions of millionaires like Moses Taylor.[4]

In cities, however, we must not tarry. The boundless prairie, the snow-clad mountain, the limitless forest, the ever-shifting river, these must be our themes; these we must explore, and these we must photograph. The prairie grouse and the quail, the wild turkeys, the ducks, snipe, swans and geese, the bear and the deer, the antelope, yes, and even the alligator;—these all we must put into our bag, and into our book. Farewell, then, to the kind-hearted matrons of New York, and the heart-breaking flirts of Philadelphia, to whom we paid a visit, but, for the sake of our peace of mind, it had been better we had not. Farewell to the Atlantic—it may rave and roar now as much as to it may seem good—and let us away to Niagara, over the four-track line of the New York Central and Hudson River Railroad, one of the best equipped in the world, and most comfortable to travel on. Four hundred and sixty-eight miles is the distance, *viâ* Buffalo, to Niagara, and the best to take is the night train, which reaches Albany early in the morning, and carries daylight with it nearly into Niagara.

At Albany a beautiful vista is seen up the hill-side street, but too much haze hung in the morning sky to permit of our photographing either that or the towering Fall River palace-steamers and pretty little yachts, with which the Hudson about here abounds; this river we, however, now leave, and follow up the picturesque Mohawk.

Scarlet shumacs, and every varied hue of autumn's dyes enriched the woods we traversed. It was very hot, the thermometer recording 80° in the shade, and the beautifully timbered, broken, and rather sandy country we bowled through, basked in a second summer, with soft and subdued lights and shades.

At the breakfast station we met that great American institution the "bummer," or "dead beat." He is a gentleman who volunteers all manner of services and information to you, and not unusually even invites you to partake of fluid refreshment at his expense;—but

"Trust him not, he is fooling thee.
Beware, beware."[5]

If you be with him, join in a game of cards, or, indeed, associate in any way for any length of time with him, your experience will be greater, and your pile of dollars much less. Our "confidence men"

Broadway, the Metropolitan Hotel enjoyed a central location that, in addition to its exceptional quality, likely made it especially appealing to travelers hoping to enjoy the best New York City had to offer. "Has Served Its Last Meal"; "New York City."

2. The Equitable Life Office housed primarily law, insurance, and financial companies and was owned by the Equitable Life Assurance Society of the United States. Considered one of the finest office buildings in New York City, it was a model of cultural, financial, and technological progress. The A. T. Stewart Company Store building housed what some claim was the first department store, and as such, the store was part of a new trend in American culture—that of shopping not only to supply needs but also as a form of entertainment. Each of the buildings mentioned here, including the offices of Tiffany & Co., would have been symbolic to any traveler of the vitality and excitement of Gilded-Age, moneyed, society. "New Equitable Life Building."

3. The *New York World* was a daily newspaper published from 1860 to 1931, purchased by Joseph Pulitzer in 1883. It is best known for its rivalry with William Randolph Hearst's *New York Journal*. Charles Hallock founded the weekly journal *Forest and Stream* in 1873. The magazine focused on outdoor life and sports. Orange Judd (1822–92) was an American agricultural chemist, editor, and publisher. His company published agricultural and scientific texts.

4. Moses Taylor (1806–82) was a New York merchant and industrial organizer. He was president of City Bank of New York from 1855 to 1881. At the time of his death, his estate was estimated to be between $40 million and $45 million. Salvato, "Moses Taylor Papers."

5. These oft parodied lines warn against a fair maiden in "Beware! (From the German)" in *Voices of the Night* (1839) by Henry Wadsworth Longfellow.

fill the same national requirement as the great American bummer or dead beat, but the bummer is infinitely the more talented of the two.

On we go through Schenectady into a more attractive country than that nearer Albany. Swelling hill and dale like North Devon is around us, but the rich golden Indian corn crops, and bright large yellow pumpkins peering through the corn stacks, show plainly enough that we are in a far sunnier land than any stay-at-home Devonian has known.

The leaves vary from the bright vivid green of the firs, to pale yellow, bright red and dark crimson, against the white limestone hills. Train after train laden with Indian corn and mineral oil for Europe rush past us, bound east. Now we run parallel to the great Erie Canal,

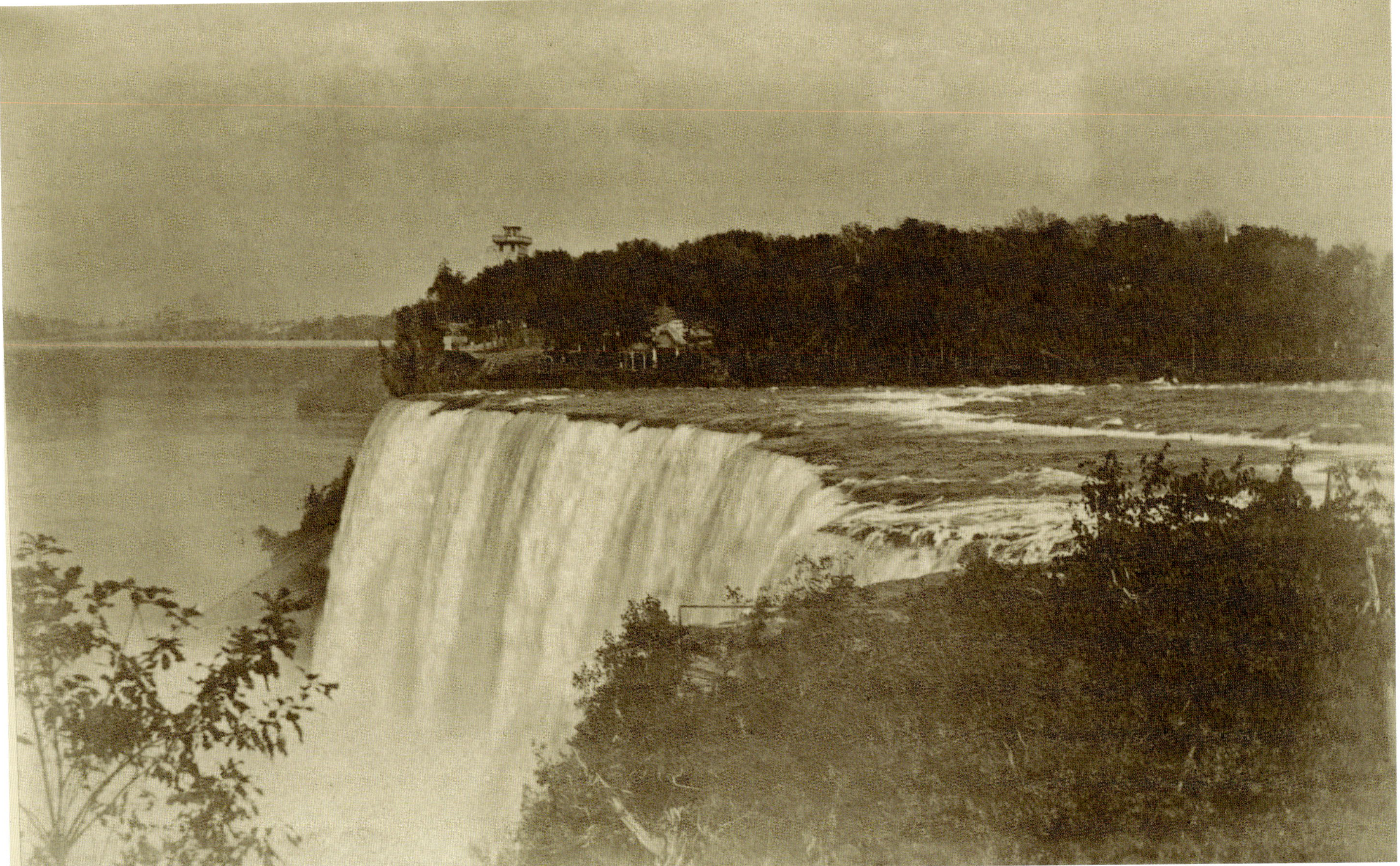

NIAGARA, AMERICAN FALLS.
Image of American Falls taken from Luna Island, looking east.

and get to Amsterdam, which the Dutch have almost abandoned.

Again we follow the narrowing Mohawk, which winds through field after field of yellow grain. Little red and white hamlets, and browsing herds dot the wooded heights and grassy vales, but the country is very roughly cultivated, and the style of farm architecture is anything rather than permanent. Four enormous freight trains within sight of each other move eastward from Utica, where the marvellous beauty and diversity of foliage-colouring was quite indescribable, and these lovely relics of the dying year never appear so much in consonance with the best taste as when, as here, they surround and enshrine the marble slabs over the homes of the peaceful dead.

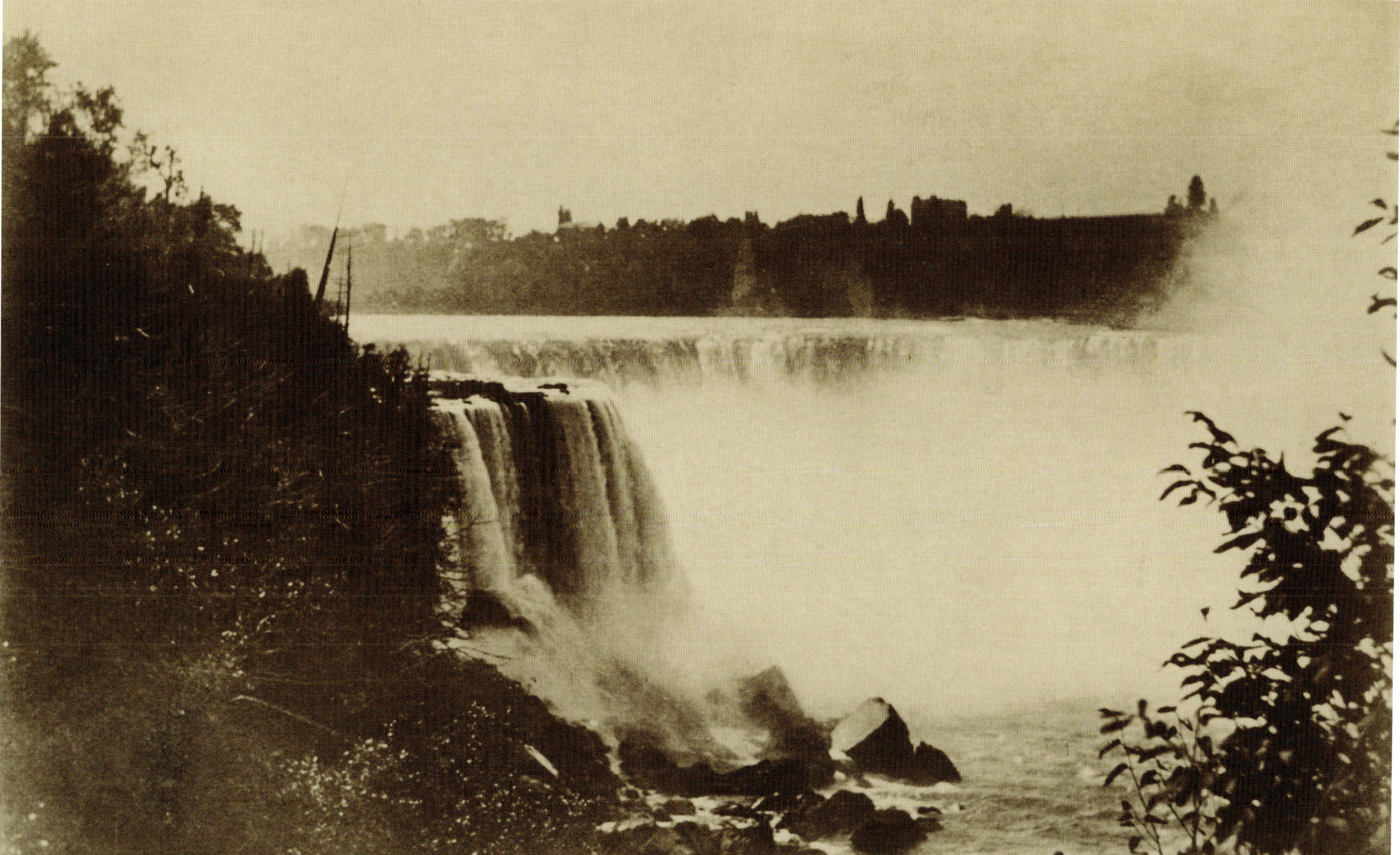

Niagara, Horse-shoe Falls.
Taken from Goat Island. The quality of the instantaneous film is evident here in the detail visible in the falling waters. Townshend notes that one can see the Catholic convent on the Canadian side.

The Mohawk contracts between steep narrow rock banks, and amidst glorious tinted surroundings the Erie Canal, covered with its big, ugly, black barges, takes a higher level than the river on the southern hill-side as we run into Little Falls.

At Utica one gets a capital lunch at noon, and thereafter sees a fertile, rather flat, and very well cultivated country, but nothing either grand or picturesque on either side of the train as far on as Rome. Here the train newsboy begins to bother us. "Oh! go away," we exclaim, "we never read." "What! never read?" he responds, in horror; "then, how in thunder do you ever know anything?"

Jordan is a station soon reached, and between this and Fort Byron a very picturesque fence is seen on the north side. This curious construction is composed of the stumps of old forest trees laid close to each other, the roots are interlaced and interwoven some six feet in height, forming a most impenetrable barrier.

Any amount of stumps standing amongst wild undergrowth are now met with, and a pretty reedy lake forms a favoured resort for snipe and duck.

The Erie Canal passes through Clyde, a town of some importance. All the smaller towns and villages in north-western New York State are composed of diminutive wooden houses, with larger ones very prettily situated around the suburbs. A powerful steam-launch towing a long string of barges through the Erie Canal adds a pretty effect to the scenery, and patches of vine cultivation west of Rochester pleasingly diversify the continued Indian-corn crops. Then it gets dark, and we run into Buffalo on Lake Erie shortly after eight. Having been capitally cared for at the Continental Hotel, which is on the railway platform, the charges being only two dollars per day, we proceeded to Niagara early next morning.

Again it was too hazy to attempt to photograph the lines of the New York Central, which runs its trains in an hour from Buffalo to Niagara, and this line follows the broad, placid Niagara river, lined with immense rafts of huge pines. Great rosy apples studded many orchards along our line, which brought us to the Falls at 10 a.m., and taking a carriage at the Niagara House, a fairly comfortable hotel, we drove to the Whirlpool Rapids, where the first of the many charges made in Niagara is levied; fifty cents each was the charge for being lowered in the elevator. Of these Whirlpool Rapids many apocryphal stories are told, but the "Maid of the Mist" steamed down them on June 15th, 1861, and our photograph of the boiling waters will show the reader that this feat was about the most perilous one attempted.[6] These rapids run somewhat in the form of an arc, over the upper end of which the great suspension-bridge crosses. The banks are clayey slate on the American side, and a purple-and-white stratification characterizes the Canadian shore. The boiling, roaring current, in a mass of seething white foam, thunders on the ear with a sound that would be stunning were it not so monotonously continuous. Our view of this wonderful sheet of water is taken looking down it from the head of the elevator mill race, towards the whirlpool, which is out of sight to the right beyond the white fir-topped headland.

From here we drove back to Goat Island, to enter which is another two-shilling toll. On from Goat Island we went to Lunar Island, and took our next view looking east from the top of the Lunar Island staircase of the American Falls, which descend 164 feet. The Fall is as green as the river blue, and more especially in views of mighty Niagara does one feel the hope that photography may yet be made to act chromatically, and give the green, red, and blue as truthfully as it does the black and the white.

Our next picture was taken from Goat Island, of the Great Horse Shoe Fall, the most magnificent sight of anything in Niagara, in consequence of the immense mass of rushing waters that eternally leap over it into its spray-hidden chasm, 158 feet below. The Roman Catholic convent, and the tower built to commemorate the visit here of the Prince of Wales, are seen in the distance on the Canadian shore.[7]

6. Townshend refers to Capt. Joel Robinson's famous passage of the rapids on June 6, 1861. "Niagara Falls Stunts and Daredevils: History," *Niagara Parks*, accessed December 2, 2015, www.niagaraparks.com/about-niagara-falls/niagara-falls-stunting-history.html.

7. Townshend may refer to either the Monastery of Mount Carmel or the Shrine of Our Lady of Peace. The tower is Brock's Monument, built to commemorate the British

The Three Sisters islands, connected by bridges, stand just where the river breaks into falls. Our view of these shows the Canada shore in the distance and the placid Niagara river extends into the far background.

The weather was glorious, but large fleecy clouds drifted constantly across old Sol, and rendered the snatching of good photographic moments no easy task, for sometimes the light would be powerful enough for instantaneous negatives, and at other periods the camera would require a two-seconds' peep at the scenery to get an accurate impression of what it was looking at.

victory on October 13, 1812, over American troops. Maj. Gen. Isaac Brock, commander-in-chief of British forces in Upper Canada, was fatally wounded in the battle to reclaim the Heights of Queenston. Brock's cenotaph also commemorates the Prince of Wales's (Edward VII) visit on September 18, 1860. "Historic Plaques and Markers," *Niagara Parks*, accessed March 1, 2015, www.niagaraparks.com/niagara-falls-attractions/historic-plaques-and-markers.html.

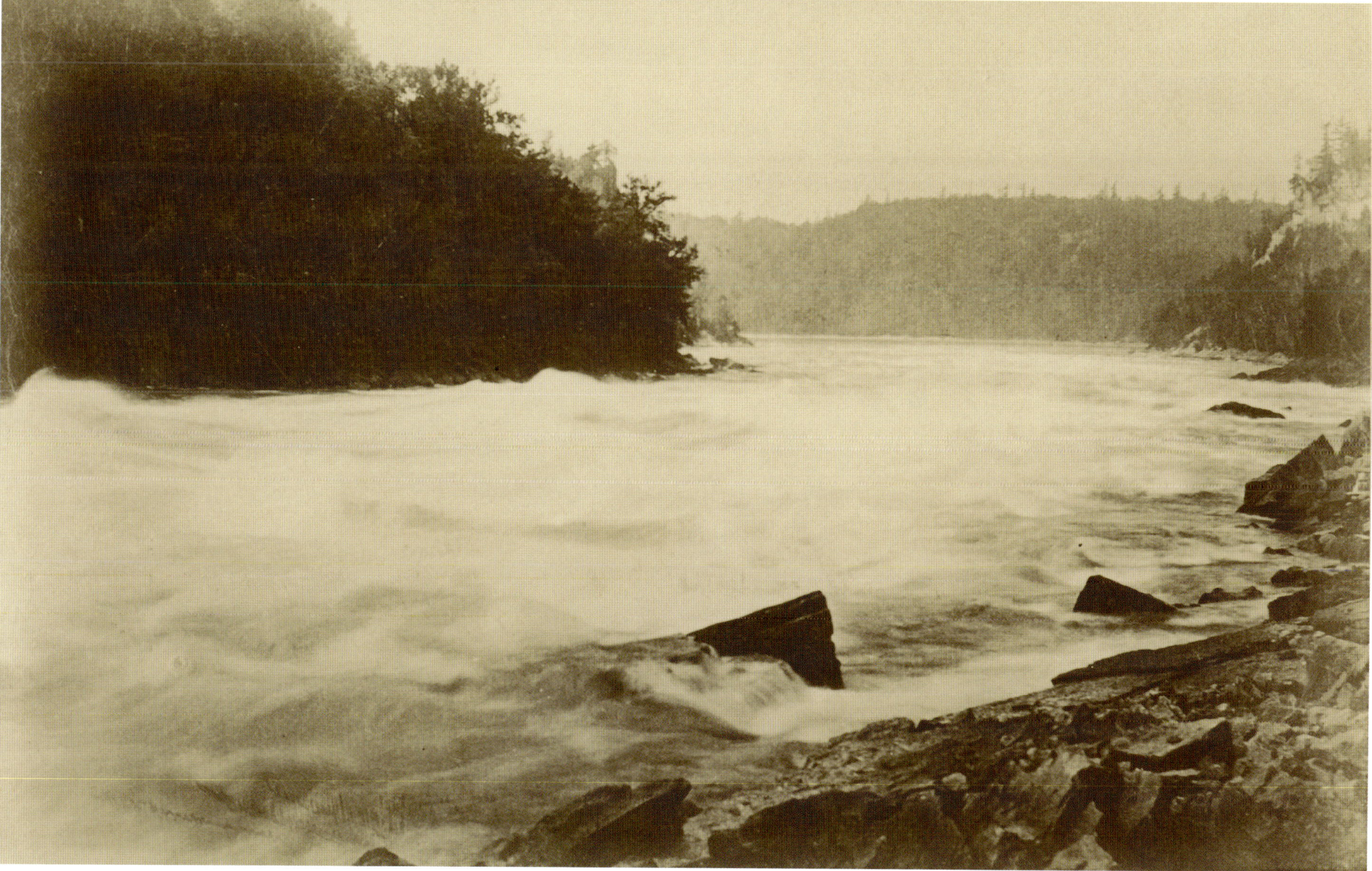

The Rapids (Two Miles below Niagara).

These are the Whirlpool Rapids below the falls.

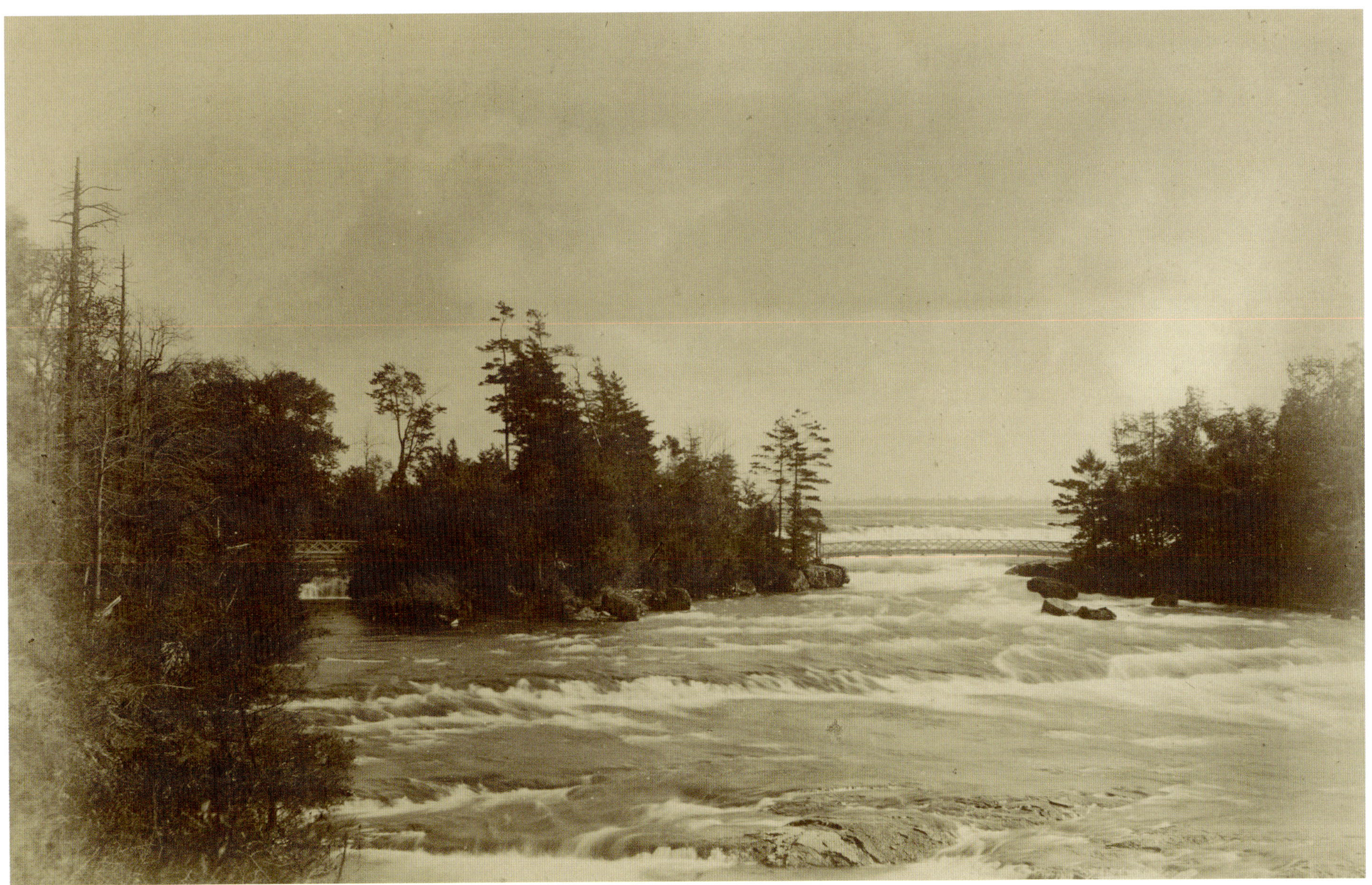

The Three Sisters Islands. (Niagara River above the Falls.) Looking toward the distant Canadian shore. The islands are joined by bridges. The sharper detail of the rapids must have pleased the photographer.

Other pretty or grand views we were unable to take, for our plates in the slides, were all used, and no dark chamber to get out others from their box could be found. The very smallest amount of light would, of course, fog the entire plates, and our object was to present as clear views as possible, both in text and photography, of this country.

The next move we made was into British North America, and after crossing with a four-shilling toll the suspension-bridge, which is 198 feet above the river, and 1,268 feet long, we found that there was rather more imposition and extortion practised on the side of Niagara that belongs to Her Majesty than in Uncle Sam's contiguous domains.

The views are, however, better from the Canadian side, for you can see from there the American and Horse Shoe Falls, and compare them together.

The everlasting, the eternal spray which hangs around these great falls, golden or silver, as the sun governs the day or the moon the night, reminds one only of the summer of the snow-clad Sangre de Criste ranges, if you could imagine them inverted, or when light sunlit or moonlit snow-clouds drift across them; but the green of the vast waters, which struggles so hard with the white of the eventually conquering foam, is a factor in which the great depths fairly outrival the great heights.

Tourbillons[8] of white spray dash back frightened from the abyss they are being precipitated into, and rainbows of every size and shape float over the wonderful scene, no matter from what point one views it.

This view is obtained from the top of a tower, the admission to which is ostentatiously styled free, but you cannot well get out of it without purchasing some presumed curiosities, and then paying a dollar to the proprietor, and another to the guide, to take you down a staircase 160 feet, and bring you out under the Falls. Here you can see almost nothing but blinding spray, and in any case you are only under a very outpost corner of the rushing waters. Some of the hackmen of Niagara are in league with the places that charge the most, and you are, especially on the Canadian side, driven not so much to the best views, as to where you will be charged the highest sum.

A long baulk of timber runs out a little below the tower and staircase to within twenty yards of the north side of the Horse Shoe Falls. From here a view of peculiar magnificence and colour is seen. On the American side all the water is white rushing foam, sea-green and semi-transparent in the middle, and darkly flowing near as just before it takes its great final leap.

Going from here through Cedar Island, and then up the Chippewa side along the Rapids above the Falls, we notice that the water in the middle of the river is much lower than that at the sides, caused by the freedom of escape at the centre of the Horse Shoe.

A graceful little miniature of the great suspension-bridge takes us into Clarke Hill Islands, and past many small falls, one of which runs twenty-seven miles per hour under Pollox Bridge. Beyond lies the hot sulphur spring, where sulphuretted hydrogen gas burns through several folds of a kerchief, and the same gas, after we have drunk two tumblers of water, is so strong in them that it lights in a clear reddish flame.

Back to Niagara we drive high up on the Canadian hills. The two grand Falls lie below. The reddish-yellow light of the Indian summer mellows everything in the distance but the Niagara river, which far above the Falls is seen like a sheet of burnished gold. Its peace is soon to be succeeded by war; first ripple after ripple, then wave after wave, last breaker after breaker.

These wonders of nature are done homage to by all sorts of bad and indifferent architecture in the near surroundings. It is 201 years since Father Hennepin discovered Niagara, and then its very solitude must have imparted a charm which we are now deprived of.[9]

8. From the French *tourbillion*, meaning a whirlwind or whirling storm. *Oxford English Dictionary Online*, s.v. "tourbillion | tourbillon, n.," accessed March 1, 2015, www.oed.com.

9. In 1678 Father Louis Hennepin, a French priest, traveled to Niagara Falls. Although he was probably not the first to discover the site, Hennepin was the first European to document Niagara Falls in *A New Discovery of a Vast Country in America* (1697), which effectively introduced the site to the Western world. An English translation appeared in 1698. *Encyclopedia Britannica Online*, s.v. Louis Hennepin, Franciscan missionary, accessed March 1, 2015, www.britannica.com/biography/Louis-Hennepin.

"And as the moon from some dark gate of cloud
Throws o'er the wave a floating bridge of light,
Across whose trembling planks our fancies crowd
Into the realm of mystery and night."[10]

10. From "Haunted Houses" in *Birds of Passage* (1858) by Henry Wadsworth Longfellow.

CHAPTER III

NIAGARA TO CHICAGO, *VIÂ* PHILADELPHIA AND PITTSBURG, AND THENCE TO KANSAS CITY—BOUNDARIES, RIVERS, AND RAILWAYS OF KANSAS—PROSPECTS OF THE UNITED STATES: THEIR COLONIZATION *VERSUS* OURS—STATES OF THE UNION CANNOT TAX EACH OTHER'S PRODUCTS AS OUR COLONIES CAN—THE CRY OF IMPERIAL DISINTEGRATION—KANSAS COMPARED WITH OTHER STATES—ITS EARLY HISTORY UNDER THE *FLEUR-DE-LIS*—ITS PRESENT STATISTICS AND CLIMATE—PHOTOGRAPH REFERENCES.

"But oh! the life in Nature's green domains,
The breathing sense of joy! where flowers are springing
By starry thousands, on the slopes and plains,
And the grey rocks—and all the arch'd woods ringing."

MRS. HEMANS, *Relics of Tasso*

Sport, and to study the progress of the settler out West, were now our only objects, and the middle States not serving as favourable ground for these pursuits, let us make a dash at once to where we would be. Four hundred and sixty-eight miles we first re-traversed to New York, for our engagements led us into Philadelphia, that great mass of red brick and white marble on the Delaware and Schuylkill. In this city of the old Quakers, a day is spent in seeing the site of the International Exhibition,[1] and the beauties of the romantic Wissahickon and Consohocken.[2] Philadelphia is only ninety miles, two and a half hours' run from New York. On we go, three hundred and fifty-four miles, to Pittsburg, through the heart of Pennsylvania, and over the Alleghany mountains—a magnificent sight on a clear sunny morning such as the one on which we passed over them. At Pittsburg our Pullman is run on to the Pittsburg, Fort Wayne, and Chicago rails, and four hundred and sixty-eight miles on these brings us to the city of the lakes, Chicago, where Lake Michigan in all its glory of autumn quietude, surrounds much of the gem-like city, as silver would a precious stone. But against cities we have now taken the pledge. Even the Palmer, or the Grand Pacific Hotels cannot keep us; so, hey! for the Chicago and

Epigraph: From "Release of Tasso" in *New Monthly Magazine* (November 1823) by Felicia Dorothea Browne Hemans (1793–1835). Hemans's work was immensely popular in both Britain and America, selling thousands of copies and earning her the respect of William Wordsworth and Joanna Baillie. Although much of her poetry focused on the domestic sphere, she often employed Romantic themes—here, Nature. "Felicia Dorothea Browne Hemans," 1179–80.

1. The Philadelphia Centennial Exhibition was the first international trade fair in the United States. The exhibition opened May 10, 1876, ran for six months, featured more than two hundred buildings and hosted more than ten million visitors. As Townshend and Hyde did not arrive in Philadelphia until 1879, they probably viewed the site and permanent buildings, rather than the exhibition. *Encyclopedia Britannica Online,* s.v. "Philadelphia Centennial Exhibition," accessed March 1, 2015, www.britannica.com/event/Philadelphia-Centennial-Exposition.

2. Wissahickon may refer to the eponymous valley or creek. Wissahickon Creek is a tributary of the Schuylkill River beginning in Montgomery County, Pennsylvania, and passing through northwest Philadelphia. The last few miles of the creek run through a deep gorge, the Wissahickon Valley, which is now one of the U.S. National Natural Landmarks. See Friends of the Wissahocken website for more: www.fow.org. Conshohocken is a borough of Philadelphia located on the east bank of the Schuylkill River. It was an industrial and manufacturing center during the nineteenth century. See the borough's website for more: www.conshohockenpa.org/visitor/history.

Alton rail, which takes us over four hundred and eighty-nine miles to Kansas City, Missouri; then only a bridge has to be crossed, and we are in the new State of Kansas, with the newer one of Colorado lying beyond it, the Indian territory and that of New Mexico lying south, and again southward beyond the former, the enormous State of Texas.

Kansas, however, we are now in, and this fine State is an old favourite of ours. We only present eight photographs of scenery in it, but this is owing to the limited number of plates we could carry with us from England, it not being possible to procure as yet really instantaneous plates, as Wratten and Wainwright's are, in the United States.[3] Kansas is splendidly rich, but cannot be called a "beautiful" State, and wishing this book to be of practical utility to the emigrant, as it will fall chiefly into the hands of those to whom the humbler classes would naturally look for advice, we will here give a short sketch of Kansas in its historical, climatic, agricultural, and emigrational aspects. Our trip as recorded in this book, it is true, is only one of three months; but we have had intimate knowledge of Kansas and the Kansans for over three years.[4]

Kansas, then, has for its southern boundary the thirty-seventh parallel, and for its northern the fortieth. The State is four hundred and thirty miles long, and two hundred and ten wide, its area being ninety thousand square miles. One hundred and fifty miles of Kansas front on the Missouri, which steamers not only ascend from the Gulf of Mexico, but which magnificent river is navigable for two thousand five hundred miles north of the northern boundary of Kansas.

The State abounds in rivers and streams, except in a portion of its very central belt, lying between the Atchison, Topeka, and Santa Fé and Kansas Pacific railroads. As one goes West on these splendid lines, which run through all Kansas into Central Colorado, there is a gradual ascent for six hundred miles; from the Missouri river to the Rocky Mountains. Where the Kansas river discharges itself into the Missouri, is but seven hundred and fifty feet over the sea level. Where the lines we have referred to cross the Colorado boundary, the altitude is three thousand five hundred.

The words "United States" have a very mixed meaning to most untravelled Englishmen. The name to most of us means an immense friendly Power—a Power sprung from ourselves, and of which we are proud; a Power which, when it fully fills up and develops the American continent, will assuredly take up the spread of civilization, and of the Anglo-Saxon race, at perhaps the point where our senility as an empire may force us to leave off, and consign to the offspring of England the perfection of the glorious task—the emancipation of the world from thraldom and tyranny—labored for by its parent for many a century, and carried out regardless of either blood or treasure. Secession or rebellion will never be tolerated in the United States, nor will one State—though the Union extended to Cape Horn—ever be permitted to tax the products of another. And who will say there are not signs of senility in us as an *Empire*?

From the Crimean war[5] down to the commencement of the Colonial reign of the Earl of Carnarvon,[6] have we not been all but inviting our colonies to cast loose the silken—but all the stronger for that—threads of patriotism and unity which rendered common the cause, liberties, and protection of every ENGLISHMAN, whether he was born in Northern Canada, tropical India, or Southern New Zealand? So-called Liberal statesmen may soon again rule our destinies, and wrapped up in their prejudiced, insular, narrow-minded views,

3. The comment here reminds us that the travelers are economizing their available plates for the journey ahead.

4. Townshend owned land in the Topeka, Kansas, area, as noted in his Royal Geographical Society application and reports in *The Field*. Pagnamenta, *Prairie Fever*.

5. The Russians fought the British, French, and Ottoman Turks in the Crimean War (1853–56). Several disputes contributed to the conflict: tension between powers in the Middle East, Russia's demands to protect Russian Orthodox subjects of the Ottoman sultan, and the privileges of the Russian Orthodox and Roman Catholic churches in Palestine. The Treaty of Paris, signed March 30, 1856, obliged Russia to surrender southern Bessarabia opening the Danube, neutralized the Black Sea, and guaranteed the integrity of Ottoman Turkey. *Encyclopedia Britannica Online*, s.v. "Crimean War," accessed March 2, 2015, www.britannica.com/event/Crimean-War.

6. Henry Howard Molyneux Herbert, 4th Earl of Carnarvon served as undersecretary for the colonies (1858–59) and as colonial secretary (1866–67 and 1874–78). In 1867 he introduced the British North America Act granting Canada self-government. He supported similar moves in South Africa and Ireland. *Encyclopedia Britannica Online,* s.v. "Henry Howard Molyneux Herbert, 4th Earl of Carnarvon," accessed March 2, 2015, www.britannica.com/biography/Henry-Howard-Molyneux-Herbert-4th-earl-of-Carnarvon.

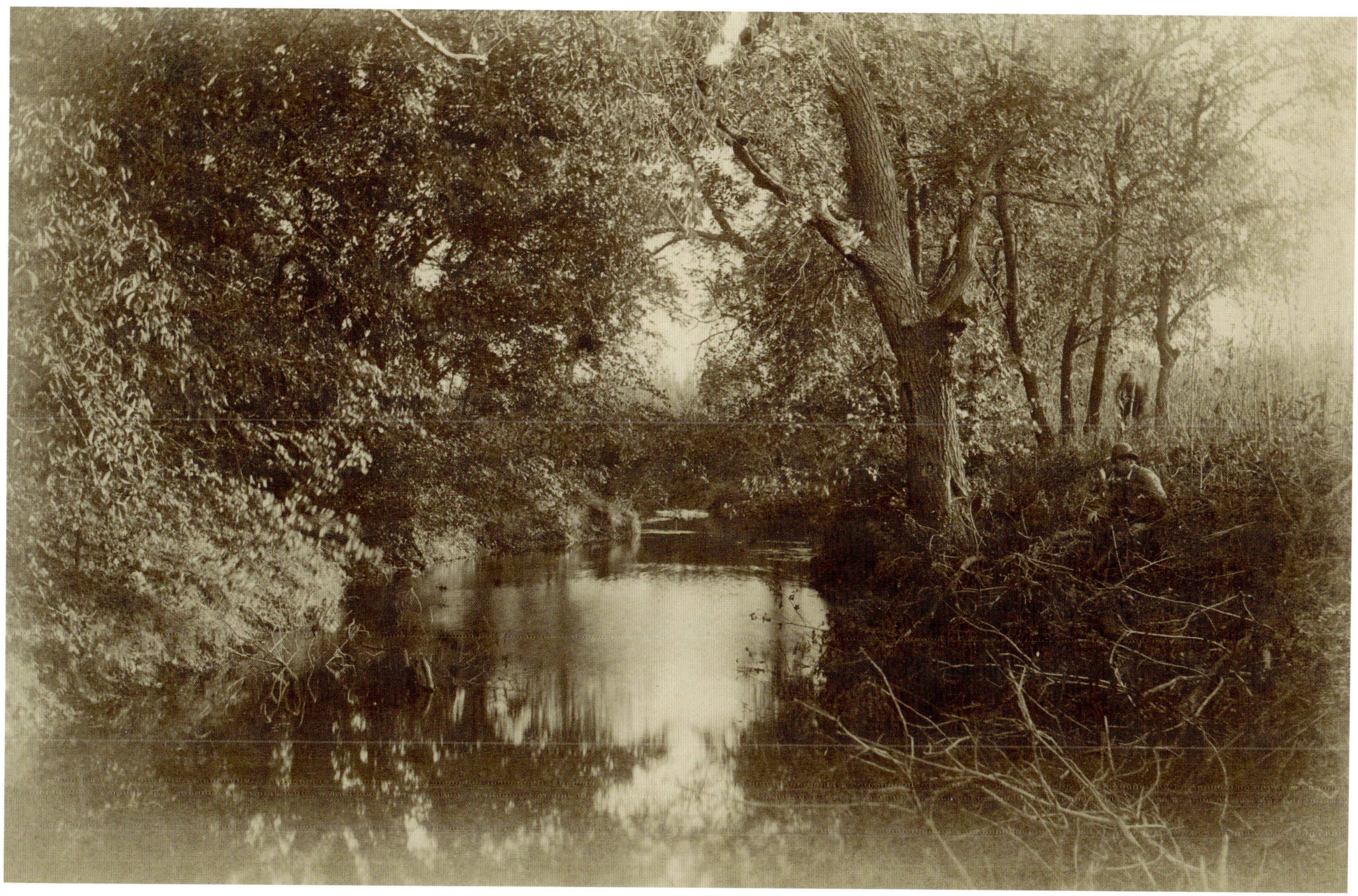

Vista on the Whitewater.

The first image of Kansas and thus the West as our travelers define it. Townshend remarks that "man has never interfered with this scene." Still, the image provides a sense not of wide open space or wilderness but of peace and solitude. The viewer partakes of the gaze of the lone figure, perhaps Hyde, a horse behind him, in the idyllic sylvan scene.

may survey the glories of Great Britain, as seen only from the top of the tower-clock in Westminster, and anew exclaim, "Perish the Colonies! Withdraw protection from our South African and Anglo-Indian colonists and interests, as we did from our brethren in New Zealand; perish Lord Carnarvon, the editor of 'The Colonies and India,'[7] and everyone else that raves of Imperial Federation.[8] Imperial disintegration is that which will suit our pockets. Give us our own sea-girt Isle, and a nice, solid, compact Government therein." So said Rome, and where now is Rome? So said Holland, and where now is the old King of the Seas? So have said, and say still a large party amongst us; and yet many of us say, "The Union is too large, it must break up." It never will; the majority of the States will, in Imperial matters (as we understand them) always rule the minority. York and Lancaster wars there may be here, but York *or* Lancaster will rule the United States as one great power,[9] probably long after our Liberal administrations have snubbed the last dependency of our Empire into unwilling independence, preceded by—as in the case of Canada and Victoria at present—our products being allowed to be gradually taxed out of their markets.[10]

So much for our opinion of what are termed the great uncertainties supposed to hang over the United States—uncertainties only borrowed by the Englishman meditating emigration from the clouds which even Lord Beaconsfield, Lord Lytton, or Lord Dufferin have not been quite able to lift from our heretofore cruelly-neglected Colonial Empire.[11] There hang no uncertainties over the future of any State here, none of them will ever be kicked or kick itself out of the Union, and of all the well and peaceably-conducted Western States give us Kansas and Nebraska—the western homes of the younger children of New England and of Germany. This may seem to be a digression, but before we get into emigrational statistics the ground must be cleared of all prejudice against the Government of the United States and the prospects of the settlers therein. Defects in administration we shall have from time to time to notice, but the laws are almost the same as our own, and with the law-abiding electors of each State rests the enforcement of them. Thus Kansas and Nebraska are almost as firmly governed as England. In West Texas and New Mexico a large proportion of evil-doers escape punishment; whilst in Arizona and Dacota there as yet appears to be no law at all, except in perhaps the law libraries of those territories.

The merits of Kansas as a country fit for settlement have only struck the world of very recent years. M. Duquesne, in 1720, hoisted the *Fleur-de-lis* of France amongst the Kansan Pawnees, and claimed the country by divine right—a puzzling theory to red men—for the Duc d'Orleans, Regent of France.[12] As, however, Duquesne fell

7. *Colonies and India* was a weekly journal published out of London, Middlesex, containing the latest colonial and foreign intelligence. The British Library holds the volumes from 1879 to 1898.

8. In response to growing concerns over the sustainability of the British Empire, some British statesmen—like the Earl of Carnarvon—supported imperial federation to allow for democratic government at the local level while maintaining the British Empire's international power and status.

9. Townshend here compares the American Civil War (1861–65) to the English Wars of the Roses (1455–85), the dynastic civil wars between the Houses of York and Lancaster.

10. The Colony of Victoria in southeast Australia separated from New South Wales in 1851 and attained self-government in 1855. British dominions, such as Canada and Victoria, were considered autonomous states within the British Empire and thus had complete legislative authority, including levying taxes. *Encyclopedia Britannica Online,* s.v. "Victoria, State, Australia," accessed March 2, 2015, www.britannica.com/place/Victoria-state-Australia; s.v. "dominion," accessed March 2, 2015, www.britannica.com/topic/dominion-British-Commonwealth.

11. Earl of Beaconsfield Benjamin Disraeli served as British prime minister from 1874 to 1880. Robert Bulwer-Lytton, 1st Earl of Lytton, served as viceroy of India from 1876 to 1880. Frederick Temple Hamilton-Temple-Blackwood, 1st Marquess of Dufferin and Ava, served as governor-general of Canada from 1872 to 1878. *Encyclopedia Britannica Online,* s.v. "Benjamin Disraeli, Prime Minister of United Kingdom," accessed March 3, 2015, www.britannica.com/biography/Benjamin-Disraeli; s.v. "Robert Bulwer-Lytton, 1st Earl of Lytton," accessed March 3, 2015, www.britannica.com/biography/Robert-Bulwer-Lytton-1st-earl-of-Lytton; s.v. "Frederick Temple Hamilton-Temple-Blackwood, 1st Marquess of Dufferin and Ava," accessed March 4, 2015, www.britannica.com/biography/Frederick-Temple-Hamilton-Temple-Blackwood-1st-Marquess-of-Dufferin-and-Ava.

12. The duc d'Orleans Philippe II (1674–1723) served as regent of France for Louis XV from 1715 to 1723. M. Duquesne refers to Ange de Menneville, Marquis Dusquesne, a naval officer and governor-general of New France from 1751 to 1755. However, Duquesne would have been only twenty in 1720 and still serving under another's command. Rather than Duquesne, Townshend probably means Claude Charles Du Tisne, one of the first French Canadians to enter Kansas and to establish the fur trade with the Osage and Pawnee.

back at once to the Missouri, the Pawnees took for granted that his divine right accompanied his retreat, and so things went on peaceably until the Spanish Commandant at Santa Fé heard of the affair, and advanced rapidly northward to claim a diviner right over Kansas for the King of Spain. The Pawnees and Missouris were then at war, and the Spanish Commander offered the Pawnees—as he thought—to join them against the Missouris. He had, however, mistaken the tribe, which was really a Missouri one; and they, dissembling for a time, suddenly fell upon the Spaniards and killed every man of them, saving only the chaplain.[13] The *Fleur-de-lis* consequently floated over Kansas for eighty-five years afterwards, but not one red man did the French civilize. No one even dreamt of getting an acre under cultivation, and not until 1854 was it proposed to organize Kansas into a territory. Since then its rise of population from virtually nothing to three-quarters of a million has astonished even the Kansans themselves. In 1854 it is doubtful if five hundred acres were turned over by the plough; in 1878 six and a half million acres were under crops of one sort or the other. In the former year there was not a mile of railroad in the State; now there are about two thousand five hundred. No newspaper was published in the State in 1854; now there are two hundred and thirty-seven. Then there were no schools; now there are five thousand and two, with an attendance-roll of one hundred and seventy-seven thousand. Then there were no churches; now there is accommodation provided for one hundred and thirty-five thousand worshippers. Wheat and all sorts of grain growing and cattle fatting are the chief occupations of the rural Kansan, and for wheat and cattle we know to our cost how good the markets are, and are likely to be. What we should do in these bad years without the unlimited American supply the poor only can tell, and their reply would be—"Starve, or go into the poor-house."

Next we come to the climate, and this is not a subject proper to generalize much about. Enough of open weather exists during winter for all agricultural operations, and Indian corn need not be gathered until the heat of summer is over. Failing any late meteorologic table, we can only say that the heat for at least six hours every day in July, August, and September is usually very great, the thermometer ranging from 80° to 100°, and even occasionally 106°, but mornings, evenings, and nights, unlike those in South Texas, are always refreshingly cool. In winter the days are, as a rule, bright, dry, and cold. In March and September it usually blows a gale during all the month, and nothing more disagreeable can be imagined, as the dust then appears to fly sky-high over the entire State. These winds do not, however, hurt the farmer at all, for his crops are then either too young to be injured, or gathered in. The rainfall is very good, and in the Central belt of the State neither floods nor droughts are experienced. In the Eastern belt the former sometimes give a great deal of trouble, and in the Western some droughts, as this year, prove almost ruinous. Nevertheless, the rain-belt is extending gradually West.[14] The rainfall last year in the Eastern belt was 37.58 inches, in the Middle one 27.89, and in the Western belt 21.73. This year in the Western belt we do not believe that the rainfall was even eight inches, and a great deal of loss was consequently experienced by farmers in that region, and by many even in the Middle belt, of which Ellis, Rush, Pawnee, and Edwards counties form the Western limits near the railway systems.

The photographs accompanying this chapter will be referred to again hereafter. The first is a view on the Whitewater river, eighteen

Dictionary of Canadian Biography, vol. 4, 1771–1800, s.v. "De Menneville, Ange"; Kansas State Historical Society, "French Settlers in Kansas," in *Kansapedia*, last modified July 2011, www.kshs.org/kansapedia/french-settlers-in-kansas/12203.

13. In 1720 Lt. Gen. Pedro de Villasur led a scouting expedition through the Great Plains to check French progress. On August 13 Indian forces attacked the Spanish camp on the Loup River, killing de Villasur and most of his soldiers. Nebraska State Historical Society, "The Villasur Expedition—1720," last modified June 2004, www.nebraskahistory.org/publish/markers/texts/villasur_expedition_1720.htm.

14. Townshend refers to the theory of climatology proposed by Charles Dana Weber, commonly known as the "rain follows the plow." According to this erroneous theory, championed by boosters, human settlement and agriculture effected a permanent change in climate, resulting in increased rainfall and soil fertility as the population increased. See chapter 6 for Townshend's full presentation of this idea.

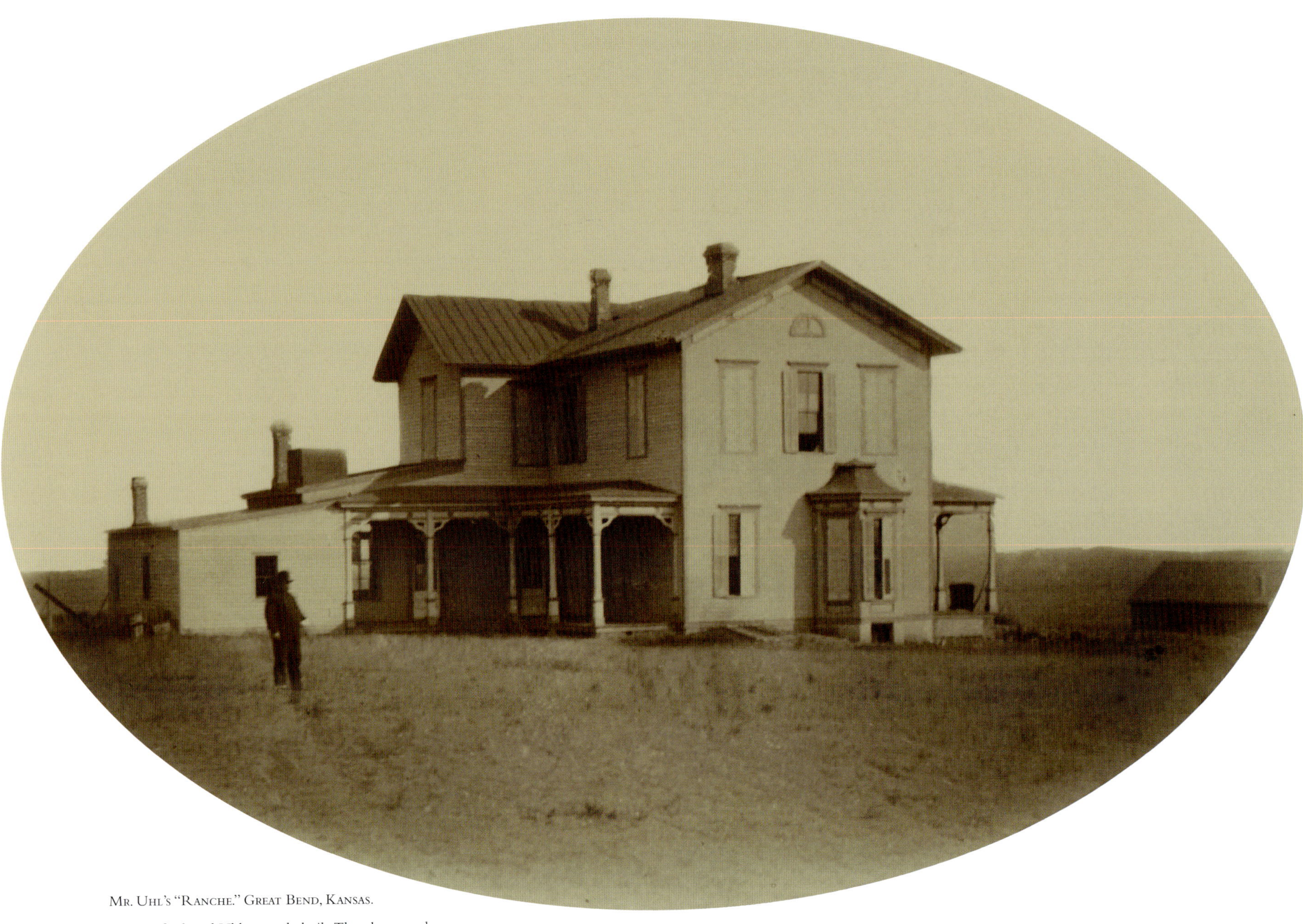

Mr. Uhl's "Ranche." Great Bend, Kansas.
House of Edward Uhl, recently built. The photograph emphasizes the gingerbread trim and gracefully roofed dormer, elegant touches for a newly developed region.

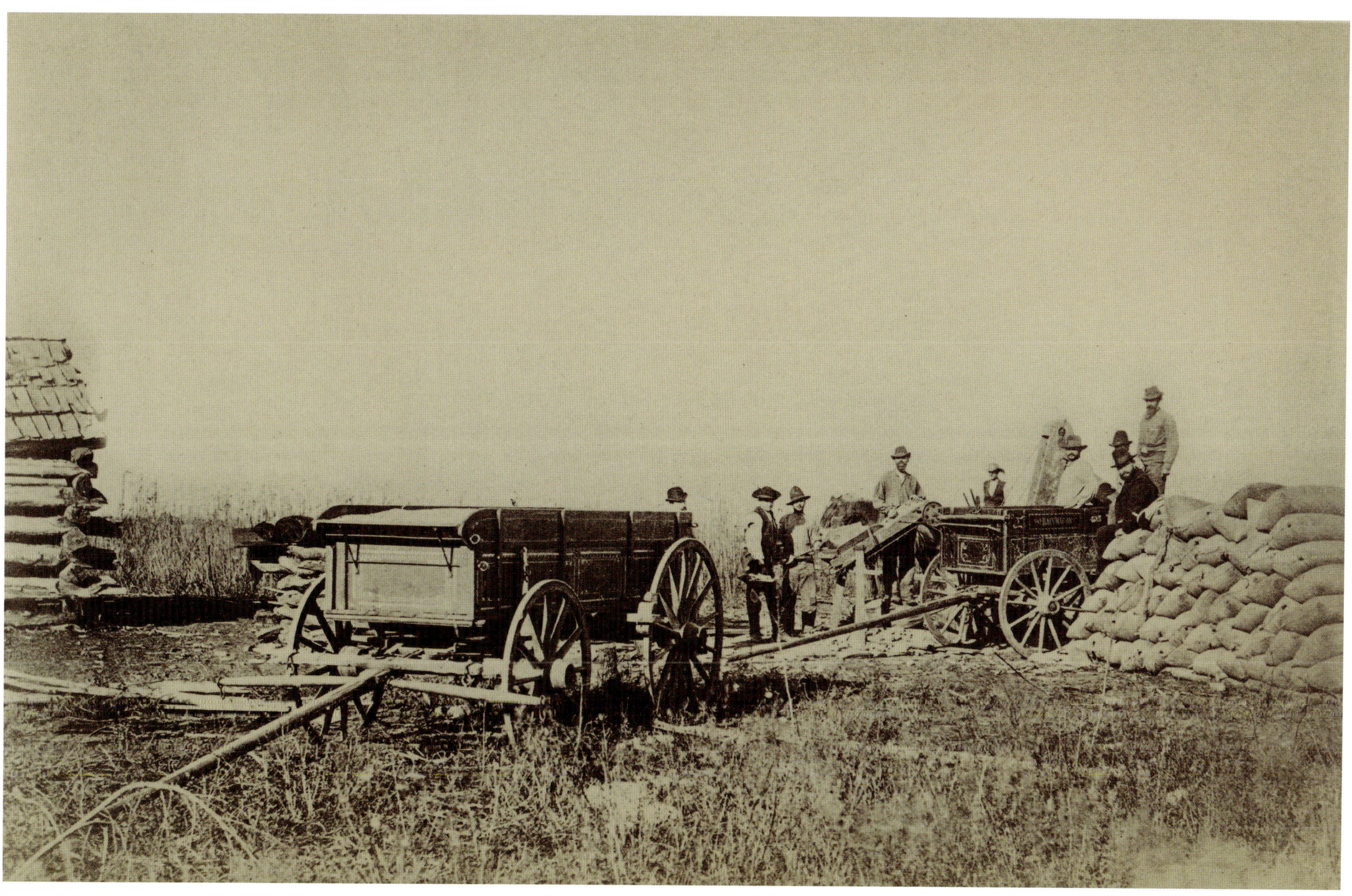

Corn-Shelling.

A well-composed and balanced image, framed by the rough cabin and the bags of corn, the wagon tongues form a strong diagonal axis, featuring the technology of the shelling apparatus and the working men.

miles south of Newton, in South-West Kansas, and man has never interfered with this scene; the second is the house of Mr. Edward Uhl, recently built on the prairie near Great Bend, on the line of the Atchison, Topeka, and Santa Fé railroad; and the third is a busy farming scene near the Whitewater, where yellow grain is jumping from the sheller into sack after sack, when

"In richest robes the hills and woods appear,
The lakes and springs lie motionless and clear,
Ruled by the fairest queen of all the year—
Beautiful harvest time."[15]

15. These unattributed lines appear under the title "Harvest Time" in *New England Farmer* 2 (1868) and again as "Indian Summer" in *Living Age* 115 (1872).

CHAPTER IV

LEAVE KANSAS CITY FOR THE PRAIRIES—THE FOUR SYSTEMS OF BUYING LAND IN KANSAS—HOW TO INVEST TWO HUNDRED POUNDS—LAWRENCE AND TOPEKA—THE COURTESY WE MET WITH THERE—ITS HOTELS—A LITTLE BIT OF GEOLOGY—CHASE COUNTY AND FREE RANGE—FLORENCE, ITS HOTEL AND ITS PHILLIPS—JOE IRWIN AND HIS PET AVOCATIONS—QUAIL MIXED WITH AGRICULTURE AND PHOTOGRAPHY—A FORECAST OF NEWTON FARMING.

"Half veiled in golden light of shimmering air,
The landscape stretches wonderously fair,
No paling beauty anywhere;
Nature is in her prime."

Poems of England

We cannot promise that this chapter is likely to be very entertaining, as in it we propose to run into detail for the information of intending emigrants, or emigrants' friends.

At Kansas City—most of which is in the State of Missouri—we left the Chicago and Alton railroad, and met Mr. Goddard and some other officers of that wonderfully dashing and enterprising line, the Atchison, Topeka, and Santa Fé—one owning about seven hundred miles of its road in Kansas, which it, as before said, runs across; about three hundred miles in Colorado, which it runs half through; and over two hundred miles in New Mexico, being the only line of railway in that territory. First, however, of the portion of Kansas which this liberally and honestly managed line traverses.

It may not be amiss to say here that we have been long in love with the way the Atchison, Topeka, and Santa Fé railroad has managed its two million five hundred thousand acre land grant, and the splendid quality of a great deal of its land. The Company's sales are of four descriptions. The valuation of the lands are all fixed, and to be had in the office of Colonel A.S. Johnson, the land commissioner, in Topeka, the State capital.[1] Here the man who has seen and selected his land in the valley of the Cottonwood, or the Arkansas Valley—through which the best portions of the railroad property run—can pay cash down, getting thirty three and one-third per cent. discount; or,

(2) He can buy on the two years' system—viz., one-third of the purchase-money down, with ten per cent. interest on the remainder, and the balance in two annual instalments. For this mode of purchase he gets thirty per cent. of the marked value off to begin on.

Epigraph: These unattributed lines appear under the title "Harvest Time" in *New England Farmer* 2 (1868) and again as "Indian Summer" in *Living Age* 115 (1872). In the original text these lines appear before those that Townshend employs to close chapter 3.

1. Alexander Soule Johnson (1832–1904) was known as the first white baby born in Kansas. He worked for the Atchison, Topeka, and Santa Fe Railroad's Land and Tax Departments from 1874 to 1890. During the period of this narrative, Johnson was also a prominent banker in Topeka and would soon become a state legislator. Bryant, *History*; James L. King, "Col. Alexander Soule Johnson," *USGenWeb Archives*, 2006, http://files.usgwarchives.net/ks/shawnee/bios/johnson123nbs.txt.

(3) The six years' system. Twenty per cent. is allowed off. The first payment at date of purchase, is one-sixth of the principal, and seven per cent. interest on the remainder. The second payment is only interest. Afterwards one-sixth of the principal, and seven per cent. interest on the unpaid sixths, until all is paid.

(4) Is the eleven years' system, the first payment being one-tenth of the principal, and seven per cent. interest on the balance. At the end of the first and second years only interest is payable, and then the payments of one-tenth, and interest, run on until the title is perfected by the liquidation of the whole.

As an example of this, we will give, say, one hundred and sixty acres, at one pound per acre. Payments would be, turning dollars into pounds, at five dollars to the pound:—

DATE OF PAYMENT.	PRINCIPAL.			INTEREST.			TOTAL.		
	£	s.	d.	£	s.	d.	£	s.	d.
May 1, 1880	16	0	0	10	1	8	26	1	8
May 1, 1881		nil		10	1	8	10	1	8
May 1, 1882		nil		10	1	8	10	1	8
May 1, 1883	16	0	0	8	19	4	24	19	4
May 1, 1884	16	0	0	7	16	10	23	16	10
May 1, 1885	16	0	0	6	14	6	22	14	6
May 1, 1886	16	0	0	5	12	0	21	12	0
May 1, 1887	16	0	0	4	9	8	20	9	8
May 1, 1888	16	0	0	3	7	4	19	7	4
May 1, 1889	16	0	0	2	4	10	18	4	10
May 1, 1890	16	0	0	1	2	6	17	2	6
May 1, 1891	16	0	0		nil		16	0	0
Total	160	0	0	70	12	0	230	12	0

Or one thousand one hundred and fifty-two dollars in round numbers.

For the new immigrant short of means, and very anxious to put what he has into agricultural stock, and pay his annual rent for eleven years from the yield of the soil, this is a splendid scheme, and another advantage is that he can throw up the land when he feels disposed; but just contrast this £230 12s. for one hundred and sixty acres with scheme No. 1. It reads thus:

	£	s.	d.
One hundred and sixty acres at £1 per acre	£160:	0	0
Cash discount off, 33 ⅓ per cent.	53:	6	8
	£106	13	4

an immense reduction over the total sum which plan No. 4 eventually gets out of the purchaser.

The land departments at Topeka have been very conservative in their policy, have made no reckless statements, and do not advise any married man to come to Kansas with less than £200, or any single man with less than £100. What has been done with £200 we have ourselves seen, and Colonel Johnson recommends the expenditure to run as follows:—First payment on one hundred and sixty acres at 19s. 4d. per acre, on the six years' system, will be £34 11s. 4d. House with two small rooms and kitchen, £50. Pair of horses and harness, £36. Breaking plough, £4 8s. Harrow, £2. Cow, £6. Interest on purchase-money unpaid, £8 19s. 4d. Total, £141 18s. 8d., and leaving a balance of £58 1s. 4d. for furniture and food until the crops come in.

It will be thus seen the Company takes for granted that with fair farming the crops will not only support the settler and his family, but, besides, pay for the land in six years. If the hardships and general newness of things and people the first year are met with perseverance, good temper, and hard, honest work, the success of the farmer may be taken to be assured.

Having thus given an outline of what has been done, and what is being done, and may be achieved for a good many years to come before all the good land is taken up, as it very rapidly is being, let us onward from Kansas City towards the setting sun, and passing historic Lawrence, where the free-labour inhabitants were all killed by

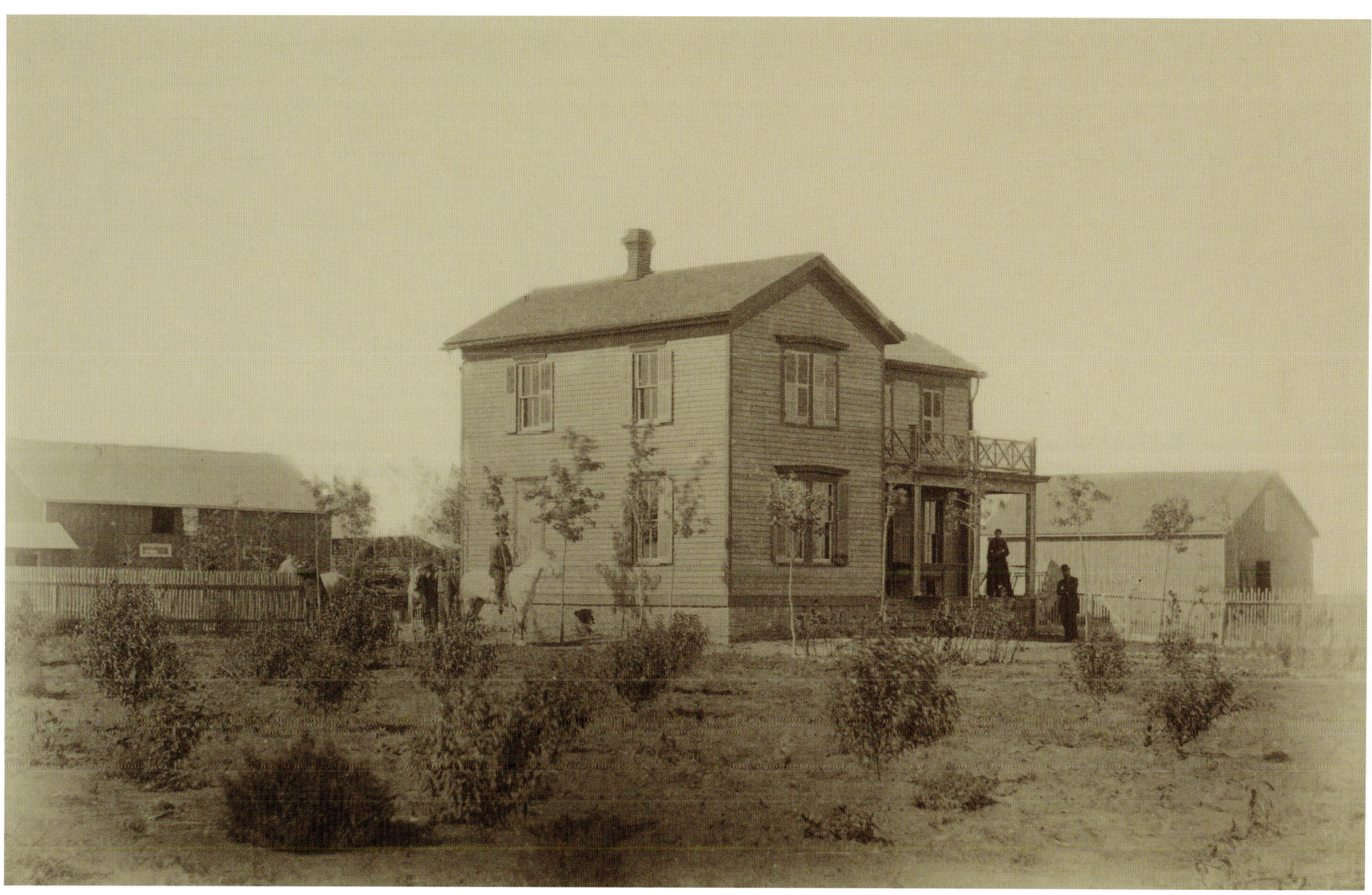

Dietrich Claassen's "Ranche." Near Newton, Kansas. The photograph highlights the fine new houses and buildings, with the young trees suggesting the new country. The well-dressed and bold figures in the foreground are Mr. and Mrs. Dietrich Claassen.

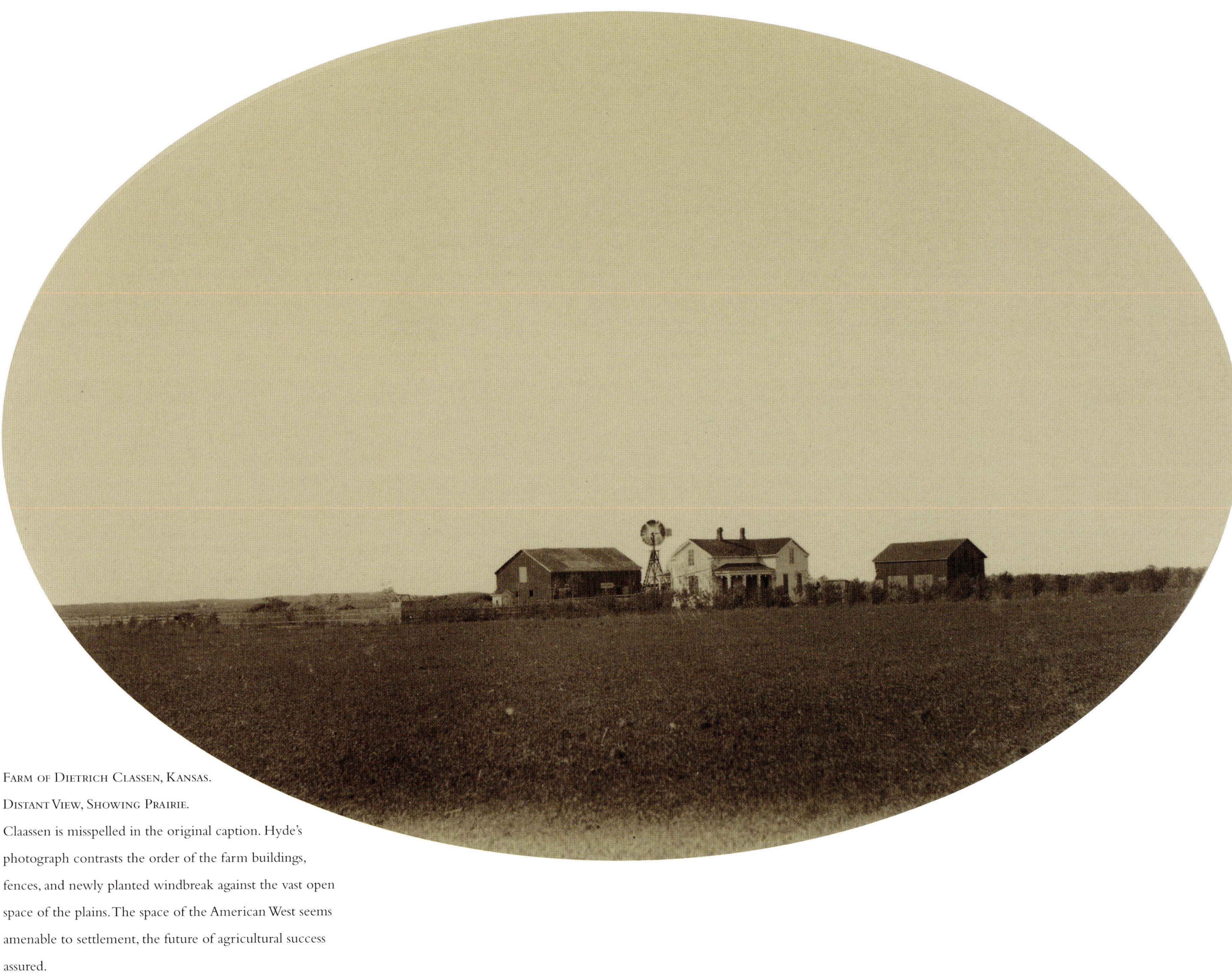

Farm of Dietrich Classen, Kansas.
Distant View, Showing Prairie.

Claassen is misspelled in the original caption. Hyde's photograph contrasts the order of the farm buildings, fences, and newly planted windbreak against the vast open space of the plains. The space of the American West seems amenable to settlement, the future of agricultural success assured.

Quantrell's slave-owning raid at the commencement of the late war,[2] we follow the Kan valley, heavily timbered, and richer than language can paint.

This land is now far too dear for new emigrants, as it is not in any land grant, nor sold on time, and it brings from £8 to £16 per acre. Topeka, the quiet New England capital of Kansas, we reach, and meet some dear old friends—friends not only of ours, but of every British emigrant. South Kansas was, indeed, our first love years ago, but we had strayed from it, and been tempted into strange and beautiful wildernesses in Utah, Wyoming, Colorado, Arkansas, Texas, and goodness only knows where, in the interests of emigration.[3] But our old Topeka friends opened their arms to us as though we had been ever constant to the Arkansas Valley, and so we were made much of, and assured we were the best writers and photographers in the world, by everyone in the General Passenger Office, Land Office, and Foreign Office; we were introduced to every Colonel and Honourable in the State House or Capitol; we were invited to all sorts of impossible things in the way of sporting expeditions, and finally we were turned loose with every sort of possible credential and introduction that was worth having by Mr. Manchester, Mr. Wm. F. White, Colonel Johnson, and Mr. C. B. Schmidt. Ex-Judges and a living Militia General—Frederick—would not permit our land-owning friends to monopolize our society in the State capital,[4] where, if any hotel will concede sufficiently to British prejudice, and establish a bath-room, we will mention their other good points, but not until then. At present the best a tourist can do is to go to the Dutton House, or Poppendick's. The emigrant will find nearly as good accommodation at far less cost in the Adams House, north of the river.

On October 17th, then, take we the Pullman car, on the South-West-bound mail train of the Atchison, Topeka, and Santa Fé, and bowl one hundred and six miles to Florence, past enormously luxuriant crops of corn, across homelike, picturesque, placid, tree-lined streams, which cut deep into the chocolate-coloured soil, geologically termed "loess," or material which ages of time have slowly drifted by rainfall from the western mountains. Alluvial deposits are found as you near the watercourses, which have all sunk and cut downwards; but everywhere you find vegetable mould, mingled with lime, iron, chlorides, carbonates, phosphates, silicates, and sulphates. The phosphates were created and for millions of years reinforced by the successive deaths of the animal race, which swarmed over these vast plains in prehistoric as well as historic times. In the fossiliferous portions of the State are found the Mastodon, *Mastodon giganteus, Elephas Americanus*, and a gigantic horse, a portion of the jaw of which is to be seen at the State Agricultural College. The Elephant was very common, and from the observations of scientific persons would appear to have had but four teeth.

We have only time to make these speculations and investigations during our journey of eighty-one miles to Cottonwood Falls, where the land grant of the Company commences. Up to this point the country had not been very much settled, except near the unlimited coal fields of Carbondale, and round Emporia Junction, where the Missouri, Kansas, and Texas line crosses our course on its way to Northern Texas. The reason why so comparatively little of the land south of Topeka is settled, is, that it is in the hands of capitalists, who are waiting a rise, which is apparently never high enough for them, though all good land has risen over ten per cent. in Kansas, since 1876. At Cottonwood Falls we reach the valley of the Cottonwood, in Chase County, which is the only one with a free cattle range, where damages cannot be brought against the stock-owner for trespass

2. On August 21, 1863, William Quantrill led 300 men, known as Quantrill's Raiders, into Lawrence, Kansas, devastating the town and killing more than 150 of the 3,000 residents. Quantrill was a Confederate supporter and called the raid on Lawrence retaliation for various attacks on Missouri by James Lane's Kansas Brigade. Davis, *Kansas*; Kansas Historical Society, "Quantrill's Raids."

3. Though employing the editorial "we," Townshend here refers to his articles published in *The Field* in January and October 1878.

4. Presumably prominent Topekans and men involved with ATSF, not all of whom can be identified with certainty. Wilder notes in *The Annals of Kansas* that William F. White was author of a pamphlet, "Rocky Mountain Tourist," and a Topeka newspaperman. Colonel Johnson is A. S. Johnson, noted in chapter 6, as is C. B. Schmidt.

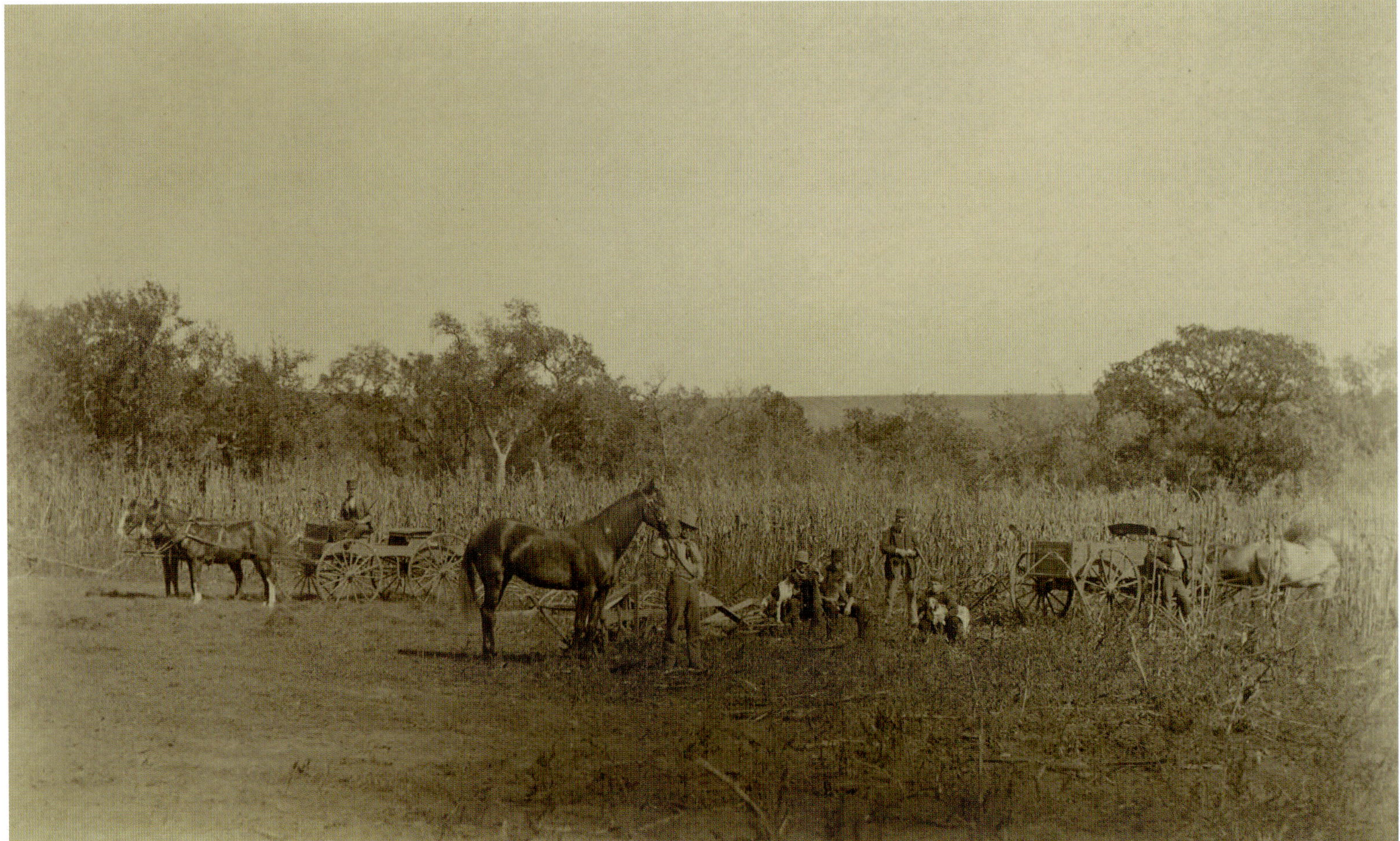

Firnell Brothers' "Ranche." Near Florence, Kansas.
The original caption is in error; the brothers are identified as "Fernald" in the narrative. The image includes two men in the main group with shotguns. The one standing appears to be Townshend. Might the other be Hyde?

of cattle, unless the farmer has his land fenced in. In all the other agricultural counties along the line of this railroad the law is the other way, and "the herd law" prevails; there no need of fences, save for shelter, exists, and the stockmen must herd their cattle.

The Cottonwood river, for most of its course, flows through a gently-rolling prairie country, adapted for every sort of agriculture; but in Chase County its two-mile-wide valley contracts between bluffs of Magnesian limestone, which crop out in many places over this district, for which reason it has been tacitly relegated to cattlemen, for whom there is a good deal of room, even yet, as Chase County contains all but half a million acres. Mr. J. W. MacWilliams, the Mayor of Cottonwood, is the Company's land agent here, and a more courteous and straightforward one it would be hard to find.[5]

Again the cry is "Forward," and this time we stop at Florence

5. John W. McWilliams founded the Chase County Land Agency in 1869 and acted as loan officer and land agent for the one hundred thousand acres of unsold land owned by the Atchison, Topeka and Santa Fe Railway. Cutler, *History of the State of Kansas*, available at www.kancoll.org/books/cutler/chase/chase-co-p2.html#COTTONWOOD_FALLS.

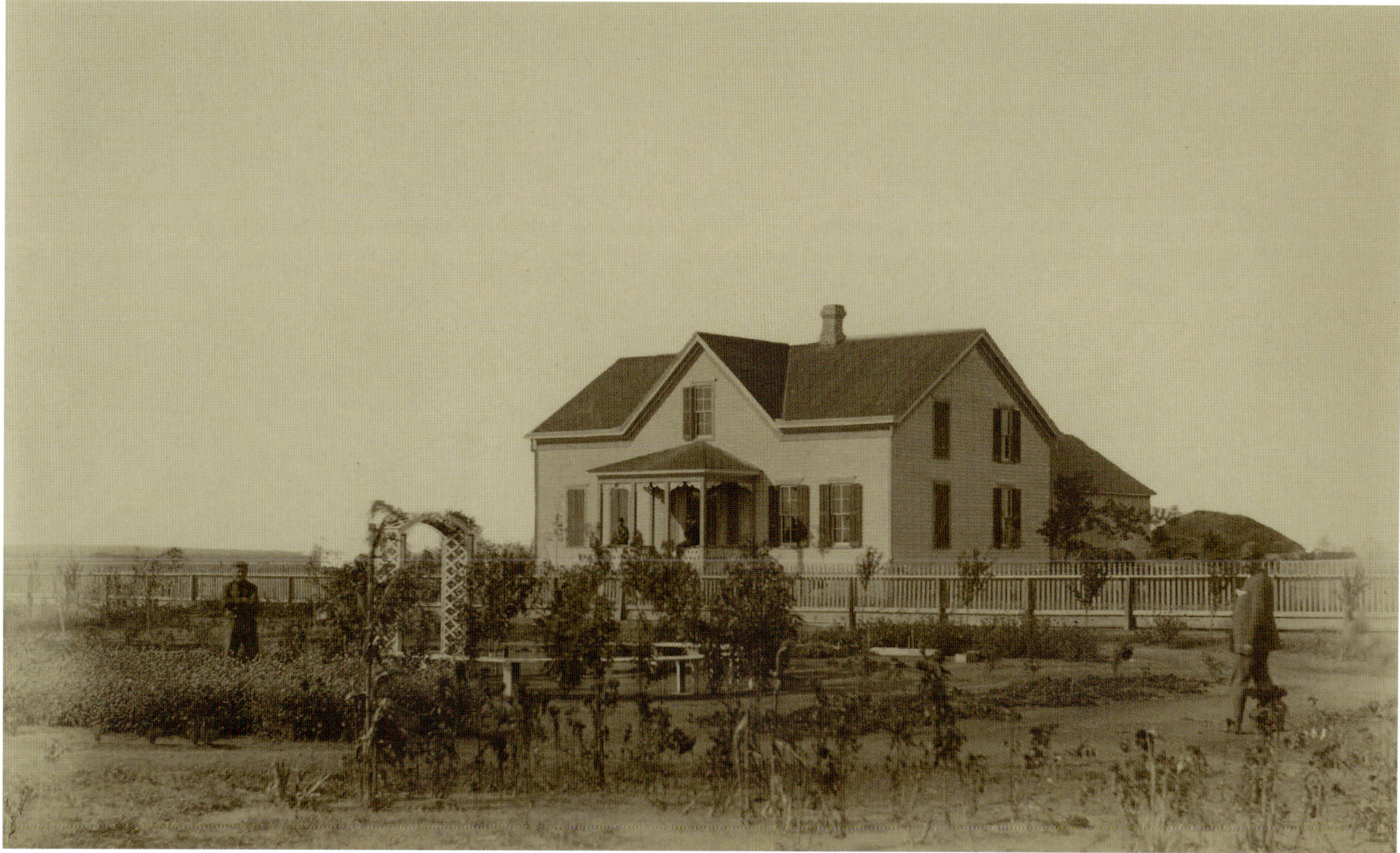

BERNHARDT HARDER'S "RANCHE," KANSAS.
Harder stands to the left of his arbor. Hyde again captures the extreme order of the farm against the wide prairies behind.

Junction, from whence run branch lines to El Dorado to the south, and McPherson to the north-west. Florence is perhaps the very best centre for the intending emigrant to stay at, for he has trains going in four different directions, and has by a long way the best hotel in Kansas to put up at. The Clifton Hotel has an English manager, and of course a bath-room. Its apartments and its cooking are very good. No more jovial or attentive host and hostess than W. H. Phillips and his good wife ever lived in "merrie England," or left it for the far West; and the chief clerk, Joe Irwin, is a sportsman to the manner born, who knows where every grouse and quail in the country reside, and is always willing to take you to see them.[6] Behold us, then, with Joe in his light spring waggon, driving merrily away West from

6. William H. Phillips was a noted English chef lured by Fred Harvey from Chicago to work at the Clifton Hotel, which became a famous Harvey House Hotel in Florence, Kansas. Townshend reviewed the hotel and its impressive dining room for *The Field*. He also met Joe Irwin, local hunter and fishermen, in Florence through Fred Harvey. Fried, *Appetite for America*.

Florence, through Marion County, on October 18th; banging away at quail, right centre and left, missing any amount of the little wretches, who *would* just hop up over a bush and down again, or round it, or across Martin Creek, on the banks of which we presently came to the rancho of Fernald Brothers, and of this we took a photograph. Joe Irwin's spring waggon is seen near a grain-sower to the right. A celebrated horse of the district is held by his groom in the centre, and a group of farmers and farm hands collecting Indian corn into a waggon are in the background. Close inspection will show the corn-stalks' height far above the waggon and horses. The Fernald Brothers have been here but two years; they bought one hundred and sixty acres, and have ninety of them under cultivation.

The two views of the farm of Dietrich Classen, which are also in this chapter, we got next day in Butler County, south-east of Newton. The first of these views shows the owner on his horse, and his wife on the balcony.[7] The other picture is a more distant view of the same farm. All these buildings and the fee simple of the farm of three hundred and twenty acres cost but £1,400, and Classen has only been out from Germany for two and a half years.

In the next chapter the reader must look for the *modus operandi* of farming, and the farm profits here, and to any practical mind they cannot fail to be interesting. This chapter and the day it is written on have run their full length, and it is in Kansas the

"Calm evening hour wherein the sun goes down,
And his last gleams fall lingering on the hills;
By the lone tarn how sweet is silence grown!
How deep a dream of rest the silence fills!"[8]

7. Dietrich and Abraham Claassen (the correct spelling is with two a's) were among a community of Russian-immigrant, German-speaking Mennonites in Kansas established around 1873–74. Juhnke, "Mob Violence and Kansas Mennonites"; Saul, "Migration of the Russian-Germans to Kansas"; Epp, *Petals of a Kansas Sunflower*. Townshend consistently misspells Claassen in the text.

8. These lines appear in a description of George Edwards Hering's landscape "By the Lonely Tarn" (1879) on display at the Royal Academy of Arts. *London Magnet*, May 12, 1879.

CHAPTER V

FLORENCE TO NEWTON—FARMING OPERATIONS WITH A CAPITAL OF £200—THE LOVE OF THE EMIGRANT FOR OVER-COLOURED STORIES—WHAT EL DORADO REALLY IS—BUTLER COUNTY—320-ACRE FARM OF DIETRICH CLASSEN—HIS PROFITS IN A BAD YEAR—RAPID GROWTH OF TREES—BERNHARDT HARDER, THE WEALTHY MENNONITE—HIS IDEAS OF THE COUNTRY, HIS GARDEN AND HIS CEMETERY—BISHOP SUDERMANN—CATTLE-FATTING FARM OF A. CLASSEN, AND HIS INVESTMENT IN IT—HARVEY COUNTY, STATISTICS THEREOF—APOLOGY FOR A CHAPTER AS DRY AS THIS SEASON IN KANSAS.

"Then ardent man would to himself be new,
Earth at his foot and heaven within his view:
Well might the novice hope, the sanguine scheme
Of full perfection prompt his daring dream."

MOORE

Twenty-nine miles south-west of Florence Junction is Newton Junction, from which the Wichita branch runs south to Arkansas City, almost in the Indian territory. All this country is extremely well adapted for wheat, and families settling here with £200 have, as a rule, prospered by adhering to the following procedure.

The settler, say, arrives in February, and his house is erected by contract in two or three weeks. The cost of a starting outfit we have previously given. As the land has no stumps or stones on it, the plough can go directly to work, and before March is over he will have a crop of rye, barley, or brown corn, and enough vegetables planted for the use of the family. A pig or two, and a few fowls, are a great help; and after the spring crops are put in, the farmer can earn a few pounds easily and honestly by working his team for his neighbours' more extended agricultural operations. In this way too he can give labour for the use of grain-drills, reapers, and such other machinery as he has not means to buy for himself at first. A reference to the last chapter will show that for his 160 acres he has no instalment to meet the end of the first year, when he puts in his wheat, which he reaps fifteen months—as the second crop—from the time he first settled, and then each year more than pays its own way, land instalments and all. Increasing areas are henceforth being annually put under cultivation. Time is found to plant Osage-orange hedges—prickly and impenetrable barriers—round his homestead. Forest trees and fruit trees follow, without expense of outside labour, and as even a partial failure of crops occurs on an average but once in five years in Kansas, and then the higher prices for farm produce almost compensate for the average wheat crop falling from, say twenty bushels to the acre to

Epigraph: From Thomas Moore, "Poems Relating to America," in *The Poetical Works of Thomas Moore, Collected by Himself*, vol. 2 (1840). The quoted verse is from the poem titled "To The Lord Viscount Forbes, from the City of Washington." The lines imagine, with skepticism, human possibility without the weight of history.

ten, the risks of the farmer here are much less than in England, where every third year has of late been almost disastrous to agriculture.[1]

The emigrant always wants to be told of districts where everything always grows, where there are neither floods nor droughts, insects nor taxes. And where these things are worst, lying agents find it necessary to explain them away altogether. "El Dorado" is, indeed, found in Kansas, but it is only a second-rate railway station, and gold has to be worked for there as hard as in most other parts of the Western States.

The farm of Mr. Dietrich Classen is a very good type of those in Butler County[2]—the buildings and steadings on it are shown by our photographs in the last chapter—and Mr. Classen told us that for his 320 acres agricultural machinery cost him £200. He has 150 acres under cultivation. This year was very dry, so had only twelve bushels of wheat to the acre, and got 3s. per bushel for it, the price after he had sold it rising to 4s. 2 1/2 d. To raise the first crop of wheat, Mr. Classen said, cost him £1 13s. per acre, so his profit nett was only 3s. per acre, but this was with an exceptionally bad crop, and the first in new ground. His second wheat crop cost him to raise £1 1s. per acre, and this showed the very fair profit also, in this bad year, of 15s. per acre.

Of Indian corn he raised thirty-five bushels on new ground, and fifty bushels the second crop. This year corn sold there for 10d. per bushel, but last year it carried only half that price. We therefore have come to the conclusion that, except very near a railway station, Indian corn only pays for fattening cattle or hogs—a business at which twenty per cent. should be and has been made. Farming, to market all the produce, cannot reasonably be expected to pay more than ten per cent. after supporting the farmer and his family. Much more has been done, but it is not the rule.

Near Dietrich Classen's house were peach-trees four feet high, from seed planted eighteen months ago, and maples of the same age were over ten feet high. The Osage-orange hedges in the neat farm—Mr. Andrews'—were beautifully clipped by machinery, and this neatness was even eclipsed by the fine order everything was in at the farm of Bernhardt Harder, a director of the Harvey County Savings Bank.[3] This old gentleman is also a new settler. Our photograph shows him, in his semi-Russian or Mennonite cap, near his garden arbour. The date was October 20th when we went to see this leader amongst the Mennonites, and the weather was warm and glorious as any of our best summer days. "Good new country. Plenty of hard work, plenty of money," the old gentleman, in his broken way, remarked to us, and then took us to see his improvements. Amongst others, a cemetery he had laid out for himself, near the garden, which bloomed even thus late in the year with a good many flowers.

All the agricultural pictures which we took here—seen in this chapter and the last—are on the farms of Mennonites, of whom ten thousand are located along the lands of the railway. We regretted not having a plate to spare for the residence of the Right Rev. Leonhard Sudermann, who, though a Prussian, lately from Berdianski, has been elected by the Russian Mennonites their bishop.[4] On the banks of the Whitewater—a pretty vista of which is shown by one of our photographs—stands at a considerable elevation the residence and offices of Mr. A. Classen, another of the numerous clan of his name who have settled in this district. Though the view is taken across the Whitewater, and at a considerable distance, the neat fences and steadings show how good and careful a farmer he is. He has only two hundred acres, of which twelve are in timber, but his land is splendid, and he paid £2 per acre for it. Out of the £4,000 which he brought over here, he has invested £1,600 in building and fencing, for the purpose of fattening and keeping in hogs and cattle.

The threshing on Plum Grove farm, Mr. Spencer's, is represented in our last chapter. A Bain and a Kansas waggon are being filled

1. British agriculture had been struggling due to bad weather cycles, economic conditions, and outdated production practices. Britain had recently, in 1876, begun importing American wheat. Pagnamenta, *Prairie Fever.*

2. See chapter 4, note 7.

3. Harvey County was formed in 1872. Gaylord, "Harvey County."

4. Sudermann was also a leading promoter of Mennonite immigration to America. Krahn, "Sudermann."

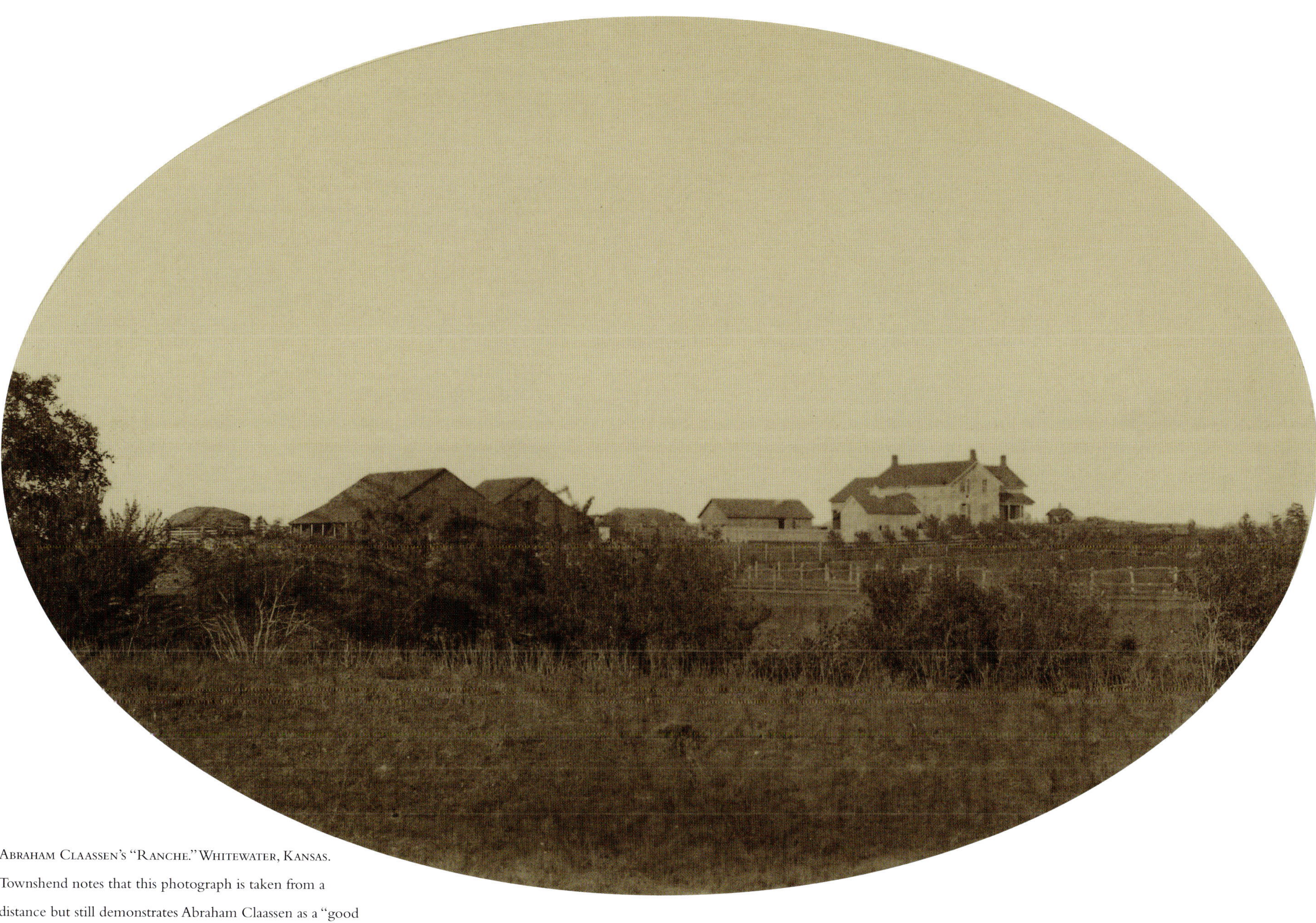

Abraham Claassen's "Ranche." Whitewater, Kansas. Townshend notes that this photograph is taken from a distance but still demonstrates Abraham Claassen as a "good and careful" farmer.

rapidly. Indian-corn stacks appear in the background, and nine farm hands just suspending work for the moment. The heads of the gentle, good, patient horses, are only just visible behind the machinery.

And now we turn back towards Newton. The leaves are still green and fresh on the bank-lining trees of the pretty Whitewater. By the time we shall reach Newton, and the comfortable home of our friend C. B. Schmidt,[5] he will have driven us forty-nine miles over the prairie during the day, with a single pair of horses. So we take the homeward drive—in mercy to our capital little nags, very easily—and begin to talk of the county. We very soon get into Harvey, which we find is in the eastern tier of zones in the Central rain-belt of the State. It is eighteen miles from north to south, and thirty from east to west, with 345,600 acres of land. Through it flow the Arkansas, Black Kettle, Sand, Jester, and branches of Emma Creek; the Whitewater, Gypsum, Doyle, Wildcat, and Gooseberry. The population last year was 8,107, and this year 10,440. Its towns are five: Newton, Halstead, Sedgwick, Burrton, and Walton, varying in population from Newton, 3,000, to Walton, 300.

The total assessed valuation of property in the county is £343,385, and the real value £472,308.

The total debt, including that of towns, is £11,419, and of this amount over £8,000 was expended on school buildings, of which there are fifty-eight, and in which the attendance-rolls amount to 3,028. In the county there are twenty-two religious organizations,—viz., four congregations of Presbyterians, ten of Methodists, three of Baptists, three of Congregationalists, and two of Episcopalians.

As to agricultural statistics, this year we have none, but the State Board of Agriculture of 1878 gives the number of acres under cultivation in Harvey County as 122,022. Winter wheat—the principal crop raised—was valued that year at £91,201, the Indian corn at half that amount, and the oats at £13,000. This year the acreage of winter wheat is 36,148, of spring wheat 1,518, Indian corn 41,167, and so on through the tables of potatoes and sweet potatoes, sorghum, castoroil beans, flax, tobacco, millet, and artificial grasses, for the spread of which the reader must go on to the next chapter.

As to animals in Harvey County, they number 27,476—viz., horses 3,348, mules 646, milch cows 2,383, other cattle 4,195, sheep 3,654, and hogs 13,250.

The reader by this time has probably been led a little deeper into agricultural statistics and emigration than he bargained for, but let him take heart. Some sport and adventure is yet to come—unless, indeed, he has fallen in love with the type of country life we present in Butler and Harvey, and elects to buy the 40,000 acres yet unsold in the latter, on the eleven years' system, from the Atchison, Topeka, and Santa Fé line, at 28s. per acre.

Both in this chapter and in the next we have, to some little extent, to apologize for—as Tommy Moore says—

"Still flying from Nature to study her laws,
And dulling delight by exploring its cause."[6]

5. Carl Bernhard Schmidt (1843–1921), a native of Saxony, was an immigration and land agent in the employ of the Santa Fé Railroad. Dubbed "the Moses of the Mennonites," for successfully recruiting many Russian German-speakers of the Volga region, he is credited with overseeing the move of fifteen thousand Germans to Kansas from 1873 to 1885. Bryant, *History of the Atchison*; Kansas Historical Society, "C. B. Schmidt"; Saul, "Migration of the Russian-Germans."

6. From Thomas Moore, "To the Invisible Girl," *The Poetical Works of Thomas Moore, Including His Melodies, Ballads, etc.* (1829). In this romantic poem, Moore argues for the truth of the spiritual essence of nature over scientific fact.

CHAPTER VI

From Newton Junction Westward—The Extension of the Rain-belt in Kansas—Mr. Hilton's Views of the Cause—Blue Grass *versus* Buffalo Grass on Wheat Land—Sheep, former Swindles—How alone Sheep will Live and Pay—The Cost of starting a Flock, or hiring a Farmer to Run them—Mr. Edward Uhl's Farm—Large Investments in general—Our Run to Pueblo—Law in Colorado as against Equity—The Grand Cañon of the Arkansas.

"In some still evening, when the whispering breeze
Pants on the leaves, and dies upon the trees,
To thee, bright goddess, oft a lamb shall bleed,
If teeming ewes increase my fleecy breed."

Pope's *Pastorals*

With that genial general foreign agent, Mr. C. B. Schmidt—an animated mass of information and good nature—we started again westward from Newton Junction.[1] The crops are still heavy, and the agriculture creditable, but the country evidently gets drier. The soil here is more retentive of moisture when once turned up than is that of Eastern Kansas, so less rainfall answers the purpose of the farmer, and *where* the limit of rainfall ceases to be sufficient for the conditions of success of the settler, is the subject we shall now consider.

Kansas as an entirety was thirty years ago described as *droughty Kansas*, or *the great American Desert*. Twenty-five years ago it was laid down as a fact that nothing would grow west of the meridian of Topeka. Twenty years ago that line was laid down at Emporia. In 1865 Florence was admitted to have rainfall enough to grow corn. Five years later to Florence and even Hutchinson were extended the full confidence of the farmer, and now new settlers have bought farms beyond Dodge City, which is four degrees and a half west of Topeka. Now for the reason, as given most admirably and concisely by Mr. H. R. Hilton, the Secretary of the Land Department in Topeka:—[2]

"Prior to settlement the plains as far east as Topeka were covered with buffalo grass, which never exceeds three inches in length, and this being burned over almost annually, left the surface of the earth exposed to the sun's rays. This surface, owing to the baking process it underwent, was so hard that the rain which fell could not penetrate it, and was instead drained off in the water-courses without materially

Epigraph: From Alexander Pope "IV. Winter; or, Daphne," *Pastorals*, first published 1709. Townshend's choice of lines would seem to celebrate the profit of lambs over the poet's celebration of nature, the traditional subject of the pastoral.

1. See chapter 5, note 5.

2. H. R. Hilton was a Kansas scientific agriculturalist and farmer who became a promoter for the Santa Fé Railroad. He developed an evolutionary theory of progress on the plains that depended upon the "Rain Follows the Plow" idea. "The Effects of Civilization on the Climate and Rain Supply of Kansas: A Lecture" by H. R. Hilton was published in 1880 by the Land Department of the Atchison, Topeka and Santa Fe Railroad Company. Townshend seems to have been the recipient of an advance copy of this promotional literature. Emmons, *Garden in the Grasslands*.

benefiting the land on which it fell. Nothing was left for evaporation. Precipitation was rendered difficult by the constant radiation of heat from the ground exposed to the sun's rays. All the air nearest the surface of the earth became heated by it, and this coming in contact with the vapour-laden air-currents, expanded them and rendered the condensation of the moisture in them almost impossible. The influence of this radiation of heat could only be overcome by the agency of electricity, and almost all the rain that fell fifteen and twenty years ago came in violent thunder-showers. The rains descended in great quantities, and were rapidly drained off, relieving only in a small degree the aridity of the climate.

"But with the industrious settlers came a change. The tough, buffalo-tramped, and sun-baked sod was broken, and the land cultivated. When the rain fell, instead of running off as formerly, it was received into the cultivated land and held for evaporation. Trees were planted, rank vegetation began to cover the ground, and the short buffalo-grass rapidly gave way to the tall blue stem that completely covered the surface of the ground, and shading it, kept the surface of the earth cool, and stopped entirely the radiation. Even the prairie sod, when shaded by the taller variety of grasses and penetrated by their stronger roots, became mellow and porous, admitting the rain into the soil that was formerly surface-drained. All these agencies of taller grasses, cultivated fields, green crops, trees, and ranker vegetation, have contributed to the general amelioration of the climate, by retaining the rain that fell on the soil, by stopping radiation, and thus letting the moistened air come in contact with the earth, by acting as condensers of the moisture brought in contact with their cooling influences, and by local evaporation increasing the humidity of the atmosphere. The result is, that each year the rains are becoming more general and better distributed over the surface, the showers more gentle and frequent, and the seasons more equable."[3]

As the line of agricultural limit extends, it is marked by the gradual conquering of the buffalo-grass, what is termed the "blue-stem," a sweet, succulent, and powerfully-rooted grass, smothering the short, thick, curly buffalo variety. Any lands whereon the blue-stem grows will produce wheat; even a little patch of blue-stem will show to the experienced land-seeker that Ceres, if invoked there, will abundantly bless the harvest. Nevertheless, plenty of districts into which as yet blue-grass has not penetrated, will grow it and wheat luxuriantly when it does reach there. We nevertheless think that settlement has been too rapidly pushing out West and that farmers would do wisely to pay a little more money—say £1 to £1 8s.—for land between Cottonwood Falls and Wichita, where the annual rainfall is constant and abundant, than buy at 12s. per acre land west of Great Bend, where once in a while they may be dried up and withered. At and west of Great Bend, however, the sheep question has begun to assume a great deal of importance, and so we will just glance at that.

Three years ago we visited every sheep flock in South-West, and indeed we may say in all Kansas. The lamentable swindle perpetrated on a number of young English gentlemen, on the line of the Kansas Pacific, at Victoria, was then fresh in all minds, and sheep in Kansas appeared determined to do nothing but die.[4] It is scarcely too much to say that each settler at Victoria lost every sheep he had. The Kansas Pacific Railway had nothing to do with this matter, but they sold a lot of land to a London shopkeeper, who advertised extensively the place as fit for sheep, and sold the land he had bought for less than 6s. per acre, for £1, actually before he paid for it. We then thoroughly hunted up the sheep question here, and came to the conclusion that nothing paid better than sheep in Kansas, though it was not in the Australian sense of the word a sheep country, and that the losses all occurred from the new sheep-owners not admitting this latter fact. In

3. The famous "Rain Follows the Plow" thesis was popularized by Dr. Samuel Aughey, Jr., of the University of Nebraska but had many other adherents and proponents, including H. R. Hilton. The theory lost credibility with the drought of the 1890s. *Encyclopedia of the Great Plains*, s.v. "Rain Follows the Plow," accessed July 20, 2015, http://plainshumanities.unl.edu/encyclopedia/doc/egp.ii.049; Emmons, *Garden in the Grasslands*.

4. Victoria, Kansas, was a British colony organized by George Grant—whom Townshend refers to as a "London shopkeeper"—in Ellis County in 1873. The colony achieved prominent attention in the press by 1876 but was defeated by locusts and drought by the early 1880s. Pagnamenta, *Prairie Fever*.

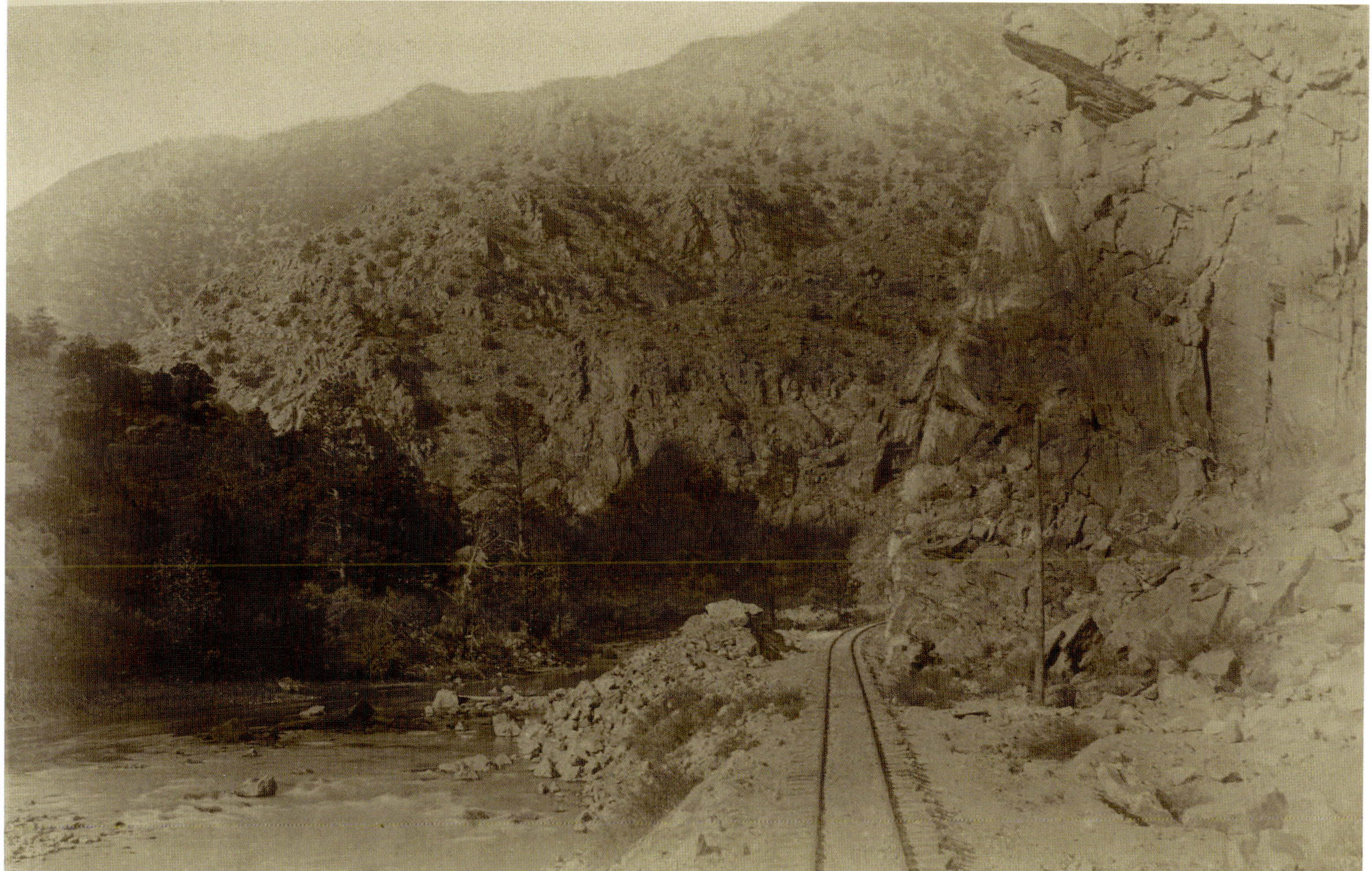

Entrance to the Grand Cañon of Arkansas. Rocky Mountains, Colorado.
This is the first photograph of Colorado, a series that Townshend calls "extremely successful pictures." He rates this scenery as more spectacular than Niagara Falls.

other words, if you shelter and feed your sheep in winter you can get ten-pound fleeces, and a regular mutton market is at your door. But a sheep country in the eye of a sheep-man of colonial experience or reading, is one that requires no shelter for sheep, and no artificial food for them; and it was from being represented as this sort of a country that caused Kansas to ruin every original sheep-man who came from abroad into it.

Sheep, then, do admirably west of Great Bend, though as yet the flocks there are but small: Messrs. G. H. Wadsworth, and S. G. Wright, each having only 2,000 sheep in Pawnee County, and Mr. Chandler the same number in Pratt County; these are the largest flocks in the State.[5] Spanish Merinos do best here, for open ranges, as they are so gregarious, but Cotswolds, and Shrops, acclimatized in Ohio, shear heavier fleeces, and bring better prices as mutton.

5. G. H. Wadsworth's pioneer success as a sheep famer in Pawnee County in 1876 is recounted in Linus Brockett's *Our Western Empire* (1882).

A settler with £1,000 could perhaps do no better, if he has a taste for sheep, than take Colonel Johnson's advice, viz.:—

Secure a good farm. The first payment on 160 acres at 16s. per acre, on the six years' system, will be £28 16s. A house will cost £100. Team, waggon, and farm implements, £120. Total, £248 16s. Leaving a balance of £751 4s. for the sheep. The farm must first be well established; so as to provide the family with requisites, and winter feed for the sheep, and then comes the sheep investment proper:—

800 graded Merino ewes, at 12*s*	£480	0	0
8 pedigreed Merino bucks, at £8	64	0	0
Corrals and sheds for 1,000 sheep	50	0	0
Windmill, pump, and well	25	0	0
	£619	0	0

EXPENSES.				RECEIPTS.			
Hay	£14	0	0	640 lambs, at 6s	£192	0	0
Indian corn	30	0	0	Wool, 4,800 lbs. at 1s.	240	0	0
Shearing, &c	60	0	0				
Shepherd	60	0	0	Total	432	0	0
				Less expenses	164	0	0
	£164	0	0	Net profit, one year	£268	0	0

All this feed is raised on the farm, but is charged as expenses against the sheep. Though the lambs are valued at £192, the farmer would naturally object to sell them, and this would bring down his cash in hand at the end of the year to £76, on which, with the surplus product of the farm, if he could manage to live for twelve months, his position would be immensely improved. We have not space here for Mr. Wadsworth's farm figures, but knowing him personally as an honest man and good farmer, we would suggest to any reader interested in the matter to write for them to Colonel A. S. Johnson, Topeka, Kansas.[6]

Capital is very scarce in all the new States, and in such a very pushing one as Kansas is, where most new farmers go into investments on a scale which double their capital would scarcely seem to warrant, very handsome profits may be realized by buying flocks of sheep for farmers, and letting them run them for half the increase and half the wool. An honest, good farmer—and Kansas abounds in such—will often pay over twenty-three per cent. as half share on a capitalist's investment in such a way; but these speculations should only be done on a small scale, say 200 sheep to each farmer.

Here we must leave this interesting subject, and being at Great Bend, drive off in the carriage of Mr. Edward Uhl to his handsome new house, a photograph of which appears in Chapter IV. Mr. Uhl has invested very heavily here.[7] He bought 8,000 acres from the Railroad Company, and has 1,280 acres in wheat. Two horses plough two acres per day, he informed us, in the Cheyenne Bottom, the old name of his estate, which is five miles north of Great Bend, in Barton County, and was once—and that, but ten years ago—the favoured home of the buffalo. Mr. Uhl said he would not grow Indian corn for cattle fatting, but millet instead, as this gives him a crop of five to seven tons per acre, and "rounds cattle out splendidly." He has purchased two-year-old heifers, with calf next spring, for £2 per

6. For information on A. S. Johnson, see chapter 4. There could be few more credible names.

7. In *History of the State of Kansas*, Alfred Theodore Andreas states that Edward Uhl came to Cheyenne Bottom from New York City. Together with William W. Carney, Uhl had a fine property of over eight thousand acres, and Uhl's two-story house, built in 1879, was said to be the finest in the county.

head, and cows for £2 12s., which, when fat, will fetch £4 12s., or—less the freight and commission at the Kansas City stockyards—£3 18s. Here the prairie is broken and the wheat crop raised and sent into market for £1 6s. per acre, and the profit per acre is 14s., reckoning the crop at twenty bushels.

With very large investments, however, we do not propose to deal, for the capitalists of to-day prefer Stock Exchange rumours to agricultural statistics, and none of them would touch the shares of the line we are on—the Atchison, Topeka, and Santa Fé—until they were sent up by speculators, with local information, from ten to fifty; and then but sparingly, until they reached ninety, when the world began to see that a second honestly-made line to the Pacific Ocean would be one of the finest investments possible to conceive. Then the capitalists made a rush, and sent up the Atchison, Topeka, and Santa Fé shares to over 100; but the men who had bought their shares very cheaply, determined to pay no dividend, but use all earnings in extensions. The capitalists bewailed the naughtiness of the Boston Stock Exchange, and so we leave them, and one of the best of them, Mr. Edward Uhl, who was wise, ere it was too late for wisdom. We proceed onward, and westward, past Pawnee Rock—the battle-field where the last of the Pawnees was killed by the Cheyenne tribe, ten years ago[8]—past Dodge City, that wicked capital of the "Cow boys," which we shall notice on our return; past one station after another, for two hundred and sixty-seven miles, to Pueblo in Colorado, all the time traversing a great plain, the upper valley of the Arkansas, which we persistently follow; and note on its nearly treeless banks, thousands upon thousands of cattle, all on a free range, which is getting already inconveniently overstocked, for its grasses, though nutritious, are sparse, its shelter against the cold Rocky Mountain winds of winter almost *nil*, and the snow-storms, only beasts in very good condition can be expected to survive.[9] We had great luck in Pueblo, for the line through the Grand Cañon of the Arkansas then belonged to the Atchison, Topeka, and Santa Fé Railroad Company, who, indeed, built every foot of it, but from whom it has since been wrested by a remarkably equitable decision of law, in Denver. Forty miles of the Denver and Rio Grande Railway intervene between Pueblo and Cañon City, and the Atchison, Topeka, and Santa Fé, having lines running east and west of each city respectively offered very liberal terms to lease the Denver and Rio Grande line. The agreement was made, and signed—that is, the agreement for a lease. Hearing of this, Mr. Jay Gould,[10] of the Union Pacific, offered the Denver and Rio Grande better terms, which they immediately accepted, and refused to be bound by their agreement with the Atchison, Topeka, and Santa Fé. Mr. John G. Adair, of Rathdair, and every other honourable English shareholder who knew the facts, at once sold out their shares in the Denver and Rio Grande line, which, thus left unhampered by any over-sensitive ideas of integrity, not only got a legal loophole out of their promise of a lease, but taking the offensive, procured a decree ordering the Atchison, Topeka, and Santa Fé to hand them over, for what it cost, its line through the Grand Cañon of the Arkansas. Law and equity, honour and good faith, have indeed appeared of late to be divorced in public matters in Colorado, and the less the

8. Pawnee Rock is today a historic site in Barton County, central Kansas. The site itself was a rock promontory (mostly destroyed by railroad construction) and an important landmark along the Santa Fé Trail as well as an important Native American site. The story of a battle to which Townshend refers is part of the site's indigenous lore. However, as typical, Townshend's sense of Native American history is suspect; the Pawnee tribe did not meet its end, and though the site did have archeological evidence of inhabitation and perhaps battles, there was no verifiable battle there ten years prior. Kansas Historical Society, "Pawnee Rock," 145.

9. Townshend's observation of "thousands upon thousands of cattle" along the Arkansas is interesting. He is correct in his observation that the free range is becoming overcrowded. Indeed, by 1890 the cattle boom and this era of British investment came to an end. While other factors like drought played a role, the dominant impediment to profit was an overstocked "free" range. Successful operators, including Goodnight and Adair on the JA Ranch, had already gone about purchasing and fencing their range. Pagnamenta, *Prairie Fever*, 262–63.

10. Jay Gould, one of the infamous "robber barons" of the era, became a controlling stockholder of the Union Pacific in the 1870s before selling out in 1882. He also bought smaller railway lines in the Southwest and was powerful in Scott's Texas Pacific Railroad. Josephson, *Robber Barons*, 222–30; White, *Railroaded*.

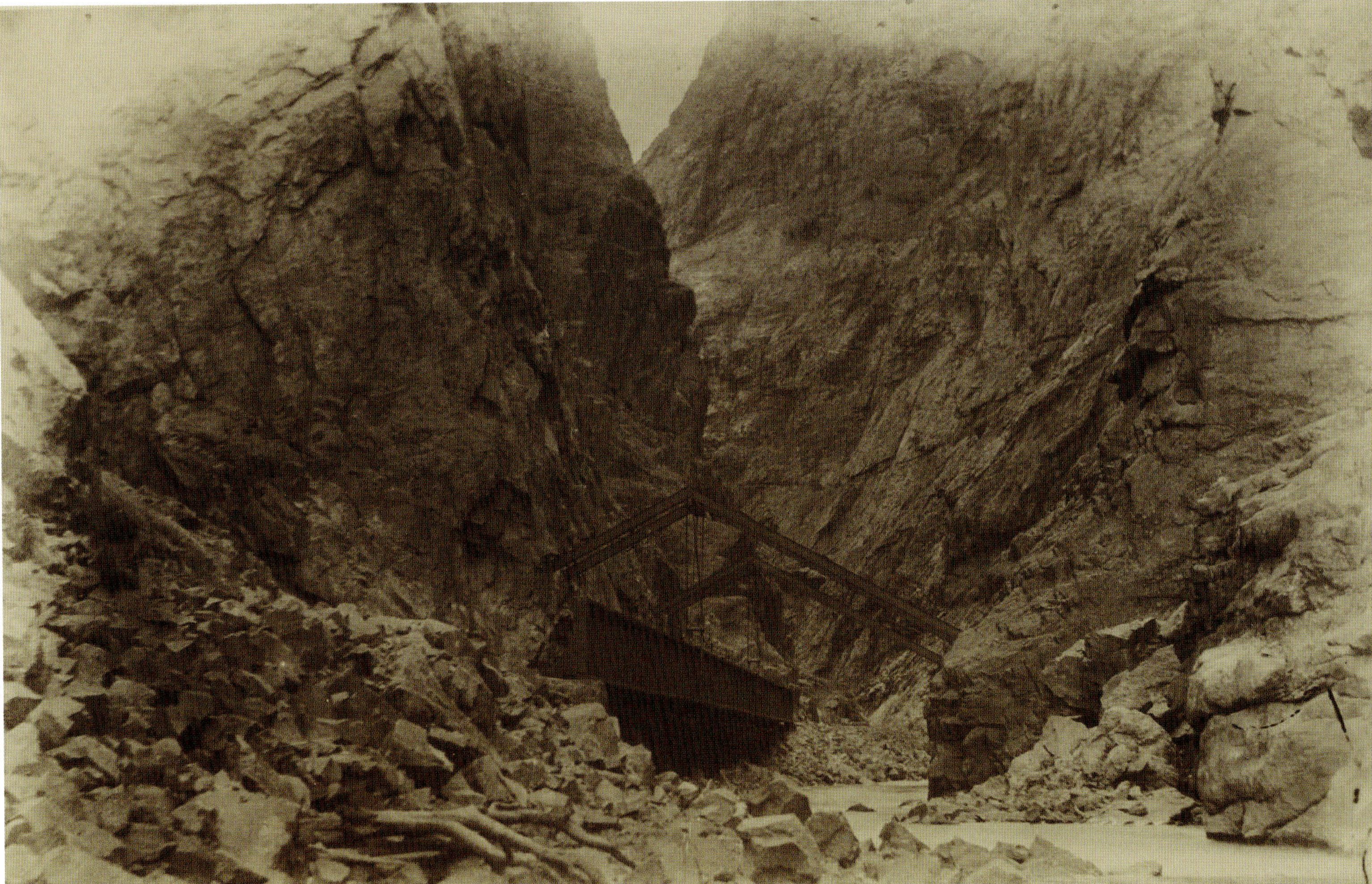

A. T. and S. F. R. R. Bridge. Grand Cañon of Arkansas, Colorado.
Our travelers found this bridge to be an admirable feat of engineering and a challenge to represent either in prose or photograph.

confiding shareholder has to say to any companies in that State, the better.[11] However, as I said, the Grand Cañon line was, in October, the property of the Atchison, Topeka, and Santa Fé; and having had the good fortune to travel westward with Mr. A. A. Robinson, the chief engineer of the line, he most kindly gave us a special train to use as we liked for two days, through the Cañon, and up Texas Creek beyond.[12] The result of this facility was to enable us to take some extremely successful pictures of this wonderful mountain and gorge road. The forty miles from Pueblo to Cañon City, up the Arkansas banks, is in itself very lovely; but when once the train leaves Cañon City, grander and grander grows each vista behind, and on each side. In front, cliffs and heights rise higher, and still higher. The graceful,

11. Adair did indeed register protests, in 1877, as did other British investors in the Denver and Rio Grande Railway and affiliated land development companies. The DRG was in a battle with the Atchison, Topeka, and Santa Fe (known as "the Royal Gorge War") for a central route through the Rockies via Raton Pass and Santa Fe. For the complete story, see Athearn, *Rebel of the Rockies*, and Bryant, *History of the Atchison, Topeka, and Santa Fe Railway*. For British investor perspective, see Brayer, *William Blackmore*.

12. Albert Alonzo Robinson (1844–1918) would eventually rise to vice president and general manager of Atchison, Topeka, and Santa Fe. Waters, *Steel Trails to Santa Fe*, 46.

trembling aspen, the delicate, many-hued cottonwood clumps are left behind with the plains, and now

"Behold the groves that shine with silver frost,
Their beauty wither'd and their verdure lost."[13]

We are indeed in the winter in the Rocky Mountains, and one massive pile of granite over another rises and rises on each side, to sometimes much over two thousand feet, completely shutting out the wintry sun. The Grand Cañon of the Arkansas may appear to greater advantage when you look down into its awful depths from above than when you gaze up its great, rough, massive two-thousand-feet-high walls from below. We have seen it both ways often, and which view conveys to the mind the greater idea of immensity, of force, of distortion, of igneous agency, erosion, and denudation, it is impossible to say. As a point to be seen in America we think even Niagara pales before it. At points such as the Royal Gorge it is too contracted for even one narrow-gauge track, and there we took our first view of the hanging bridge, which it is quite impossible to describe. The walls of the cañon are here so perpendicular, and the Arkansas so fully takes up all the space between them, that a long bridge is necessary. It will be seen that one side—the outer one of the structure—is held up by two girders of unequal length, arranged like a roof, the apex of which just comes over the outer edge of the bridge—the inner edge of it resting on a ledge of rock. Without sunlight it is impossible to give a really good photographic representation of this unique piece of talented engineering, but the subject is too remarkable to permit any sense of false pride in our art, forbidding us to present what our critics may safely call a rather inferior picture.

Our next photograph is of a scene near the Royal Gorge. A solitary cottonwood tree, but a very fine one, diversifies the rugged, arid, face of titanic nature here. No camera, however, can show the heights, as the eye has to traverse a long way up before they are reached.

The Arkansas River, now very low, brawls and dashes amongst big boulders, which it usually covers and tears over with a noise like thunder. Many accidents have occurred in this Grand Cañon. Before the advent of a railroad it could never be traversed save during intense frosts, and Indian tradition tells of a beautiful young dusky maiden who, in endeavouring to rescue her lover from the broken ice, was swept to rapid destruction from the upper end of the gorge.

"Her fate is whisper'd by the gentle breeze,
And told in sighs to all the trembling trees.
The trembling trees in every plain and wood
Her fate remurmur to silver flood.
The silver flood, so lately calm, appears
Swell'd with new passion, and o'erflows with tears."[14]

Beautiful maidens, however, there are still to be found by following up the Grand Cañon of the Arkansas, on the iron trail, secure from snow and ice; and of the habitat of these beautiful maidens our next photograph gives a distinct idea.

This view is of the summer camp—not yet, even in late October, abandoned—of Mr. C. C. Bigelow.[15] The sun is so strong in the cloudless sky that some degree of shade is preferable, and the verandah of the tent just gives this desired medium. This tent is erected on a substantial wooden platform, and has large glass windows. Indeed, to look at the picture one would think it a regularly-built house, yet it can all be moved into the train in a day, and the protecting huge cottonwood tree which overhangs it, left to protect nothing, save perchance a stray deer or two. The flower-pots will go too, but the tasteful beds of cacti will remain as souvenirs of the fair hands that selected and transplanted them. Piano strains

13. Townshend here returns to Alexander Pope's "Winter" pastoral that he used as the chapter's epigraph.
14. Again, Pope's "Winter."
15. The Bigelows are mentioned as a prominent family of Cañon City in *Southern Colorado*, a promotional guide to the region that was published by Brinckley and Hartwell.

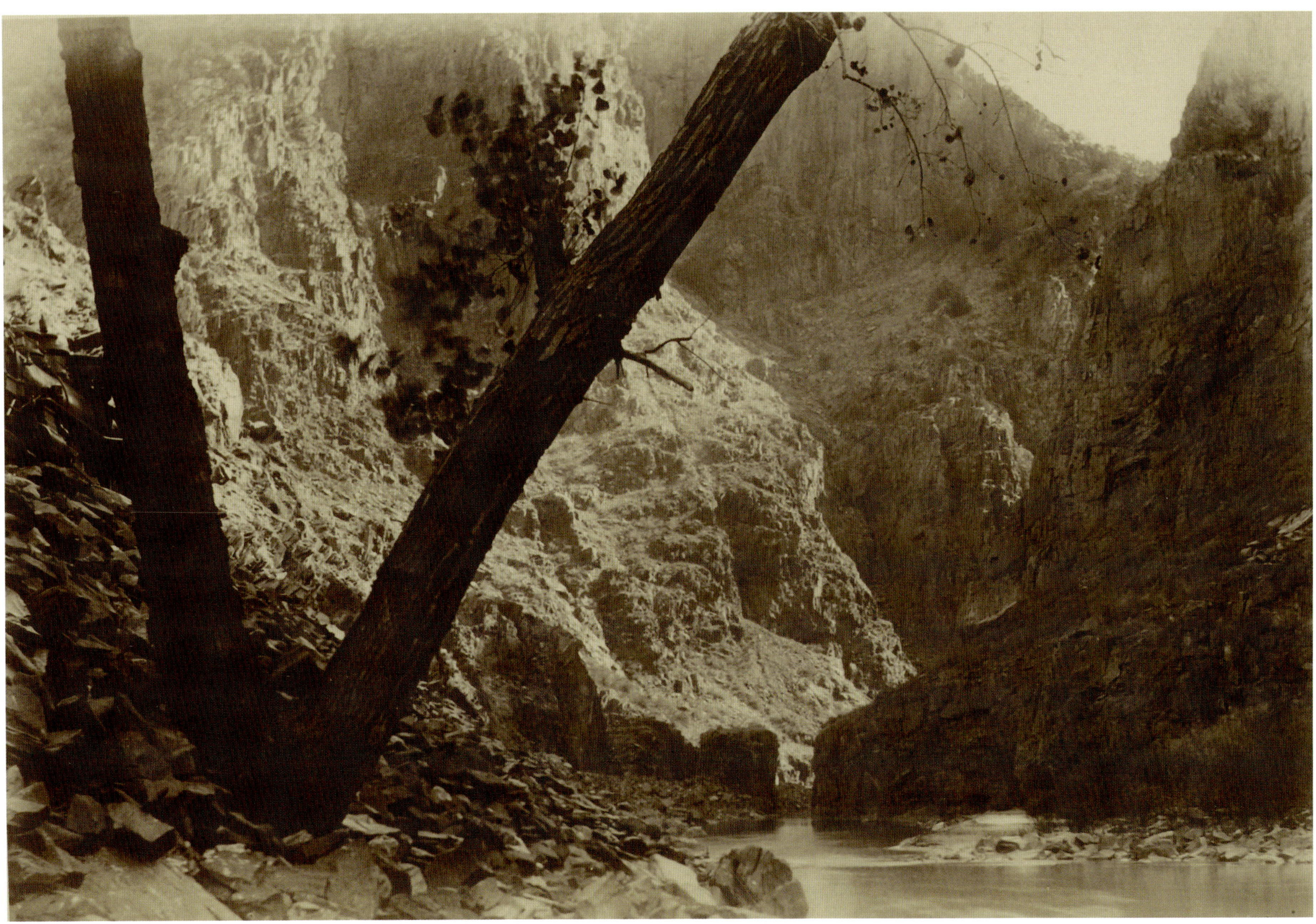

View in Grand Cañon of the Arkansas.
One of Hyde's most self-consciously artful attempts at using natural features to frame the scene; here several interlocking Vs are composed of tree, cliff, and sky.

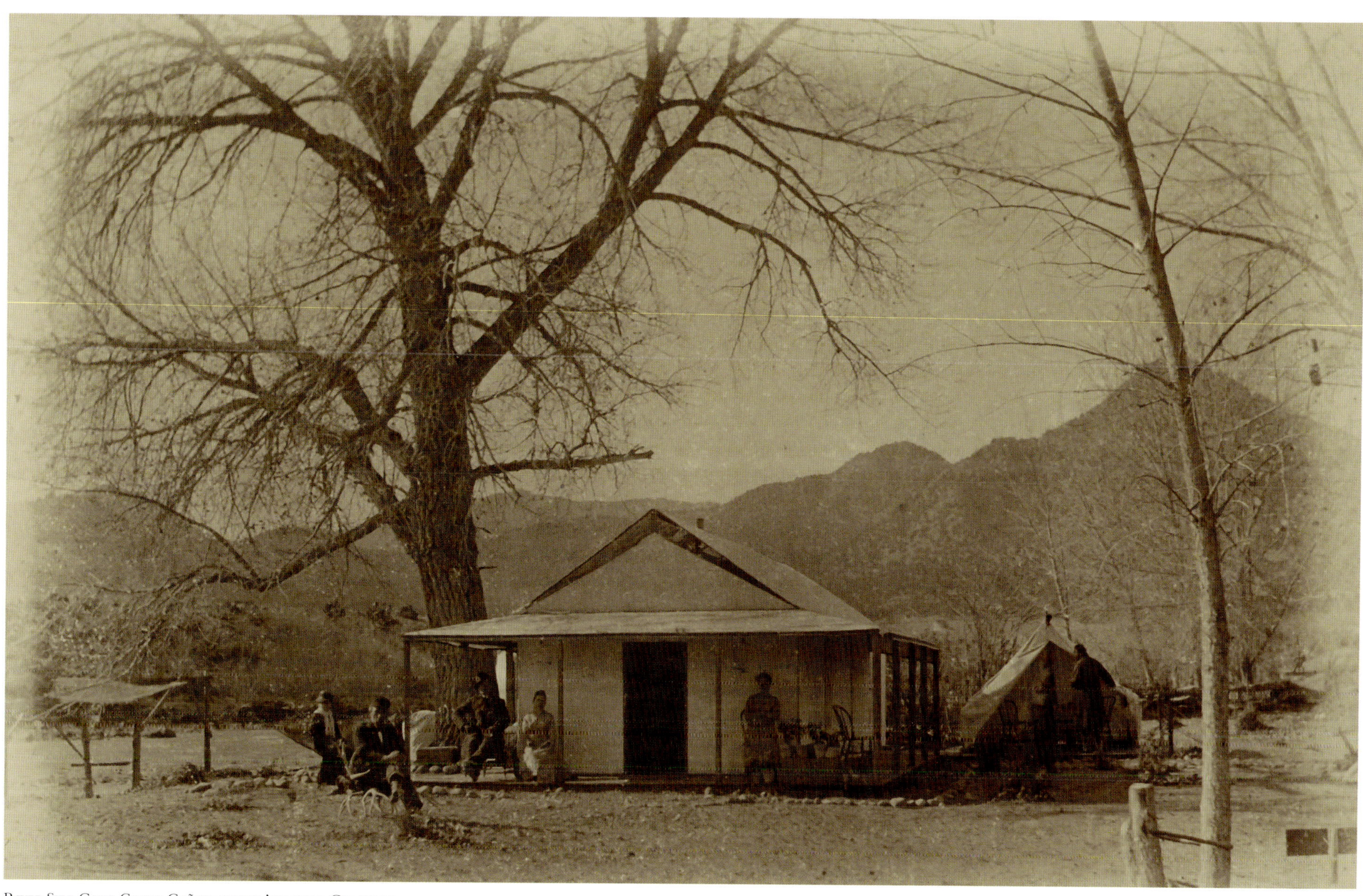

River Side Camp. Grand Cañon of the Arkansas, Colorado. These formally dressed campers, one of whom is seated on an antler chair, are identified as the party of C. C. Bigelow.

floated merrily from the tent. The cedared massive cone to the east is gloriously lit up by the morning sun. The yellow-and-white stratification to the east, and the brilliant red formation to the north, all charm the eye as they rise from the blue or foam-flecked Arkansas, the course of which we now leave for that of its tributary—Texas Creek—and after a few miles' run stop to photograph the Upper Section House. Our train is here seen in the distance, and a bit of the bright, pleasant, ever-singing mountain stream, which appears to the traveller only less brilliant in its granite setting at morn, than—

> "When falling dews with spangles deck'd the glade,
> And the low sun had lengthen'd every shade."[16]

16. From Alexander Pope, "III. Autumn; or, Hylas and Aegon," *Pastoral*, published 1709.

CHAPTER VII

VIEWS OF THE UPPER END OF THE GRAND CAÑON—COLORADO CLIMATE AND GAME—ESTER PARK—DENVER, ITS ATTRACTIONS AND THE SNARES SET THEREIN—A NEW DEFINITION OF AN ENGLISH HOUSE—JOINT STOCK COMPANIES—COLORADO AS A PLEASURE RESORT—NATIONAL PREJUDICES—THE PRESENT PROSPECTS OF SHEEP AND CATTLE OWNERS IN COLORADO—START FOR NEW MEXICO, *VIÂ* THE NEW MEXICO AND SOUTHERN PACIFIC RAILROAD—MORE VIEWS OF COLORADO.

"Oh, fly to the clime where he pillows the death
As he cradles the birth of the year.
Bright are your bowers and balmy their breath,
But the snow spirit cannot come here."

MOORE

The views we present of the Upper Section House, and of the end of the railroad as we saw it, give the reader a fair idea of rugged nature and the extreme difficulty of railroad construction here. The view of the Upper Section House perhaps illustrates these best; the immortal old "Rockies," bold and grand, as seen from the (then) end of the worked line, presenting, perhaps, an appearance as if they might be wound round a great deal more easily than is the case.

Colorado is indeed a most lovely State. For weeks, for months, even for years one may explore new streams and lakes, valleys and gorges, mountains, hills, and natural parks. Rarely, save in June, does it rain; save when a passing winter snow-storm comes over the sky, it is eternally clear blue, even at night. The mountainous regions are seldom visited by winds, and the air is clear, pure, and life-giving; but for a long time to the newly-arrived tourist—except he be a Swiss or a Khiberee[1]—exercise in Western Colorado necessitates frequent rests, on account of the rarefication of the atmosphere.

The amount of game to be met with in Colorado is getting every year rapidly less for inquiring miners, who live chiefly upon the fruits of their rifles, have penetrated almost every corner of the State, and driven the deer, elk, bear, and mountain sheep into fastnesses most difficult and expensive to penetrate. The bison or buffalo has been altogether exterminated in that portion of the Rocky Mountains in Colorado, but the mountain grouse is still plentiful, and the fishing on the upper Rio Grande could not well be better. The duck and general wild-fowl shooting on the lake in the San Luis Park, west of Cañon City, and easily got at from Alamosa Station, on a more southern branch of the Denver and Rio Grande, is very good also, and in Ester Park, the property of the Earl of Dunraven, in Northern Colorado, it is said the shooting is very good.[2] Whether it

Note on chapter-opener: The use of "Ester Park" is a consistent error. It is clearly meant to be Estes Park.

Epigraph: Thomas Moore, "The Snow Spirit," *The Poetical Works of Thomas Moore,* vol. 2, *Juvenile Poems, Poems Relating to America* (1840).

1. Khiberees are natives of the Khyber Pass region of the Spin Ghar mountain range between Afghanistan and Pakistan.

2. Properly Estes Park. The Earl of Dunraven purchased more than six thousand acres of land in the area that became Estes Park and the Rocky Mountain National Park. The controversial purchase fueled Anglophobic sentiment. Pagnamenta, *Prairie Fever.*

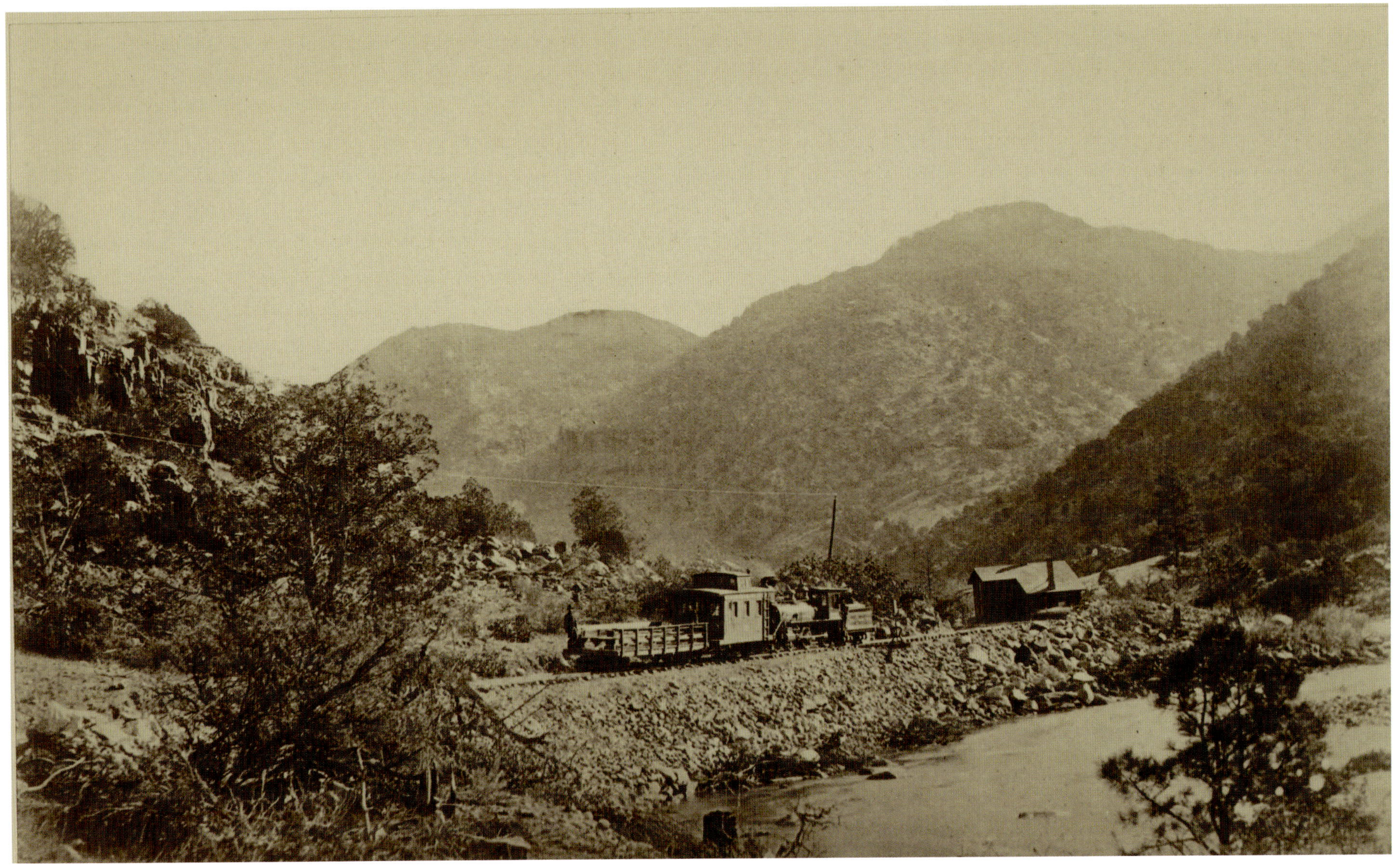

"Our Special." Section House, Grand Cañon of Arkansas, Colorado.

The text describes the location as along a tributary, Texas Creek, shown in brilliant morning light.

is or not, about the best hotel in the State is situated there, and the scenery is lovely. We arrived, however, much too late in the season to be able to cruise about Northern Colorado, which was then very much snowed up; even in our campaign in the Rockies, as far south as Central New Mexico, we got more than enough of the grasp of the icy king.

Denver, the capital of Colorado, is a most charming city, and no attribute of civilization or luxury is absent there, though one's expenses are sometimes rather startling in that metropolis, from which every line of railway in the State, saving and excepting the Atchison, Topeka, and Santa Fé, radiates. In Denver, the naturalist can enjoy himself to the full at Taylor's Free Museum in Larimer Street.[3] He can get any sort of game he likes at Charpiot's Hotel, and—wonder of wonders!—can get a bath there, a luxury not to be had—save at Phillips's in Florence—for a thousand miles east, even to St. Louis, and not for two thousand miles west, even unto the Sacramento.[4] Of course you can get a bath everywhere by dressing and going off to some barber's shop—a most uncomfortable and unsatisfactory sort of arrangement. From Denver, the most lovely run one can make is on the Colorado Central, up Vasquez, or Clear Creek Cañon, to Georgetown, or Black Hawk; or on the South Park line to Leadville, that wonderful mining town, which stands 10,000 feet above sea level, in the heart of the Rockies, and which has risen from a population of three souls in 1876, to over twenty-five thousand in 1880. The great gold and silver reduction works of Professor Hill, at present United States Senator for Colorado, are also at Denver, and his managing partner, a fellow-countryman of ours, Mr. Richard Pearce, never lets a Britisher go away ignorant of the business nor of his genial good nature.[5]

Mr. G. W. E. Griffith has been a valuable "Child's Guide" to many a young would-be English settler in Denver, where what the Yankees term "wild-cat" schemes are always rife, and set for the unwary English capitalist.[6] This has really made Denver what it is, though few Englishmen have ever got either principal or interest from the "rings" which rule there, especially in mining matters. That splendidly rich mine, "The Terrible," called in London the Colorado Terrible,[7] is a pretty fair specimen of this, and when once one gets behind the scenes and becomes intimate with an old inhabitant, it is interesting to walk round the suburbs and view the palace villas, whilst your companion explains, "That is an English house." "Oh, really!" you say, quite warming up with pleasure at the success of your fellow-countryman. "Does an Englishman live there?" "Bless you, no," is the reply. "That lot of houses was built out of (we will say) the great Bonanza Land Grant, in New Mexico. That residence was built with a portion of the money made by selling the same Bonanza Land Grant to a second party. This street cost a lot of the cash paid by a third party—a railroad company—to get the vendor to upset the title of the second purchaser of the Bonanza Land Grant. This investment was made by jumping an English mine; that by 'freezing one out,' the other by going to law with them about nothing–trying the Evil

3. George L. Taylor, a naturalist, was the proprietor of Taylor's Free Museum of Rocky Mountain Curiosities. Townshend, *Colorado*.

4. Charpiot's Hotel on Larimer Street in downtown Denver was owned by Col. Jerome S. Riche and was billed as the "Delmonico of the West." See the photograph at http://digital.denverlibrary.org/cdm/singleitem/collection/p15330coll22/id/26696/rec/1.

5. Nathaniel Peter Hill had been a professor at Brown University and is credited with the first successful gold and silver smelter in Colorado's Rocky Mountains, founded in 1867 at Black Hawk. He was the U.S. senator from Colorado from 1879 to 1885. One of Hill's partners, Richard Pearce, was associated with the Swansea Works of Wales, where Hill learned the smelting process. The company was called the Boston and Colorado Smelting Works. "Hill, Nathaniel Peter," *National Mining Hall of Fame and Museum*, accessed August 13, 2015, www.mininghalloffame.org/inductee/hill; *Quarterly of the Colorado School of Mines* 8, no. 2 [July 1913], accessed August 14, 2015, http://babel.hathitrust.org/cgi/pt/search?q1=colorado+smelting+works&id=umn.31951000591320l&view=1up&seq=1.

6. This reference is obscure. In Griffith's 1929 memoir *My 96 Years in the Great West*, he relates his role as a banker in Kansas mediating between municipalities and bondholders in railroad construction difficulties. It is possible that Townshend had business with Griffith in Kansas, but it is unclear what, if anything, Griffith had to do with the English in Colorado.

7. The Colorado Terrible Lode Mining Company, formed in 1873, was a company with heavy British investment. The operator of an adjacent mine, Silver Ore, broke through into the Terrible, whether by accident or by design, forcing British investors to purchase the other company for £220,000 in shares. British investors lost heavily in American mining frauds. Spence, *British Investments*, 127–28.

One for arson, with the jury selected from Pandemonium, and the Court held in Hades." This is the worst side of Denver, but there are bright sides everywhere found, even without looking for them, here. Mr. Hermann Beckurts—the worthy proprietor of the splendid city waterworks—Colonel Archer, and a host of other hospitable and distinguished citizens of Denver, have made splendid fortunes honestly and easily; but they never touched foreign capital, nor if they could help it, those who did, and who used the money of one English capitalist to upset the legal rights of another, in the remarkably constituted, nominated, and elected territorial Courts previous to 1876.[8] And even now that Colorado is a State, and its Courts State institutions, Tom Moore's couplet holds true:—

> "You may break, you may shatter the vase if you will,
> But the scent of the roses will cling to it still."[9]

Only that you must substitute "Court" for "vase," and "corruption" for "the roses."

The town companies, the improvement companies, the coal companies, and every other sort of company in Colorado, are bottomless pits for capital. Only when some scheme has notably failed, is it turned into a company, and the few salient points where these schemes have been found to pay are always reserved as royalties for the promoters in the company charter. The number of Englishmen who have become demoralized in Colorado, and deliberately put their best and oldest friends at home in for schemes that they have tried themselves and failed in—just to get out of loss themselves—is terrible to think of, as this state of things is not only not the rule in Kansas, Iowa, Nebraska, New Mexico, or Texas, but is exactly reversed, and old British settlers there always think it their duty to protect and befriend newly come-out buds from the old parent tree.

Colorado, to camp-out in during summer, is little short of Paradise, and when one considers that Pueblo or Denver is only seventeen days from Liverpool, the wonder is it is not a more general resort of health and pleasure-seekers. Horses, mules, and waggons are very cheap; and with a waggon and pair, a tent and blankets, a few cooking utensils, a good English No. 12 shot gun, a Winchester rifle, and a couple of fishing-rods, a man and his wife might have three months of the most delightful wanderings amongst grand and silent nature, undisturbed by any of the ills or annoyances that flesh is climatically or financially heir to, for £250. Many refined Eastern State families do this, but the British tourist is always in too great a hurry,

> "And never is, but always to be, blessed."[10]

Therefore he returns to his own country, having seen various peoples and things, but knowing even less than before he came amongst them, for then—if an educated man—he probably had correct ideas drawn from standard books on the subject. When he returns home his well-founded knowledge has been upset, because his prejudices drive him to conclude that a nasal twang is more than a set-off to virtue; that no man who dines at noon can be honest; that an absence of bath-rooms means absence of morality; that chewing tobacco means absence of mental culture, and the fiery railway-car stove indicates a dislike to all foreigners, which feeling, as regards the railway-stove itself, is certainly fully reciprocated by every one of us.

But it is surprising to find how much human nature is alike every where, especially amongst the fast-spreading English-speaking race over the globe. A man now prejudiced against England in the States, or one in England who declares that he hates the land of Uncle Sam, is always snuffed out before he travels far in this line. The people most prejudiced of these two classes are not, curiously enough,

8. Herman Beckurts was the owner of the *Denver Tribune*. In 1877 this paper was billed as "Devoted to the Mining, Agricultural and Political Interests of Colorado." It was Colonel Archer who ran Denver's gas and water works. Strahorn, *Handbook of Wyoming*.

9. Thomas Moore, "Farewell! but whenever you welcome the hour," *The Irish Melodies* (1826).

10. Though far from Townshend's ironic usage, the quoted line is closest to Alexander Pope's lines from *Essay on Man* (1734): "Hope springs eternal in the human breast: / Man never is, but always to be blest."

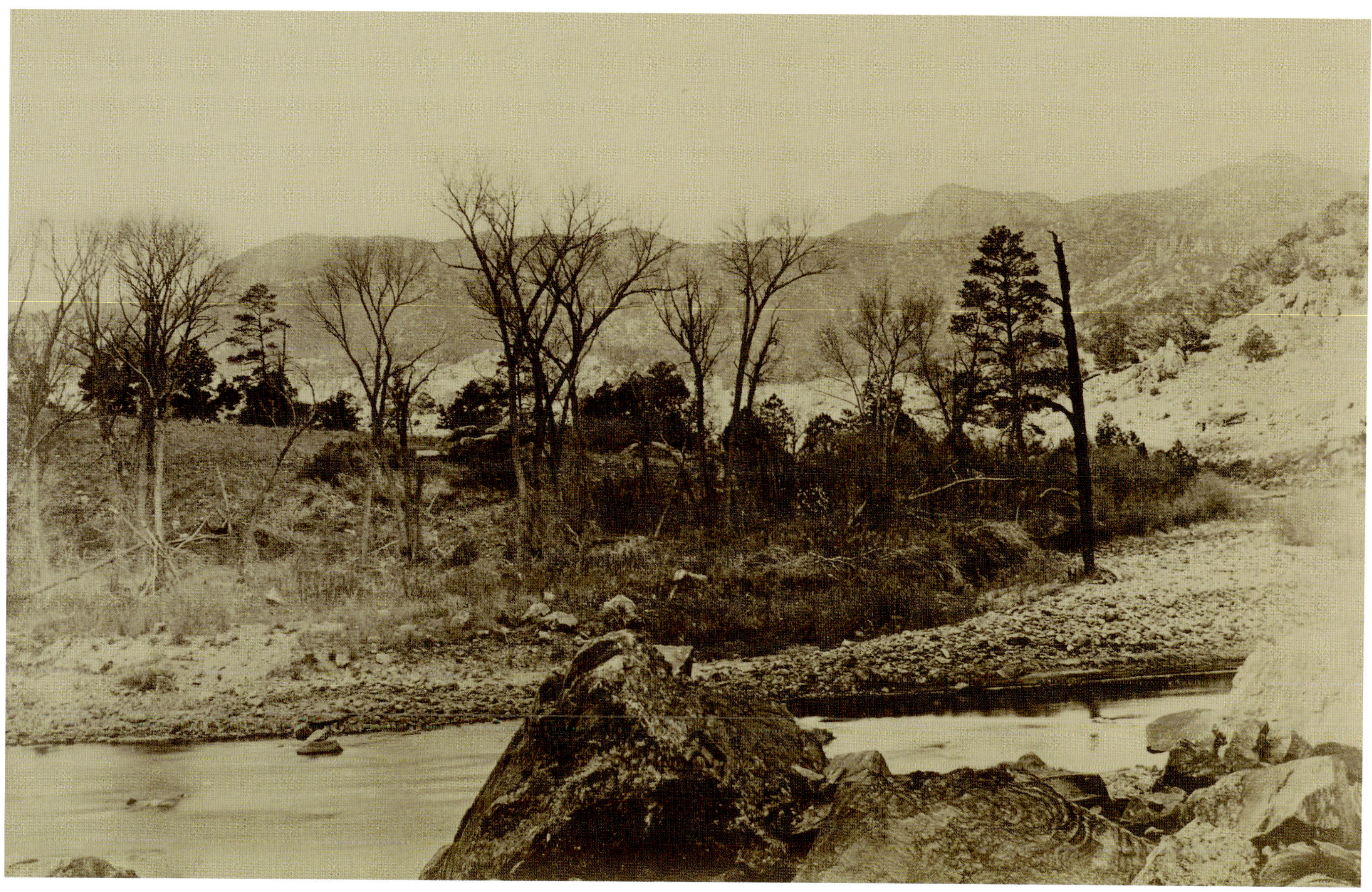

Head of the Grand Cañon of Arkansas. Rocky Mountains, Colorado.
An artfully composed shot, balancing the rock in the foreground against the mountains on the horizon, the river gliding between.

the untravelled, but those who have merely made flying visits to the other country. The bitterness of a Yankee who can't get his morning cocktail at his hotel in Liverpool, who has to walk perhaps half a mile to find a barber to shave him, or, worse, who in a large village can't get one at all, who misses every single convenience in one of our railway carriages that he is accustomed to in his own cars, who can't get his baggage checked, say from London to Queenstown nor from Bath to Brighton,—this Yankee has his bristles raised at every point; and if he does not remain long enough in the country to find out that if we have not telephones and lifts in our average hotels, we have really better food and infinitely better attendance than he has been accustomed to; and that if we do not provide Horton's reclining chairs free for railway passengers, we run them so quickly over their journey that they do not want to recline. If, in short, he stays long enough, he likes us and our ways; if he does not, he hates both. So it is with the average tourist in the States. He is always pitied and often disliked, until his tact, if he has any, shows him that weighing corn by apothecaries' weight will not do, and that American social pricks are a great deal too hard to be successfully kicked against. Then he begins to run smoothly on American rails, and finds no law compels him to chew tobacco, nor prohibits his carrying a portable india-rubber bath with him. He finds also that he can make a capital dinner at the Western six o'clock supper, and need by no means gorge himself at high noon or starve. In short, he finds that he can engraft himself very pleasantly on the American social system, by accepting what he likes of it and evading the remainder without grumbling or growling. Here we shall not say how good, true, and generous is the inner great heart of America, and few have had better opportunities of testing it. In our future records will be seen many acts of thoughtful kindness shown us, and as the emigrant has been to a great extent neglected in this chapter, we now towards the end of it devote a little space to cattle and sheep, which in former years appeared to have no end or limit of development in Colorado.

The "Chicago Times'" correspondent, Mr. J. F. Finerty; an intimate friend of ours,[11] thus fully expresses our sentiments and experience as well as his own:—

"The season of 1879 has footed up only a fair average for the stock growers of Colorado, and some of them, more unfortunate than the rest, are a little blue over the prospects for the future. The year opened auspiciously enough, and the percentage of increase was not below that of preceding years, while most of the young stock survived the April storms, which are usually so fatal, particularly to lambs. But the dry season was destructive to stock. Grass was short, and during the season prairie fires swept over immense areas of the range, which was already crowded along the water ways. Later in the season the water began to fail, and herds were moved from place to place in search of grass and water. The large drive from Texas came in due season, and sold well in spite of the unfavourable season, but the buyers were pretty generally 'bit'—at least they did not make the profit which the investment and risk seemed to demand. The rush to sell broke down the market in October and November, and for the first time in the history of Colorado stock-growing, there appeared to be an over-production and a glutted market. This was more apparent than real, but the effect on prices was the same. The returns of stock for taxation showed only a natural increase over the report of 1878, but as these returns are notoriously defective, little importance can be attached to them. For example, the returns of cattle showed only about half a million head in the State, while almost any schoolboy knows there are nearly, if not quite, a million. There is some excuse, however, for this deception. The law requires all property to be appraised for taxation at its 'full cash value,' and cattle are assessed at an arbitrary rate per head. If the 'brand-count' was returned to the assessor, stock-growers would pay more than their proportion of the state and county taxes, and would also pay on missing stock, infirm cattle, &c.

"Probably one hundred thousand cattle and three hundred

11. John Frederick Finerty, a native of Galway, Ireland, is best remembered as a correspondent for the *Chicago Times* who covered Plains Indian military campaigns and authored two books, one on Gen. George Crook and another on Irish history. Timmons, preface to *John F. Finerty Reports*.

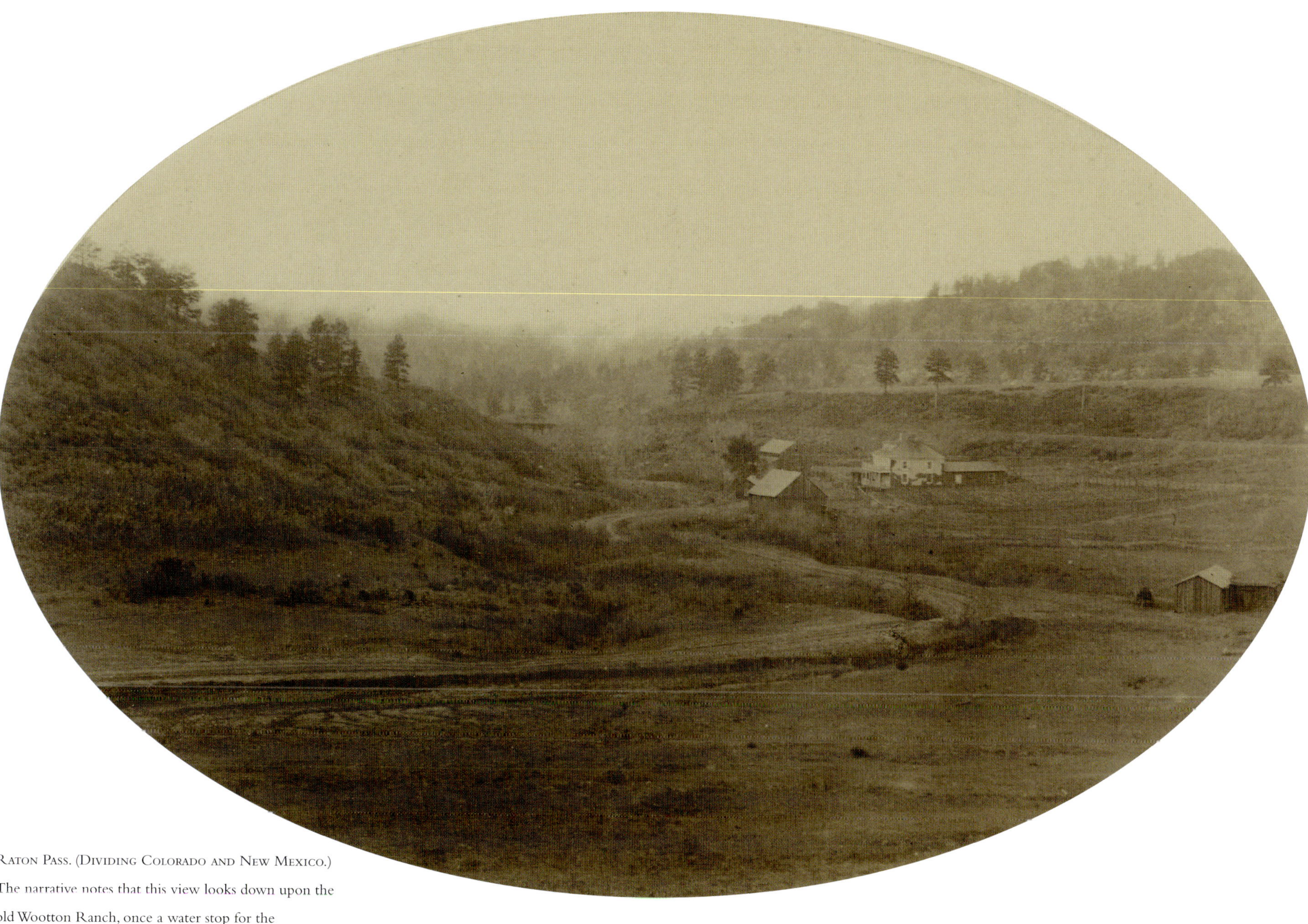

Raton Pass. (Dividing Colorado and New Mexico.) The narrative notes that this view looks down upon the old Wootton Ranch, once a water stop for the Santa Fe Stage.

thousand sheep have been added to the actual number in the State last year, making, in round figures, one million cattle and one and a-half million sheep in Colorado to-day. Stockmen say this is quite enough, and discourage further investments, especially by 'outsiders.' Agriculture is rapidly monopolizing the water of the State for irrigation, and each advance of agriculture lessens the area of profitable stock-raising. It is true that water may be secured by artificial means, by drawing it from wells with windmills, or perhaps artesian wells will eventually be found practicable, not only for stock, but also for irrigation; but these methods have not been developed at the present time.

"The stock business is still a mine of wealth to the State, yielding larger returns than any other investment, save an occasional venture in mines. Transportation rates to the East have been reduced by railway competition, the home market has improved materially, and the losses by Indian raids and white thieves are practically at an end. The cost of herding is about the same. Herders are paid from $25 to $40 per month, with board. The latter is not up to the mark of the Grand Pacific in Chicago, or even of the Gage's Grand Central in Denver, but the men manage to live well at a small expense. Cattle are cared for a little closer than formerly, and have to be moved more frequently than when grass and water were plenty. The additional labour involved is not great, and indeed the handling of cattle costs next to nothing, so that, after the first investment is made, and a complete outfit secured, $5 will pay the ordinary expense of bringing a steer from foal to market.

"Western Colorado is the finest stock range on the continent. The valleys of the Western slope are wild with luxuriant grasses, upon which cattle keep rolling fat all winter, and make splendid beef in the spring, when Eastern-slope cattle are unfit to kill, 'Snake-river beef' is known in Chicago as well as Denver, where it is sold in the spring at almost fabulous prices. Unfortunately, Snake and Bear rivers are too near the Indian reservation to invite settlement, and, unless the Indians are removed, I could not advise anyone to venture there with any character of 'portable property.'"

And now having disposed of Central Colorado, let us have a peep at its New Mexican frontier. In pursuit of the Colorado beeve we have returned to La Junta, and from that junction take the New Mexico and Southern Pacific Railroad—one operated and leased by the Atchison, Topeka, and Santa Fé—across the plains to Trinidad, a lively little town on the Purgatoire, or, as it is locally spoken, "Picketwire." The United States Hotel is a very good one at Trinidad, and we left it with shivering regret at 5.30 A.M. next morning, to take a slow run up the Great Raton Pass of the Rocky Mountains, on a freight train, to see sunrise.

The Colorado sky was even at daybreak perfectly cloudless and blue, and the surroundings were dark-green, scrubby, round-headed cedars, golden buffalo-grass, brown earth and rocks, and cottonwood trees with autumn leaves of every colour, from red to nearly pure white. Square adobe or "doby" houses of Mexicans, are dotted along our road up the pass, along the Purgatoire. These residences are low, one-storey, square buildings, without, as a rule, any glass windows, the apertures in the walls being closed, when needed, with heavy shutters, like many of our barns. Our train was a very heavy one, for we were carrying an immense quantity of rails, to extend the honest iron hand of Boston to the far distant shores of the Pacific; and three of the heaviest of the Baldwin locomotives—two pulling and one pushing—panted, snorted, and struggled hard in getting us to move along at much beyond a respectable footpace, over the stiff grades. In a short time we get to Wootton's Ranche, where of old the Santa Fé stage used to stop and water.[12] The Santa Fé stage is now a thing of the past—peace be with it! for it was in life a horribly slow, yet anything but peaceful mode of conveyance. For the sake of bygone discomforts, we photographed the old ranche, as seen from a great

12. Richens Lacy "Uncle Dick" Wootton is famous for collecting a toll for his trail over Raton Pass between Colorado and New Mexico from 1865 to 1878. Thrapp, *Encyclopedia of Frontier Biography*.

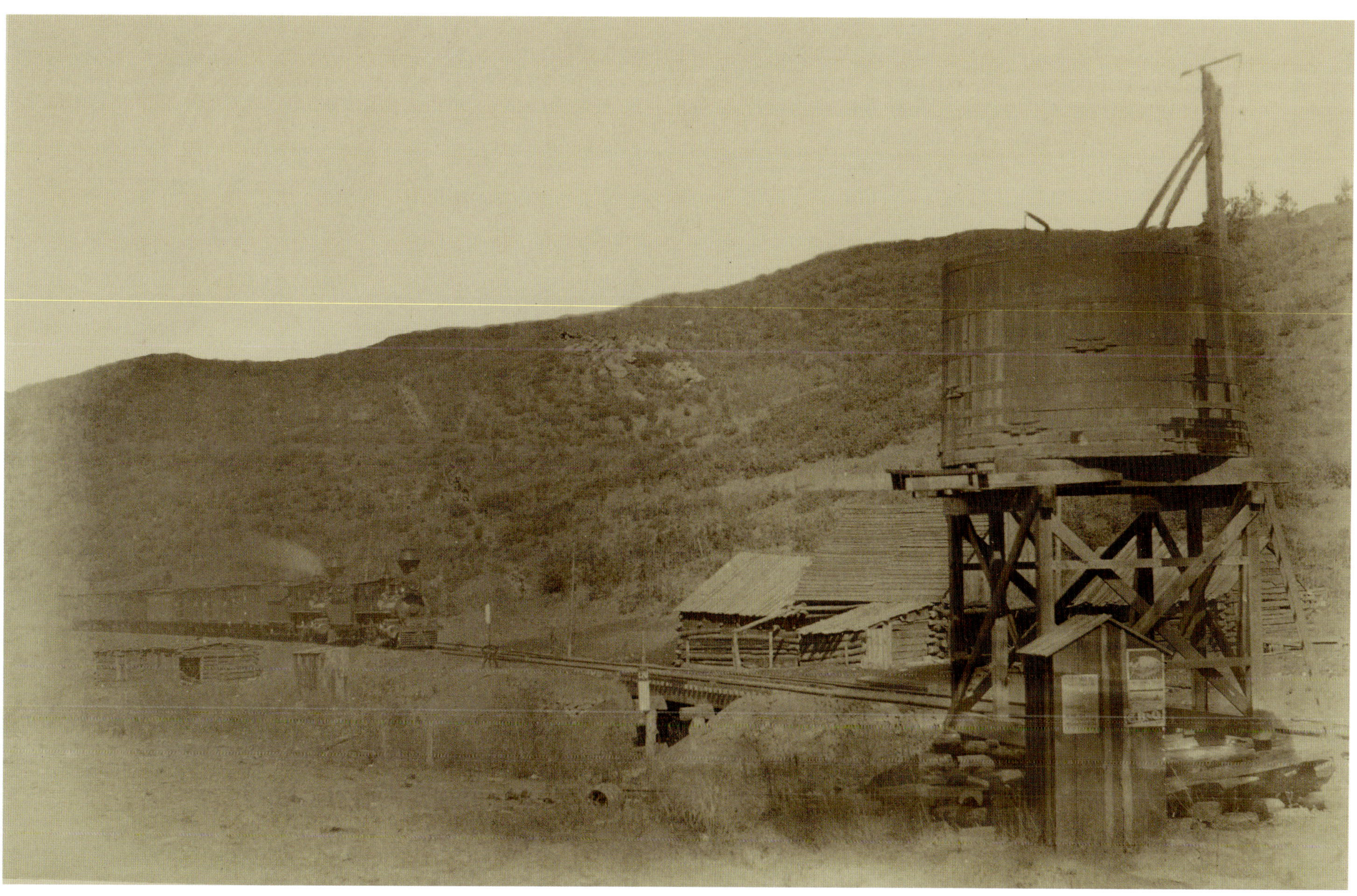

Raton Pass Water-Tank. A. T. and S. F. R. R.

Hyde captures a fine sense of motion in this photograph, showing a train using two engines to reach the pass.

distance; and at the end of the lovely pass, which will take a great deal of the next chapter to describe, we took a view of the freight train, standing at the summit, with two engines attached. This view also shows the railway water tank, a bridge, and the pointsman's house.

Old Sol—Fisher's Peak in the background, snow-clad—here also appears to say,

> "Weave the frontlet, richly rushing
> O'er my wintry temples blushing."[13]

13. Thomas Moore, "Ode 78," *Odes of Anacreon* (1800).

CHAPTER VIII

Approaching New Mexico—An Old Mexican Superstition—Appearance of the People—The Burro and his Music—Scenery at the Raton Pass—Difficulties of Travelling—Amateur Photographers—Mr. Moore's Railroad Yacht—A lot of Truth Spoken almost in Jest by an Officer of the United States Army.

"And many an alter in my way
Has lured my pious steps to stray;
For if the saint were young and fair,
I turn'd and sung my vespers there."

Moore

Though yet really on the Colorado side of the Raton Pass, we were to all intents and purposes in New Mexico. Strings of *burros* (the Mexican term for donkeys) were being heavily loaded—driven along the roads by swarthy Mexicans, with outrageous sombreros, huge spurs, and more or less tinsel on their trappings. From out of each house door, little bronze coloured Mexican children, each in a very scanty garment, peered curiously with large jetty-black eyes at the New Mexico and Southern Pacific puffing monster, as it toiled away upwards past them to carry civilization, commerce, order, and law into the old domains of their Montezuma, whom they firmly believe will come on earth again, and rule the children of the Child of the Sun, with his old accustomed benevolent and mild sway.[1] Here and there amongst the children is seen a pretty Mexican maid in her favourite dress of pink. The native Red Indian, her ancestor on one side, is still remarkable for his erect and proud bearing, the natural gait of that inborn freedom which is absolutely unconquerable. Her ancestry on the other side come from the haughty Don and Donna; and the lissome, yet softly dignified grace of every movement which the Spanish girl has been ever conspicuous for, has descended to her Mexican cousin intact. A gipsy complexion, eyes full of softness and fire, redundant tresses of silky, jetty hair, a beautifully rounded figure, *petite* limbs, and a dress

"Leaving every beauty free
To sink or swim as Nature pleases,"[2]

complete the one redeeming feature of the Mexican race, its girl, who becomes often a faithful, good wife, and *always* an excellent mother.[3]

Onward and upward we toil, bearing with us what we term the necessaries of life, towards New Mexico—necessaries, there

Epigraph: Thomas Moore, "The Shrine," *The Poetical Works of Thomas Moore*, vol. 1 (1853).

1. While Townshend does not bother to describe "Indians" he must see along his travels, "Mexicans" draw his invidious attention. This seems a function of his nationalistic feelings toward Hispanic as opposed to Anglo colonial histories and his strongly negative attitudes toward miscegenation.

2. Thomas Moore's "Lesbia Hath a Beaming Eye" describes a long and flowing dress.

3. The stereotypes of the Mexican American woman as epitome of dutiful wife and mother was alive and well at this time, connected to the pejorative image of these women as submissive. Deutsch, *No Separate Refuge*.

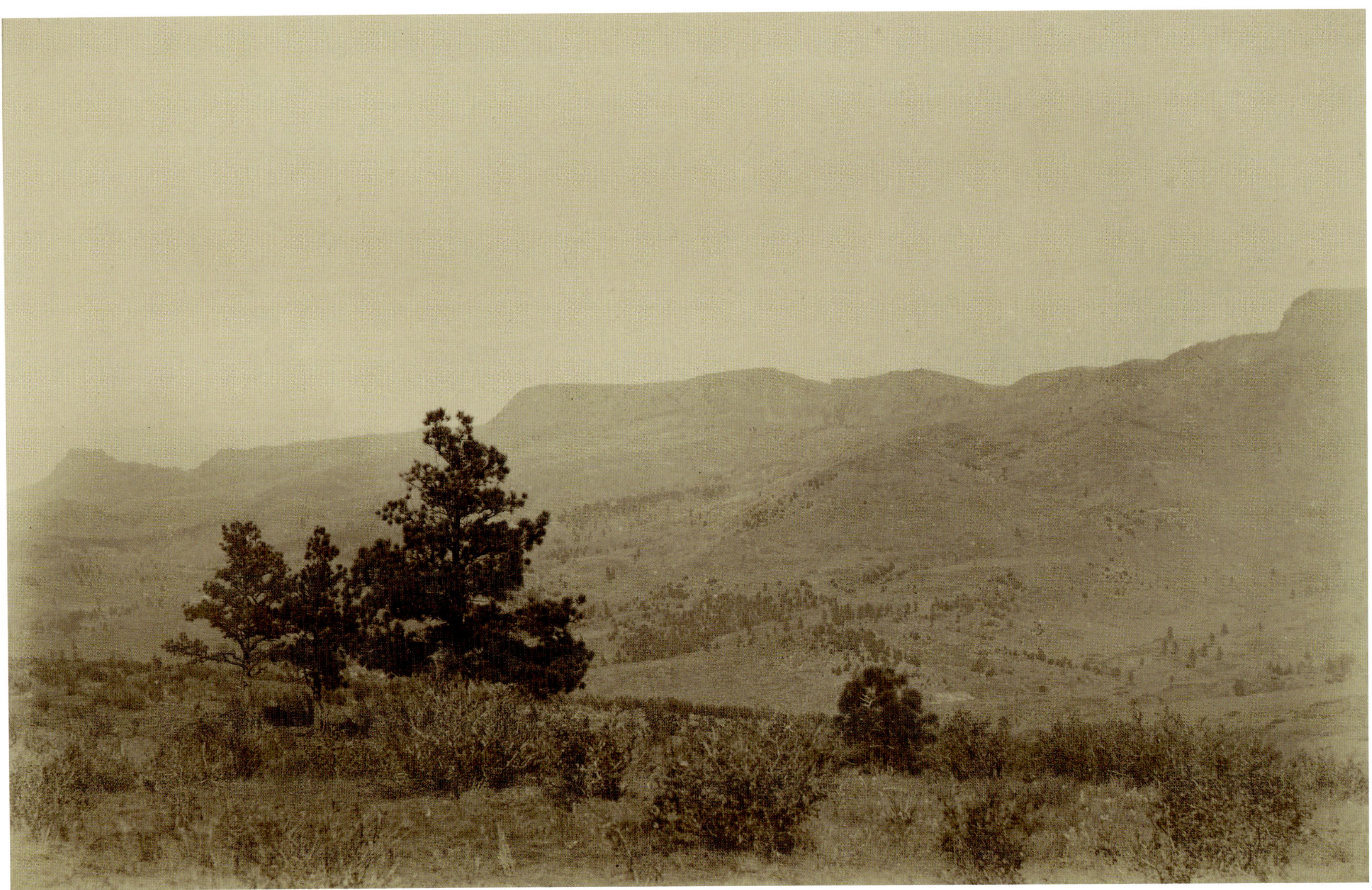

Raton Pass. Fisher's Peak Range, Colorado.
This conventional landscape photograph, which Townshend references in explaining the geography and climate of the region, serves documentary purposes. He notes, interestingly, that the more distant peaks of the Rockies are impressive but too distant for their camera to capture.

considered luxuries. Snow-crowned Colorado fades away behind us as we approach the territory of the Montezumas, which was so completely plundered and demoralized by its Iberian conquerors that a century of Anglo-Saxon rule under the stars and stripes will scarcely restore even the Montezuman primitive civilization and habits of industry to the New Mexican.[4] Upwards, past conical hills, crowned with stumpy cedars, past deep valleys, lined with graceful, delicate cottonwood; distant mountains on all sides of us, and the formidable Raton Pass straight ahead.

Still we are in Colorado; and the go-ahead spirit of that new State appears to have infused some unwonted energy into the Mexican here; for he has brought under cultivation some very unpromising-looking patches of land by irrigation.

A Mexican hairless dog is now seen with his master, accompanied by the ever-present patient *burro*, whose disagreeable way of saluting the rising sun in his dissonant manner has been here temporarily cured by tying a stone to his tail the previous night. A donkey cannot, it is said, bray without elevating and knocking about his tail, and the Mexican has discovered that a very small weight attached thereto prevents this.

Our sixteen miles of up-grade is now nearly conquered. The pull has been almost throughout an extremely severe one, though the passenger-trains with two engines attached make light of it. Scrub oak and pines appear around, and lo! we are at the Summit Station, where we spend the day photographing, often with one foot in New Mexico and one in Colorado. A scene at the station is in our last chapter, and here we present a view of Fisher's Peak Range, as seen from a hill one mile east of the summit of the pass. Fisher's Peak, the peculiarly-shaped mountain to the left, watches over the town of Trinidad. The cedar-trees in the foreground show how these "mountain inhabitants" can grow in rocks, almost without rainfall. Close inspection will also show a number of these cedars dotted along the mountain range in the background. Walking about and climbing these mountains over the pass was tiring work, especially as we carried our photographic impedimenta with us. So little has man disturbed these solitudes that even the magpies hopped about us as we lay resting on the grass, so close that we could touch or catch them. Were we not both witnesses to this fact it would, in consequence of its apparent improbability, have been better not stated here. The views from these mountain-tops were very grand, but too distant for photographic record. Below we see valleys crossed by the iron viaducts of the North Mexico and South Pacific Railroad, curving, like the celebrated Horse Shoe in the Alleghanies, in the Pennsylvania, or Mule Shoe, near the Veta Pass, on the Denver and Rio Grande lines. For forty miles or more in every direction the prospect is glorious. Not an acre of apparently level land is anywhere seen. Fisher's Peak rises some six miles to the north-east. The magnificent Spanish Peaks, which sentinel El Moro, and tower over it nearly 14,000 feet, are far to the north-west, and further off westward lie the snowy range of the Rocky Mountains, glittering and sparkling in all their frosty, icy, wintry beauty. Underneath is the tunnel of 2,000 feet long, which leads under the State line of Colorado into New Mexico, the great northern plains of which lie spread before us, skirted away far to the south-westward by one hundred and fifty miles of perhaps the most picturesque portion of the Rocky Mountains. A beautiful wilderness which as yet has been but very partially explored.

No matter how the mind may feast on glorious scenery, the flesh is invariably weak, and a motion to adjourn for dinner was carried *nemine contradicente*. So down to the Railway Section House we scrambled, and obtained an excellent dinner of roast beef, tomatoes, potatoes, apple-pie, tea, coffee, and iced-water, for 2s. Then away up another mountain to the east we go, and get eventually upon a little *mesa* or elevated plateau, with two pines on its top and several on it sides. From here we faced the clear-sighted little camera—the *lens* of which had gazed unmoved upon so many beautiful scenes in

4. Townshend's sense of the benevolent and improving nature of Anglo-American imperialism almost requires this criticism of the improper imperialist practices of the Spanish empire against the Aztecs and other peoples and what he views as its unfortunate results still visible in New Mexico.

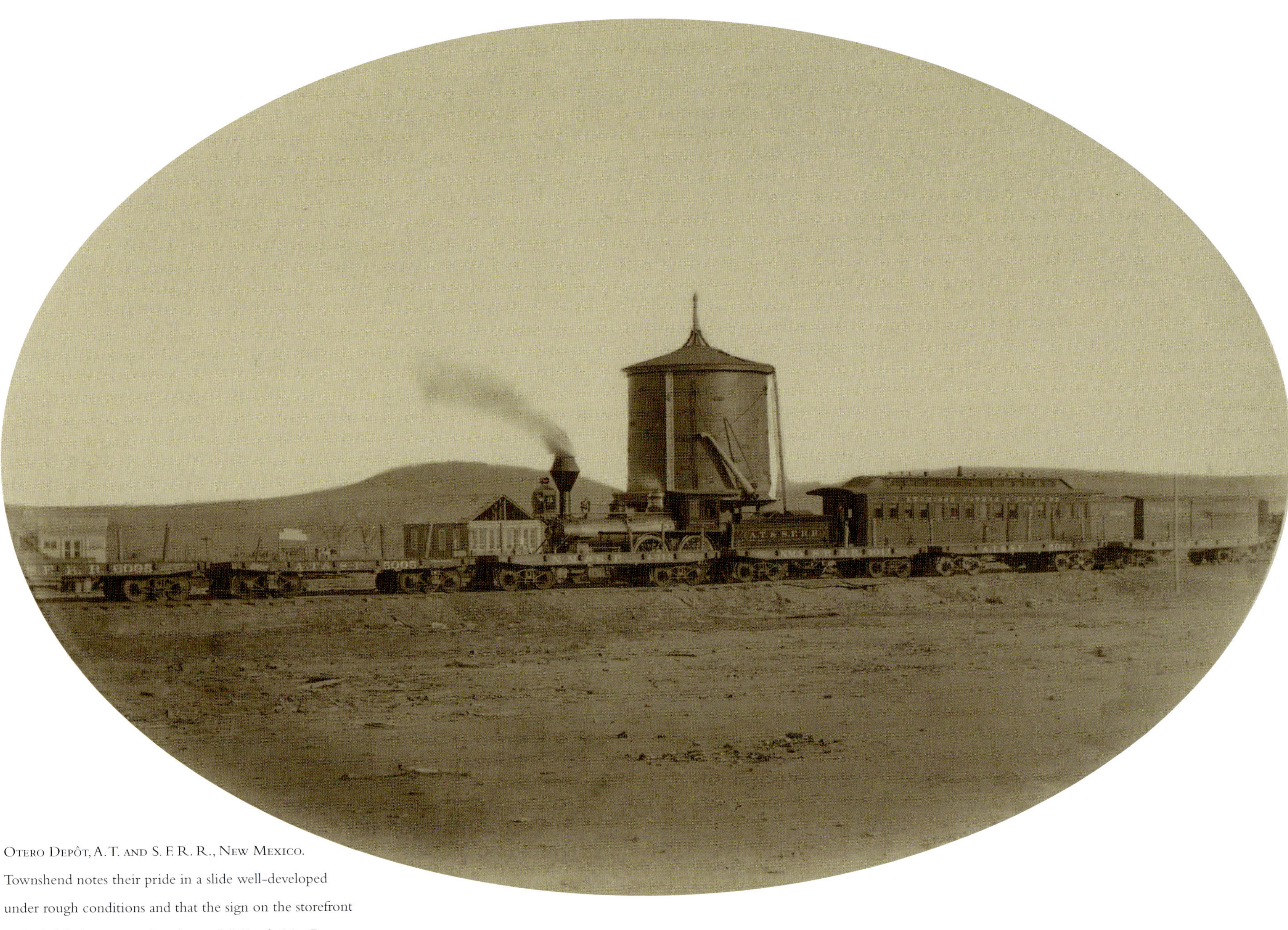

Otero Depôt, A. T. and S. F. R. R., New Mexico. Townshend notes their pride in a slide well-developed under rough conditions and that the sign on the storefront at the left is sharp enough to be read: "Tienda Mas Barata de Otero," or "The store of most cheapness in Otero."

the Holy Land—towards Fisher's Peak, and taking off his veil gave him a three seconds' glimpse of it—about three times as long as we generally permitted him to stare with his big eye at anything or anyone. Fatigued, we lie down for an afternoon nap, one selecting a decayed pine log for a pillow, and the other using a hat laid on a sage bush for a similar purpose.

As evening began to approach it became necessary to develop the last six plates we had taken in Colorado, and put new ones in the slides ready for New Mexico the next day, so to a dug-out we repaired, and as this residence had no window, it appeared only necessary to hang our rugs and coats inside the door, and across the hearth, to insure perfect darkness. But once shut in, various pencil-rays of light appeared through cracks in the mud walls, and the nautical expression "caulking" is the only way to describe our efforts to cure these defects in our required dark-room. At last, a newspaper here, a cushion there, our portable bath in another place, and planks stood on end everywhere, rendered our laboratory perfect. Miners' gunpowder-cans contained all the water we wanted, and the expiration of two hours and a half saw our six plates turned out beauties; ready for printing. This time would appear great to professionals; but in an extempore dark-room, a miner's hovel, where water has to be fetched from a distant well, and one tumbles from time to time over picks and boots, dishes, and powder-cans—everything general disposed to go wrong—and one has to not only develop six plates, but open the plate boxes, and put six new ones into the slide-cases, the time consumed here was not greater than that occupied in most other camping-places. Our first picture in Northern New Mexico, Otero Station, with the special train on which we travelled, and of Mr. Moore, the pay-master of the line shows that no light got at our plates before use, as the little shop's inscription, "Tienda Mas Barata de Otero"—"The store of most cheapness in Otero"—can easily be read in this picture.[5]

But we are as yet in our dug-out—virtually a hole in the ground, with a roof over it. Satisfied that our work was done according to programme, and well done, we permitted a pipe and a glass of grog to reward our labours, and walked off thus rejuvenated to supper in the little station-house.

Now the scene changes from travelling in a heavy freight train, to the special one of the paymaster of the Atchison, Topeka, and Santa Fé (Mr. Moore), who most kindly—though we had never met before—invited us to leave the regular trains, and join him. This, besides saving a great deal of time, enabled us to get the best information as to the country and prospects. It also enabled us to get most admirable meals, for Mr. Moore carried his cook and cooking-stove in his railroad yacht, which had, in addition, six sleeping-berths. The photograph specially of this luxurious conveyance and of the special engine which spun it along at fifty miles per hour, gives a fair idea of our mode of conveyance over the New Mexico and Southern Pacific road, one only just opened, and one which when the Raton Mountain tunnel was completed, brought trade, strangers, civilization, and the nineteenth century into the midst of the sixteenth, without the aid, and scarcely with the consent, of the New Mexicans.[6]

The invasion, indeed, of New England capital and New England culture into New Mexico, was scarcely less startling to the semi-red man than was the unwelcome appearance of Cortez and Pizarro, with their dreaded horses and burnished suits of mail, to their forefathers. But the dollar is more mighty than the sword, the musical ring of the locomotive-bell more potent than the rattle of the drum, the thrust of the piston-rod more irresistible and permanent in its effects on civilization than that of the lance; and the throb of the engine in its peaceful conquest, is more frequent than was the sob of the widow and orphan in New Mexico in its warlike conquests of bygone days. We emerge from the long tunnel. Widely over hillside and plain resounds the weird echoing shrill scream of the iron horse; and the

5. The introduction includes discussion of photographic technology here described.

6. Probably James Moore, listed as a former paymaster of the Atchison, Topeka, and Santa Fe Railroad who died in 1916. Camp, "Necrology, 1916."

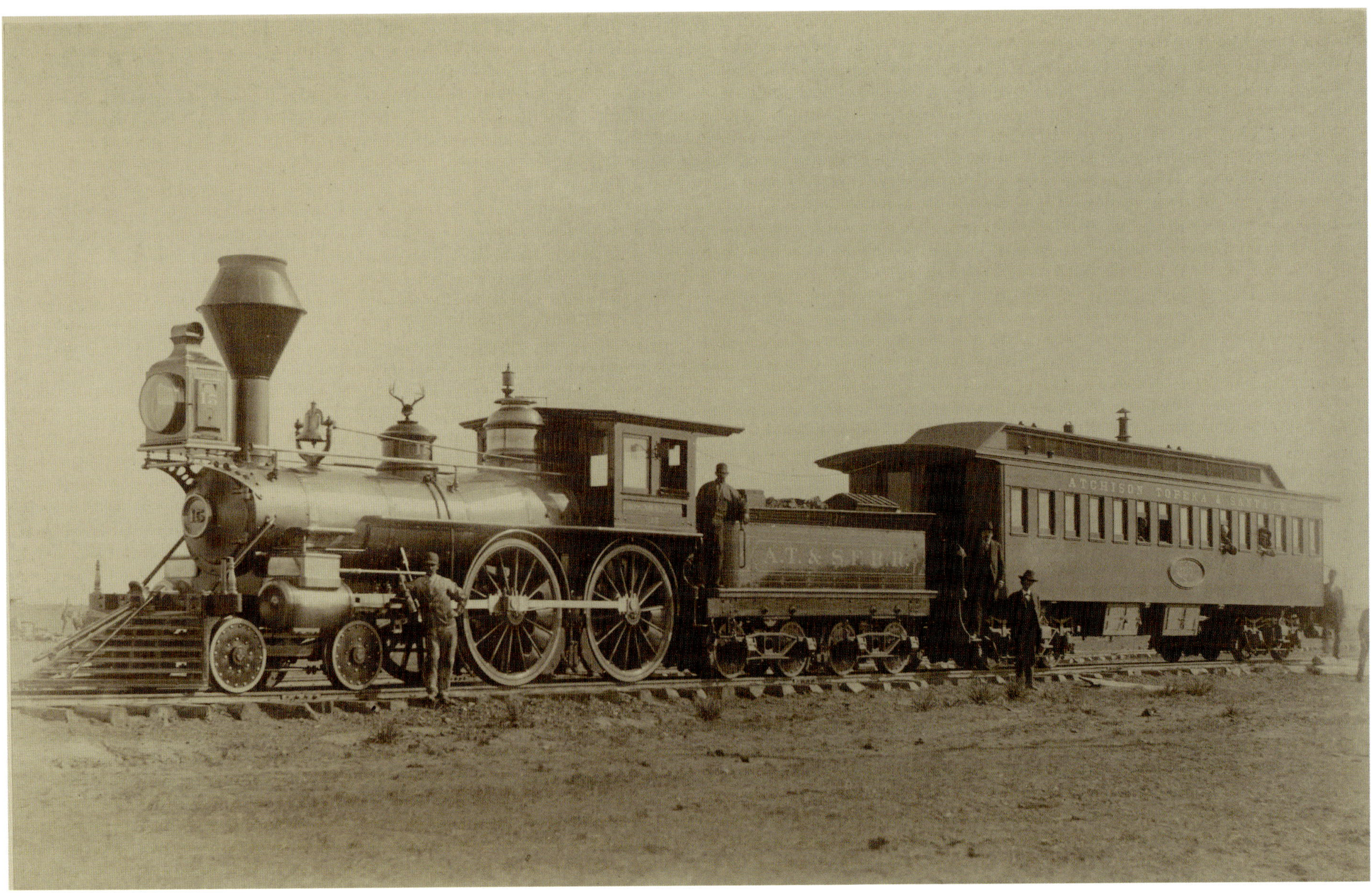

"Our Special." Springer Depôt, A. T. and S. F. R. R.
The special train belonged to Mr. Moore, who is one of the figures in the photograph. Note the decorative deer antlers mounted to the engine.

shock-headed Mexican teamster, who holds in his arms a little, wee, shock-headed teamster junior, at his mud cabin door, looks with mingled feelings of disgust and sorrow at a conveyance which he cannot rob, and which he sees is destined in every way soon to ruin the career of the highwayman—the one most dear and most natural to every true Mexican heart. Of the 221 miles of the New Mexico and Southern Pacific Railroad at present built, more than half are in Colorado, and except the splendid scenery of the Raton Pass, nothing at all approaching the beautiful is found along it up to Las Vegas. An English settler tells us the country is not as dry and good-for-nothing as it looks, and how it looks, perhaps, is best described by an officer of the United States' regular army. This gentleman had been quartered at Fort Bascom, New Mexico, for some years, and evidently studied the race of man as well as the topography around him. The entire poem we regret that pressure on space prevents us giving. The production is, of course, viewed as a most wicked and inexcusable satire by everyone in New Mexico.[7] It runs:–

"Why paint things in a rosy light,
And never chronicle the facts—thus—
How one sits down to rest at night,
And often squats upon a cactus.

"The stinging grass, the thorny plants,
And all the prickly tropic glories.
The thieving, starved inhabitants,
Who look so picturesque in stories.

"The dusty, long, hot, dreary way,
Where 'neath a blazing sun you totter,
To reach a camp at close of day,
And find it destitute of water.

"The dying mule, the dried-up spring,
That novel-writers seldom notice;
The song of blood mosquitoes sing,
And midnight howling of coyotés.

"Tarantulas and centipedes,
Horn'd toads, and snakes, and mesquit daggers,
With thorny bushes, strings, and weeds,
To bleed the traveller as he staggers.

"And oft at night the sentinel,
Who dozing dreams of distant battle,
Is roused in fright to hear the yell
Of Indians who have nabb'd his cattle."

The following graphic sketch is then given of the Apaches:—

"As desert, mountain, rock, and sand
Comprise the topographic features,
There's nothing left at my command
Except to paint the living creatures.

"Each mountain chain contains a hive
Of these marauding sons of thunder,
Who somehow manage and contrive
To live upon mescal and plunder.

7. The poem was published, in expurgated form, in J. H. Beadle's book *The Undeveloped West* (1873), as "Arizona and New Mexico." The poem was also published, in somewhat different form, in *Locke's National Monthly* of November 1874 as "Photographic Views of Arizona and New Mexico," signed "Ute, in Camp." *In Two Thousand Miles on Horseback* (1868), James Florant Meline presents some of the less offensive lines of the poem and attributes the work to "George Canterbury, private, Company C—Regiment Cavalry." None of these sources present the same outtakes that Townshend does, but clearly Canterbury's racist screed was widely distributed in print culture, both periodicals and travel narratives. While Beadle's remarks concerning the poem's reception match Townshend's, only Townshend includes the claim that the poet was an officer stationed at Fort Bascom, which was located on the Canadian River just west of the Texas border and operated from 1863 to 1870.

"From towering crags they watch the route
O'er which a bullock train is creeping,
And with a wild, blood-curdling shout
Across the desert come they sweeping.

"But here their valour takes a turn
On meeting with the least resistance:
They shun the fight, and quickly learn
To keep a most respectful distance."

Then in language some of it too strong to put in print, though it is just what the late Jonathan Swift, D. D., Dean of St. Patrick's,[8] would have enjoyed, the gallant officer comes to the Mexican race proper.

"Now turn I to another race,
Inhabiting this sunny region,
In calm and fearless truth to trace
Their manners, habits, and religion.

"These natives in a Yankee's eyes
Have neither virtue, brains, nor vigour:
A most unhappy compromise
Between the Indian and the nigger.

"Their language is a mongrel whine,
From which all meaning seems to vanish
Like strength from their own beer or wine,
A parody upon the Spanish.

"On what they live besides the air
You may perchance be interested;
They have the queerest bill of fare
That human stomach e'er digested.

"They eat frigoles, and carné, corn,
And on a hog's intestines riot.
Tortillas, sheep's heads, hairs, and horn,
With chili is their fav'rite diet.

"Pinoche and water-melon seed,
Bad eggs, strong onions, and pinolé.
And when hard in truth for feed,
They live upon mesquit-beans solely.

"'The greaser' seldom eats or drinks,[9]
His mind is wrapped in scanty clothing;
Of books he never dreams or thinks,
And labour is his special loathing.

"But little care he ever feels,
So he but apes the Spanish hero,
With monstrous spurs upon his heels,
And on his head a broad sombrero.

"Smoking and lolling in the shade,
Their lazy nerves no thought perplexes,
But make a chimney undismay'd
Out of their noses—both the sexes.

"They tell a thousand barefaced lies,
To all the saints in heaven appealing,
Confess their sins with tearful eyes,
Devoutly pray—but go on stealing.

8. Jonathan Swift (1667–1745) is famed as the author of *Gulliver's Travels* and "A Modest Proposal." Townshend here refers to Swift's often pungent satirical poetry.

9. "Greaser" as derogatory term for Mexicans and Mexican-Americans is of unclear origin but dates to at least the Mexican War period and was in common usage in the Southwest in the 1850s. Bender, *Greasers and Gringos*.

"The women dress upon a plan
Resembling French Zouaves, or Turcos;[10]
And thus God's last great gifts to man
Appear but little else than scarecrows.

"With face conceal'd from human sight,
And legs exposed to all that passes,
Their colour varies in the light
'Twixt that of leather and molasses.

"Upon their heads, in triumph reign,
Great swarms of vermin, fat and saucy.
These rovers of the Spanish mane
Cruise fearless o'er the ocean glossy.

"They dwell in hovels built of mud,
Where dogs and goats at will may wander,
Whilst slop and filth, a balmy flood,
In streams around the door meander."

Having given an account of the Mexican mode of travel and agriculture, and reflected severely upon the morals of the race, the gallant officer suggests that the greatest possible improvement in New Mexico would be for the ocean to rush over it, after it had sunk below the level of the adjacent States by earthquake. Finally, he indulges in prophecy, as follows:—

"When Gabriel sounds the final trump,
And all the nations are paraded
For grand inspection in a lump,
This race will prove the most degraded."[11]

10. Referring to North African or Turkish style of robed, flowing dress.

11. The poem and Townshend's enjoyment of it reflect a particular distaste toward racial and ethnic hybridity, the New Mexican as "mongrel" is characteristic of British and American racial prejudices of the day. The racist hostility demonstrates the fear, based in pseudoscientific thinking (prefiguring eugenic theory), that inferior races, through miscegenation, would corrupt the European or "white" and superior race. Such anxieties of miscegenation were the typical product of colonialism, and the U.S. Southwest was and continues to be a place characterized by a history and strong tradition of hybridity. Levine,"Anthropology."

CHAPTER IX

THE MAXWELL GRANT IN NEW MEXICO, AND THE SWINDLES ATTENDING ITS TITLE—THE COMING ROUTES TO THE PACIFIC—OTHER OLD SPANISH LAND GRANTS—ALBUQUERQUE, ITS WINE AND MINES—LAS VEGAS—PROSPECTS FOR EMIGRANTS—THE HOT SPRINGS OF LAS VEGAS—HEALTH GENERALLY IN NEW MEXICO—OUR START UP THE GALLINAS CAÑON AND OUTFIT FOR BEAR HUNTING.

"See the bold youth strain up the threatening steep,
Rush through the thickets, down the valleys sweep,
Hang o'er their coursers' heads with eager speed,
And earth rolls back beneath the flying steed."

POPE

Once through the Raton tunnel we are in the great Maxwell Grant, and there so much of the timber has been cut, that although naturally the prettiest portion of Northern New Mexico, the scenery is much disfigured.[1] To go into the history of this Maxwell Grant would be very instructive to the intending investor. Mr. Morley, the resident engineer on this line of railway,[2] has no objection to enlighten the traveller on the matter, if he wants a warning respecting titles declared good when vendors wish to sell, and bad after they have sold. As the law courts in the Maxwell Grant case veered round, we have ourselves heard, from men considered very leading ones in Colorado, first that the Maxwell Grant title was good and undoubted, and then, as their interests in it appeared to be going into other hands, that not only was the title bad, but that we actually lied, to have ever written that they had said the reverse, though fortunately we had not only taken a memorandum of the conversations with us, but had the title offered to be vouched for in their own handwriting. Millions have been lost by the Dutch and English in these Mexican land grants, but chiefly in this Maxwell one, and all to enrich a patriotic republican ring to be found in Denver and the regions for sixty-six miles round thereabout.

"That party-coloured mass which naught can warm,
But quick corruption's heat—whose ready swarm
Spread their light wings in Bribery's golden sky,
Buzz for a period—lay their eggs, and—"[3]

Epigraph: Alexander Pope's *Windsor Forest* (1713) celebrates British power through its commemoration of the Treaty of Utrecht and the ending of the Spanish War of Succession, which had huge implications for European nations and empires.

1. When the United States annexed New Mexico in 1848, the state contained some three hundred land grants, most made under the authority of the King of Spain. The way in which these commons fared in the transition to U.S. territories is a complex history. The Maxwell Grant (originally made by a Mexican governor in 1844) comprised two million acres of land that, with the advent of U.S. annexation, became the scene of massive fraud and conflict that led to the Colfax County war of the 1870s and had long implications in legal and social history. As Townshend notes, English and Dutch investment syndicates had control of the Maxwell Grant during the 1870s. Sánchez, Spude, and Gómez, *New Mexico.*

2. William R. Morley had been a heroic figure in the ATSF's victorious race against the Denver and Rio Grande Railroad to control the Arkansas River Canyon during 1878, part of the famed Santa Fé Wars. Waters, *Steel Trails to Santa Fe.*

3. Thomas Moore, "Corruption, an Epistle," *Corruption, and Intolerance, Two Poems Addressed from an Irishman to an Englishman* (1809). It is hard to ignore Townshend's implicit comparison between English-Irish colonization and Anglo-American investment.

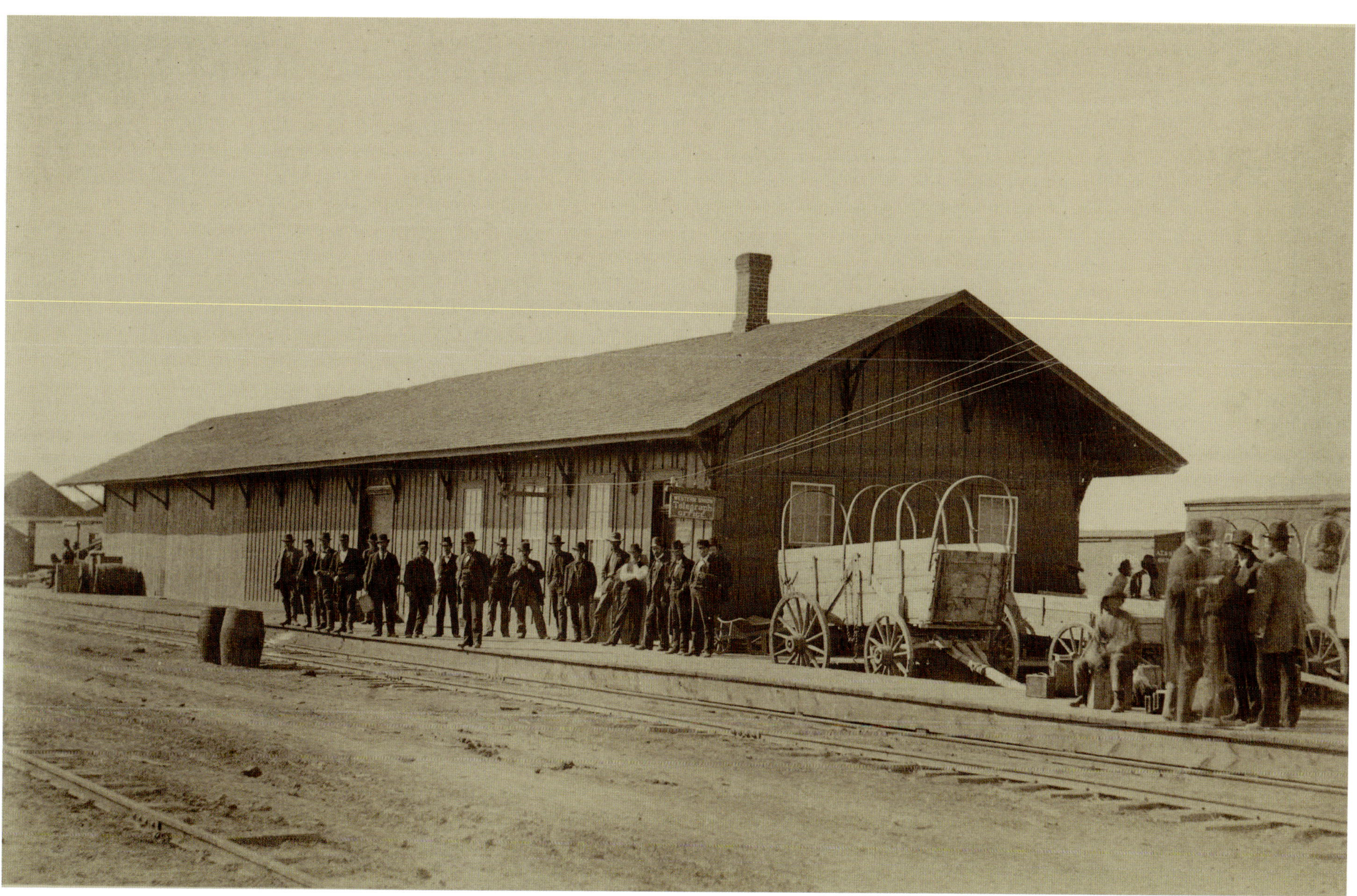

Los Vegos Depôt. A. T. and S. F. R. R., New Mexico.
Las Vegas is consistently misspelled in the original captions. This wonderful image captures the bustle of the new train station contrasted to the idle freight wagons. One can also make out the Western Union Telegraph sign behind a row of interesting characters.

Tom Moore says "die," but here, so far from doing this, they live most remarkably well, and are the envy of all weak minds and the model of all would-be sharp ones.

But we return, passing Otero–the scene of one of our photographs—to the subject more immediately before the reader—viz., travel southwards in New Mexico.

The good engine "Thomas Nickerson," named after the worthy Chairman of the line,[4] pulls us along over hill and dale, at nearly fifty miles an hour, over a fine substantial line, with very even grades. This railway has, indeed, been built evidently not for local traffic merely, but for the extremely heavy business that must come over it whenever it reaches the Pacific Ocean, which at the rate it is being extended—viz., one mile per day south-westward—is a consummation that will ere long be attained. Perhaps few matters will interest the reader who has any concern in our Pacific colonies more than to learn of the chances of increased communication with them across the American continent, a route which heretofore has been a grinding monopoly of the Union and Central Pacific railroads, to all intents and purposes one, as the Union Pacific ends at Ogden, in Utah, and from that on to San Francisco the Central Pacific only runs.[5]

The Southern Pacific, it is true, is fast extending across the continent from California, and the Atchison, Topeka, and Santa Fé, through its leased line, the New Mexico and South Pacific, purposes to connect with it at El Paso, or thereabouts, next summer. But no confidence appears to be placed by anyone in this being of much advantage, for it is believed that the Southern Pacific is very much under the control of the Union and Central Pacific roads, and will not lower upon the existing exorbitant tariffs of the latter. This connection, then, only because it would be more southerly, and therefore a pleasanter winter route, and perhaps a more picturesque one, would appear of advantage to the public. The Atchison, Topeka, and Santa Fé do not, however, propose to trust their eggs in any one such basket. Away they go south through Old Mexico, to Gyamas, on the Gulf of California. The Mexican Government is very anxious to assist this enterprise, and make Gyamas a port of some consideration, and no doubt through here it would be found shortest to send most of our mails to Melbourne and Auckland.[6] If so, passengers would, as they always have done, follow the mail route. This would offer at any rate such a serious opposition to the existing transcontinental line, that its through passenger fares should be of necessity reduced. But as if the interests of Mr. Jay Gould's monopoly were not up to the present sufficiently threatened, a close understanding has been entered into by the Atchison, Topeka, and Santa Fé with the St. Louis and San Francisco Railway, which already runs into Southern Kansas direct from St. Louis, and has a valuable charter, but no money, to go along the thirty-fifth parallel to San Francisco. This charter, the Atchison, Topeka, and Santa Fé propose to take up westward from their station Albuquerque in New Mexico, and jointly with the St. Louis and San Francisco road build away from Albuquerque merrily to San Francisco. Mr. W. B. Strong, the Vice-President of the Atchison, Topeka, and Santa Fé, is given as authority for all these statements regarding the three routes, by the "Denver Tribune," and so far as the first two of them are concerned they may be taken to be almost absolutely certain of speedy fulfilment.[7]

The magnificent markets that the mining territories of New Mexico, Mexico, Arizona, Nevada, Utah, and Southern California

4. Thomas Nickerson (1810–92) became president of the ATSF from 1874 to 1880 and was also in a leadership position in other railway lines, notably the Atlantic & Pacific. Waters, *Steel Trails*.

5. The effective Union Pacific monopoly was indeed the case and would be until the ATSF connected with the Southern Pacific in Deming, New Mexico, in 1881 (Riegel, *Story of the Western Railroads*, 189–90). The ATSF would complete its own independent line in 1887 (Bryant, "Entering the Global Economy," 210).

6. The Sonora Railway had been purchased by Nickerson and the ATSF in 1879, though completion of these lines did not occur until after 1882 (Riegel, *Story of the Western Railroads*, 192). Remember that Townshend had various interests and wrote a pamphlet (clearly commissioned by the ATSF), "The New Southern Route from San Francisco to the Atlantic Seaboard," which was aimed at Australian and New Zealand travelers coming to the U.S. East Coast.

7. The ATSF's line (completed in 1887) would ultimately run from Albuquerque to Los Angeles.

will present to grain and cattle-raising Kansas, is a subject that perhaps would have been more properly dealt with whilst we were writing on that State, and given as a reason why we did not select other lines of railway running through it, in an emigrational way. We had, however, carefully considered the matter beforehand, and preferred to devote all our space to those districts which the railway extensions of the United States seem to destine for prominence, in the great rise of values which the far West is yearly realizing.

Onwards, southwards, we push; and waiting a few minutes at the little station of Springer—where, as may be seen in our last chapter, we immortalized Mr. Moore's pay-car—we ran through a second celebrated Mexican land grant—the Nolan one—and so on to Watroots, which is in another immense grant—the "Scolly."[8] These grants, singularly enough, were all made by the Spanish Government to Irishmen, chiefly for having fought hard in what they considered "the holy cause," one which has to the generations of all ages sanctified in those ages every conceivable atrocity towards the minority, who in civilized lands differed in religious matters with their rulers. Savage Mexico really never was until subdued by Spain; the holy cause of the conquerors was then driven by lance and petronel[9] into all those who failed to be convinced by the then less recognized pontifical weapons of bell, book, and candle.

Though the buffalo-grass round us is thicker than in Colorado, there are very few cattle on it, which can only be accounted for by the scarcity of water. Here we were informed that blue-grass, and other good varieties, will not as a rule, in New Mexico, follow the destruction of the native varieties, as in Illinois, Missouri, and Kansas; but that weeds of the worst sort—viz., burr weeds, spring up on all turned-up ground, and fairly take possession of it. A series of long valleys lead into Watrons[10] and past it; but only after leaving Las Vegas, going southward, does the scenery become pleasing, and settlement and cultivation appear in the valley of the Rio Grande. Southward, however, beyond Las Vegas, we shall not long detain the reader, though the line extends to Albuquerque, one hundred and twenty-five miles beyond, having on its way to cross the Pecos River. Albuquerque has a population of 2,500, and does an immense trade in wool, hides, and ores with Southern New Mexico and Arizona. The Jesuit padres of Albuquerque possess very extensive vineyards in the teeming, rich valley of the Rio Grande. The wine they make is said to be little if at all inferior to Hungarian, which it much resembles; but as we have not had a full opportunity of testing this much-lauded drink, we shall not now say more about it. New Mexico, no doubt, will be the scene of a heavy emigrational rush in a year or two, for doubtless it possesses both as much coal and precious mineral as Colorado, but without a railway system such wealth profits a State very little. Rich gold and silver ore are claimed to have been discovered in the Cerillo mountains, ten to fifteen miles from Las Vegas, and also in the Sandia range, one hundred miles south of the same town. Coal-measures to a great extent have also been struck at Gallistro, between Las Vegas and Santa Fé. Silver Butler City—at present a phantom corporation—has been located in the aforesaid Sandia range, on the veins of gold, silver, and copper; and if all is truth that is spoken, Silver Butler City may yet become a second Leadville. Between the two highest ranges of the Sierra Sandia, thirty-five miles from Albuquerque, are to be seen the traces of an old Spanish settlement, and the ruins of a church. Extensive building and piles of broken ore lying about prove that in olden times mining was carried on here to some very considerable extent. Returning, however, to Las Vegas, a typical Mexican town of eight thousand inhabitants—half of these, however, followed the railway there, and will probably follow it

8. Like the Maxwell Grant, the Nolan and Scholly (not "Scolly") land grants were made during the 1840s, when the region was a Mexican province, by Governor Armijo. The government made land grants to foreigners as a way of guarding against invasion and encouraging economic growth. Both Noland and Scholly had New Mexican partners. Nevertheless, these grants were controversial and brewed great local resentments of long standing. Sánchez, Spude, and Gómez, *New Mexico*, 96–98.

9. A petronel is an early cavalry firearm, something between a pistol and a carbine.

10. Both "Watrons" and (previously) "Watroots" seem to refer to Watrous, a railroad stop and community near Fort Union, just beyond Las Vegas.

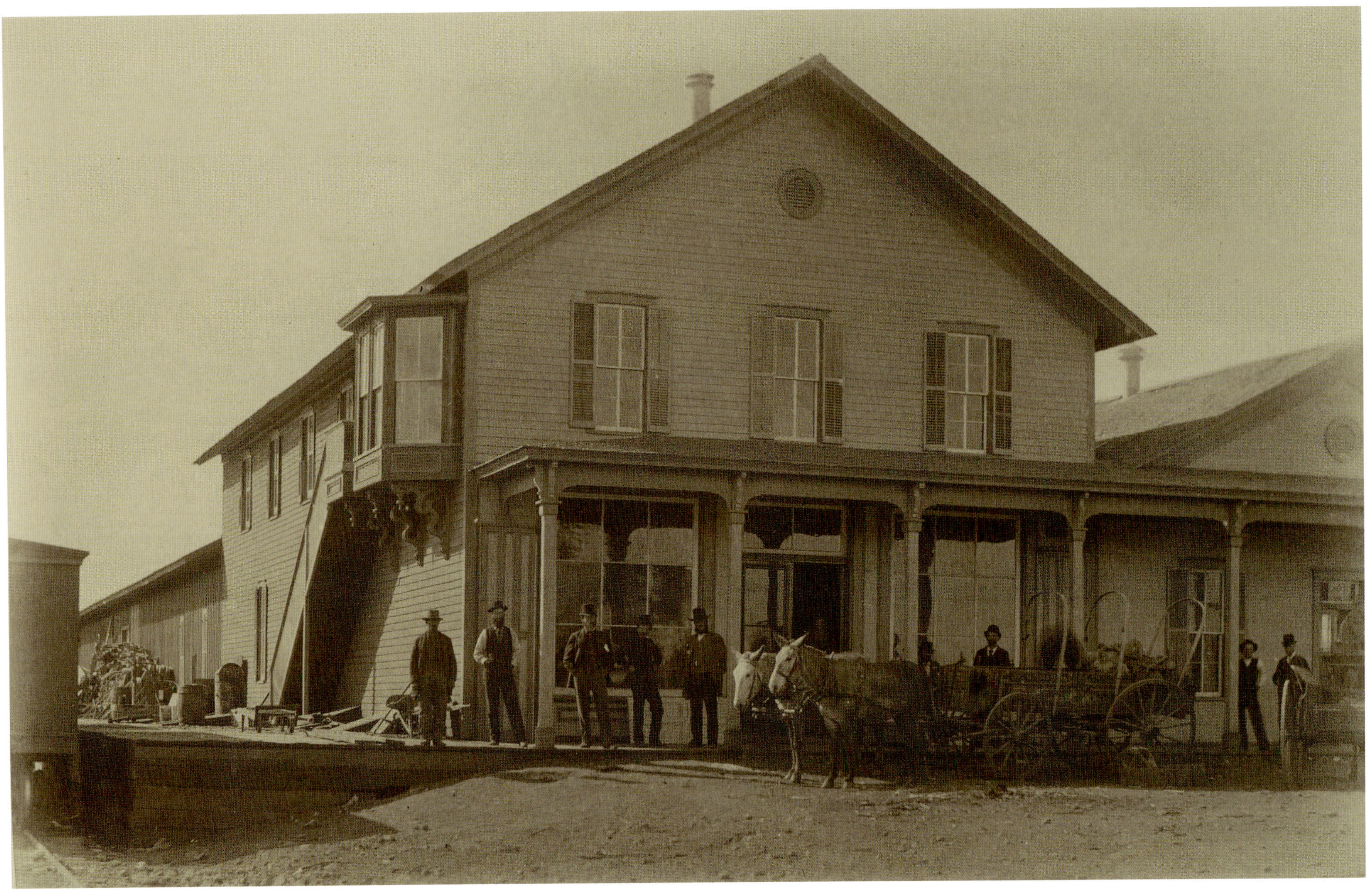

Otero Sellar's "Store." Los Vegos, New Mexico.
The image includes fine architectural detail and an unidentified cast of locals.

to Albuquerque and further—we, on reaching Las Vegas, drove across the American Gringo, or new town, to old Las Vegas, and put up at Parker's hotel, the want of comfort in which is almost atoned for by the extreme civility of the landlord.[11] Mr. Blyth, a successful English settler, dined with us here, and said in effect that though the streams are small, and the grass does not grow to any great extent, yet that it was really a far better cattle and sheep country than most outsiders believed.[12] He ranges over seventy thousand acres, and felt quite satisfied with his returns. Just about Las Vegas, and indeed from most of the road down from Maxwell Grant to it, the country looks barren, desolate, and rather forbidding, and would not captivate the taste of anyone much. The emigration will be chiefly one of miners, though doubtless the present easy terms at which lands in the Rio Grande and Pecos valleys may be bought from the Mexicans, will attract far-seeing agriculturists to feed the mining districts in increasing numbers. At first such an enterprise would not be pleasant, for though the Central New Mexicans are a quiet, inoffensive people, easily ruled and easily attached to employers, they would be scarcely desirable neighbours. A Mexican you may trust almost anything to, but he will to a certainty steal anything you don't trust him with. A negro will generally steal small things, whether you trust him or not, as anyone of experience in the Southern hotels knows.

Sheep's, and goats' flesh, corn, bread, milk, and chili, or red pepper, the Mexicans live on altogether; and their houses on the way from Las Vegas to the Hot Springs, on Gallinas Creek, some three miles west of Las Vegas, are picturesque, and browsed round by goats and donkeys of almost every colour. A browny-yellow plain stretches from Las Vegas towards these hot springs; every bit of grass has been eaten off along the road, but where the Mexicans had irrigated to the right, fair herbage grew amongst corn-stalks, and good herds of cattle appeared happy enough amongst them.

The plain is now becoming broken. Rocks of very contorted stratification surround us. Then winding round a gravel hill, and across the beautiful clear stream of the Gallinas, pronounced Geanas, we sight a very handsome hotel—far the best in New Mexico—and a Grecian bath-house, very pretentious, with its long colonnaded balcony, and very graceful scene in front of the Cañon of the Gallinas. The new hotel—a photograph of which we give—was not then open; but it has been so since the commencement of this year. We put up in the old Adobe hotel, kept by Mr. Moore.[13] This curious-looking structure is far from uncomfortable, and is seen to the right, and more in front of the new hotel in the photograph. The cooking at Moore's was far better than the average, but as there were only about three bedrooms, and fifteen guests, the sleeping accommodations may be supposed to be no better than they really were.

Major Hawley, of Topeka, and Dr. J. B. Wheeler, of Lawrence, Kansas, we found at Moore's, getting ready to start on a shooting expedition up the Cañon next day, and the Major being an old friend of ours, invited us to join his party.[14] Opposite the next page will be seen the Major on his *burro*, surrounded by some of the most magnificent scenery of the Cañon of the Gallinas, twelve or fifteen miles up it, from the hot springs; and further on, an extended idea of

11. The first ATSF train arrived in Las Vegas in July of 1879. Its coming created economic development and divided the community. The "new town" with the depot lay to the east side of the Gallinas River. The Parker Hotel was located on the old town plaza. Wilson, *Historical Sketch*.

12. In *My Life on the Frontier*, vol. 2, Miguel Antonio Otero mentions meeting Herbert C. Blythe in London in 1885, describing him as "formerly the senior member of the old firm of Blythe Brothers and Anderson of Glen Mora" (67). Possibly the man Townshend speaks with is this man or his brother.

13. The grand hotel under construction (a project of ATSF investors) opened in 1882 and burned down in 1884, but the same location at the hot springs would become the site of Fred Harvey's famed hotel known as the Montezuma Castle, which opened in 1886. Montezuma became an important location for western American tourism (*New Mexico: A Guide*). The Old Adobe Hotel at the hot springs was run by W. Scott and Minnie Moore, as related by Miguel Antonio Otero (*My Life on the Frontier*, 1:176), who met Jesse James at the hotel in July of 1879. See also Stanley, *The Montezuma*.

14. Major Hawley of Topeka may be Charles E. Hawley, who had affiliation with finances of the ATSF and later was prominent in the First National Bank of Topeka; Dr. J. B. Wheeler of Lawrence may be the founder and first president of the State of Kansas Dental Association in 1870s. Patterson, *Western Dental Journal*; King, *History of Shawnee County*.

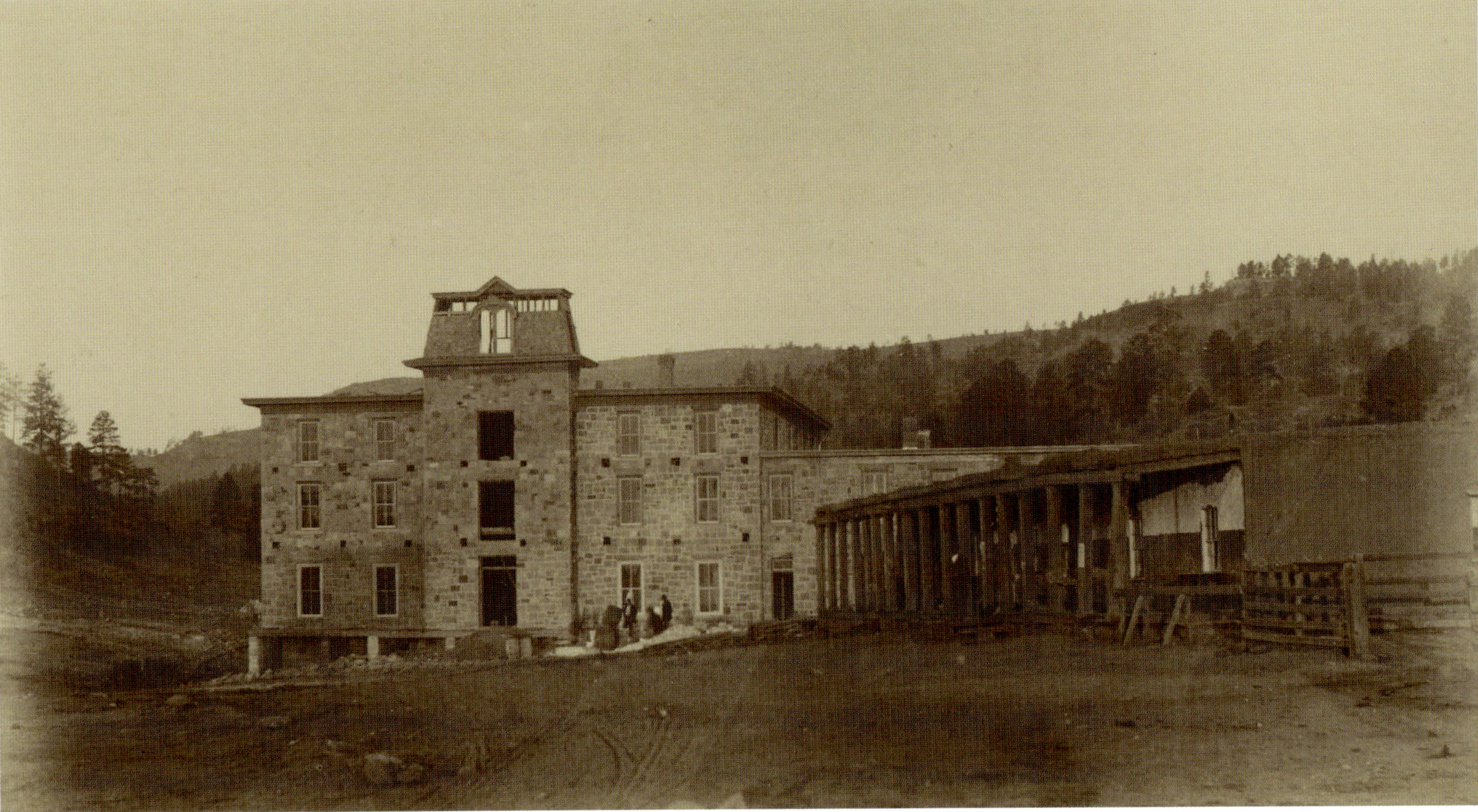

A. T. and S. F. R. R. Hotel. Los Vegos, New Mexico.
The image provides a fine contrast between the modern stone hotel still under construction and the older "Adobe Hotel" to the right.

this *burro* travelling will be photographically conveyed to the reader; but as we are at these hot springs, a sketch of them may prove of interest to the traveller in search of health.

These remarkable springs have had a local reputation for many centuries, but not until the New Mexico and South Pacific Railroad ran within a few miles of them, were they properly analyzed.

The Las Vegas springs having an altitude of 6,400 feet, and being two hundred and fifty miles south of Maniton[15] springs in Colorado, and about four hundred and fifty south of the great hot springs of Salt Lake City, enjoy a more equable climate than either, and combine the fine mountain air with the mineral waters. The horribly disagreeable summer weather at the hot springs of Arkansas, which are only 600 feet above sea-level, makes a summer residence there most disagreeable and trying. With now a good hotel, nothing can be better for rheumatism, gout, neuralgic affections, and various other diseases than these hot springs, which are the most southerly attainable on the elevated plateau of North America.

Of the springs there are twenty-two, and the analysis Prof. Hayden of the United States Geological Survey made of three of them is as follows.[16]

15. Manitou is the correct spelling.

16. Ferdinand Vandeever Hayden (1829–87) was a geologist known for his leadership in the Geological and Geographical Survey of the Territories, 1869–79, through which the U.S. government gained vast amounts of information about its holdings. Chambers, *Hayden and His Men*.

In one hundred thousand parts of water are contained parts as follows:—

CONSTITUENTS.	SPRING NO. 1	SPRING NO. 2	SPRING NO. 3
Sodium Carbonate	1'72	1'17	5'00
Calcium Carbonate / Magnesium Carbonate	1'08	10'63	11'41
Sodium Sulphate	14'12	15'43	16'24
Sodium Chloride	27'26	24'37	27'34
Potassium	Trace.	Trace.	Trace.
Lithium	Strong trace.	Strong trace.	Strong trace.
Silicic Acid	1'04	Trace.	2'51
Iodine	Trace.	"	Trace.
Bromine	"	"	"
Temperature	130° F.	123° F.	123° F.

These springs vary in temperature from 110° to 140°, and the native population have a high opinion of their efficacy in all skin-disease cases. Dr. Symington, of the United States' army, says that there is less catarrh and consumption in New Mexico than in any other country he knows.[17] He adds, that when the troops were sent to New Mexico in 1861, there were 350 cases of catarrh amongst them, and at the expiration of a year no cases were reported. In eight years' service in New Mexico, the doctor further adds that he only heard of two cases of consumption amongst natives. To the extraordinary electricity of the atmosphere, the healthfulness of New Mexico is attributed, but this field of research is rather too speculative for our purpose. The climate here is certainly a great help to the physician at the hot springs, Dr. P. H. Ellsworth, who is reputed a very good one.[18]

Leaving Moore's hotel, and the hot springs—having had therein several most enjoyable baths at 2s. each—one fine frosty morning our steeds were brought to the door, and the Major gave the order, "boot and saddle." These steeds were *burros*, some of them very small; bridles were no portion of the outfit, and the saddle-girths were composed of very dry and worn raw hide. To the heaviest of us were assigned, by the dictum of the Mexican owner of the little animals, the smallest *burros*. We were all soon in the saddle, and picking their way carefully along frosty planks, our little mokes crossed the Gallinas, and headed up for Mac's Ranche,[19] which was about twenty miles off, up the Cañon—in fact, at its head. At Mac's we were assured of a welcome; so we took no guides, but packed one of the *burros* well with our photographic apparatus, a large sack of flour, side of bacon, and some whisky, for fear Mac might prove to be on short allowance. Our guns and rifles too we carried, and of ammunition a goodly stock; for up the Cañon were reported bears, deer, turkeys and ducks, and we vowed that we would pour libations to Nimrod and Diana, ere many suns had set.[20]

The clouds thickened over splendid pines as we wended our way up the Cañon, round rocks that looked sheer down over precipices, up nearly perpendicular cliffs by zig-zags; then snow began to fall, and our pack donkey coming in contact with a tree got rid of his load, and gave the Major and the Doctor a lively time to catch and repack him. The snow now came on thickly, and two of us suffered from

17. Dr. John Symington (1846–94) was a leading medical authority in New Mexico of this time. He married into the influential New Mexican Armijo family. Speer, *Encyclopedia of the New West*, 338; "John D. Symington, Jr.," *Find a Grave*, accessed August 13, 2015, www.findagrave.com/cgi-bin/fg.cgi?page=gr&GRid=58994624.

18. P. H. Ellsworth was a physician of long tenure in Hot Springs, Arkansas, who had expertise in the health benefits of hot springs and perhaps had some position at the New Mexican hot springs at this time. It is also possible that Townshend has him confused with Dr. S. N. Pettijohn, proprietor of Montezuma's drug store and author of a book on the hot spring's beneficial healing powers. Stanley, *The Montezuma*.

19. Identified in chapter 10 as John McCalla, of whom more is related in that chapter.

20. Nimrod is depicted in the Bible as a mighty hunter; Nimrod was also the pen name of Charles James Apperly, a writer of hunting (died in 1843), with whose work Townshend was likely familiar. Diana is the Roman goddess of the hunt.

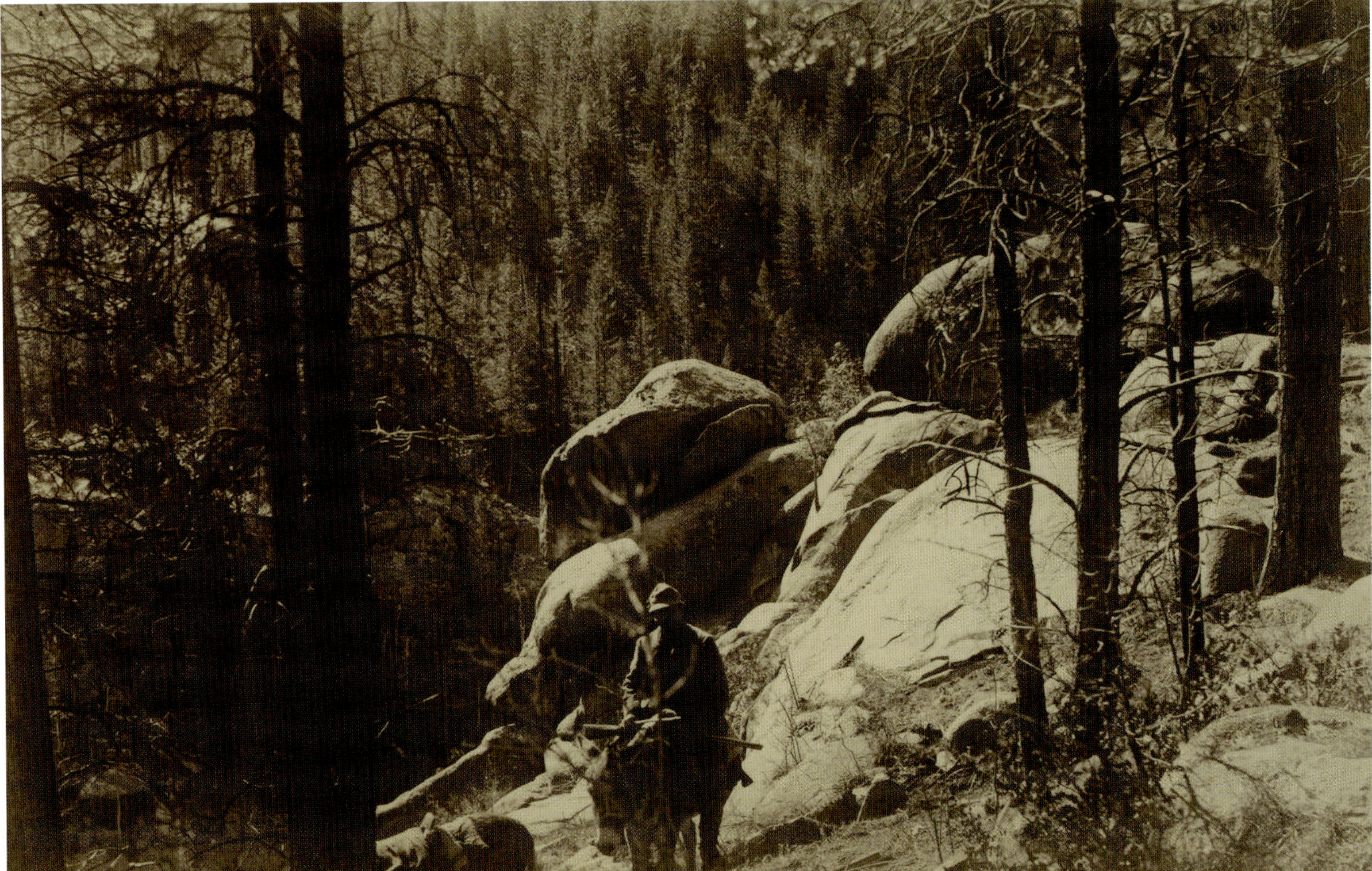

GUYEMOS CAÑON, NEW MEXICO.
Gallinas is consistently misspelled in the original captions. The rider is identified in the text as Major Hawley.

headache—a common ailment when taking exercise in these altitudes for the first time. Hopes of seeing a bear, however, kept us on the *qui vive*, for the previous evening nothing but bear stories had been in vogue, and by the people who were last up this Cañon we were told that a very large bear had come out to look at them, and sat so unmoved as they passed, that they feared to fire on such a perilously narrow ledge path. We scanned the light grey and purple stratification all round us for a bruin, we peered through the tall straight pines in all directions with the same object, until our eyes watered and ached. The pack donkey afforded us, however, a good deal of occupation. Once he headed directly for his home, and we had an exciting "round up." And on a donkey without a bridle, a brute that you can only direct with a stick laid on one or other side of his head, a "round-up" even on a plain is not easy work, but on a mountain road only three feet wide "in parts," we do not like it, and prefer our camp life as shown in illustration.

CHAPTER X

Up the Gallinas Cañon on *burros*—Game on a Cattle Drive—A Laughable, and a Serious Accident—Camping under Difficulties—Mac's Arrival—Our Quest of Game—The Stalking of the great Black Bear—Mica Mining—Conclusion of New Mexico Rambles.

"Or looks on heaven with more than mortal eyes,
Bids his free soul expatiate in the skies,
Amid her kindred stars familiar roam,
Survey the region, and confess her home!"

Pope

The snow did not prove too sufficient to obliterate our mountain-path, or sorry indeed would have been our plight. To follow up the course of the Gallinas would appear the best way up the Cañon, but this, in consequence of the depth of water often found in it, and the precipitous surroundings, which generally forbade you to leave the river once you got into it, forced us to wind perpetually up or round very steep hills. Even our sharp-pointed sticks which cruel incentives the Mexican donkeys alone understand—only kept our little steeds going at the rate of about two miles per hour. We continued the discussion of bears as we thus slowly progressed to Gallinas Village, which is about half-way to the head of the Cañon.

Major Hawley and the Doctor had both seen from the train an enormous bear between La Junta and Trinidad, on the open plains, from the train; and a cattle-drover just in from Texas had informed us that during all the four months he was upon the road through Texas and North-East New Mexico, his camp had abundance of game, antelopes, and turkeys, and that on the Cimmaron River they had struck a band of two thousand buffaloes. The man believed he was telling the truth; but the number in a band of buffaloes is almost invariably over-estimated, and having been all over Texas during the past two years, we very seriously doubt if there are two thousand buffaloes left in the entire State.

With hearts beating high at every turn in this beautiful and romantic portion of the Rocky Mountains, we yet looked in vain for any trace of game, and after rounding several mountains and striking the river at sundry picturesque points from time to time, we reached Lower Gallinas Village. The Mexican belles shrunk from the ardent gaze of the Gringo, or white man, as we rode through it, headed by the stalwart Major. This village is situated on a high mountain valley, or plateau, which is very rich, and capable of being for the most part irrigated by the Gallinas; this, indeed, the Mexicans have to some degree done very well already. Presently we came to Upper Gallinas Village, and tried hard to get some information as to the *lie* of Mac's ranche, but we could, alas! amongst us not muster one

Epigraph: Alexander Pope, *Windsor Forest* (1713).

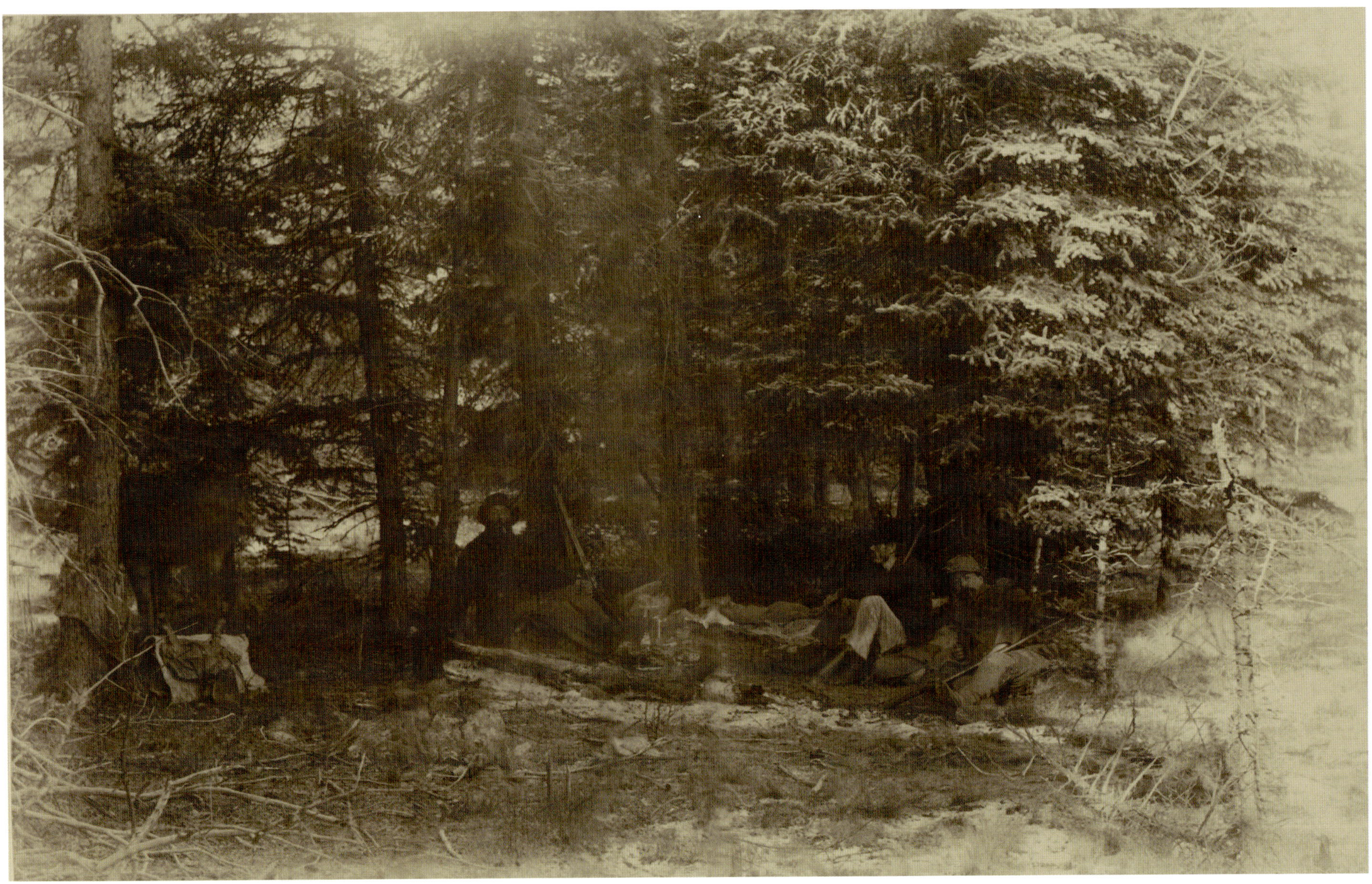

Our Camp. (Guyemos Cañon, New Mexico.)

The individuals shown here appear to be (*left to right*) Townshend, Dr. Wheeler, and Major Hawley.

word of Spanish, and so had to proceed, hoping all would end well.[1]

The plateau now ended, and the Cañon road again commenced with increased difficulties—indeed, nothing but a donkey can possibly go over it. The haste we were in to reach Mac's before night made the slow pace of the *burros* a little tiring, but all went smoothly as we crossed and recrossed the mountain stream, until at length going up a very precipitous bank the wretched girth of one of our saddles gave way, and over the tail of the pleased *burro* went the bold rider, rolling, gun, saddle, and all down quite a sharp declivity. As no bones were broken, this incident served but to give renewed vitality to our spirits, because of the mirth it created. Shortly after this, however, an accident which narrowly escaped being in the dread category of "mortal," occurred, by one of our *burros* rushing under a fallen tree, which lay, supported by its roots and branches, about four feet above the ground. The rider had to dismount, of course, and as the brute of a donkey forced his way on, one of the many branches caught the hammer of the gun suspended to the saddle, another caught a trigger, off went the charge, and those in front could distinctly see that it passed between the side and uplifted arm of the dismounted member of the party. This escape was a great deal too close to be pleasant, and is an argument against carrying a loaded gun strapped to the saddle, although the custom is universal over all Texas and New Mexico, and an accident of this sort we never heard of before.

Very soon, however, even the remembrance of it was banished from our minds, for it was getting quite dark. Snow, which had fallen more heavily here than on the lower levels, had obscured the trail; and as we got into another little mountain valley of some two or three hundred acres, the path and daylight came to an end together. In crossing the Gallinas at this point, the pack *burro* rushed under a bough, and got rid of his load, which it took two of us a very long time to collect and pack again in the dim, uncertain light and in the river-side brush. There was nothing for it but to camp, and a most unwelcome alternative this was, for not only had we so reckoned on reaching Mac's ranche as to be quite unprepared for it, but Dr. Wheeler was an invalid, and the air was laden with frozen snow. But needs must, where the evil spirit drives, and a camp we had to make. For this purpose we went amongst the thickest firs and pines, where overhanging and intertwined boughs prevented the frost falling directly on us. Then to windward we built a wall of boughs between the tree trunks, so as to break the force of the biting norther. Dried sticks and limbs in abundance lay around in the forest, and made an admirable fire to begin with, but not a lasting one, and we had no axe wherewith to fell a pine. Here fortune befriended us. An enterprising settler had at some former period commenced to build a corral in the valley; this enclosure, when we found it, consisted simply of four small pine trees, laid out as a square. Our joint efforts very soon, however, dismembered this, and the pines were hauled in triumph to the fire, into which their ends were stuck; and as these burned, the trees were pushed further and further in. Tough Mexican beefsteaks we now roasted on forked sticks before the blazing pines. Our tea and coffee were made successfully in a preserved-beef can, and then a cup of the fluid that cheers without inebriating those who "know when to stop," put us into a frame of mind fit for slumber. The Major and the Doctor had fortunately some blankets, we had none; and the miseries we endured that night were so great as to make it painful to recall them. Our feet would be roasted by the fire advancing a little, and our noses would be frozen at the same time. Then we would get up, push the pines further in, and rouse up the fire. Another pipe, half a glass of grog, to sleep again, and in an hour or so, the fire would have retreated so far, that we felt like icebergs looking at the light of an ocean steamer, in the half-dreamy, drowsy state that sleeping in a temperature of about 18° is invariably calculated to produce. Moore's mud-hotel was not very comfortable, but it was paradise compared with this utterly unprepared-for camp, and we quite disagreed with the poet, when he says

1. Upper and Lower Gallinas Villages were located along Gallinas Creek about twelve miles northwest of Las Vegas and about five miles apart. The name refers to "gallina de la tierra," the wild turkey. Julyan, *Place Names of New Mexico*, 143.

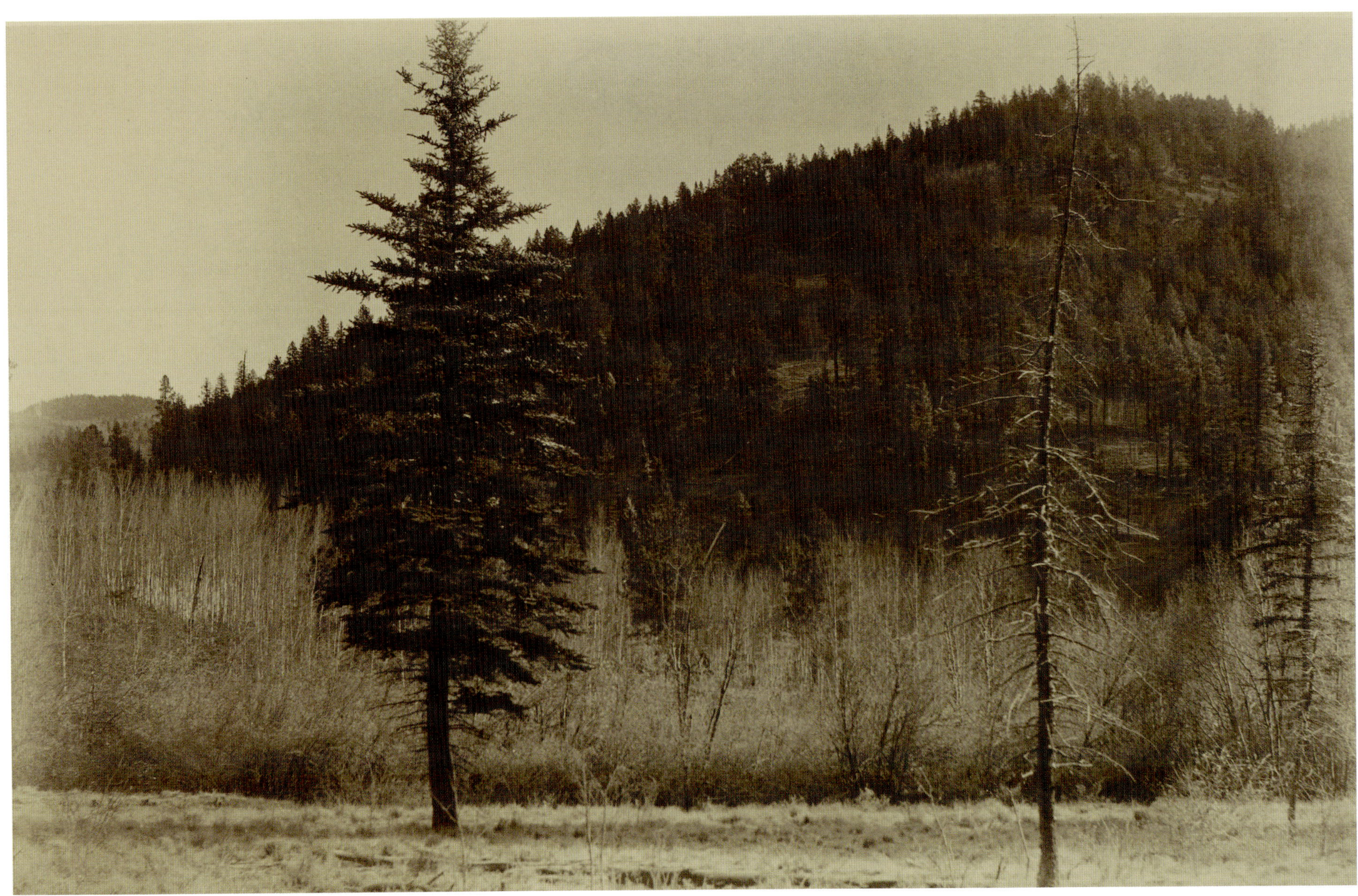

View Looking North from Our Camp.

Not one of Hyde's more impressive efforts, the interest here appears to have been the types of trees found in this mountainous environment.

"The light of bliss in these lordly groves,
Shines pure as it did in the lowly shed."[2]

However, fortunately, all things have an end, and very little the worse for our night's Arctic nightmare rest did old Sol finds us, when he peeped through the icicle-hung boughs, and illuminated the fretted frostwork on the faded cottonwood leaves next morning. The fire was soon stirred into renewed activity, and breakfast gladdened all eyes, hearts, and indeed stomachs, for these Rocky Mountain breezes are the most appetite-provoking arrangements that a poor fellow with an insufficiently stocked larder ever cursed.

Our camp is seen in the photograph, and the view that follows is that seen from the camp looking northwards. The latter view shows pine and fir-clad mountains, with the all but leafless cottonwood trees, which line the banks of the Gallinas, in the foreground. Just as the photographic arrangements were completed, a tall Scotch-looking man walked up to our camp. "You are Mac," we instinctively remarked. "I am," replied the mountain miner; "but who are you?" "This letter of introduction tells," we responded: and then Mac opened the letter, and his heart to us, and led us to his ranche; the photograph of our arrival at which will probably call a smile to the reader's countenance.

We were only a mile from Mac's cabin, and, though he may have seen our fire the previous night, took no note of it, for there is a class of persons in New Mexico who camp out because society forces them to do so. Of course Mac had no means of knowing that we were not of that distinguished order, and so did not come near us until daylight. In the photograph, Major Hawley is in the centre; Mac, who mounted the *burro* of the one of us who took the photo, is on one side; and Dr. Wheeler, with one of the authors of this book, appears on the other. Behind us is seen Mac's shanty. In the next photograph, however, the photographer is seen deer-stalking near Mac's, in the Gallinas Cañon.

An extended account of our three days' exploring of these mountains in search of game of any sort might possibly be interesting, but it certainly would deter sportsmen from coming from any distance to the Gallinas Mountains. We did see a few deer out of range, and also a flock of wild turkeys, of which we rendered no better account to our game-bag. Fate had ordained that not here, but in Texas, were we to be able to present a good sporting record of our doings, and reap gunning laurels.

"With slaughtering guns the unwearied fowler roves,
When frosts have whitened all the naked groves,"[3]

is scarcely metrical verse, though it is Pope's, and exactly describes our doings at Mac's. Be it, however, understood, our guns were slaughtering in intent only, and not in fact. The adventure of one of us with a bear here, however, must be chronicled.

Having drawn lots for partners,—as we carried shot-guns, and the Major and Doctor rifles, and we wanted—so to speak—a branch of each service represented in each party,—the Doctor and one of us were selected to go together south, up a rugged cañon, tributary to the one of the Gallinas. The Doctor, not being very strong, soon fell back, and the shot-gun, with its owner, ascended the mountain. The silence was intense. The winter—but be it remembered, sub-tropical–sun poured down brilliant rays from a perfectly cloudless sky over the mountain; though the frosted Cañon, with its ice-bound stream, had become, with all surroundings, solidified for the winter.

Besides the pine of Colorado—but much straighter, more luxuriant, and handsomer here—were two sorts of firs, which lent by their lighter shade a variety not seen in "the Centennial State" to the mountain prospect. In that dream of the beautiful, of the grand, and,—as he ascended higher,—of the sublime, was wrapped the carrier of the shot-gun. Creation and all its glories had long ousted from his mind thoughts of destruction, when, suddenly lowering his eyes from the distant vista—mountain over mountain—to the

2. Thomas Moore, "You Remember Ellen," *Irish Melodies* (1808–34). Ellen, "the hamlet's pride," marries a stranger who is later revealed to be a lord. In these lines, we learn she shines as well in her rich surroundings as she did in her "lowly shed."

3. Alexander Pope, *Windsor Forest* (1713).

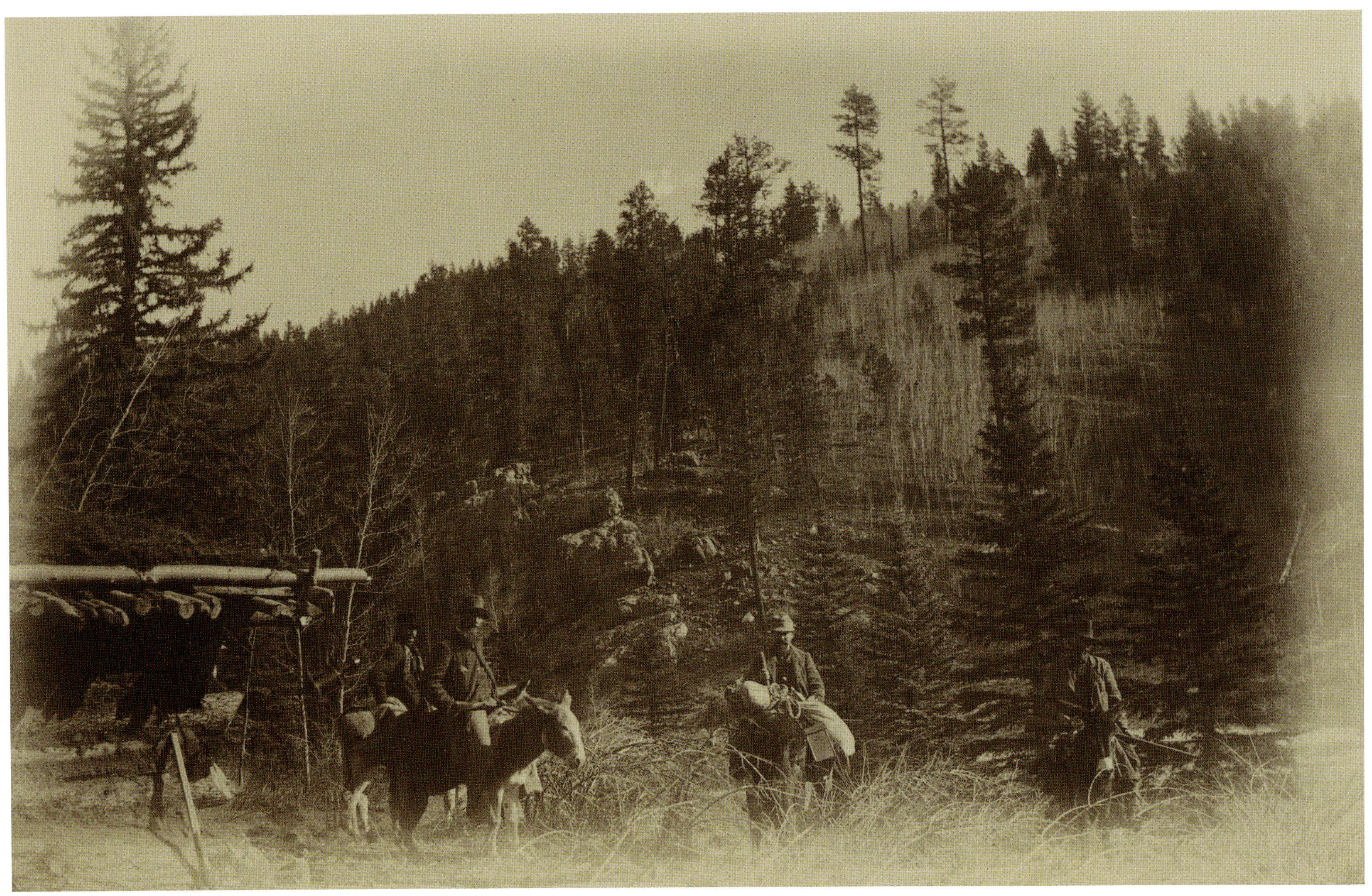

"Mac's" Log Hut. (Guyemos Cañon, New Mexico.)
The text identifies the figures captured in this image (*left to right*) as Dr. Wheeler, Townshend, Major Hawley, and Mac.

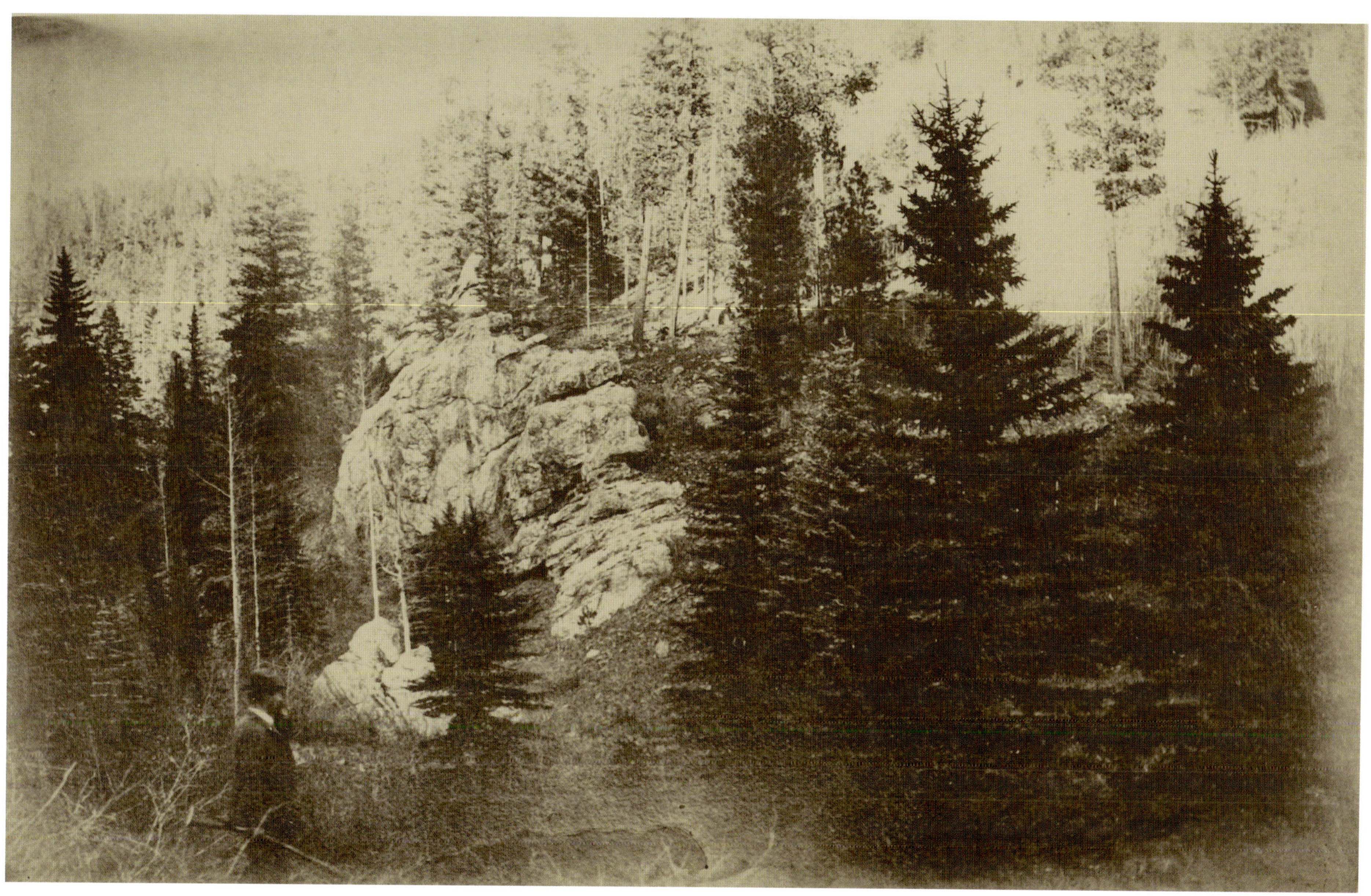

Guyemos Cañon, near Santa Fe, New Mexico.
This is the only photograph for which the text explicitly identifies Hyde ("the photographer is seen deer-stalking"), though it seems evident that Hyde is captured in other images.

immediate foreground, he beheld, about sixty yards ahead, a large black bear, lying crouched on a log, looking straight at him. Now a bear who does not appear to have any idea of running away from you, who looks straight at you, and who, for aught you can tell, seriously contemplates an advance towards further acquaintance, even to the extent of an embrace, is not a pleasant sight when a man has only a shot-gun and No. 6 cartridges. So the member of our expedition came to a halt, and returned the bear's gaze for some considerable length of time. To retreat were eternal disgrace, even though there were none to witness, and might not the Doctor have got up somewhere near?

No; an advance was demanded by all the laws which bind every member of every exploring expedition to add his mite to the sum-total of that distinction which from every exploring expedition is expected by those who stay at home at ease. So an advance, being deemed the right thing to do, was slowly, and in a cat-like manner, entered upon. A charge of No. 6 even, at ten or fifteen yards, followed by another at six or ten, might place any bear *hors de combat*. But then, again, it might not, our sportsman thought, as he neared the monster. Retreat was now, however, out of the question; the bear's eyes got supernaturally large, but he never moved a muscle. His outline became more angular, his paws—with those awful claws—why, they appeared to be severed from his body. Surely something is amiss with our Nimrod's vision.[4] Another forward step and the mystery is revealed. The black bear is a burned stump of wood, resting on another; and the eyes with the baneful yellow glare? why, they are but knots in the pine, which rain or snow having lodged in, have decayed, or turned grey.

Our sport up the Cañon of the Gallinas was thus a healthful, amusing failure. The mountain scenery was most exquisite and glorious, and Mac's mica mines, near the top of one of the highest peaks, very interesting. Mac—John McCalla[5]—is here by himself, and has already 400 lbs. of good mica taken out. The price of this varies from 1s. to £1 8s. per lb., according to the size of the slabs, and even the waste fetches 6d. per lb. for patent piston packing.

This little instance of the mineral wealth of the Rocky Mountains in New Mexico, may, as one of our personal experiences, prove interesting. With it we have reluctantly to close our very partial sketch of a territory which will ere long ring with the miners' pick, from the Raton Pass through the Jemery, Los Ladrones, Socorro, San Mateo, Membres, and Burro Mountains.[6] There is very little disposition now to any violence or lawlessness in New Mexico, but so-called civilization will possibly at its first mining advance call these concomitants of mineral wealth into existence, and the New Mexican may for a time say:—

"With the pure dawn of revelation's light?
Yes—rather plunge me back in Pagan night."[7]

4. See chapter 9, note 20.

5. "Mac," John McCalla, is likely the same John McCalla who was a successful miner in the Kelly-Magdelena area of the Black Range by the mid-1880s. Judging from Fayatte Jones's 1902 study of New Mexico mining, mica mining was not a successful endeavor in the Gallinas Canyon area (Jones, *New Mexico Mines*). See also the Library of Congress, "Chronicling America" (http://chroniclingamerica.loc.gov/) for various newspaper articles out of Socorro County, New Mexico, and Las Vegas, New Mexico, referencing McCalla's mining.

6. Townshend's list names mountain ranges running toward the south of New Mexico. In general, Townshend takes care with Spanish place names, using tildes correctly. However, in this list he misnames the Jemez and Mimbres mountains.

7. Thomas Moore, "Intolerance, A Satire," *Corruption, and Intolerance, Two Poems* (1808). The poems are a broad-sweeping diatribe, the first in a series of verse epistles on England's ills.

CHAPTER XI

The Indian Territory—Two North and South Routes through it—The Traits and Management of Indians, and the impending doom of the Red Man in the United States—Through the Indian Territory *viâ* the Missouri, Kansas, and Texas Railway—Another way through it *viâ* Dodge City—Characteristics of that place—Hospitalities of Camp Supply, and of Western Life generally.

"Here waving groves a chequer'd scene display,
And part admit, and part exclude, the day;
As some coy nymph her lover's warm address
Nor quite indulges, nor can quite repress.
There, interspersed in lawns and opening glades,
Thin trees arise that shun each other's shades."

Pope

There are two methods of getting through the Indian Territory from north to south. One abounds in very picturesque and home-like scenery, but is not a particularly good one for sporting purposes. This is the route of the Missouri, Kansas, and Texas Railway, which runs from St. Louis and Hannibal, through Missouri and Kansas, and then traverses the country of the Cherokees, Creeks, Choctaws, and Chicasaws, to the Red River, and through six miles of Texas to Denison, where the Houston and Texas Central line meets and virtually continues it to the Gulf of Mexico. The other route is from Fort Dodge in Kansas, *viâ* Reynold's Stage line, first through some sixty miles of Kansas, and then through one hundred and twenty miles of the country of the Cheyennes and Arapahoes, into the Pan Handle of Texas, near Fort Elliot, in Wheeler County.[1] The latter is a very good road for the sportsman, and about Camp Supply the number and variety of game—deer, antelope, duck, prairie grouse, and quail—is very great, we are assured by the officers of that garrison.

We propose to sketch both routes in this chapter, but as there is nothing whatever remarkable or even very pretty on the way from Dodge to Texas, photographs only of the scenery on the Missouri, Kansas, and Texas Railway, through the Indian Territory, or "Indian Nations," as is more commonly the expression out West, are presented to the reader. The Indian Territory is in about the same latitude as Tennessee and North Carolina, and than its eastern half no finer or richer piece of land is in the United States, or perhaps anywhere else. The Missouri, Kansas, and Texas runs through the very prettiest portion of this country, and at its stations may be seen in comparative civilization the "noble red man," who will not dig, and to beg is anything but ashamed. Indeed he seldom begs, unless in a position to enforce his request, and, despite the assurances of the Indian Bureau to the contrary, he levies toll off many a herd of Texan cattle which are being driven northwards. A rather ludicrous case in point

Epigraph: Alexander Pope, *Windsor Forest* (1713).

1. Philander Gillette Reynolds (1827–88) ran as many as six stage lines out of Dodge during this period. He is not to be confused with Albert E. Reynolds, an important freighter in the region, though the two may have been distant relatives. P. G. Reynolds's line from Dodge to Camp Supply was the first such established and was extended to Fort Elliott in 1878. Camp Supply was located south of Dodge City in Indian Territory. Haywood, *Trails South*, 183–84.

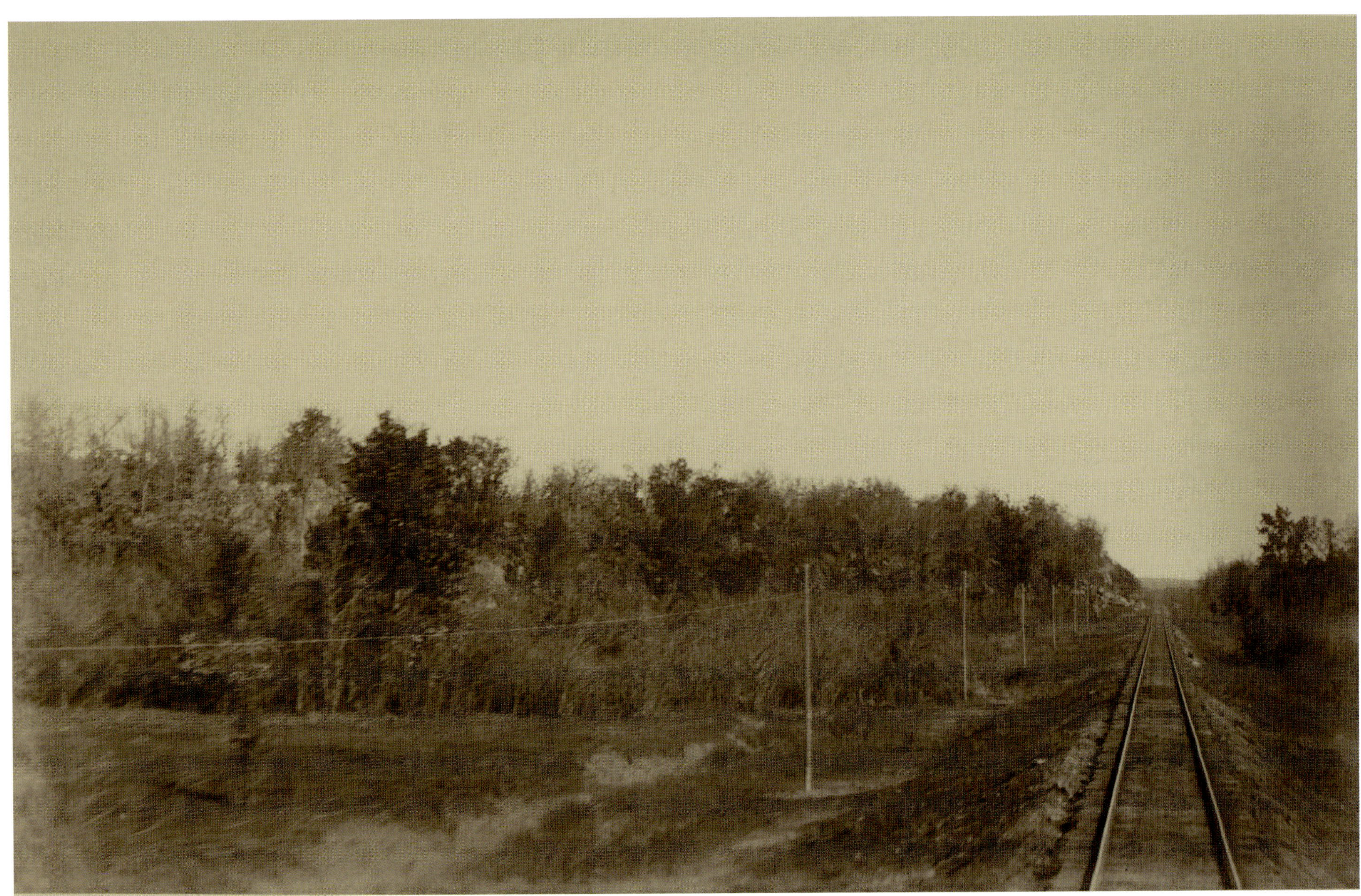

TRACK OF THE M. K. AND T. R. R. INDIAN TERRITORY. Taken near Muscogee, this image highlights Townshend and Hyde's interest in railroad development, which was much contested at this period. The telegraph line to the side is clearly visible.

occurred not long since, when, out of eighteen hundred cattle, Mr. Arthur Gorham, the ex-land-commissioner of the Atchison, Topeka, and Santa Fé line, lost three hundred head one night, and trailed the animals, and the Indian ponies after them, into the mountains.[2] To his intense astonishment he shortly afterwards read an official statement from the chief of the Indian Department in the Territory, "that none of his cattle were stolen." This reminded us a good deal of the plan generally followed by nurses, when their charges fall off chairs and nearly break their noses, of assuring them they have not been hurt. It fortunately is not usual, however, to meet Indians on the Texas cattle trail through the Territory, and it is only when they are nearly starved by the non-issue of government rations–which rations are regularly sent to the Indian agent—that they steal cattle. The Indian agent, who is paid for rations which he is thus relieved from issuing, very naturally denies that "the wards of the Nation" steal anything. The truth is, that it is he that steals from the Indians, and they in turn have to recoup themselves, which he objects to admit, as if Government paid the person robbed, it would very properly and probably mulct the Indian agent in just that amount.

The degree of civilization in the Indian Territory is rather overstated, for, though schools exist throughout it, and missionaries have left no corner unoccupied, yet the fact remains that the Indians will not do any sort of work. The elevation of the race therefore seems impossible, and its absorption into the mass of the great Anglo-Saxon republic surrounding it, appears to be totally out of the question.[3]

The Government of the United States is really far more liberal to the red man than we are in Canada.[4] Every Indian in the United States costs Uncle Sam three times as much as does each of Her Majesty's red subjects in the Dominion; but our red brethren are peaceful and contented, they are amenable to every law, and the individual, not the tribe, is held responsible for acts of violence. In fact, a couple of Canadian mounted police can go into an Indian camp, and summon the chief, on a charge of being drunk and disorderly, before a magistrate, and the chief forthwith goes with them.

In the United States, the republican theory of freedom and equality—which amongst the Anglo-Saxon race in it is merely a beautiful theory—becomes as regards the Indians, a treaty practice. Every Indian nation is theoretically independent, and has a treaty with the United States. None of the Indians are citizens of the United States, and theoretically none of them are subject to any of the United States' laws. Practically, every treaty with them has been, or will be broken, just as the stipulations of these treaties conflict with the advances or usages of Western civilization. Savages, according to modern practice, really have no rights, whether guaranteed by treaty, or otherwise, which civilized Powers respect, when the exercise of those rights inflict wrong on trade, travel, or commerce. The liberal theories, and extremely illiberal practices of a republic, do not agree with any wild, uneducated race. They expect everything, and get little. The rule of an autocratic empire best suits the savage or semi-savage all the world over. The sway of a mild limited monarchy like ours will usually suffice to preserve law and order amongst them; but the theory of indefinite rights, which they are forbidden practically to exercise, has stung, and will sting, every Indian tribe into open war with the United States, and such war cannot, in the case of a theoretically independent nation—as each tribe is,—be in any legal way construed as rebellion. The prisoners are prisoners of war, and the destruction of small detachments of one of the finest bodies of men, for its too limited size, in the world—the United States' regular army—is and can be only dealt with, as having occurred through the

2. Arthur Gorham, of Kinsey, Kansas, was employed by the ATSF as an assistant land commissioner in the late 1870s. By 1882, Arthur Gorham is listed in a Kansas Stockman's Convention Brand Book as a rancher of the Cherokee Strip. *Brand Book*, 54.

3. The Indian Territory was a shifting entity comprised of areas granted to tribes removed from their indigenous lands from its inception in the 1820s to its eventual partition from Oklahoma Territory (1890) and ultimate statehood as Oklahoma (1917).

4. Townshend's ideological orientation, much on display here, is discussed in the introduction to this volume.

fortunes of legitimate warfare, and a repetition thereof only prevented by strengthening the cordon round the more hostile of the tribes, and destroying them as speedily as possible when they go on the war-path.

Thus it appears that the red man must eventually disappear off the face of the United States, before a civilization that is too liberal to coerce him into its ways, yet too illiberal to permit him to live in any other. The doom of the red man might be for a long time averted by placing him under the control of the army, the rigid rules of which he respects, as well as the independent and impartial character of its officers; but, under the Indian Bureau at Washington, nothing but petty frauds on the tribes has even been experienced by them, and nothing else is ever expected.

In no way do we wish to reflect upon the chiefs of the Indian Bureau, but the pestilent petty Indian agents appointed to each tribe have made civilization distasteful to every red man, and most whites, west of St. Louis.[5]

Returning, however, from this general Indian subject to the matter more immediately before us—the Indian Territory. The land there is held in common by each tribe, which cannot sell or alienate any portion of it, but may lease to whites for twenty years, which has in a few instances been done. Another curious feature in the treaty laws is that the descendant of an Indian, where the wife or husband is not an Indian, is entitled to all tribal privileges. A man may therefore—and very often does—marry a dusky maiden, and his eldest child can lease to him at the age of twenty-one, any portion of the tribal lands.

Nothing but the hereditary dislike of the various tribes in the Territory prevents their uniting in a general outbreak, as occurred last year amongst the Utes in Colorado.[6] Such an outbreak, had it occurred in the Indian Territory, could not have been coped with by all the troops in the department of Texas, and scalps would have been lifted probably for three hundred miles south. The old chiefs, however, have of late years totally discountenanced all violence, for no matter how successful a general rising might be at first, it could end only in either Indian extermination, or the removal of every tribe to Arizona or Dacota, a consummation which very probably the next decade will see, in any case, accomplished.

The route we will first refer to for the ordinary traveller, through the beautiful abode of the red man to-day, is, however, over the rails of the Missouri, Kansas, and Texas. This route we took from Emporia Junction, where the Missouri, Kansas, and Texas crosses the line that brought us up from New Mexico, the Atchison, Topeka, and Santa Fé. For over one hundred and thirty miles we go through Kansas, chiefly in the Neosho Valley; and then, a little past Oswego, we run into the Indian Territory, past Vinita, where the St. Louis and San Francisco line at present ends, and, crossing the Arkansas on a very fine bridge, stop at Muscogee; an idea of the scenery around which may be gathered from the first photograph in this chapter. The north fork of the fine Canadian, and then the Canadian River itself is crossed. Beautiful English-like hill and dale, just timbered enough for shelter, intervene between the water-courses, which are throughout heavily and abundantly wooded.

The next scene we present is Limestone Gap, the prettiest view along the entire line; and then comes a scene at the dining station of Atoka. The usual lot of roughs were gathered together near the lunch stand, and we could not resist the temptation to immortalize them; but the really very nice dining-room of the company is not included in the picture, and we owe the Missouri, Kansas, and Texas an apology for this, which we make in the following explanatory way—viz., that all through our travel we have endeavoured to portray as much as possible ordinary life, instead of, like the *genus* emigration agent, picking out very pleasing but perhaps very exceptional bits of civilization in the districts we traversed.

In autumn there are few lovelier vistas than those seen in this

5. The Indian Agent (a role existing in some form from 1849 to 1908) was a notoriously corrupt figure, though naturally there were many exceptions to the rule. *Encyclopedia of the Great Plains,* s.v. "Indian Agents," accessed July 22, 2015, http://plainshumanities.unl.edu/encyclopedia/doc/egp.pg.032.xml.

6. Townshend refers to what became known as the White River War of September 1879, which included Ute, U.S. Army, and civilian fatalities. Ultimately the White River Utes were removed to Utah. At this point in Townshend and Hyde's trip the events were very recent, no doubt coloring Townshend's remarks. O'Neil, *Southern Utes.*

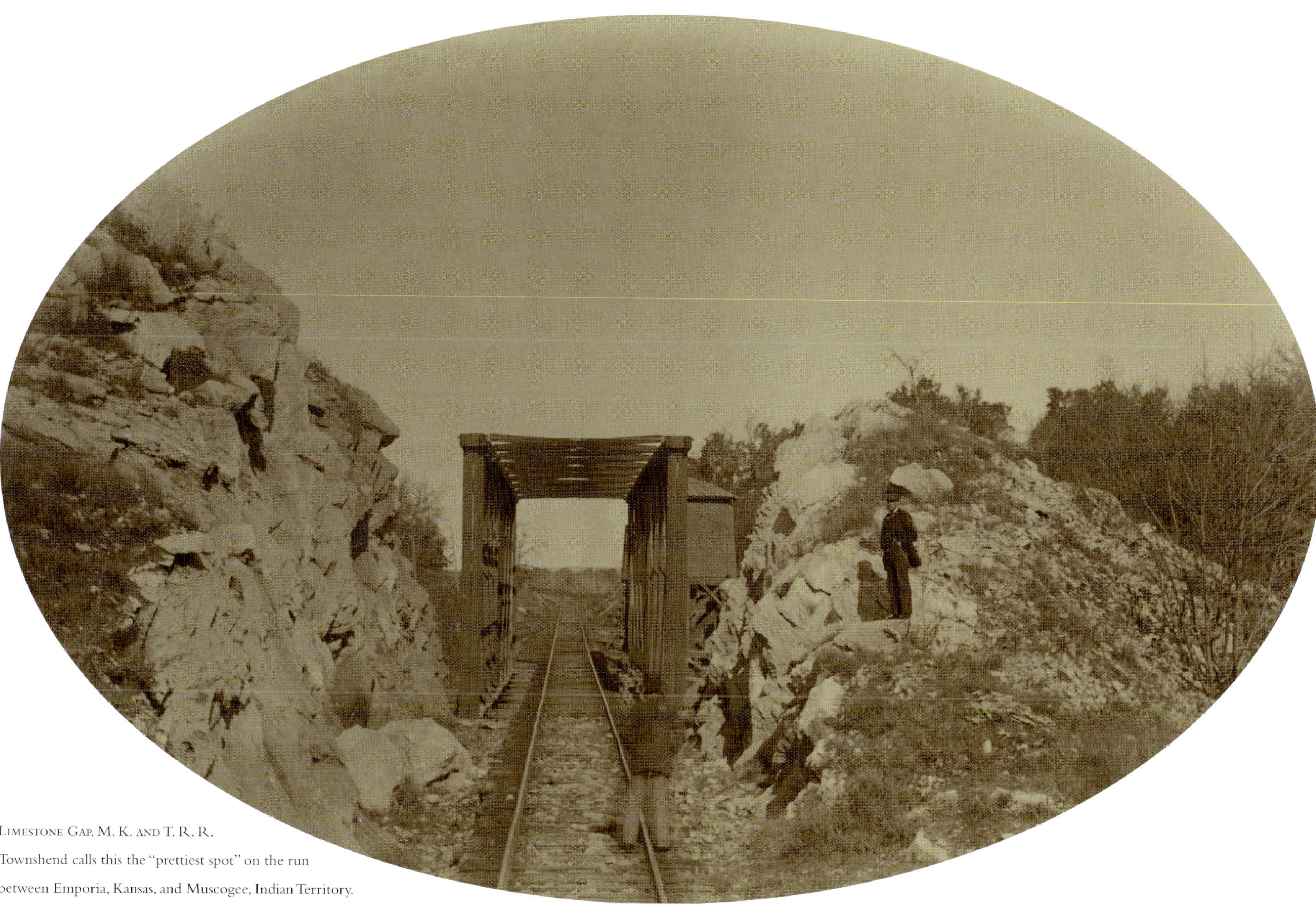

LIMESTONE GAP. M. K. AND T. R. R.
Townshend calls this the "prettiest spot" on the run between Emporia, Kansas, and Muscogee, Indian Territory.

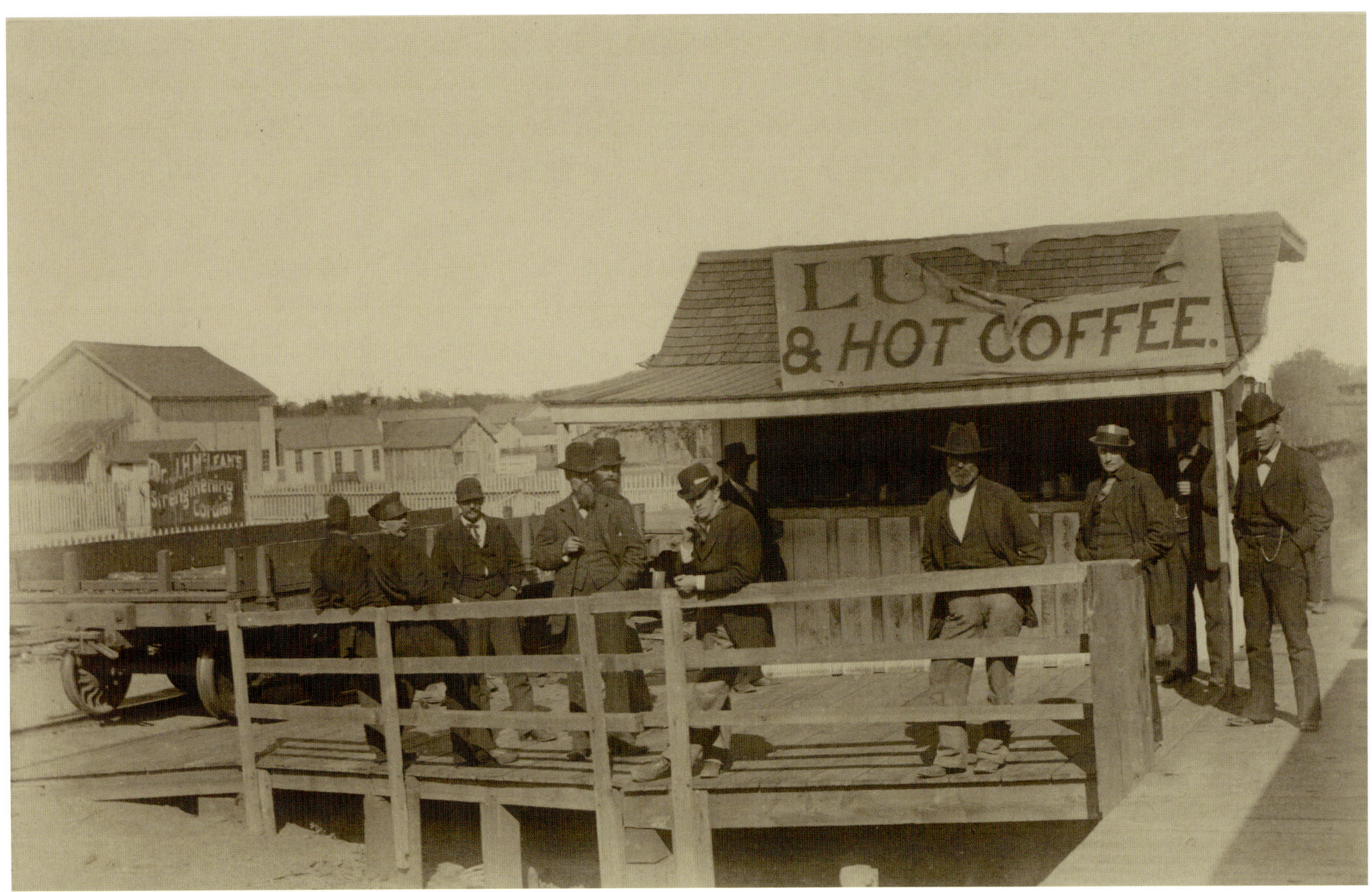

Muskogee Depôt, M. K. and T. R. R. Indian Territory. The caption is in error. The narrative identifies the scene as "the dining station of Atoka." Townshend says he cannot resist gaining an image of the "usual lot of roughs," who seem unamused.

portion of the Indian Territory, and, indeed, summer and spring may safely be added, but in winter all grass and all green vanishes in the Indian Territory, and then the Iron Mountain Road from St. Louis to Texarkana in Texas is our favourite way of travel. This railway, however, does not go in any way near the Indian Territory, the second road through which, as we have said, is from Dodge in Kansas, *viâ* Reynold's stage coaches.

On one of these we journeyed south from Dodge City early in November. Dodge City in itself demands more than passing notice by the way, for it is the great head-quarters and usual stopping-place of the Texan cattle-drivers or "cow-boys." But as Dodge is only otherwise celebrated for its extreme wickedness, where greenhorns are wont to be bamboozled, and where the most villainous whiskey in America finds its largest and most constant market, the reader will perhaps kindly pardon us for saying no more on this subject, save that as a redeeming feature, its mayor, Mr. Kelly, keeps the best greyhounds in the West, and runs down antelopes with them every time he tries.[7]

From Dodge, then, let us depart, over a rather dry and altogether uninteresting portion of Kansas, in a small two-horsed coach, for a two-hundred mile drive to Fort Elliot. New coaches have since been placed upon this line, therefore the old ones we shall not abuse—now they are no more. In any case, the drive is not a very cheerful or pretty one.

Camp Supply, a large fort, offered us every sort of hospitality, but being bound direct to Texas, we had to decline the pressing invitation of Lieutenant O. W. Budd, of the 4th Cavalry, and push on across a number of more or less dry creeks and rivers. On this route we did not see a single Indian; but that game was abundant, we had every evidence save their living presence about the coach road.[8]

Delicious wild turkey was served on the wayside stations where we changed horses; but as the strictest laws are in force against the sale of liquors in the Indian Territory, the wayfarer had better bring his own supplies with him, unless he follows the late lamented Father Mathew's footsteps.[9]

We had more luck than most people, for, having the good fortune to have Mr. Lee, the post-trader of Camp Supply and Fort Elliot, with us, as far as the former place, he not only gave us an excellent dinner in his private apartments, but presented us with a bottle of the very best Bourbon as we left, and wrote on to his agent at Fort Elliot to receive us with open arms, which he did. This kindness and hospitality of Mr. Lee is only a sample of similar acts of generous goodwill, which when travelling in the great West, we, as strangers, received.[10] It is true that our names as votaries of literature had to some extent preceded us, and all leading men in the West are very anxious to be friendly with the English, and attract English emigration. Happy the emigrant here whose experience shall be like ours; but it will be a good deal his own fault if it is not.

7. James H. "Dog" Kelley (1833–1912) was mayor of Dodge City from 1877 to 1881. Mallory, "Dodge City War."

8. Camp Supply (later Fort Supply) existed from 1868 to 1894. It was an important base of operations in military actions against Southern Plains tribes. Lt. Otho W. Budd was an officer at Supply during the 1870s and 1880s. Carriker, *Fort Supply*.

9. Father Theobald Mathew, an Irish temperance reformer, came to the United States in 1849 and spent two years in the country. *A Compendium of Irish Biography* (1878), s.v. "Theobald Mathew," accessed July 22, 2015, www.libraryireland.com/biography/TheobaldMathew.php.

10. William McDole (W. M. D.) Lee is most noted for his partnership with Albert E. Reynolds, which involved freighting and trading, the commercial buffalo hide business, and ranching. At this time, Lee and Reynolds were the most significant businessmen in the southern plains region. Schofield, "Lee, William Mcdole."

CHAPTER XII

Fort Elliot, Texas—Lieutenant and Mrs. Manning entertain us right royally—Differences between our Army and that of the United States—The Civil Service on the Frontier—Extraordinary Scenes at the Capital of Wheeler County—Mr. A. B. Legard's chivalrous Conduct—Prairie Grouse Shooting with the Commanding Officer—We borrow his Cartridges, and say Good-bye to the Fort.

"When milder autumn summer's heat succeeds,
And in the new-shorn field the partridge feeds,
Before his lord the ready spaniel bounds,
Panting with hope, he tries the furrow'd grounds."

Pope

A general sketch of the State of Texas, which we now enter near Fort Elliot, must be given; but for the present, as we are about only to explore the Pan Handle, which, though a portion of the State, may in many ways be said to be only a dependency of it, we will not follow up the, to many, rather dry line of statistic writing, with which a new country should be for practical purposes always introduced to the public. In other words, we stave off for the moment hard work for ourselves and our readers, and select life in the frontier fort as our theme, until, before entering settled Texas at Denison, we are forced for the sake of our characters into statistics.

We neither of us were born to luck, but luck has at intervals obtruded itself pleasingly in the way, and our arrival at Fort Elliot was an instance of this sort.[1] Our only friend at this post was its commanding officer, Captain Nolan, of the 10th Cavalry, and had we arrived a couple of hours later he would have been gone, as his company of coloured troops were in the act of mustering for a march to Fort Sill, when Reynold's stage-coach drove up with us in it, in front of the post-trader's.[2]

To photograph this company, as in light marching order it stood prepared to start, was of course a duty and a pleasure. Mrs. Nolan's charming sister was induced to head the company that was to escort her to other fields of conquest, and then our old friend the Captain turned us over to the kind hospitalities of Lieutenant and Mrs. Manning, who made us as much at home in their quarters as though we had been life-long friends. The first photograph in this chapter gives a general view of the fort as seen from the settler's store, and the last gives Captain Escridge's company of 23rd Infantry, the garrison consisting of three troops of cavalry and three companies of infantry.[3]

Epigraph: Alexander Pope, *Windsor Forest* (1713).

1. Fort Elliott (which Townshend consistently misspells "Elliot") operated in the eastern Texas Panhandle from 1875 to 1890. Soldiers based there primarily helped oversee settlement in the region, kept native peoples on reservations, and assisted in keeping cattle herds from running afoul of Indian lands. Kyvig, "Fort Elliott."

2. Capt. Nicolas Nolan commanded Company A of the Tenth Cavalry, an African American (Buffalo Soldier) unit. It is remarkable that Townshend has no comment on African American cavalry troopers, who served on the southern Plains and Southwest with distinction during the Indian wars of this period. Lt. Henry O. Flipper, the first African American graduate of West Point and a U.S. Army officer, was part of the Tenth at this time. Odintz, "Buffalo Soldiers"; Dinges, "Rattlesnake Springs"; Dinges, "Flipper, Henry Ossian."

3. Richard I. Eskridge was a captain of the Twenty-Third Infantry. U.S. Department of the Army, *Register of the Army*, 170.

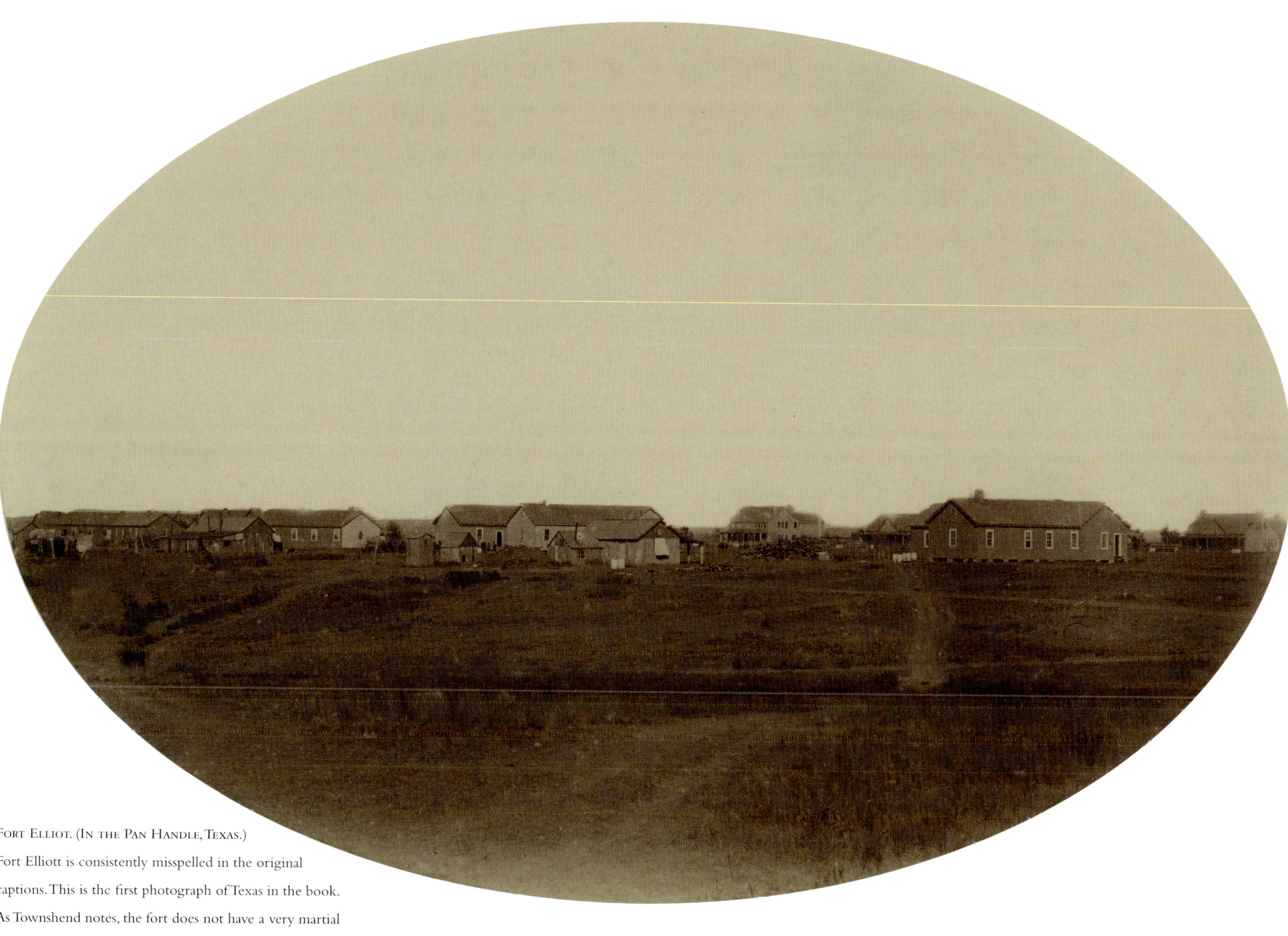

Fort Elliot. (In the Pan Handle, Texas.)
Fort Elliott is consistently misspelled in the original captions. This is the first photograph of Texas in the book. As Townshend notes, the fort does not have a very martial appearance.

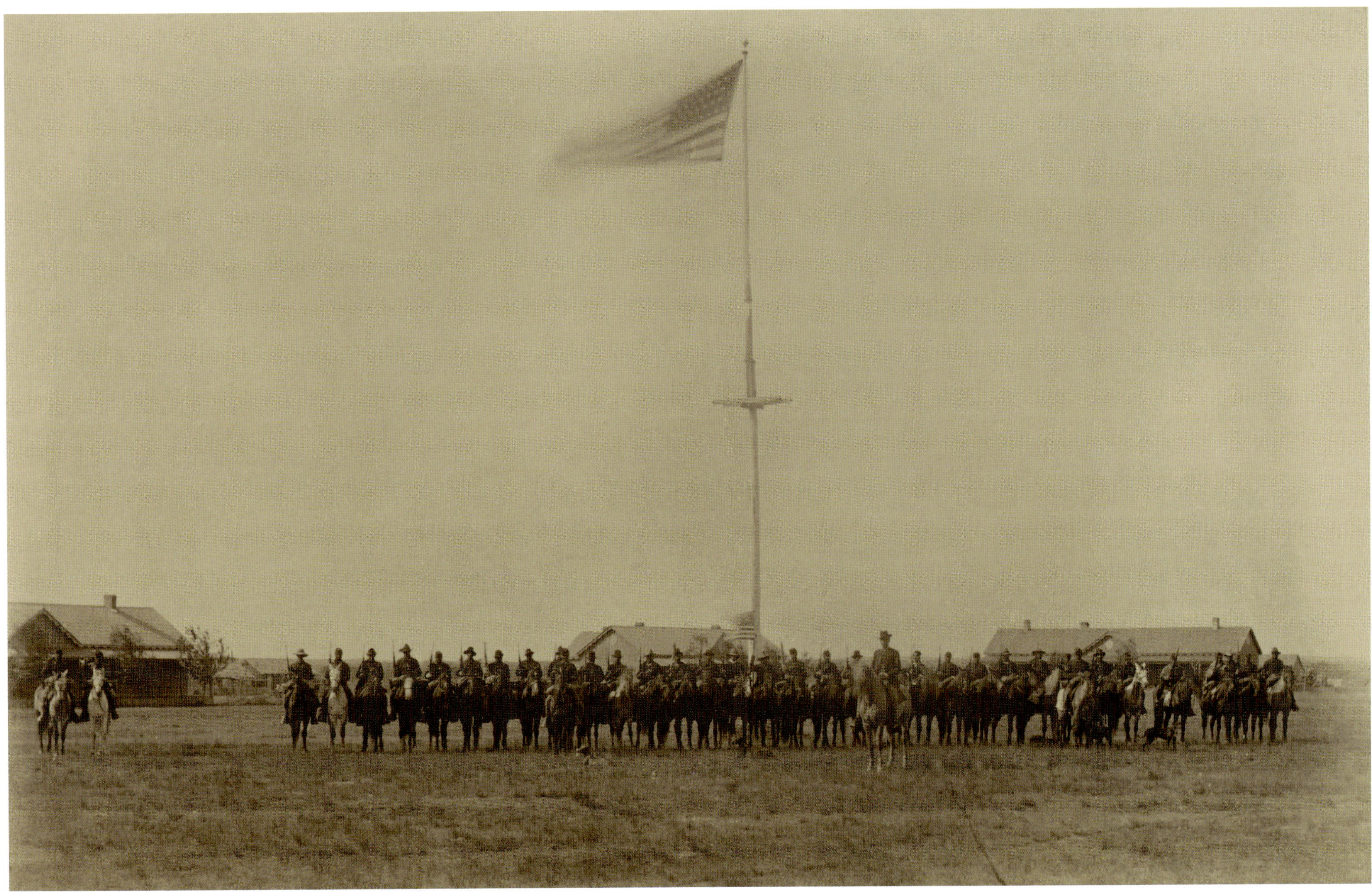

A Scouting Party, Fort Elliot.

These are African American troopers of the Tenth Cavalry, commanded by Captain Nolan, preparing to ride out. The American flags call attention to the Texas Panhandle wind and Hyde's impressive instantaneous film.

These frontier posts of the United States, though termed forts, are nearly all quite incapable of being defended. They are really barracks, not forts; but call them by what name one may, they are the most charming possible oases in the desert of civilization which surrounds most of them.

There is no regimental mess in the United States' army, except at the military academy of West Point, where the military education given to all cadets for the line, as well as more scientific branches of the service, is about as superior to our Sandhurst course as it is inferior to that of Woolwich.[4] Thus, ordinarily, *ex officio*, the officer of the line of the United States' army is a better-educated man than one of our line officers, and in the same way our artillery and engineer corps are more able and scientific than their prototypes in the United States.

A regimental mess keeps up, no doubt, to a very desirable extent, the *esprit de corps* of the regiment, and has many other virtues, not the least of which is the greatest culinary comfort with a minimum of expense. But the American system has its good points too, and they are that nearly all the officers are married, and have their families with them in the forts. This relieves outpost duty of all its horrors, and creates a most charming society, into which a traveller with good introductions is always warmly welcomed.

The daughters of the regiment are usually dashing *equestriennes*, graceful dancers, good talkers, heart-breaking flirts, and as a rule enjoy the robust health which the demi-semi wildness of their surroundings fosters, and which is denied to so many of Columbia's daughters, more especially in the Eastern States.

Discipline is not much *seen* in the United States' outposts, but it is felt all the same to an extent quite sufficient for the wants of the service, which is virtually a police one with respect to the Indians. Scouting parties have to start off very often, at short notice, after "the wards of the nation," who have broken out of their reservations, and taken to acquiring cattle *per fas aut nefas*.[5] It therefore appears to be considered a waste of time to get up in "full fig," as fatigue dress for a scout may so soon have to take its place. The United States' soldier in his barrack, therefore, looks rather slovenly, and the officers, who seldom wear any uniform except trousers, present a rather motley appearance to an eye accustomed to the rigid dress or undress, uniform or mufti, of European armies.

The United States' army is the best-paid, and perhaps fed in the world, but it certainly is not the best-dressed, even though that dress costs much more than ours per man. As a service, the United States' army is also the hardest-worked in the world. Think of a force, not effectively larger than our metropolitan police in London, holding all the Indians in the country in check, and furthermore, some three thousand of them having always to be on the Rio Grande, watching the Mexican Indians, who are a dangerous and sanguinary class of savages, preferring to kill children to women, and women to men. All this work the nominally 25,000 men of the United States' army has to do, and besides, it has to be ready to quell civil disturbances, annex Canada or Cuba, furnish perpetual escorts to all distinguished persons who travel in the wilds, and uphold the honour of the stars and stripes, mentally, morally, and by the display of hospitality, as well as physically.[6] If for all these trying duties an American second lieutenant gets the same pay as does our major,—viz., about 16*s*. per day,—why, he works pretty hard now and again to earn it. And if an American general only gets £800 per annum, why, he commands very few men, and as a rule every bit of his work that is well done is performed by his adjutant-general, and he need never leave his head-quarters, but send his aides-de-camp round to inspect. The great hospitality of the United States' general officer is what has endeared him to the world, otherwise there would only be one or two of

4. Woolwich and Sandhurst (England) were locations of Royal Military Academies.

5. *Per fas aut nefas* translates as: by right or wrong; by fair or unfair means; by any means (good or bad). *Oxford English Dictionary Online*, s.v. "per fas aut nefas, adv.", accessed March 26, 2015, www.oed.com.

6. Townshend was correctly informed: the U.S. Army force size at this period was about twenty-six thousand (Stuart, "Winning the West"). His ironic gibe concerning annexation reminds us of U.S. imperial aspirations of the period.

them found on the army-list, for none of the United States' generals command regiments, as with us, though the colonels of regiments are usually brevet-generals, which entitles them to command brigades if required.

So much for the general constitution of the army. To describe its *personnel* would be a task too great for us. Genial and unbounded kindness and hospitality, a general liking for all things English, an independent, manly bearing, these are all found in every fort amongst the officers, who as a rule are excellent sportsmen, and freely place every facility that they can at the disposal of the fortunate guest. To draw any distinction between the graduate of West Point and the volunteer officer who has been transferred into the regular army, would be invidious. There are as many good fellows of one class in the service as of the other, though a great deal of jealousy usually exists between them.

Now, by an easy transition, we come to civil life on the frontier—that is, official civil life, and behold, a wonderful and fearful contrast!

Such an extraordinary set of officials as appeared at Fort Elliot, probably never were concentrated anywhere before, and certainly never deported themselves in so eccentric a manner.

Some large estate-owners—ranchers, as they are locally termed—had been prosecuted for keeping tobacco in their station stores for their men, by the Inland Revenue. The United States' marshal, to whom the matter was referred, arrested the ranchers, and brought them into Sweetwater, a little town that nestles under Fort Elliot. There the county judge discharged them all on bail or otherwise, which so annoyed the United States' marshal, that he arrested judge, sheriff, county attorney, and everyone, in fact, who had anything to say to the administration of State law, and then he re-arrested his prisoners.

The greatest excitement at once was got up in the county. Everyone went about armed to the teeth; the people swore the marshal should not carry his prisoners away, and the jurisdiction of the United States apparently conflicting with that of the State of Texas, the troops were ordered not to interfere. That the United States' marshal would be lynched, there appeared no reason to doubt, and the county court authorities, whose duty it was to protect him, had been deprived of all jurisdiction by being under the marshal's arrest. We were exceedingly glad to be in the Fort, and certain of protection, whilst this most extraordinary set of civil proceedings was going on, and we left everything in a highly hostile state of armed neutrality, a few days afterwards. The affair subsequently terminated without bloodshed, we heard; which goes far to prove that the days of miracles have not as yet ceased. We could not help thinking that had there been even one single county official, judge, sheriff, public prosecutor, or magistrate, of any social standing or influence in the place, no such conflict between jurisdictions—of which the executive officers on both sides were grossly ignorant—could have possibly occurred.[7]

But life on the frontier would be nothing—existence deprived of all interest—were not some occasional excitement got up, and we felt that a great deal of experience in law—State and National—had been gained by us in the study of a farce which promised to merge into tragedy at any moment. Everyone felt proud of having asserted his independence, and happy smiles wreathed the countenances of all who were out of pistol-shot of Sweetwater, where promiscuous fusillading was momentarily expected. An English ex-officer of our 60th Rifles, Mr. A. B. Legard,[8] was one of the parties arrested for supplying his farm-hands at cost price with tobacco, which *had* paid duty, but for the sale of which he had *not taken out a hawker's or dealer's licence*. How this absurd straining of the law was ended was, that Mr.

7. The judge, the first elected in Wheeler County, was Emmanuel Dubbs, the marshal, Walter Johnson. Dubbs had no legal background, but in this colorful incident Dubbs got the upper hand in the end. After finding the marshal and Fort Elliott soldiers guilty of contempt, he was himself brought to Dallas for trial but acquitted. He was subsequently reelected as county judge. Anderson, "Dubbs, Emanuel"; Harris, *Hide Town*, 25.

8. Allayne Beaumont Legard wrote a book titled *Colorado* (published in London in 1872, "for private circulation") detailing his western travels. This volume bears some comparison to Townshend's, though written in diary format and lacking photographs.

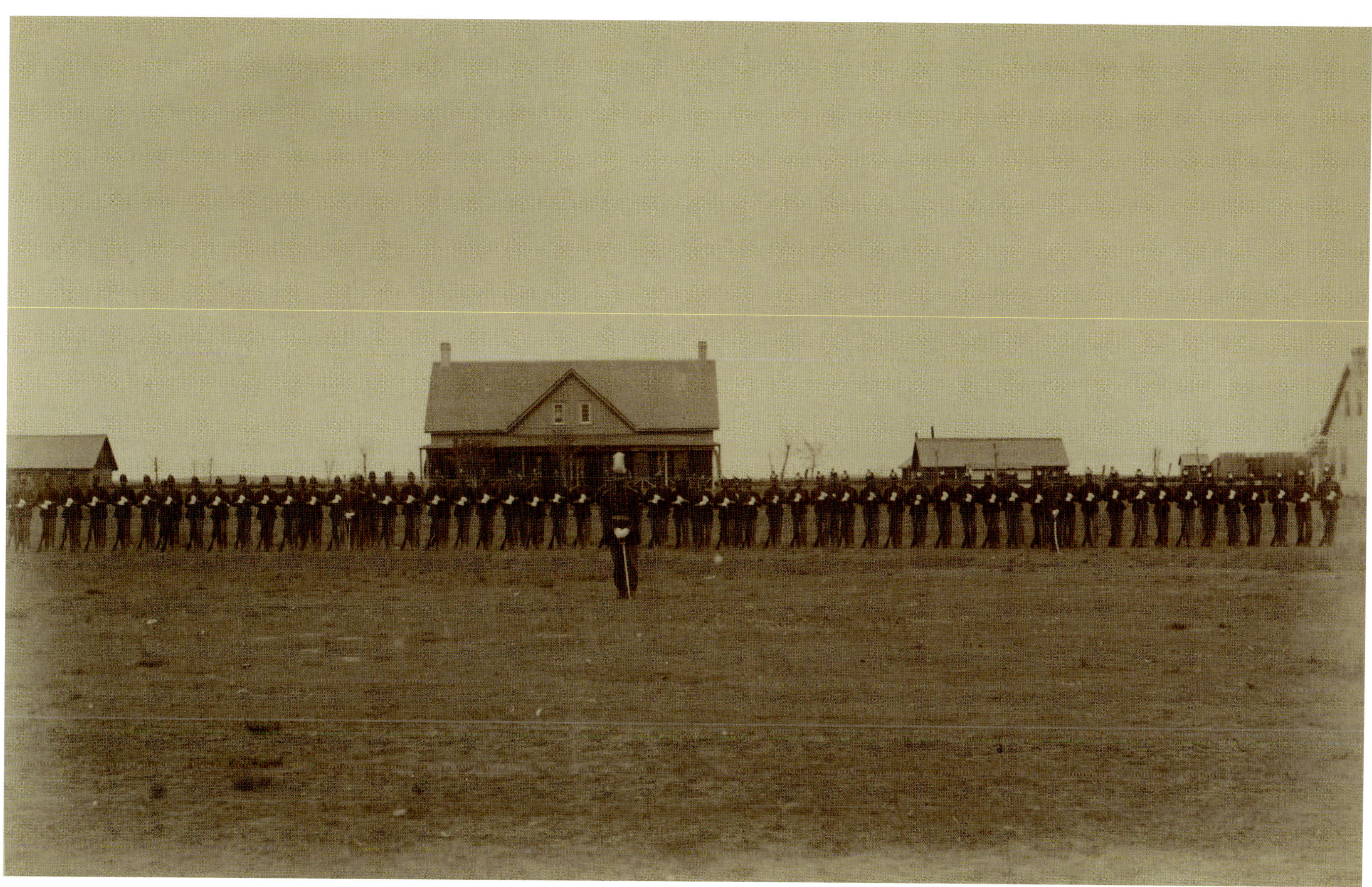

23rd Infantry, Fort Elliot. Pan Handle of Texas. The narrative identifies the officer out front as Captain Escridge. The white of the gloves and Escridge's plume contrasts with the surrounding tones. Similarly, the sense of martial order foregrounded in the photograph lends a sense of security and order to the frontier country.

Legard was fined about £2, and had to pay as costs and travelling expenses over £100. Forgiving very nobly all this annoyance, he most chivalrously protected Johnson, his arrester, from violence, and thereby sacrificed no small portion of his well-earned popularity in a place where the new construction of the law will occasionally force farm-hands to come in one hundred miles to a town to procure tobacco, or else subscribe to take out a vendor's licence for their employer. Civil life in its agricultural and pastoral phases we will deal with further on, for now we want the reader to come with us over the rolling brown heathery-looking prairie, on a prairie grouse hunt, in Captain Escridge's light spring-waggon. The prairie is heathery-looking, but it is not heathery. Thin, golden, curly, buffalo grass lies amongst, and around, large tufts of red, coarse herbage, which, had it been cut in May, would have made some of the sweetest hay, that in a horse's opinion could be found.

On, over many hills of this grass, we drove, quite discarding the slight road or trail. The commanding officer's pointer worked hard to the right and to the left of us, but his spirits and ours at length began to flag. Of course November was outrageously late for grouse, which are in season here as at home on the 1st of August. However, presently our dog pointed unmistakably to something feathered. Whirr went the bird,—bang went one of our guns,—and our first prairie grouse of the season, a lovely dark-brown bird, fat as a quail, and rounded as a partridge, came to earth, as dead as her late majesty, the lamented Queen Anne.[9] This sort of practice, we were not, however, able to keep up, and only got four brace; for the birds, which we met in fair abundance during the afternoon, were too wild to let us within range of some wretched cartridges we had loaded in Topeka. Nothing, indeed, so puts out a British sportsman as the varying strength of American powders. The orange powder is perhaps generally best, but even of that four drachms is but equal to three of Curtis and Harvey's, and of other powders, five drachms are not equal to three of theirs. English sportsmen, however, rarely will believe this, or they forget it; and not until they miss shot after shot will they become convinced of the fact, that it is just as well to come armed with a few useful hints of their predecessors to America, and not insist on buying every experience at the expense of other persons in the party, who have, perhaps, not more than enough properly loaded cartridges for themselves, but who, nevertheless, will always offer to lend,—as Captain Escridge most kindly did to us.

And now we had to move perforce onwards, though Fort Elliot is a place more pleasant to spend a month than a week in. To Mr. and Mrs. Manning, Lieutenants Dyer, Wieling, and Nicholls, and Captain Escridge, we had gratefully to say farewell, leaving them perhaps under the impression that

> "We, brave Britons, foreign laws despised,
> And kept unconquer'd and uncivilized."[10]

9. The expression "Queen Anne is dead" is listed by *Brewer's Dictionary of Phrase and Fable* as an appropriate response to the conveyor of old news.

10. Alexander Pope, "Essay on Criticism" (1711). In this poem, Pope identifies his positions as poet and critic and addresses the ongoing debate centered on how poetry should be written—"naturally" or according to predetermined rules inherited from the classical past. The final section of the poem, in which these lines appear, addresses the proper conduct and character of the "good" critic.

CHAPTER XIII

Our Outfit from Fort Elliot—Camp on McClellan Creek—Rural Honesty in Texas—Barnsey's Tales of the Border—A Native Sportsman—We arrive amongst the Turkeys—The Llano Estacado—The Texas Northers—Prairie Fire—Clarendon—"A Tough Old Cuss."

> "Why must the soul through Nature rove,
> At variance with the general plan?
> A stranger to the Power, whose love
> Soothes all save Man?"
>
> Lord Lytton

In this chapter are seen our last views of Fort Elliot—viz., the officers in their handsome full-dress uniform, grouped in front of the very comfortable quarters of Captain Escridge; then some of the ladies and little ones of the regiment; and lastly, the comfortable and picturesque conveyance that Mr. Lee, the post-trader, very kindly lent us to continue our explorations south-westward, and as this equipage will be more or less before the reader for some time, we shall commence by giving the additional description of it required by those who have scanned its photograph.

The conveyance, then, is a military ambulance which can be quite, or partially shut in with curtains of white cotton canvas, which button down so tightly as to exclude rain, and, to a great extent, wind. Behind is a platform on which any amount of baggage can be lashed. Inside are straps to hold guns, and the hood projecting in front shelters the driver from sun, and partially from rain. The springs are very strong elliptic ones; between the centres of these heavy blocks of india-rubber are bolted or clamped so that no shock can break them, for beyond the usual calculated amount of give and take, the india-rubber receives all the heavy knocks.

Strapped on behind we had a military tent, supplies of preserved meats, fruits, and vegetables, ammunition, blankets, and our india-rubber bath. In front sat Charles Barnes Austin, commonly known as Barnsey, an old Californian stage-coach driver and mail contractor. Beside him was Frank, a Mexican servant of Mr. A. B. Legard's. Frank and our pair of wheelers had been lent to us by Mr. Legard, and the two leaders belonged to Barnsey, whom we had engaged to drive us.[1]

Off south-west from the Fort we drove with light hearts, but over very heavy, sandy ground for several miles. Then the country got bold in contour and a good deal broken, as we neared La Forces Ranche, some ten miles out of town.[2] Along from here capital

Epigraph: Robert, Lord Lytton (pseudonym Owen Meredith), "The Heart and Nature," *The Wanderer* (1859). *The Wanderer* is a collection of autobiographical lyrics concerning Lytton's many travels. These lines appear in book 4, *In Switzerland*.

1. Both Charles Barnes Austin and Frank are difficult to identify. No information was found about Austin to confirm or refute the information provided by Townshend. As far as Frank is concerned, it is worth noting that Hispanic immigrants from New Mexico, notably Casimero Romero, were among the earliest settlers of the southern plains. Anderson, "Romero, Casimero."

2. "La Forces Ranche" is Townshend's misunderstanding of "Lefors." Rufe and Perry Lefors came to the Texas Panhandle in 1878 and became significant players in land and ranching interests. Their first ranch was on Cantonment Creek, near Fort Elliott. Peterson, "Lefors, Rufe."

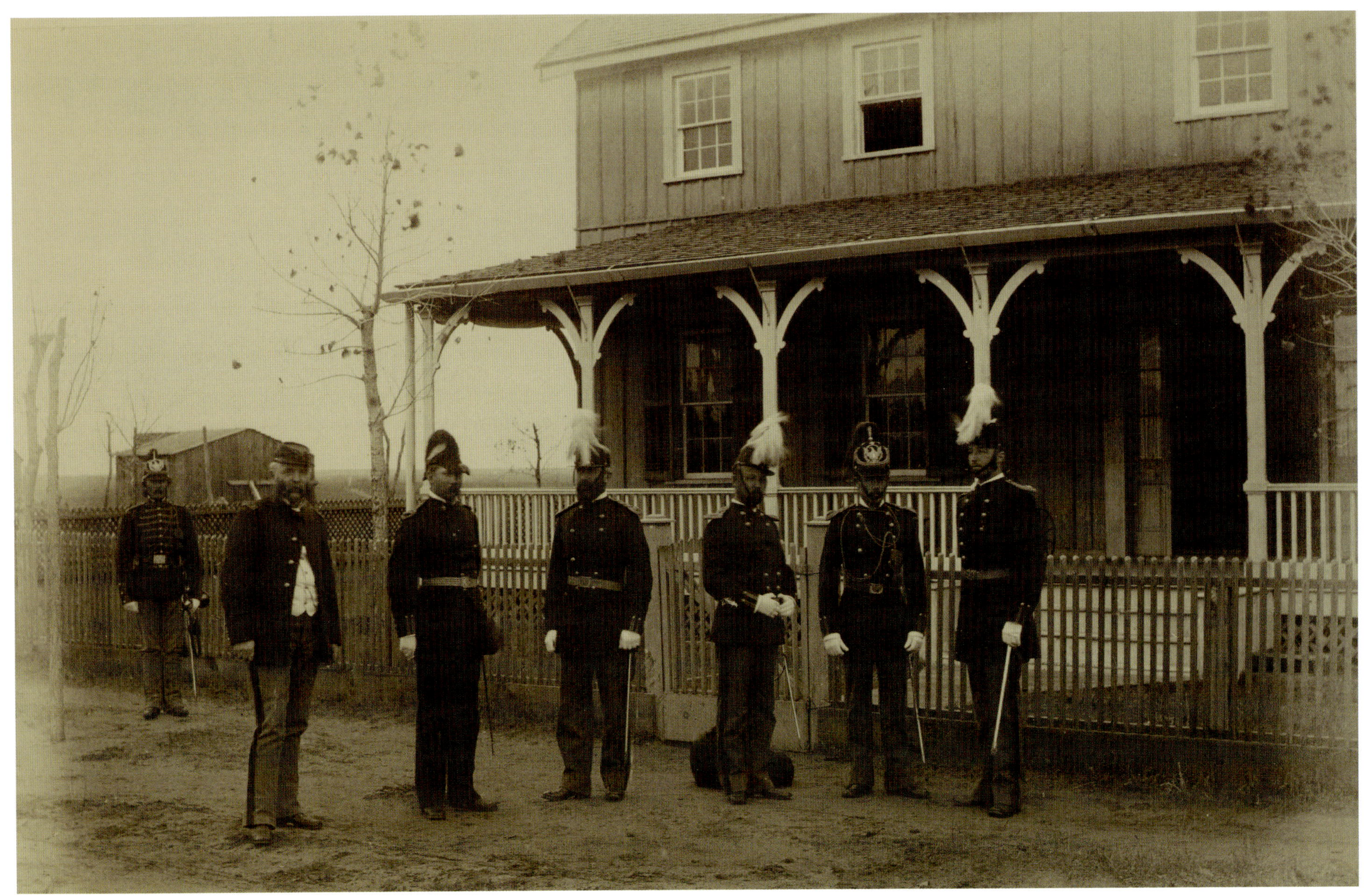

Officers at Fort Elliot, Pan Handle of Texas.
The officers in their dress uniforms and white gloves (excepting the slovenly put together man second from left), along with the picket fence and gingerbread touches to the building, make a claim for order and coming progress in a wild landscape.

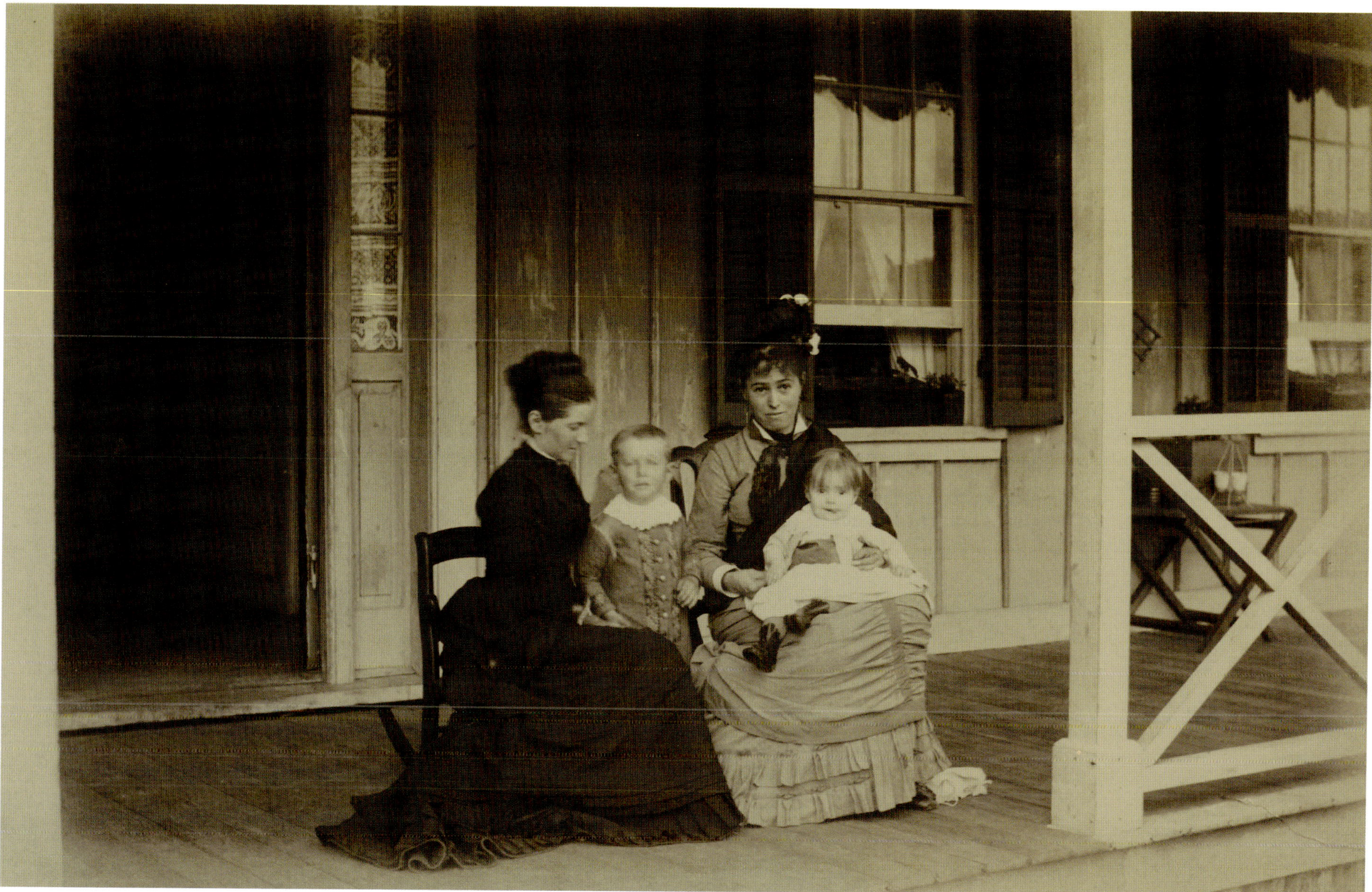

Officers' Quarters, Fort Elliot.

A valuable scene demonstrating the role of officers' wives in maintaining a sense of civility in this frontier outpost.

buffalo-grass grew even close to the road. The valley we drove in was sheltered, and cottonwood trees here and there proved that water was very little below the surface. Just before dark we reached McClellan Creek, a pretty swiftly-flowing, clear stream, and on the banks of this we decided to camp; so pitching our tent, and carpeting it with blankets, was the first arrangement made.[3] Then the horses had to be attended to, and dinner cooked. Near us was a fine hayrick, of which our horses evidently liked the quality; but on going to the ranche-house to pay for this, we found the settler was not at home. The house—as is usual in Texas—was unlocked, and all the little necessaries of simple life on the prairies were scattered about the two rooms. We borrowed some crockeryware wanted for dinner then, as also when we were returning, and found not a thing stirred during the interval, though the ranche was on the main and only road to Clarendon, and the house not a hundred yards from the road. Very soon Frank had tea, preserved beef, hot Boston-baked beans, and a hot cake ready for us. Then Barnsey told us many tales of original settler's life in California and Oregon. How with his six-shooter he had made a place too hot for one desperado; how another had rendered another place too warm for him; how a mining town had been deserted, until at last every man in it was an official, and the constituency still dwindling; how at length one man was mayor, sheriff, justice of the peace, postmaster, and constable of the city, where no one lived but himself. During the progress of these historical narratives, the calumet[4] had been in free use amongst us all. Now Frank retired to the ambulance, and coiled himself away in the bottom thereof; and we, stretching weariedly out on the buffalo robes and blankets in the tent, slept the sleep of the righteous until an hour before daylight, when Barnsey had us all astir, so as to have breakfast over, and be ready for the road whilst the morning star was yet in temporary command.

At six sharp we were off again, winding along a stream which we found on our way back was full of ducks and geese. Green and gold cottonwoods lined the banks of McClellan Creek, but as yet we saw no game, nor, indeed, since leaving Dodge City on our drive of 218 miles to this place, had we seen aught save two antelopes, a skunk, a rabbit, and the prairie grouse with Captain Escridge. A curious-looking sportsman we now, however, beheld. Burned almost black with exposure; his gun, Belgian make, was double barrelled—shot and rifle—one barrel under the other, the hammers pulling out sideways, and one trigger pulling off whichever was cocked, or both simultaneously if both were cocked. A pretty and comfortable-looking ranche-farm on the river we now reached, and Frank's quick ear detected the calling of numerous turkeys. In a twinkling we were out, following the Mexican lad; our guns loaded, and the turkeys very politely responding to Frank's long-studied and perfect call. Frank borrows my gun, fires, and misses, as the flock of gobblers walk not so much towards as round him. Then the splendid birds take to the thick brush, and some of them to high peccan trees, out of which we brought down one. A long hunt in the brush is productive of nothing, save that we stumble on a poisoned wolf and a poisoned skunk. We get a few long shots at ducks, and then return to our ambulance just as the sun rises. And now, as Saxe says:—

"Unfriendly hills no longer interpose
As stubborn walls to geographic foes."[5]

We follow up the valley of McClellan Creek, and having first taken the photograph of our ambulance, with Barnsey in his celebrated

3. McClellan Creek heads in southwestern Gray County, Texas, and flows northeast to the Red River, providing a good route for our travelers onto the caprock and toward Clarendon, Texas. "McClellan Creek."

4. A calumet is an American Indian ceremonial pipe, as in a peace pipe.

5. John Godfrey Saxe (1816–87) was a lawyer, politician and poet from Vermont. His popular, humorous, and often satirical verse appeared in *Knickerbocker,* the *Atlantic Monthly*, and *Harper's* throughout the mid-nineteenth century. His collected work *Poems*, first published in 1850, went through forty reprints. These lines from "The Good Time Coming" allude to the English poet William Cowper's *The Task. The Vermont Encyclopedia,* ed. Duffy et al., s.v. "Saxe, John Godfrey (1816–1887)."

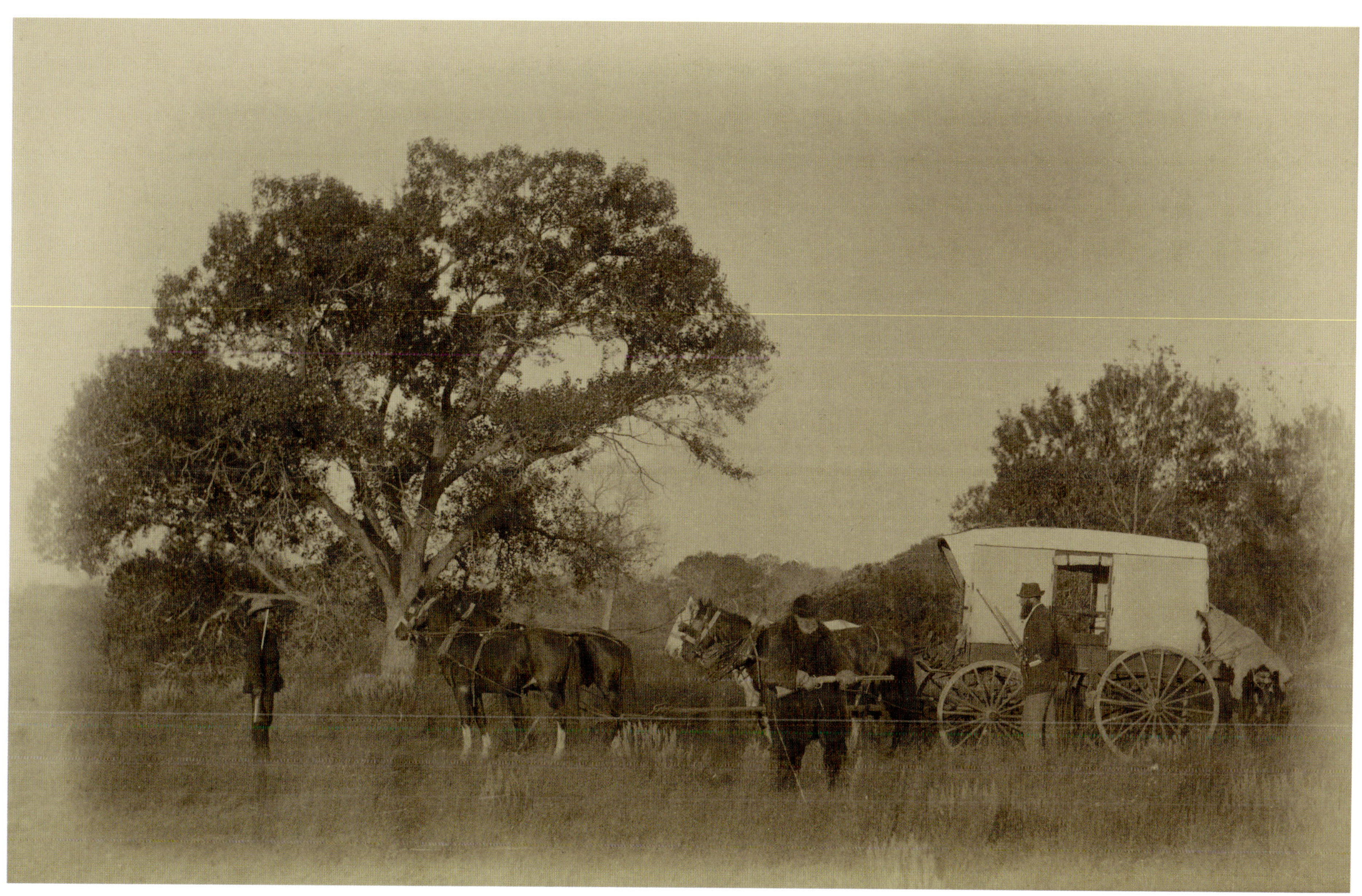

The Surprise (on M'Clellan Creek, Indian Territory). The caption is in error as the location is in the Texas Panhandle between Fort Elliott and Clarendon. It is unclear from the text what the "surprise" is. The figures (*left to right*) are the Hispanic youth Frank, Charles Barnes Austin, and Townshend. The photo seems uncharacteristically posed into an odd tableau.

buffalo-coat in the foreground, and Frank at the horses' heads, with the beautiful cottonwoods in the background, proceed onwards and upwards, and get on the Staked Plains, or *Llano Estacado*.[6]

The Staked Plains comprise nearly all of North-West, and a great deal of West Texas proper. They were, according to the majority of authorities, called "staked," because the original Spanish explorers, doubtful of being able to find their way back from such a trackless desert, drove stakes at intervals along their trails, northward and westward; and, as even scouting parties of the United States' army have been for a time lost on the Llano Estacado very recently, the precautions of the Spanish would seem to have been indicative of a great deal of the common-sense which the rapidity of modern progress so often leaves behind. The mesquite, *Acacia Algarobia*,[7] is first noticed now as a little thorny shrub with thin and fernlike leaves. As one gets south into Texas, this, however, develops into a large tree, the pods and beans of which are used as nutritive food for cattle, horses, and sheep.

The Staked Plains are high plateaux with no streams, and but few springs on them; immense rifts in the dry, light, yellowy-brown soil, however, very often occur, in some instances forming yawning gulfs of three to four hundred feet deep, bristling with large detached boulders and pointed limestone rocks. The scenery on these plains is wild in the extreme: no ocean could be lonelier. A passing "prairie schooner" is even a rare sight, except on the trails between the several forts. The grass is tall and feathery; away from these trails, a brown bunch grass now and again takes possession of thousands of acres. The stone-strewn distant hills, or rolls, are quite treeless, and no sign of human or any other life is anywhere visible.

Up to this it had been very hot, and we had slept the previous night without any covering; but now the sky darkens, and a long expected "Norther" is upon us from the Rocky Mountains. The brown prairie grasses bend low and wave frantically before the rude minions which Aeolus has let loose from his silver-lined caves in Colorado. Even the sharp, hard, unyielding spear and bear grasses tremble and sway stiffly in the presence of the unwelcome visitor. We at once fasten down our canvas curtains, and regret that our cellaret is strapped on where we cannot get it, behind, for the temperature must have fallen at least twenty degrees in as many minutes. To grumble is, however, an exercise banished by agreement from our programme; so we simply congratulate each other on the glorious sunshine which all the morning afforded us such splendid opportunities of seeing and photographing the country.

The Texas Northers are, indeed, the chief drawback to its otherwise perfectly Italian climate, and what the Texan norther is may as well here be discussed.[8] Savants in Texas tell us that the Rocky Mountains have no influence on their northers, that they are merely caused by a continuous stream of hot air which ascends from the Gulf of Mexico, causing, after a while, a vacuum into which cooler air from every State, as well as Colorado, rushes. But if this were exactly true, Florida would too have its northers, which it has not; and even if this did not upset the Texan theory, the fact that it is occasionally colder during a severe norther in Texas than in any other State except, Colorado, near it, shows clearly, that though a norther may be still, and the icy air descend apparently from the clouds even in Southern Texas, yet that the real theory of the matter is a continual succession of compensating currents of air between the Rocky Mountains and the plains of Texas. Kansas suffers little, if at all, from these northers, because the variation of mean temperature between it and Colorado is not very great. The further south in Texas you, however, go, the more sudden and severe are the northers. Cattle have been frozen to death by them in great numbers,—though this very seldom occurs,—and even the Morgan steamers, which ply down the Texan

6. The Llano Estacado, or Staked Plains, is a flat tableland of thirty-two thousand square miles that comprises much of the Texas Panhandle and plains to the south and a swath of eastern New Mexico. Townshend's account of the origin of the name follows familiar tradition though the term probably instead refers to the "palisaded" appearance of the escarpment from below. Leatherwood, "Llano Estacado"; Morris, *El Llano Estacado*.

7. An obsolete classification; the mesquite today is classified in the genus Prosopis. Sosebee, "Mesquite."

8. The Blue Norther is a well-recognized weather phenomenon on the High Plains of Texas. Barkley, "Blue Norther."

coast, have had their weather-rigging a mass of ice and icicles. That the norther has its uses, kills the fever germ, purifies the air generally, and destroys millions of noxious insect eggs, there is no reason to doubt, and though it interferes sadly with the orange, the banana, and other plants that should naturally flourish in these latitudes, as they do in Florida, and even Louisiana, we view the Texas norther as far from being an unmitigated evil, even when it brings down the thermometer—as it does once in a while—from 70° to 10°, and very often, as this winter, from 72° to 22° at San Antonio in the course of a few hours. Chiefly as affecting invalids, who, in annually increasing numbers, seek Texas as a winter home, do we deal with the norther. To the farmer it is perfectly harmless, for it never comes before all his crops are gathered, nor after they are put in to do them any damage. Having just, therefore, sketched this matter, we proceed duly on our voyage in the Pan Handle. The brown yellow-topped prairie waves surround us, as the blue white-topped ones would at sea; and the excitement on board our conveyance at sighting anything, is strongly akin to that experienced in the mariner's craft. "Hallo! There's a horse, or is it an antelope?" "Is that a waggon-cover or a tent on the horizon?" Time alone proves what each are. Then we light our pipes, and carelessly throw overboard the lucifer match. Are not the consequences startling? Away bounds the flame in an ever-spreading sheet, rolling, fizzing, crackling, over tuft and bunch grass to leeward like mad. Happily, the salt fork of the Red River lies in its course a couple of miles off, so it cannot get to any settlement. We swear never again to turn loose fire on the prairie, and get on to the little new settlement of Clarendon, in Douley County, for dinner,—and what a dinner!—rusty pork, and half-boiled beans. It lasted us for days after in point of digestion, and the memory thereof shall be lost to us—never. An Englishman, Mr. Rowe, we found here, with eight hundred head of cattle on Mulberry Creek, and he was much pleased with the country as a cattle-raising one, though he said, even so far out, free range was getting more and more restricted, and most new-comers would have to buy or lease land.[9]

Here on getting out our note-books and cellaret, we asked Barnsey whether we should describe him as an elderly saint of temperance principles, or a middle-aged gentleman of dissipated habits. "Call me a tough old cuss, gentlemen," he said, as he tossed off a horn; and so we do.

9. Alfred Rowe (1853–1912) came from England to the Texas Panhandle in 1878. Charles Goodnight assisted him in his efforts at founding what became the RO Ranch. Rowe died in the Titanic disaster. Anderson, "Rowe, Alfred."

CHAPTER XIV

More respecting the Colony of Clarendon—Enter Mr. J. G. Adair's property of half a million acres—Game near Grande Vista—Up the Palo Duro Cañon—Indian Fights—The Bed of the Red River—Turkey Creek Ranche—A Bear and some Deer—The Tulé and Que-ta-que Ranches—Mr. Charles Goodnight—Profits and Outlays in Ranching.

"The month was in the downward year,
The breath of autumn chill'd the sky;
And useless leaves, too early sere,
Mutter'd and eddied by."

Lord Lytton

Clarendon, the only town in Douley County, is a new settlement, and locally termed "The Colony." We cannot compliment the reverend gentleman who founded this colony, either upon his selection of a site, or on the manner in which the scheme has been carried through. Great numbers of the settlers have left a place where everything is extremely expensive, and where there are no markets, even if they could raise or produce anything; and we fear that Clarendon will ere very long be numbered with Herculaneum, Pompeii, Troy, and other cities of the more or less past.[1]

At 3 p.m., we drove out of Clarendon, and very soon entered the magnificent property of Mr. John G. Adair, of Rathdair, in Ireland.[2] A large, open, well-grassed plain leads for miles up to the eastern ranche-house of this estate, of over five hundred thousand acres. The ranche-house is called Grande Vista, and is not yet completed; a photograph of it is the first one seen in this chapter.

Driving across the plain, we got shots at a band of five antelopes, and at a fine pack of prairie grouse, but did not succeed in bagging anything. Grande Vista is the head-quarters of Palo Duro Ranche, which contains over three hundred thousand acres, and over these range about nineteen thousand head of cattle, which are valued on an average at about £5 per head, one with the other.[3] On the open

Epigraph: Robert, Lord Lytton (pseudonym Owen Meredith), "The Fount of Truth," *The Wanderer* (1859). These lines appear in book 3, *In England*.

1. Also known as "Saints' Roost," Clarendon was a "Christian colony" founded in 1878 by members of the Methodist Church who wished to form an agricultural community to which other Methodists could immigrate. Interestingly, an English investment firm bankrolled the project, a fact of which Townshend doesn't seem aware. At the time of our travelers' visit, Clarendon was known as a temperance community. Despite Townshend's predictions, Clarendon continues as a thriving community. Townshend misspells Donley County. Anderson, "Clarendon, Texas."

2. As discussed in the introduction, Townshend is a distant relative of the Scotch-Irish John George Adair (1823–85), to whom the volume is dedicated, and it seems probable that Townshend and Hyde were currying favor in hopes of investment partnerships. Adair was (and remains) infamous in Ireland for his eviction of 244 tenant farmers from his newly acquired Glenveagh estate in 1861. Adair came west to Denver in 1875 looking for investment after marrying American heiress Cornelia Wadsworth Ritchie. In 1877, he entered into a partnership with Charles Goodnight, forming the JA Ranch. Well connected to raise funds from overseas, Adair provided capital to purchase land and cattle to be managed by Goodnight; by the time of Adair's death in 1885 and following a $350,000 loan from the Texas Loan & Mortgage Company, the operation was the largest investment of British capital in Texas. Haley, *Charles Goodnight*; Kerr, *Scottish Capital*; Burton, *History of the JA Ranch*; Vaughn, *Sin, Sheep and Scotsmen*.

3. By "Palo Duro Ranche" Townshend refers to the Palo Duro section, the primary part of the JA Ranch, as opposed to Tule and Quitaque divisions. Goodnight originally bought

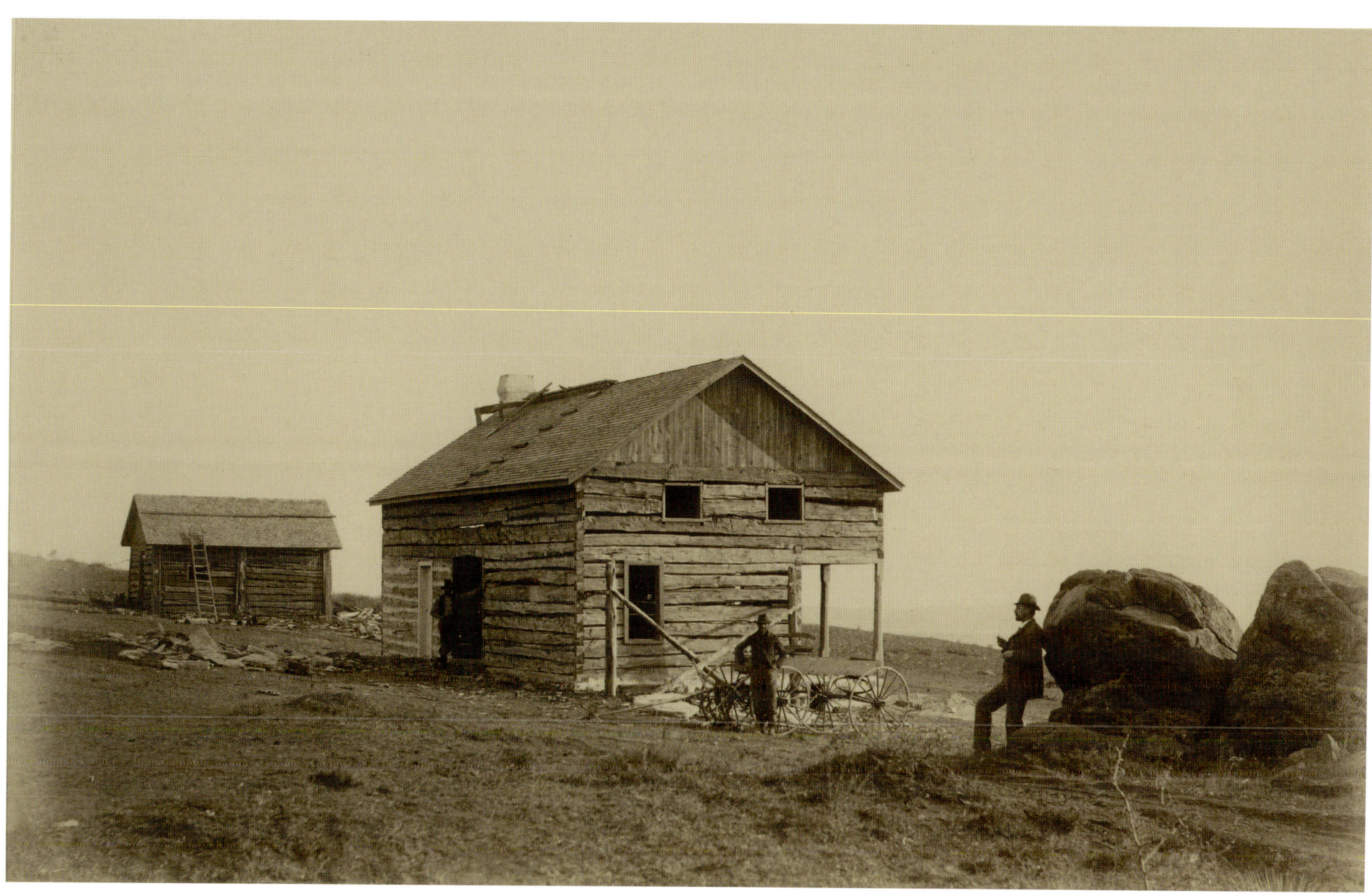

A Lonely Home in Texas. (Grande Vista.)
The JA Ranch's new and still unfinished ranch house is called "Grande Vista." The figures in the photo are difficult to identify with certainty. Perhaps Mary Anne Goodnight peers from the window. The man leaning against the boulder in the foreground seems to be J. G. Hyde, the photographer.

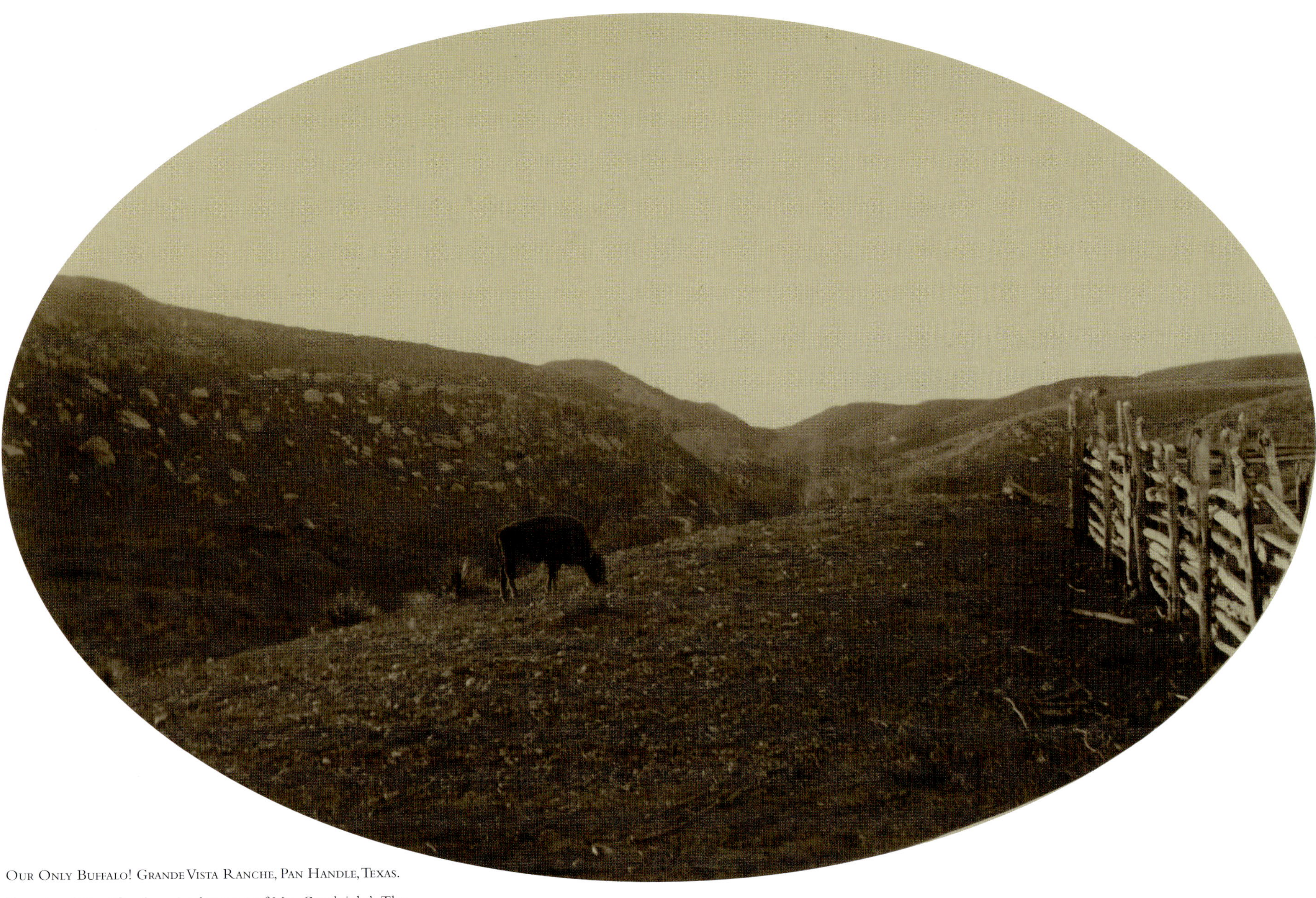

Our Only Buffalo! Grande Vista Ranche, Pan Handle, Texas. Townshend identifies the animal as a pet of Mrs. Goodnight's. The travelers had no real expectation of seeing any buffalo on their journey.

plains, these beasts range all the summer; but when winter sets in, they are "rounded up," and driven into the cañon, which is really the bed and valley of the Red River, and from half a mile to nearly three in width, enclosed by such precipitous cliffs that only at one or two places, very easily guarded, can anything get out or get in. It is, indeed, a most extraordinary property; for its fencing cost nothing, its fee simple was less than 2s. per acre, and its nett profit is over twenty per cent. Adjoining, or all but adjoining, this Palo Duro estate, Mr. Adair has two others,—the Tulé, and Que-ta-que; each of virtually a hundred and fifty thousand acres, but these as yet are not stocked, or used in any way. Mr. Charles Goodnight, one of the most celebrated stockmen of the West, is sole manager here, and excessively full his hands always are.[4] When we arrived, he was twenty miles up the cañon, sorting and branding cattle, but Mrs. Goodnight, though we brought no letters of introduction, nor did she expect us, proffered the hospitalities of the ranche,[5] and right glad were we to partake of her excellent supper, and then retire to the ranche store-room, where we spent a few hours developing our negatives, and then, spreading out the rugs, enjoyed sweet repose.

Next morning, after an early breakfast, our four steeds were again called on to transport us up the cañon. This was very hard on them, as two days' hard driving over such roads is enough for any amount of equine endurance, and we fully expected to have been able to borrow horses from Mr. Goodnight, whom we had met long before in Colorado.[6] But neither Mr. Adair's worthy manager, nor any of his horses, were to be found without going twenty or thirty miles further, so as needs must,—first having photographed a pet buffalo of Mrs. Goodnight's,[7]—off we drove, on a beautiful autumn morning, across the head of Battle Creek, on the rough, rugged, and steep road at which the last photograph in this chapter represents us and our conveyance. Magnificent views of red clay rifts and red clay cliffs now surrounded us. The rifts all ran into the centre of the valley, in which lots of very fat cattle of all sorts—from the shorthorn to the Texas longhorn, horns from six inches to six feet in length—grazed contentedly.[8]

Before leaving Battle Creek, we should remark that this cañon, before Mr. Adair purchased it, was the home of the Comanche Indians; and at Battle Creek, General Miles, of the United States' army,

---

a strategically selected patchwork of twelve thousand acres that accorded control of adjacent range through control of water. Goodnight was aggressive about buying more land, so that by 1882 the JA Ranch owned over ninety-three thousand acres. The 1877 contract between Goodnight and Adair specified a maximum of fifteen thousand head of cattle, though by 1879 this was already well exceeded, as Townshend attests.

4. Charles Goodnight (1836–1929), a native of Illinois, is a legendary westerner known as a Texas Ranger, cattle driver, and rancher. He had lost out in his Colorado ranching venture through the panic of 1873, leading him to borrow money through Adair at 18 percent interest. He subsequently entered into the JA Ranch partnership with Adair. Goodnight and Adair made handsome profit with the ranch, and Goodnight continued the partnership with Cornelia Adair after her husband's death. That partnership was not renewed, and in 1887 the two split, Goodnight taking the Quitaque. Burton, *History of the JA Ranch*; Haley, *Charles Goodnight*.

5. Mary Anne "Molly" (Dyer) Goodnight (1839–1926), a native of Tennessee, married Charles Goodnight in Kentucky in 1870 and moved with him to Pueblo, Colorado, where he had a ranch. After the panic of 1873, she came to the JA Ranch with her husband at a time when the region had virtually no Anglo women residents. She is remembered as "mother of the Panhandle" for her kind treatment of cowboys and travelers. She is also known as a philanthropist and founded Goodnight College in 1898. She and her husband had no children. Roach, "Goodnight, Mary Ann Dyer [Molly]."

6. This is not mentioned in Townshend's *Colorado*, and no documentation of this visit is to be found.

7. Molly Goodnight was distressed at the commercial slaughter of the southern plains herd of buffalo that was finishing up as she lived at the JA Ranch. Charles Goodnight himself hired hunters to come onto his range so that he could save his grass for his cattle; they killed fifteen thousand animals there. Beginning in 1878, Molly convinced her husband to save several calves, which grew to a small herd kept on the ranch. As a financial venture, Goodnight crossbred some with cattle and sold the resultant "cattalo," but it was not profitable. Molly's buffaloes were the nucleus of what is today the Texas State Bison Herd, denizens of Caprock Canyons State Park, not far from Quitaque. Hamner, *The No Gun Man*; Hunt, "Hunting Goodnight's Buffalo"; Roach, "Goodnight, Mary Ann Dyer [Molly]"; Price and Meinzer, *Charles Goodnight*.

8. Goodnight is credited with laying the foundations of superior beef cattle in West Texas by crossing Texas range cattle with Durham and Shorthorn bulls. Burton, *History of the JA Ranch*; Haley, *Charles Goodnight*.

inflicted a crushing defeat upon the noble red man, who from the Palo Duro fastnesses had annually sallied forth, and devastated the realms of the hated pale-face from time immemorial.[9]

Mr. Goodnight has been doing a great deal to the roads here, but nevertheless they were intensely bad, and nothing less than the seasoned wood and splendid fastening of a Government ambulance would have stood the awful joltings, shakings, shocks, jumps, and rolls that our conveyance had perpetually to endure. White limestone and red-clay cliffs we drove past, and amidst this startling contrast of vivid colouring, the green mesquite trees showed in the foreground to great effect.

We are now in the bed of the Red River, dry, however, as a limekiln. From each side open small rifts and cañons, which in all weathers afford ample shelter to stock. Grass dried to hay was everywhere abundant in these cañons, and on the little red conical hills we picked up some very pretty, but inferior mica, which might, if searched deeper for, prove abundant and good. Toro Cañon and Creek run now away to the right, up to scrub-cedared hills. Here we understood was the head-quarters of the "Antelopes," "Buffalo-eaters," and "Honeyeater" bands of the Comanches, until Generals McKinsey and Miles made the place too hot for them. At Tulé Cañon, General McKinsey killed eight hundred Pawnees, and captured fifteen hundred ponies; seven hundred of which he, however, subsequently lost. Not very long since have these battles taken place, but even now there is a haze and an air of unreliability connected with all narratives on the subject, which renders one indisposed to recount the local tales on these subjects to any great length;[10] therefore, we move on from records of Indian war, to the next creek, Gypsum, a photograph of which is seen in the next chapter. From this point the gramma grasses are more abundant in the extremely beautiful wild valley of the Red River; and the shades of evening found us crossing that babbling, plashing, rapid stream, Turkey Creek; and thereafter almost immediately, we drew up at Turkey Creek Ranche—a photograph of which, with Mr. Goodnight in front, his accountant, Mr. Kimball, in the doorway, and our Jehu, Barnsey, behind, is seen in our next chapter.[11] That photograph, however, was taken next morning; for when we arrived, Mr. Goodnight had not yet arrived, and there was no light to immortalize him photographically, even if he had.

Turkey Creek Ranche was the former head-quarters of the Palo Duro, but now it is only a way or supply station. The well-filled provision-basket with which Mrs. Goodnight had despatched us in the morning, was now heavily encroached upon. About midnight our worthy host arrived, tired out by his day's unceasing riding, and early next morning we started for a general survey of the romantic mountain and gorge surroundings. A distant view of these from the ranche door is seen in the next chapter, and though the photograph gives literally no idea of the exceeding wildness of the scenery, the reader will not be surprised to hear that it is a place where bears much do congregate, and that we came upon a splendid black specimen of the genus Bruin, who, like ourselves, was taking his morning constitutional. His bearship, however, was out of range when he emerged from the brush, in which he made an immense crackling,

9. In a major battle of the Red River War (1874–76), fought between the U.S. Army and loosely confederated Comanche, Kiowa, and Southern Cheyenne tribes, Col. Nelson A. Miles routed a party of an estimated five hundred southern Cheyenne warriors. Miles's troopers (cavalry backed by Gatling guns) suffered only light casualties while the Cheyennes suffered an estimated seventy-five fatalities. Rathjen, *Texas Panhandle Frontier,* "Battle Creek."

10. Ironically, given Townshend's doubt about his sources, he presents much error here, particularly mistaking Col. Ranald Mackenzie with "General McKinsey." Similarly, Townshend is mistaken in naming the Pawnee tribe, which had no role in this conflict. Also, Townshend seems to conflate two incidents between Mackenzie and the Comanches. In 1872, Mackenzie charged a probably friendly encampment of Kotstkea Comanches and captured thousands of horses, most of which the Comanches stole back in the night. Subsequently, in the decisive Battle of Palo Duro in 1874, Mackenzie captured and ordered slaughtered some one thousand horses; however, human casualties were light on both sides. No Indian battle in the region (or indeed in the West) claimed eight hundred indigenous fatalities. The Battle of Palo Duro was decisive because in addition to killing the Comanches' horses, the army also burned their camp and supplies, forcing the tribes back to their reservations in Oklahoma. Rathjen, *Texas Panhandle Frontier.*

11. "Barnsey" refers to Charles Barnes Austin, who is discussed in the preceding chapter. Charles H. Kimball, in addition to being employed as Charles Goodnight's bookkeeper-in-residence, also acted as official record-keeper for the region (not yet at this time formed into counties). "Jehu" is an ironic title meaning driver, after the Old Testament Israelite King Jehu, who was known for his fast and furious chariot driving. Burton, *History of the JA Ranch*; Hagan, *Charles Goodnight.*

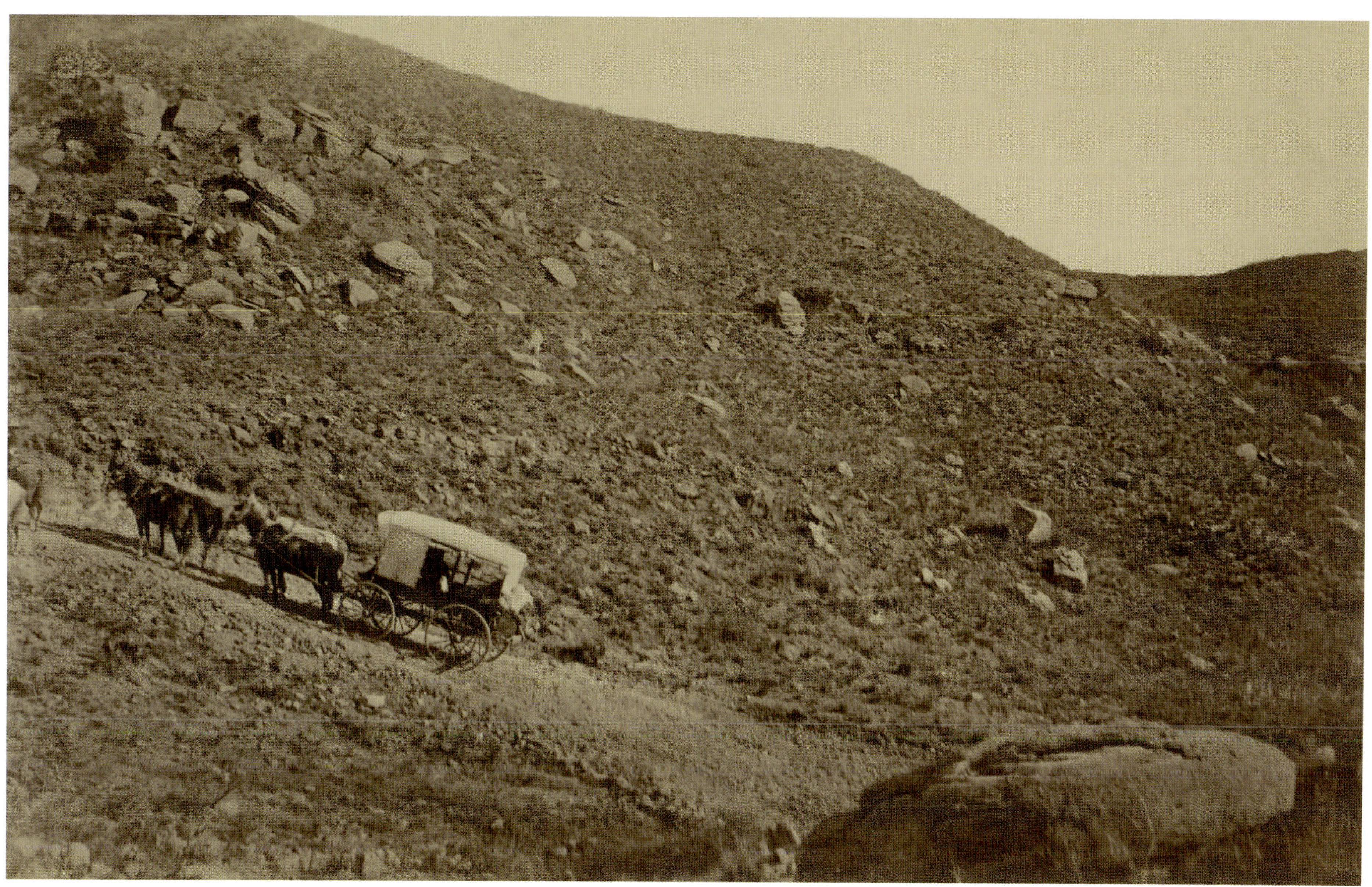

"Goodnight's Turnpike." Battle Creek, Pan Handle, Texas. The JA Ranch was founded around reliable water and shelter found in the caprock canyonlands off the eastern edges of the Llano Estacado, necessitating the construction of a steep road down.

and then, when he had reached the clear hill-side, he deliberately turned round, took a long look at us over his shoulder, and then trotted off at a pace that defied any pedestrian to follow with chance of picking him up.[12]

Indeed, without dogs, it is only by the merest accident that a bear is ever tracked or killed; the animals appear to grow more timid and cautious every year—unlike the antelope, which gets almost accustomed to civilization, and becomes emboldened, after a while, by contact with it. Game laws are not needed to protect Master Bruin, he takes very good care of himself. He will, probably, be always numerous in the Rocky Mountains, for even two hundred years of the persecution of civilization has failed to drive him out of the Alleghanies, or even out of the Catskills in the State of New York.

Besides the bear, we interviewed, at a respectful distance, two deer, and heard that a great many flocks of turkeys frequent the place, but did not see any; chiefly, no doubt, because we had not time to look for them, being anxious to learn all we could from so eminent a stockman as Mr. Goodnight, who to our own knowledge made money—though, of course, very little—whilst he was borrowing capital at eighteen per cent to run cattle up the Arkansas, from Pueblo, in Colorado.[13]

Mr. Goodnight had been twenty years in the cattle business (one of very hard work), but his vigour is quite undiminished; and even the magnitude of the undertaking he is now engaged in only appears to weigh on his mind very lightly. "When I came here, two years ago," he said, "there were buffaloes, Indians, thieves, and no grass. Now, you see, we have banished the first three, and have more grass than we know what to do with, simply by preventing its being burned, which we have done by fire guards—that is, ploughing two furrows, a few feet apart, all round the estate, and burning the grass between these furrows."

Having understood that Mr. Adair, satisfied with the magnitude of his stock-raising venture at Palo Duro, was willing to sell or lease the Tulé and Que-ta-que estates, we found that the Tulé head-quarter ranche is about twenty-five miles from Goodnight's head-quarters, and the Que-ta-que one about forty-five miles. The rent of either would be about £600 per annum, and they would each carry safely about 15,000 head, in Goodnight's estimation, if twenty-five miles of fencing were put up on the Que-ta-que, or twenty miles on the Tulé, which is the best watered, whilst the other one is most sheltered, and has its home ranche on the Pease River. Abundance of curly mesquite and brown grass are on both these ranches, Mr. Goodnight says; and he thinks the raising and sale of yearlings on either of them would be extremely remunerative. Indeed, he said that thirty per cent on the outlay might very fairly be looked for. These statements may strike the home reader as being vastly too good to be true, but we assure them that many men besides Charles Goodnight, who, in fact, has been by no means an exceptionally lucky man, have made from twenty to thirty per cent. of cattle, and as high as forty per cent. of sheep; but the latter profit has never been a constant one for any series of years. The main and great difficulty is to get hold of a good range, where shelter and water are found in abundance, and the expense of herders can be dispensed with by fences, natural, or erected.[14]

12. Black bears, as well as wolves and cougars, were indeed part of the southern plains/Llano Estacado ecosystem but were eradicated by ranchers and the professional hunters they hired. Goodnight took part in this practice, common in the late nineteenth century. Flores, *Caprock Canyonlands*.

13. Economic conditions in the 1870s were such that wealthy or well-connected British businessmen such as Adair could borrow money in Britain for 3 percent and lend it in America at rates as high as the 18 percent mentioned here. These were the terms of an earlier arrangement, in Colorado, between Adair and Goodnight. For the JA Ranch partnership, Adair provided funds that Goodnight would use to build the ranch. Under the terms of the five-year agreement, Goodnight earned a $2,500 salary, and at the termination of five years, the initial investment would be repaid at 10 percent interest and Goodnight would receive one-third of the final proceeds. The contract was renewed for a second five-year term. Burton, *History of the JA Ranch*; Haley, *Charles Goodnight*.

14. Townshend's estimate is consistent with other reports. Goodnight and Adair did make a handsome profit. At the end of the first five-year contract, after expenses, salary, and the repayment of initial capital at 10 percent interest (totaling $205,272), the partners netted a profit of $512,000. Burton, *History of the JA Ranch*; Haley, *Charles Goodnight*; Hagan, *Charles Goodnight*.

Really good, efficient, and honest managers or head men are readily enough procured in a State like Texas, where half the really good men in the place have been trained to cattle and the cattle-market; but a treasure like Mr. Charles Goodnight, who can be trusted with one hundred thousand pounds' worth of stock, is not easily found, and Mr. Adair is greatly to be congratulated upon having such a managing agent.

We asked Goodnight what sum would stock one of the adjacent ranches, and he gave us the following estimate:—

	£	*s.*	*d.*
Three thousand improved Colorado cattle, from yearlings to old cows, at £3	9,000	0	0
Thirty horses	200	0	0
Wages of six men and foreman	400	0	0
Stores for the year	200	0	0
Waggons	120	0	0
Four waggon horses—very heavy	150	0	0
Total	£10,070	0	0

Which sum various incidental expenses before the concern was properly going, would probably bring up to twelve thousand. Better bulls than those which cost in Colorado £15, Goodnight says can be purchased in Kentucky for £10. The stock should double in number every three years, and the expenses *in toto*, after starting, of running the ranche ought not to exceed 6s. per head of stock per annum. We have seen Mr. Adair's accounts at Rathdair, and Goodnight's on the ranche, and can vouch that the business is done within these figures.[15] It is too late in this chapter for us to go into the general stock question of Texas, but in our next we hope to present some little sketch of this subject to the reader.

15. Townshend here appeals not to the small-scale potential immigrant but to the aristocratic and investor class who are the primary audience of his book. He is honest in his statement that not every would-be investor would be so fortunate as to have a manager like Goodnight and in suggesting that the best range has perhaps already been claimed. The idea that the Tule and Quitaque ranges might be available for sale or lease is clear enticement.

CHAPTER XV

Origin of Texas Cattle—Their Characteristics—Difficulties of getting a Range—"Controlling" a Range—History of the Cattle Trade, its rise, decline, and almost fall—The Spanish Merino and the Vermont one—The Sheep Mania—What has been the experience of Sheep Owners here—Sheep Diseases and Drawbacks—The Texan Mustang and the Park Pony—International Swindling.

"The world improves; with slow, unequal pace,
'The good time's coming' to our hapless race.
The general tide beneath the refluent surge
Rolls on, resistless, to its destined verge."

Saxe

Following the long-horn through Texas on his way north to the markets of Kansas and Missouri, or south *viâ* the Morgan line of steamers to Havanna, New Orleans, and thence goodness only knows where, once gave us six months' continued and very pleasant travelling.[1] The knowledge gained on that trip we shall try to recall to some extent for the benefit of the readers of this chapter. The cattle in Texas were originally introduced, as were the sheep, by the Spaniards, either directly, or more probably through Mexico, of which Texas was then an integral portion. Centuries of neglect, bad feeding, and interbreeding, brought both cattle and sheep to a miserably low ebb, both as regarded stamina, frame, and meat-producing quality. But in each case the breeds were perfectly pure, and the slightest infusion of new blood always brought up in grade Texan or Mexican stock, with a rapidity quite unexampled elsewhere. We have ourselves seen the immediate descendants of the Texan or Mexican merino—an animal with bare face and legs, and producing only a fleece of about two pounds of hairy wool—rounded and wooled down to the eyes and toes after the importation of Vermont merino bucks. Cattle follow just the same rule. The awkward six-feet-long horns of the Texan steer fade quickly away after one or two crosses with the Durham. The back like the edge of a saw straightens out into a line which would not discredit Smithfield, the bone gets smaller, and what covers and surrounds it—the flesh—develops and grows soft and fat, instead of being semi-cartilaginous. There is, therefore, a wide field for the improver and raiser of both beef and mutton in Texas, for a perfectly pure, but terribly run-down breed forms the basis from which very uniform herds and flocks can be raised and annually improved. To get the local knowledge necessary is, of course, the first step for the emigrant, and this local knowledge is rarely acquired without at least a year of wandering to and fro in the track of the cattleman. Then when the knowledge of what to buy, and where and how to buy, is mastered, the question of range comes in every day with increasing anxiety to the cattle-owner. A nomadic life on free range is a thing

Epigraph: John Godfrey Saxe, "The Good Time Coming," *The Poems of John Godfrey Saxe* (1868).

1. Townshend presumably refers to his earlier travels with the British Agricultural Commission and/or in his role as correspondent for *The Field*. Charles Morgan (1795–1878) was an entrepreneur in trade who developed extensive steamship lines out of southern ports. Baughman, *Charles Morgan*.

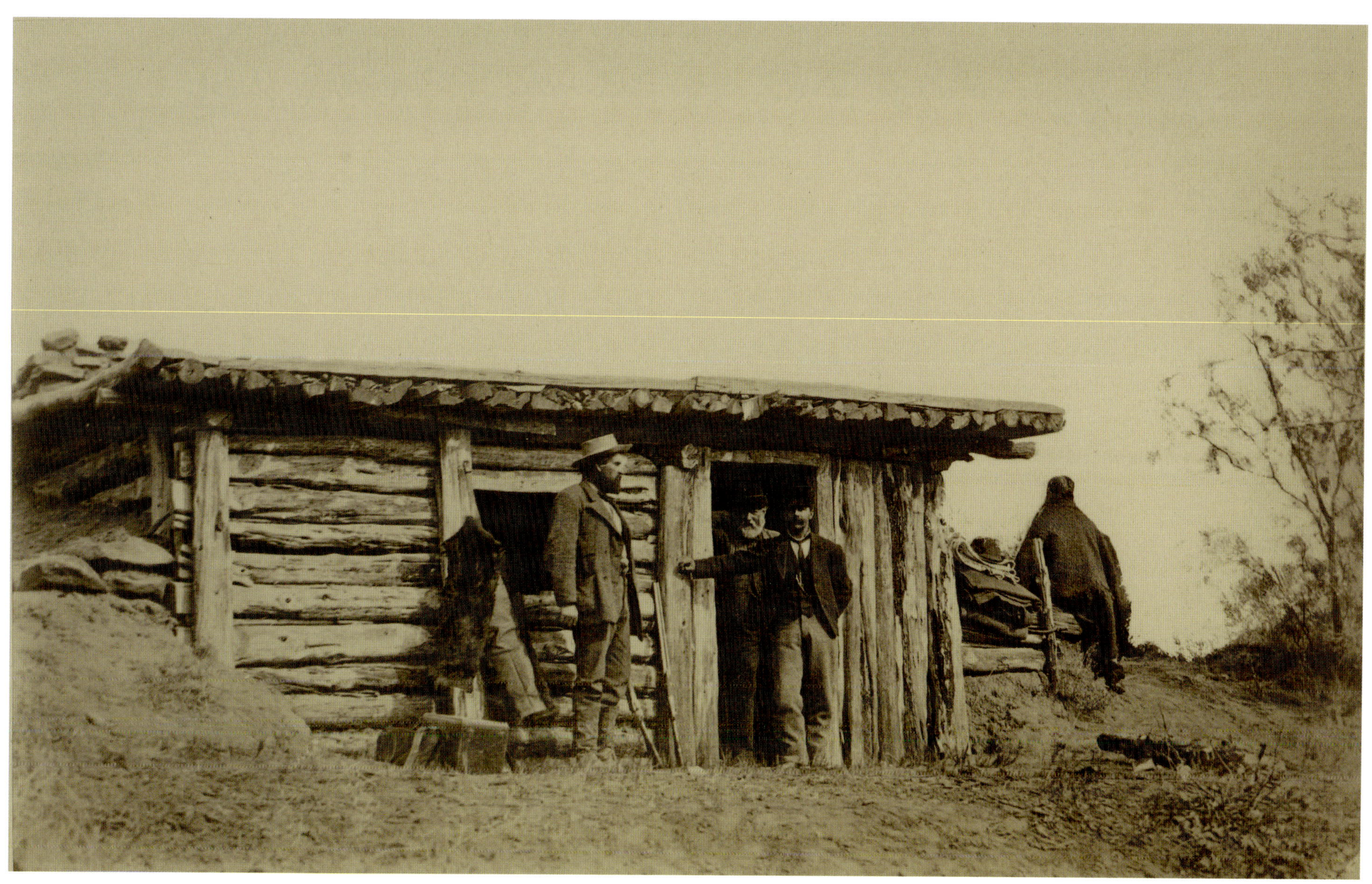

Log Hut on Turkey Creek. Pan Handle, Texas.
This older headquarters of the JA Ranch is a dugout structure. Goodnight stands at left, Kimball in the doorway, Barnsey behind him.

we read of as being the rule in Texas, but let us assure the reader, that having been all over the State we found no such thing existing there. What does exist is the possession of some spring, or stream, being held by a cattle-owner, simply by dint of stock, who eat the grass so closely near the water, that nothing can from any distance get sustenance to reach it. A very great deal of land is held in Texas in this way, and the persons who hold it, so far from being nomads, stick like leeches to their location, which may be State or School land, or it may belong to one of the large railway land-grant companies. For instance, most of the land about Mr. Adair's is owned by the Texas Pacific, and the Houston and Texas Central Railway is the owner of half Lipscomb, and more than a quarter of Ochiltree Counties, to the north. Through both of these counties flows Wolf Creek, which runs into the Canadian, close to Camp Supply, in the Indian Territory.[2]

Water is the great want almost all over Texas, and the possession of water-front almost invariably means the free use of a great deal of land behind. One spring that only takes up a small portion of a quarter of an acre may thus, as is said, "control" a range of half-a-million acres; and the great questions the intending purchaser of land in Texas should ask, are: What water-front am I acquiring? and, In the past droughts, has my spring or river ever gone dry?

As may very readily be imagined, very few "water-holes" now in any part of the State, are not either purchased, or held by heavy herds of cattle; therefore, the free range system is drawing to a close; except, indeed, that when one has only to purchase a few hundred acres of water-front, in order to control and get the use of thousands, the Texas range must always in this sense remain to a great extent free.

The entire of West and most of South Texas was free range until after the American War. During that fearful fratricidal struggle, whilst the heads of most families were at the front fighting for what they considered their liberties, a few men of obscure origin, and of no patriotism, declining to fight in either army, devoted their entire energies to stealing and branding the neglected herds, which in vastly increasing numbers roamed the plains. Thus 1868 saw the cattle of Texas in the hands of but a few owners, and these to protect themselves had to fence in enormous pastures, and, in at least one instance, to fortify their houses. These cattle-kings had, like Spain after the conquest of Peru, come to the conclusion that there was no end to wealth. With them it had been a case of *Veni, vidi, vici*, which in cattle *parlance* in the days of the war meant:—I came (upon an absentee's range), I saw (his herds), and I branded and took them away. Acquiring cattle thus easily there appeared no end to, and, when the markets of Texas opened, a ceaseless extravagance necessitated a ceaseless flow of cattle to be sent to market; not only in the immense cattle-drives north by Wichita, or Dodge, but by rail in all directions, and by steamer from every port,—Galveston, Clinton, Indianola, Rockport, and Corpus Christi. One man alone, in 1870, is said to have sent off one-tenth of the total number that left the State last year—viz., 502,196 head; and this drain continued so severely, that whilst the world thought Texas was exporting but her increase—her surplus stock—the fact was, that nearly every cattle-man in the State was virtually drawing on his principal and selling from ten to thirty per cent. more than his increase.

Thus Mr. Richard King, of Santa Gertrudes, who once drove out to Kansas fifty thousand head in one year, has on his ranche of five thousand fenced-in acres, now but twenty thousand; and minor cattle-kings have to a greater or less extent followed his footsteps.[3]

Only last season have wiser counsels prevailed, and the cattle export this year from Texas is likely to be the smallest on record, probably not over two hundred and fifty thousand, valued at, say £800,000. The scarcity of animals will put up the prices in Texas to possibly even an artificial level, and even last year it took a great deal of time to get a herd together for a fairly good start on the part of the new-comer.

2. Townshend's description of land tenure accords with the example of Goodnight's hold on the Palo Duro country, as Goodnight likely explained to him during this visit.

3. Richard King (1824–85) founded the King Ranch in south Texas in the 1850s. It was a vast holding that grew even larger following the Civil War. Cheeseman, "King, Richard."

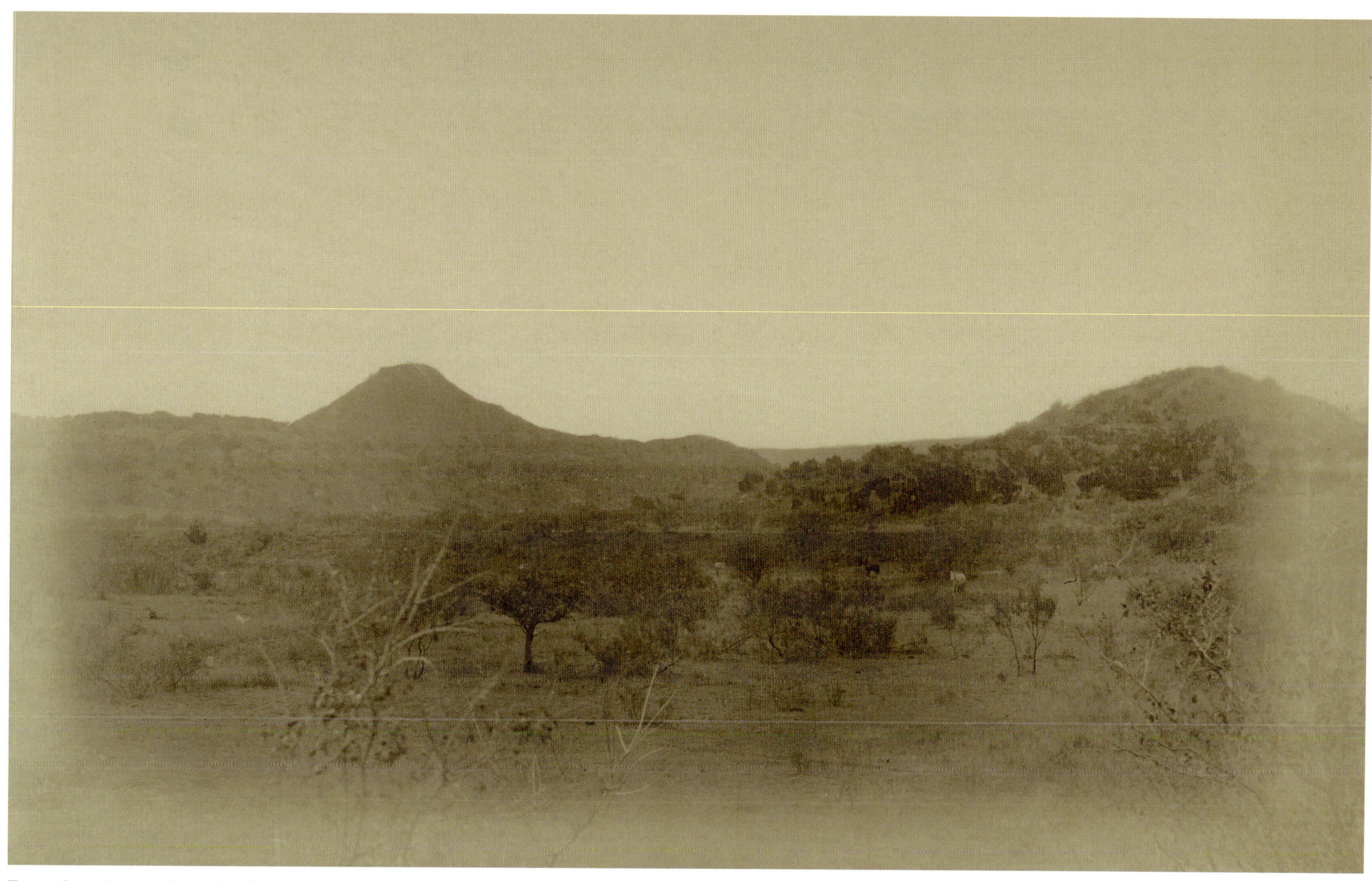

Turkey Creek, Looking South. Red River Cañon,
Pan Handle, Texas.
Several grazing horses are visible in this scene from the JA Ranch.

If cattle and the cattle market have thus run so counter to the interests this year of an intending emigrant, sheep have by no means done so; and at this branch of grazing let us now glance.

As cattle diminished in numbers, or as all a man's cattle were stolen by wealthy neighbours, or Mexican Indians from across the Rio Grande, desperation drove a considerable number into sheep, even on the Gulf coast, which was notoriously ill-adapted to them. Although there has been no instance of any great and continued success in sheep in Texas, a fair living had always been made by men with flocks ranging from two to ten thousand. Occasionally eighty-eight per cent. of lambs would be saved, and fifty per cent. on the invested capital shown by the ranche books, in which, however, from causes to follow, these profits usually remained.

There came, in short, a brief sheep mania. Everyone wanted a flock; the demand was greatly short of the supply, and far into Mexico—even six hundred miles to Zacetecos—went spirited New Yorkers, Bostonians, and Britishers, to buy ewes. The late Charles Callaghan, now represented by Mr. Macdonald of Laredo, got up a flock of ninety thousand head, and was followed at not very long distances behind by others.[4] The sheep-men were all honest and good, and were a great advantage to the society of the State. The time, however, came when everyone had sheep enough. Vermont bucks had graded the flocks of many to a high standard; the increase of sheep, which on the ranche books was written down as increase of capital, must needs be sold; and then it was suddenly discovered that there was no mutton market in Texas, and that, to use a local vulgarism, you could not throw a sheep at a man's head. Sheep of a class which in 1877 cost and would fetch 16*s.*, this year went begging in San Antonio for a purchaser at 4*s.*, and could not find one. Despite Mr. Macdonald's greatest exertions, his ninety thousand would not increase; for old sheep died as quickly as new ones were launched on their quiet, peaceful, uneventful careers, and this was the experience of everyone. Sheep in Texas now, therefore, means simply wool proceeds, and wool proceeds there are not very great: an average of about four pounds per head, and the price 10*d.* per pound. This, whilst rather more than enough to cover all ranche expenses with good management, necessitates many weary years of work and privation before a man can see his way to a retiring competency. The sheep business in our South Pacific colonies is only better because the average fleece is so much heavier; but land is far cheaper in Texas than in any of our colonies,[5] and for the man that thoroughly understands the ovine race, presents, perhaps, a better prospect to a small capitalist than does any other place, as no winter food is required for sheep in Texas, though some rough cheap winter shelter during northers is indispensable, if one wishes to avoid very serious risks of lamb loss. The vast western plains, west of the Pecos, and even west of Fort Davis, are as yet quite unoccupied, and will, in consequence of their scant supply of water, become if anything only great sheep-walks of the future. At present, however, there is little law, order, or protection from Mexican Indians out there; and it would require a strong colony, of say at least ten white men, and their twenty Mexican shepherds, to be able to defy risks south or west of Fort Davis, which has a lovely climate, an elevation of nearly five thousand feet, and luxuriant grasses for unlimited distances in every direction all round.

Sheep scab is very prevalent in Texas, and the laws on the subject are most ineffective. A poison weed, the *rumex acetocella*, is in some districts also found, and burrs and thorns which give sheep sore eyes and feet are very numerous in the south-west and south of the State, but nearly disappear as one gets north and north-west.

So far as has been ascertained, the wool sales last year were 14,568,920 pounds, which, at 10d. per pound, would have netted £607,038 6s. 8d.

Horse-breeding is, perhaps, better also glanced at in this chapter. The horse of Texas, the little wiry mustang, is, like the cow and the

4. Charles Callaghan operated a huge sheep ranch around Encinal, Texas. After Callaghan's death in 1874, William R. Jones built the operation to a vast concern of over one hundred thousand sheep and goats. Carlson, *Texas Woollybacks*; Wellman and Taylor, "Callaghan Ranch."

5. Townshend refers to New Zealand and Australia.

sheep, of Spanish, nay, even Arab stock. He is of great endurance, and his wind cannot be broken; he is rarely shod, and his constitution is such, that there is positively never anything the matter with him. His size is against him, for the Texas horse is virtually a pony, averaging from fourteen to fifteen hands high. He is capable of being made—with all his spirit—as gentle as a dog; the fiery, snorting, curveting horse of the desert is really only found in Tom Hood's nightmare, and occasionally in Mayne Reid's works;[6] nevertheless, the Texas pony requires a great deal of education after you buy him, for from four to six pounds, before you could put him between the shafts of your basket-phaeton in Hyde Park. It has always astonished us that some respectable horse-dealing firm in London should not have a sort of partnership with men who breed horses largely and who are of undoubted integrity in Texas. Such men, for instance, as Mr. G. H. Noonan, of San Antonio, who has been for a long time county court judge, and, as that position is attained by general election in America, it means a great deal as to character.[7] Why, we say, men in Texas who can probably turn out ponies gentle and trained at £12 each, cannot sell through good men in London, we fail to see.

As a matter of fact, the only time the thing was ever attempted, each party tried so hard to swindle the other, that they both succeeded; and the public, of course, met no better fate. The *trained* ponies shipped from Texas proved to be a pack of vicious brutes never off a prairie until they entered the ship, and our fellow-countrymen, not to be got the better of, never paid for them, which in any event it appears probable they would not have done.

The only manner in which the number of horses in Texas can be estimated, is by looking at the exports of last year. These were 37,860 head, and their declared value was £84,650, not quite £2 5s. each, on an average. Horse-raising in Texas, therefore, can scarcely be said to be a very remunerative business at present, unless with it the horse-trainer's profession is combined, as also that of the metropolitan horse-dealer.

Now the length of our chapter is run, and

"'Tis something that our Pegasus, though slow,
Don't stand curveting when he's bid to go;
And clear at least of one egregious fault,
Knows, like a major, when and where to halt!"[8]

6. The reference is probably to Thomas Hood's "Nocturnal Sketch." Capt. Thomas Mayne Reid (1818–83) wrote a series of dime novels including, *The Helpless Hand*, *The Scalp Hunters*, *The White Squaw*, and *The Yellow Chief*.

7. George Henry Noonan (1828–1907) moved to Castroville, Texas, in 1852. He was a Republican and Union sympathizer whose standing as a jurist in Texas endured through the Civil War and Reconstruction eras. Hooker, "Noonan, George Henry."

8. John Godfrey Saxe, "El Dorado," *Poems of John Godfrey Saxe* (1868).

CHAPTER XVI

The Grasses of North and South Texas compared—The Indians—Their Agents and one of their Chiefs—Antelopes, Ducks, and Turkeys—Tales of Lynch Law, by Barnsey—Stupid Geese and Lively Ducks—Good-bye to Fort Elliot—Through South Kansas again into the Lone Star State.

"And hears once more in vision'd trance
That voice commanding to advance
Where wealth is gained,—love, wisdom, won,—
Or deeds of danger dared and done."

P. J. Bailey, in *Festus*

We have detained the reader over long at Turkey Creek Ranche, so as to give him a general survey of the businesses most in the line of the stranger in that part of Texas; but now we get ready to start for Fort Elliot again, taking with us as far back as Grande Vista, Mr. Charles Goodnight, who pours every sort of interesting information into our ears as we jolt along in our ambulance. Why the grasses here last so much longer than in South Texas, where they spring earlier, is because there is so little rain here, and the herbage soon becomes natural hay. The scarcity of rainfall prevents this hay rotting, which it does quickly along the moist regions near the Gulf, and thus leaves the cattle sometimes little or nothing to eat between November and February. "It is the fact of the sparse grasses of Colorado remaining good and nutritious and eatable to the last, that has given that State a good name as a grazing one," remarked Mr. Goodnight; "and," he added, "any place where there is heavy rainfall is never a really money-making wild-cattle country."

On the way down we were shown where the Indians encamped when they broke out of their Territory not long since. A great deal of apprehension was naturally felt on the ranche, at the vicinity of such unwelcome tourists, who, by the way, were starving—the great end of so many Indian agents' exertions to economize out of the appropriations.[1]

Goodnight gave, on the requisition of an officer commanding a detachment of the United States' army, all the beef the red-skins wanted. He thinks the Government will pay him; but if it does it will prove a most remarkable exception to the rule, and the bill has been lying in the Circumlocution Department for over twelve months.

"One of the Indian chiefs made friends with me," Mr. Goodnight said. "He came to my house and dined; to prove his friendship he eat enough for five men; and then pathetically asked if my friendship for him was as great as his for me. I replied, 'It most

Epigraph: Phillip James Bailey (1816–1902) published *Festus* anonymously in 1839.

1. The incident was the 1878 Comanche outbreak during which Goodnight negotiated with Quannah Parker (the chief to whom Goodnight refers) for their peaceful return to the reservation, though the rancher lost a good many head of cattle to the Comanche hunters. Burton, *History of the JA Ranch*.

certainly was.' 'I would refuse you nothing I have,' he said; 'now I want powder and lead from you.'

"There is a tremendous penalty for supplying the Indians with ammunition,"—Mr. Goodnight explained,—"and even if I thought doing so was advisable, I dared not. So I remarked to him that only his enemies would give him powder and shot, for that his having them would very much displease the great white father in Washington, as he well knew, and would get him and me into trouble. Though the chief took this speech very well, he evidently believed it was all gammon, and soon afterwards departed, having, however, first promised that as I let his braves have all the beef they wanted, there should be no fires, and no cattle-killing, on the property, and he kept his word."

Having been this night again most hospitably entertained at Grande Vista by Mrs. Goodnight, and our ambulance quite laden by her and her good husband with everything eatable that they thought would be useful to us on our back-trail, we departed next morning; and seeing two bands of antelopes, one of nine, and one of thirty-two, on the Grande Vista prairie, made several attempts to get within range, but only partially succeeding, crippled one, who unfortunately had vitality enough to be able to get away.

At Clarendon, we got Indian corn for our horses at about fifty times the price of that commodity in Kansas. Soon after we left the village, we saw a lot of ducks on a pond, so near us that we were certain they were tame; this, however, proved not to be the case. When they got up, we let them have rights and lefts, getting five, but of these only three proved eatable, the remaining two being very fishy, though many hundred miles from the sea. The ducks we shot afterwards *on* the Gulf of Mexico were not one of them fishy-flavoured, so that the only rational explanation we could find was, that the Gulf being intended by nature for a winter shooting-ground, the ducks there, when they found themselves becoming unfit for food, emigrated to the Pan Handle, where sportsmen had no right to expect or look for them.

At Barton Ranche, seven miles out of Clarendon, we camped for the night.[2] This ranche was deserted, and by no means uncomfortable. The photograph depicts it, with its verandah of wattles. Barnsey is seen at the door, a wild turkey hangs to the end of the hut, and one of the authors holds a lot of ducks near a dug-out at the end of the ranche-house. This turkey and the ducks have, however, yet to be accounted for. Barton Ranche House stands on the banks of a very pretty creek, which looked to us as though it must harbor in its tree-belts sundry flocks of turkey, and on its bosom various sorts of wildfowl; so we started to explore forthwith, and walked down stream along the willows—a fine grassed and well-watered country extending at both sides—but one large mallard and one blue crane were all that rewarded our scrutiny, and these flew off before we got at all near them. Luck, however, did not altogether turn her back on us; for later on, in the evening, we beheld a flock of turkeys flying into a peccan tree, and with a Winchester rifle brought one to grass.

This night we ran out of both stimulants and milk, and the green tea we had to drink caused us to sleep—when at all—the sleep of the unjust; so we very little regretted seeing some glimmer of light in the east at 5.30 A.M., when we were up and off down the stream again, to look for ducks and turkeys. On the river itself nothing was found, but following up a little tributary, we found it proceeded from a sort of pond or lakelet; and the centre of this was simply covered with a dozen different varieties of ducks, their many-hued plumage being faintly reflected in the mirror-like breast of the unruffled sheet of water.

"Then Morning rose, and smote from far
Her elfin harps o'er land and sea;
And woodland belt, and ocean bar,
To one sweet note, sigh'd 'Italy.'"[3]

2. S. B. Barton operated a horse ranch on McClellan Creek for a period. "Barton Creek."

3. Robert, Lord Lytton, "The Magic Land," *The Wanderer* (1859). "The Magic Land" is the first poem in book 1, *In Italy*, in which the speaker approaches Italy and describes its natural, seductive beauty.

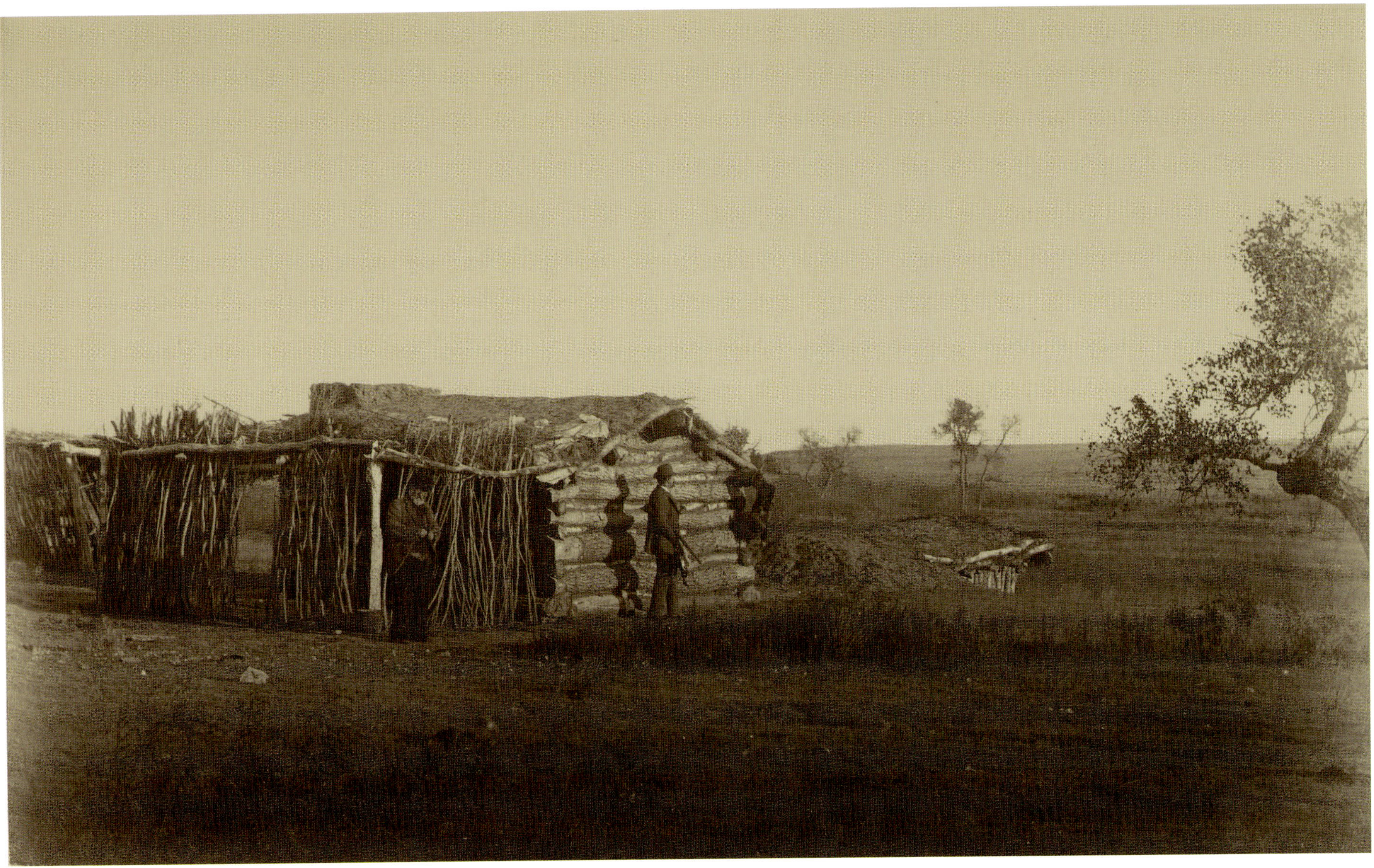

Turkey Camp, Indian Territory.

The original caption is in error. The text describes the photograph and the place in detail. This is Barton Ranch near Clarendon, Texas. The men shown are Barnsey and Hyde.

This verse very often strikes one's memory in Texas, especially as the wanderer therein gets more south and nearer the Gulf. To revert, however, to the scene more immediately before us. After gazing on the beautiful prospect for a few minutes, we crept cautiously round the lakelet, but from no spot were the feathered beauties to be sighted within sixty yards. Not caring to disturb saucy creatures who appeared to lift their noses into the air as though in contempt of things in general, especially human foes, we walked back to breakfast, getting *en route* a shot at a turkey in a peccan tree. The distance proved to be two hundred yards, and, as we probably did not estimate it at quite so much in the clear morning air, we missed emphatically, and turned to the consumption of tinned beef, salmon, and lobster, with considerable energy. 7.40 saw us off again eastward, and we soon left behind the last vista of the "Cap Rock," a thin limestone stratum, which marks everywhere the limit of the Staked Plains.

Tales of the carrying-out of the penal code of Judge Lynch, Barnsey treated us to this morning, and some of them were roughly pathetic.

"Oh, yes!" he said, "I was often a member of the jury, or committee, but it never fell to my personal lot to take a man's life. Once I had a mind to. A miserable devil who had committed no end of crimes, of which murder was not the worse, had been sentenced by us to walk the plank in Montana. I knew the man well; he had once been good, and he begged me so hard to blow his brains out that I felt kinder like doing it. But then, I thought, the wretched coward had killed so many, and creatures that couldn't protect themselves, that I had no right to make death any easier for him than the rest thought right; so I didn't."

"And you hanged him?" "Well, gents, someone *did* accidentally kick over a bar'l that he stood on, at a time when his neck was by a singular coincidence tied to an oak-limb. More usual, however, was the plan of driving a cart, or waggon, or even a horse, from under a man when he got hitched in that way."

"No," said Barnsey, contemplatively, "I never had nothing to say to the sentence of a man but what he deserved it long before, and out West you will find very few who had; that's a fact, you bet!"

This rude justice, shocking as it is to minds trained in civilization, is so absolutely necessary out in unorganized districts, that very shortly after arrival the most respectable foreigners become leading men on the vigilance committees.

Rough law and equity is measured out sharply, but were it not so, hell itself could contain no blacker record of atrocities than would the vicinity of a mining camp out West. Such, at any rate, was the impression that the narratives of honest old Barnsey made on our mind. The subject, however, was—not disagreeably—turned as we reached once more McClellan Creek, and saw a large flock of wild geese settling on it. To leave the ambulance at once was the move; and though the "stupid goose" had a great deal too much sense to permit us to come to close quarters with him, not so the ducks, which for a long time gave us beautiful rocketing shots as they rose through the tall reeds, over the spreading cottonwoods. Several of our victims fell on the opposite bank, and the creek unfortunately proving too deep to wade, we had to leave them there; thus reducing the bag which we were trying to make up for the ladies at Fort Elliot very considerably. Still, they took the will for the deed, and thanked us very kindly for what we did succeed in bringing them,—an infinitesimally small return for the unbounded hospitality we received at the Fort, both going and returning, and for the touching farewell given us, as shown in the photograph. In order to get from this Pan Handle of Texas to any other civilized portion of the State, the fastest route is *viâ* Dodge City in Kansas, and thence per rail to Denison, as sketched in Chapter XI. From Fort Elliot to Dodge is nearly two hundred miles; and a fatiguing stage-coach run it is, through the most uninteresting portion of the Indian Territory. However, once at Dodge, everything gets brighter and more beautiful. Increasingly heavy trains of golden grain leave station after station along the line of the Atchison, Topeka, and Santa Fé Railroad, the extraordinary increase of acreage in crops leaving until this year the Kansan railways unable to cope with their haulage, often for months after it was required by the farmers. On leaving the flourishing land-grant and settlers of the Atchison, Topeka and Santa Fé at Cottonwood Falls, we could not help recalling Pope's lines:

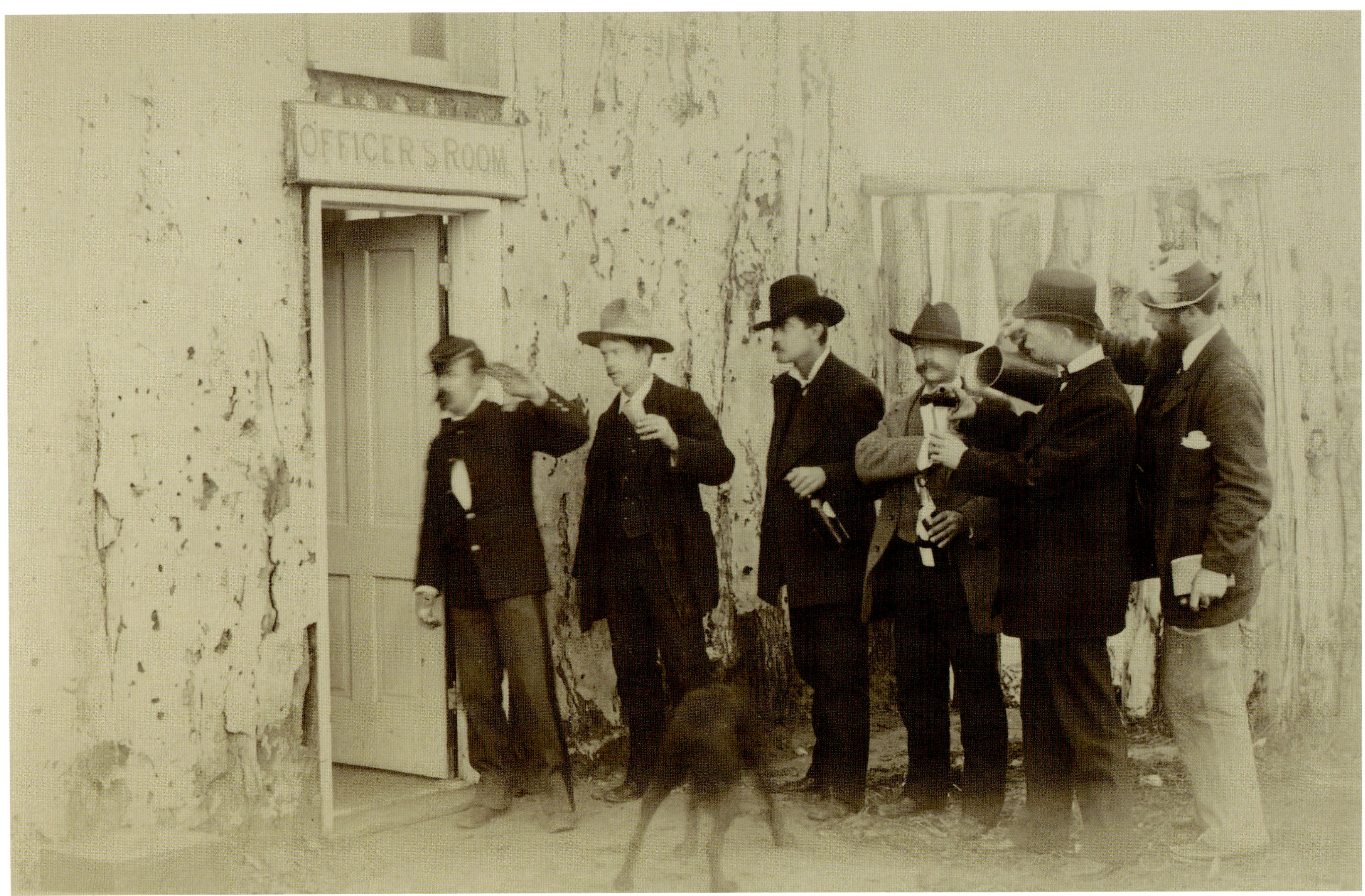

THE "DOCH-AN-DORIS." FORT ELLIOT, TEXAS.
"Doch-an-Doris" is Gaelic for drink at the door, or parting drink. The photograph seems calculated for comic effect. Townshend is last in line, possibly Hyde before him.

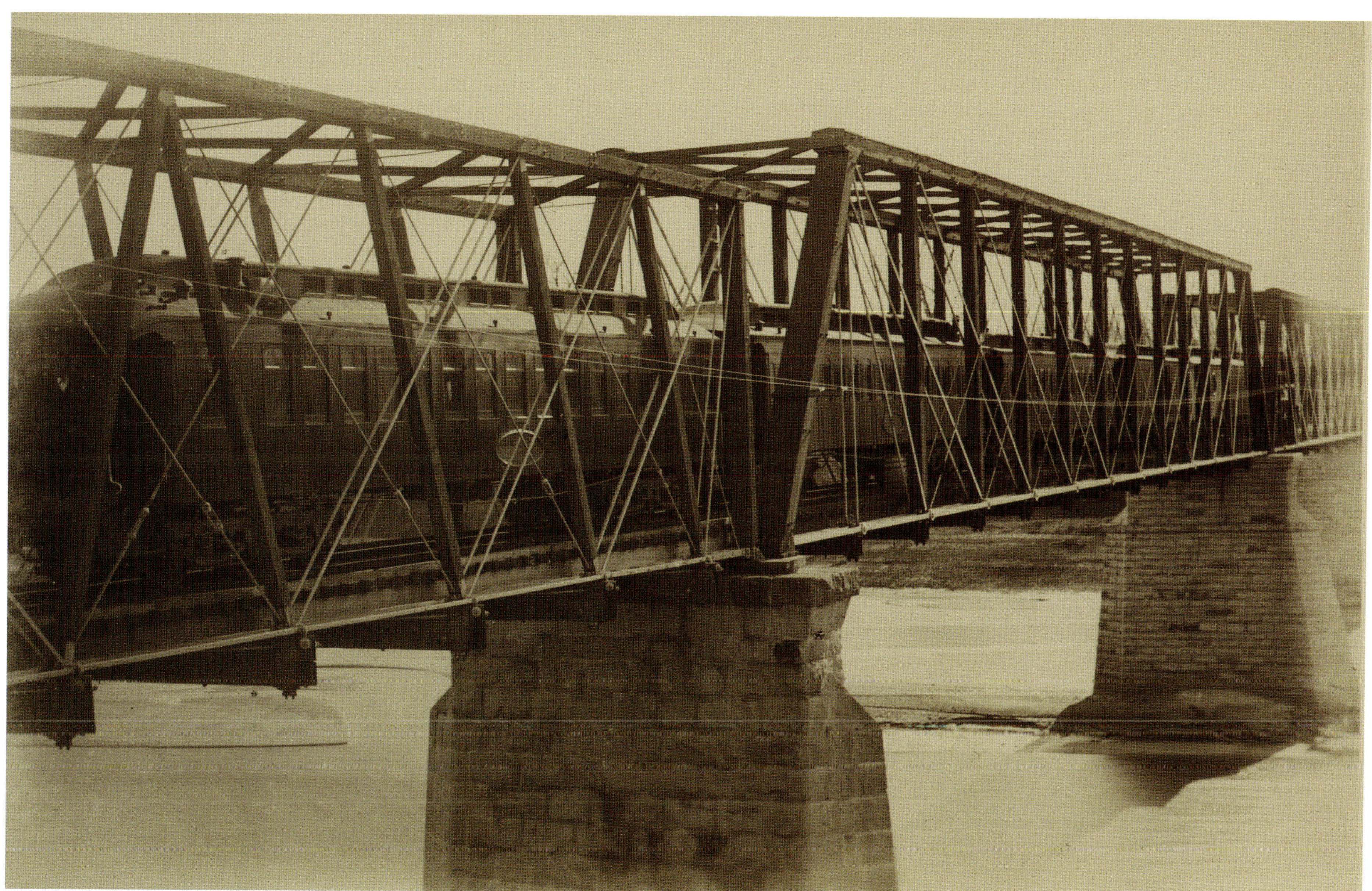

Bridge, Red River. M. K. and T. R. R.
The photograph is well-designed to emphasize modern technology of the train and the steel bridge. The scene suggests movement though the train must be standing still since men are visible on the back deck.

"See Pan with flocks; with fruits Pomona crown'd;
Here blushing Flora paints the enamell'd ground;
Here Ceres' gifts in waving prospects stand,
And, nodding, tempt the joyful reaper's hand."[4]

These lines, however, recall Kansas in June, not November. We bid a kind farewell to the State of Governor St. John; and next day, running all the time over the rails of the Missouri, Kansas, and Texas, re-enter Texas over the great Red River bridge, shown in our photograph.

4. Alexander Pope, *Windsor Forest* (1713).

CHAPTER XVII

Again in Texas—Denison and its Fruit-culture—The Wheat Regions of Texas—Dallas—Prices of Lands along the Houston and Texas Central—Waco—Houston—Fireflies, Roses, and Magnolias in November—The Mighty Dead—The run from Houston to Austin—The Royal Humane Society and Governor Roberts—On the proposed new Rail Route to San Antonio—San Marcos and New Braunfels.

"Singing through the forests,
Rattling over ridges,
Shooting under arches,
Rumbling over bridges,
Whizzing through the mountains,
Buzzing o'er the vale;
Bless me! this is pleasant,
Riding on the rail!"

Saxe

The broad Red River we now span, on the Missouri, Kansas, and Texas railway-bridge; but the autumn glories that we have passed through in the south-eastern portion of the Indian Territory are to grow more beautiful and more vivid as we approach the southern coast. The brilliant red banks, red cliffs, red foliage, and red water of the very red Red River are left behind. The train slows, the musical engine-bell rings forth warning that we are coming to Denison, and in a few minutes we are in that city, and at the terminus of the main trunk line of Texas, the Houston and Texas Central.

Denison is one of the liveliest and most enterprising places of its age—about six years—in Texas. First, the splendid powerful cotton-compress, with its busy surroundings, strikes the eye. A photograph of this we present to the reader. Now, just glance round, and have a look at the advertisements in the station; here is one, the enterprising firm's name only altered:

"Gate City!! Infant Wonder!!!
If You Wish To Invest in A Live City,
Call at the Office of
Mac-Brown, Jones, Fitz-Smith, Robinson & Co."

This sort of advertisement gives us very much the spirit of the verse:

"Let the bold sceptic who denies our worth,
Just hear it proved on any 'Glorious Fourth,'
When patriot-tongues the thrilling tale rehearse
In grand orations or resounding verse."[1]

Epigraph: John Godfrey Saxe, "Railroad Rhyme," *Poems of John Godfrey Saxe* (1868).
1. John Godfrey Saxe, "The Times," *Poems of John Godfrey Saxe* (1868).

Denison is chiefly celebrated for its fruit exports and culture. Recent as has been the growth of this business, last year there were shipped from Denison

				£	s.	d.
1,000 boxes of Tomatoes,		at 4*s.* 0*d.* per box	=	200	0	0
11,750 "	Peaches,	at 2*s.* 6*d.* "	=	1,468	14	0
250 "	Grapes,	at 5*s.* 0*d.* "	=	62	10	0
8,000 quarts of Strawberries,		at 0*s.* 9*d.* per quart	=	300	0	0
1,500 "	Blackberries,	at 0*s.* 5*d.* "	=	31	5	0
		Total		£2,062	9	0

Neither will time, tide, nor, it may be added, the Houston and Texas Central, wait for any man; so away we roll through a succession of forests and open lawns, where a great many cultivated fields,

> "Which crown'd with tufted trees and springing corn,
> Like verdant isles, the sable waste adorn."[2]

The northern portion of Texas, is, indeed, the wheat-belt of the State. For some time it was thought the more southerly counties would produce cereals of equal quality; but the result of these experiments was not sufficiently good to encourage a continuance of them; so that, though in 1875 Texas produced six million bushels of wheat, the estimated crop for this year will be but two and a-half million, according to Burke's "Texas Almanac," a work published in Galveston, and one which would be simply invaluable had it only an index.[3]

The good wheat district lies along the northern third of the Houston and Texas Central, and along the central third of both branches of the Texas Pacific. One of these branches we meet at Sherman, where it stops. The other, and more important, crosses us at Dallas, and goes on to the confines of civilization at Weatherford.

Dallas, where we get a very good supper, is the capital of the county of the same name. Dallas is the seat of the episcopal bishop of Northern Texas—Dr. Garrett,—"the emigrants' friend," as he is called, and a kind practical friend he is.[4] Good land anywhere near this railway junction costs a great deal; in fact, as high as £20 per acre near town, but a little distance out, it is as low as £4 per acre. The average products of this country, as given by Mr. Robert Elgin, the land-commissioner of the Houston and Texas Central, are:—

Cotton	per acre	¾ bale.
Indian Corn	"	40 bushels.
Wheat	"	30 "
Oats	"	35 "

And fruits and vegetables of every variety, and in great abundance. For purposes of agriculture, farmers, if they will go to Texas, should go to Northern Texas, where the climate is not altogether unbearably hot, and where the crops they are accustomed to, will grow.

The Texas Pacific, International and Great Northern are business-like, courteous, and straightforward corporations; indeed, the fault found with the latter company's land-office is, that it is very hard to buy or lease any land of it, presumably because the property of this International and Great Northern will much increase in value by the extension of its line to San Antonio.[5]

We find black, waxy, and sandy soil in Ellis County, about Ennis.

2. Alexander Pope, *Windsor Forest* (1713).

3. The *Texas Almanac* was first published in 1857 and continues today, but it was not published between 1873 and 1904. One alternate guide during this period was *Burke's Texas Almanac and Immigrants Handbook*, published between 1875 and 1885. Crawford, "Texas Almanac"; "Emigrants' Guides to Texas."

4. Alexander Charles Garrett (1832–1924) of Ireland became the Episcopal bishop of northern Texas, then a vast new missionary district of one hundred thousand square miles, in 1874. Morgan, "Garrett, Alexander Charles."

5. The Texas and Pacific Railway was a federally chartered company based in San Antonio. The International–Great Northern Railroad was the Texas portion of the Missouri Pacific. Both were actively building tracks in Texas at this time. Werner, "Texas and Pacific Railway"; Werner, "International–Great Northern Railroad."

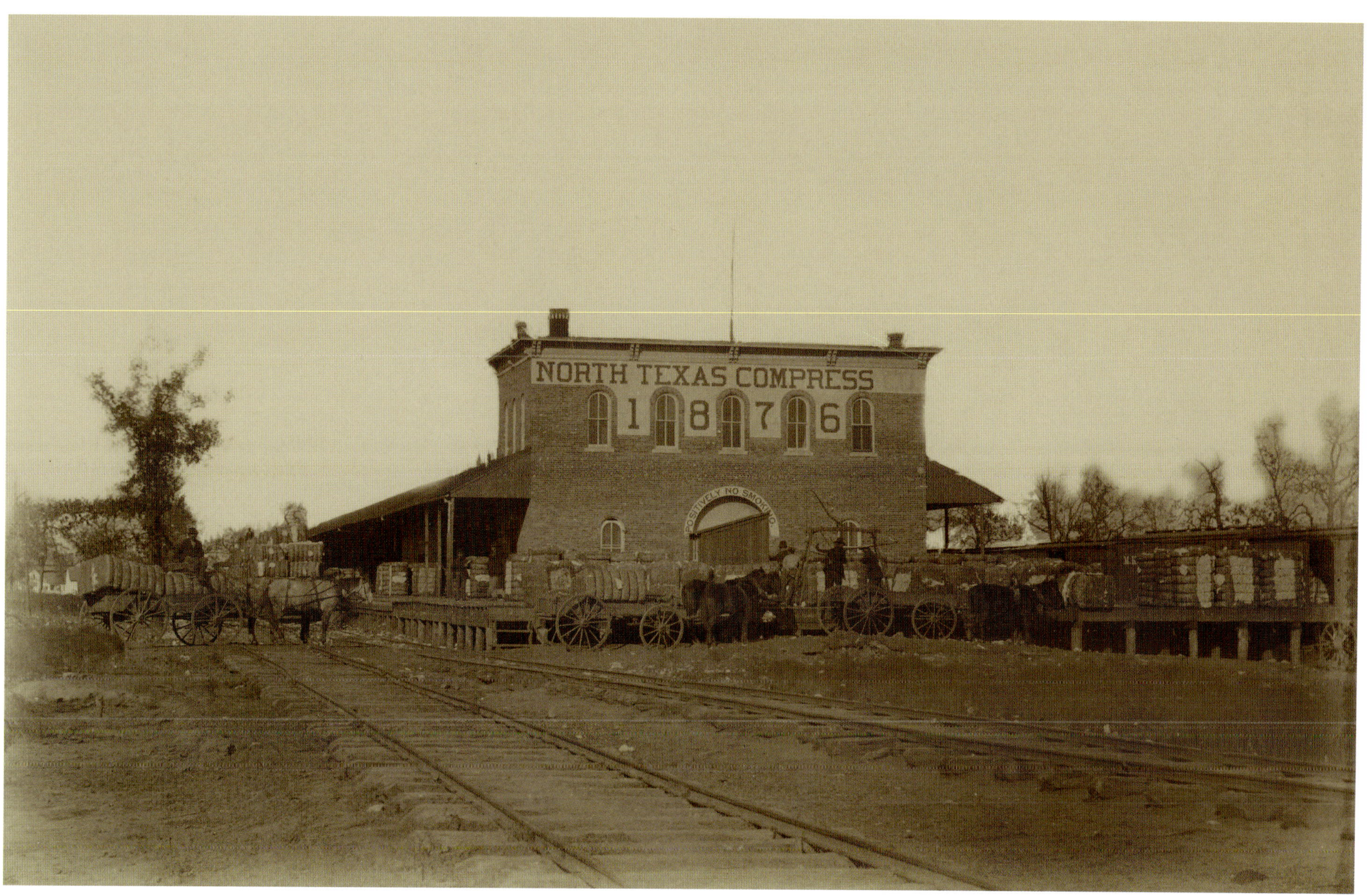

"Cotton Press."

In this wonderful scene of the work of the cotton press near Denison, Texas, the laborers are loading bales onto wagons.

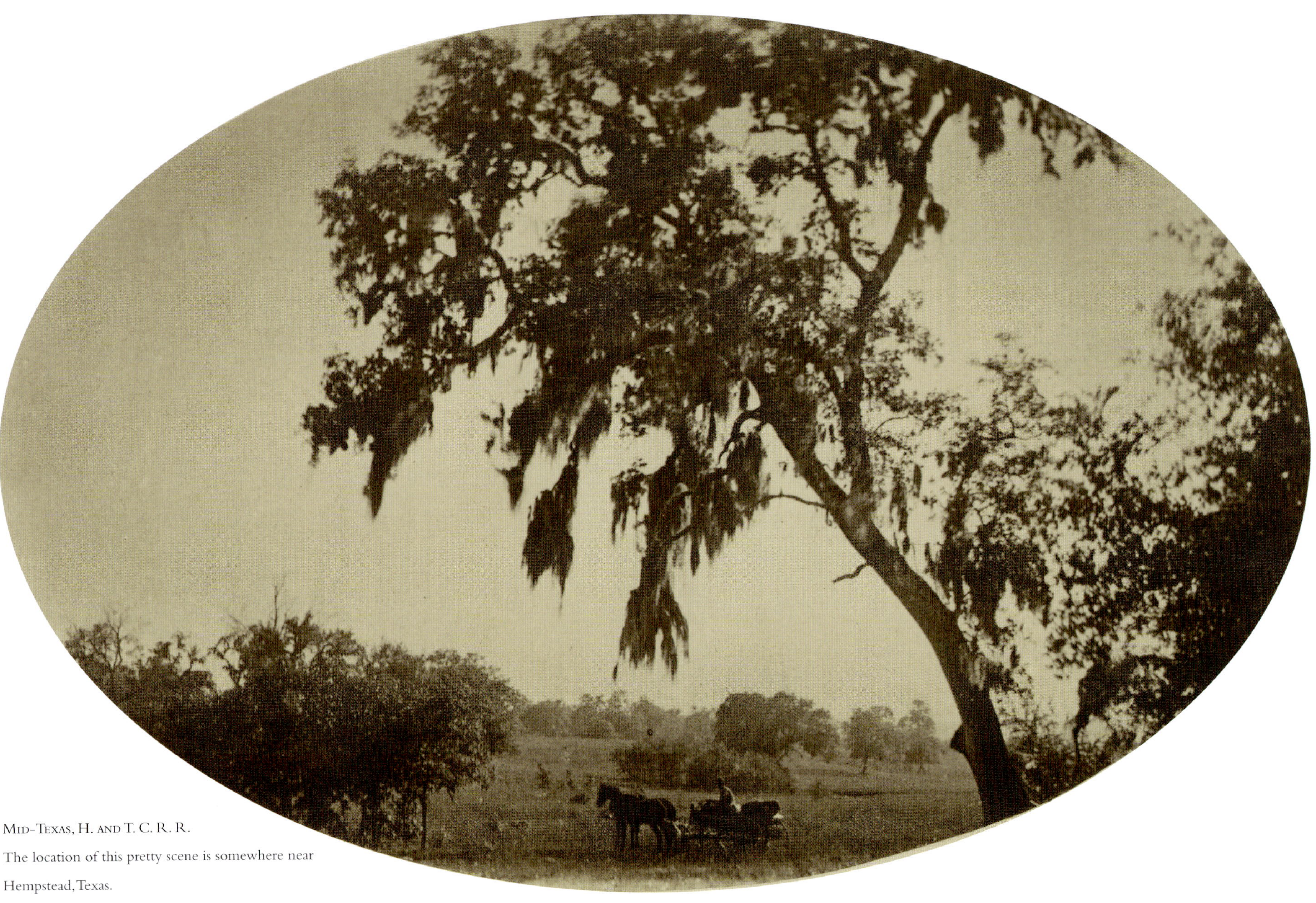

Mid-Texas, H. and T. C. R. R.
The location of this pretty scene is somewhere near Hempstead, Texas.

This sort of land sells from £1 to £4 per acre. Cotton and oats are the best crops; wheat only averaging twenty bushels per acre, and in the next county, Navarro, only eighteen. Trees are interspersed with clumps of rounded scrub very picturesquely all over this country, and the vistas are rolling and homelike. The scenery after a while gets very destitute of water. At Bremond, a pretty branch of seventy miles goes north-west to Waco, which is charmingly situated on the fine Brazos river, and is the capital of McClellan County, where land sells from 15s. to £3 per acre. Sheep and cattle do well there, and though wheat only averages fifteen bushels, oats and barley each return forty, and Indian corn thirty-five. The fact that this pretty new town has already a population of 25,000, speaks volumes for it.

At Hearne, further south, we find the main line of the International and Great Northern crosses us on its way to Austin, the State capital. Hearne is in Robertson County, and wheat here comes down to but an average of ten bushels to the acre, but cotton yields one bale, or 1,000 pounds, a splendid crop, and greater than that of any more northern county. Only those English farmers who learn to grow and manage cotton will do much good any further south. Land in Robertson County varies in price from 10s. to £6 per acre, according to the manner in which it is improved, or lies in the bottoms. Sixty schools and sixty-five churches are found in this county. We cross the little Navasota river, and run down the valley of the Brazos, to Hempstead, where an important branch of this Houston and Texas Central strikes off for Austin; but, though later in the day we went on this line, now we pursued our way to Houston, to see the extraordinary drooping moss, which, in funereal wreaths, covered all the trees; one of which we photographed and present to the reader in this chapter. Houston is a fine business-like city; the rose and magnolia bloom all the year round in its gardens, and every house has one. The firefly at night lights every street up with its spark, together with the one broad plank laid down in the middle to save the poor feet of the patient tramcar mule. The cemetery in Houston is the most charming scene in Texas: roses, moss, and magnolias ever cluster lovingly round the white marble tombstones of men who had bled, and fought, and fallen gloriously in defence of everything the noble deem best worth contending for,—for almost every man in Texas was a soldier of necessity. First, to fight the cruel Mexican, and free Texas for ever from the hand of the oppressor. Then, after a brief independent career, Texas thought it best to mingle its lone star with the stars and stripes, from which banner it strove hard and manfully again to re-pluck it, but in vain. Houston, however, for us had lost most of its charm, for our oldest Texan friend, Mr. J. Waldo, the general passenger agent of the Houston and Texas Central, was then not at home;[6] and retracing our railway run to Hempstead Junction, we went off to Austin, through an extremely lovely country, especially near the Brazos. The land is very similar to that of the Galveston, Harrisburg, and San Antonio Railway, which lies only seventy miles to the south, and a great many farmers, we were told, had come from there here, without bettering themselves very much, as the level is only some fifty feet higher.

None of the trees, though in late November, had lost all their foliage, and large clumps of Texas laurel and live-or-evergreen—oak-trees delighted the senses with beautiful variety. Indeed, emigrational prospects apart, we see no risk in, like Pope, saying:

> "See what delights in sylvan scenes appear!
> Descending gods have found Elysium here.
> In woods, bright Venus with Adonis stray'd,
> And chaste Diana haunts the forest shade."[7]

As a winter resort for the invalid, or the person of leisure, it would be difficult to match almost any part of South Texas, were the hotels better, which they are slowly becoming.

Evening had already descended as we reached Austin, the capital of the State, where we were expected and welcomed by Major Brackenridge, president of the National Bank of Austin, and

6. J. Waldo was subsequently an original board member for the Houston Belt and Magnolia Park Railway. Werner, "Houston Belt and Magnolia Park Railway."
7. Alexander Pope, "Summer, the Second Pastoral, or Alexis" (1709).

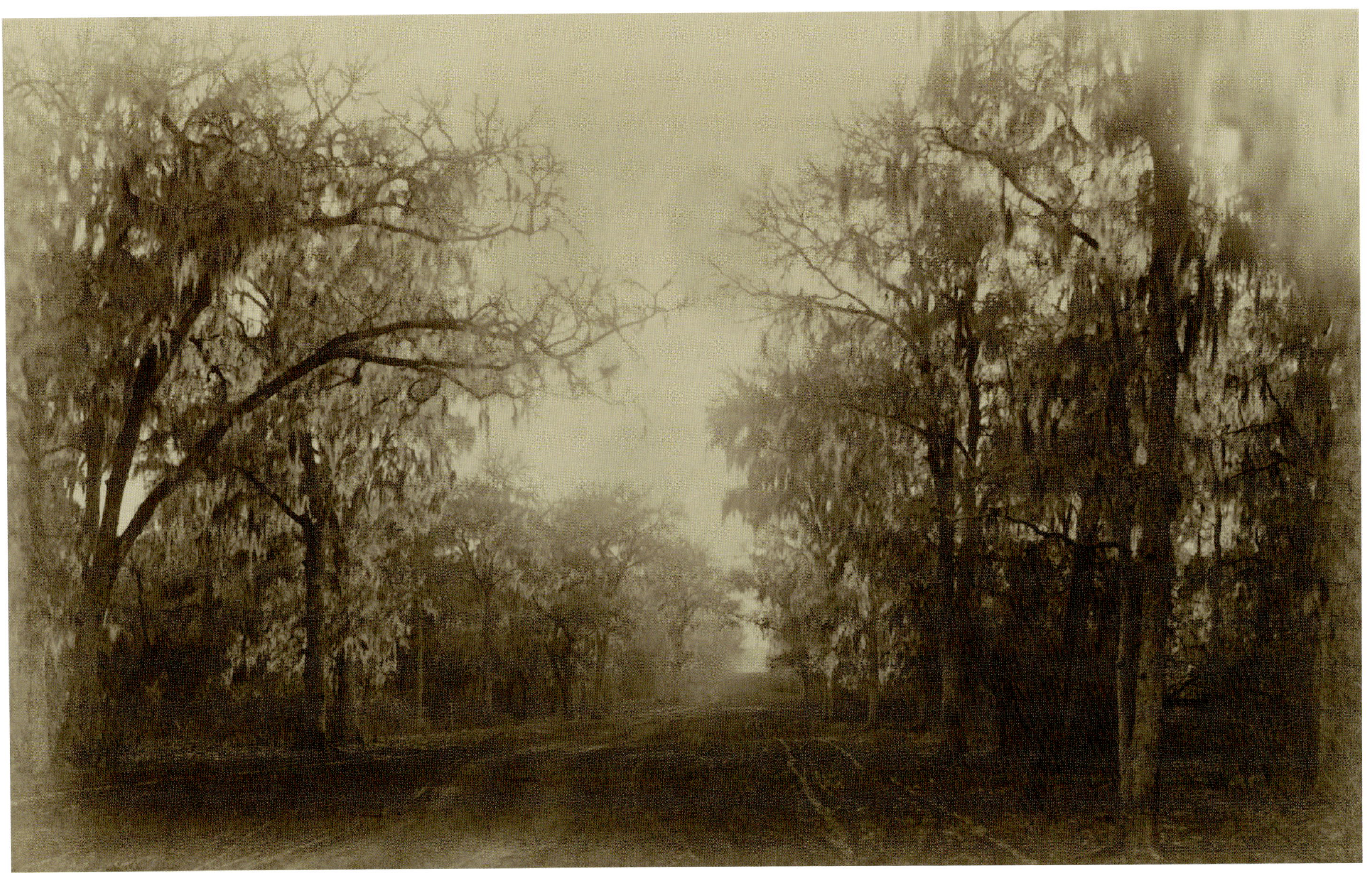

Avenue near San Mercos, Texas.

San Marcos is misspelled in the original caption. Townshend's remarks about this region are chiefly of its agricultural prospects, fine trees, and pleasing climate.

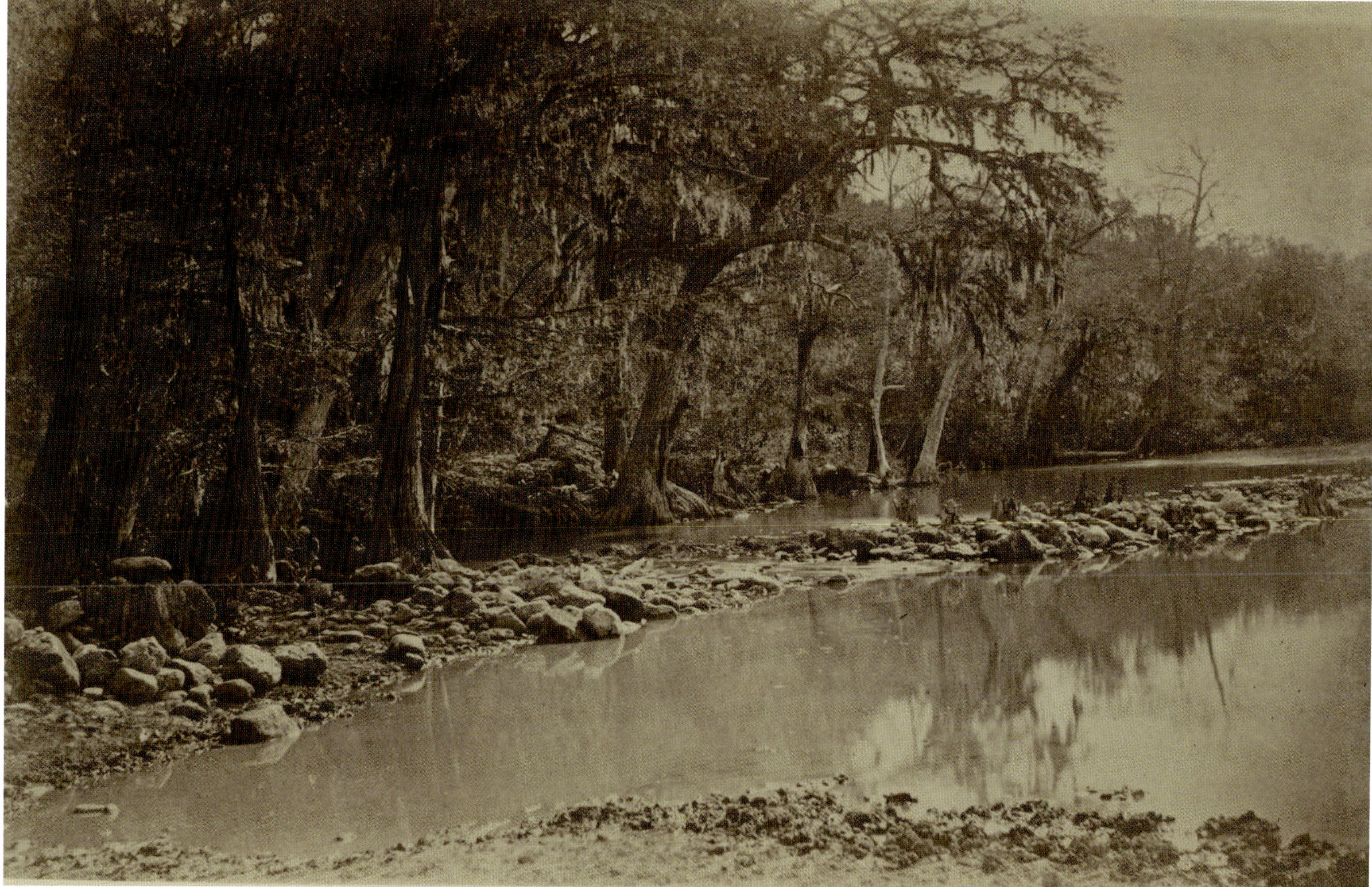

Guadaloupe River, Texas.
Guadalupe is misspelled in the original caption. The image emphasizes the lush vegetation and ample water, rather different from the Texas Panhandle and other western scenes viewed.

brother of an old and dear friend of ours in San Antonio, shortly to be introduced to the reader. Austin is a dangerous place for it is full of the most charming and accomplished flirts, who had broken our hearts several times on previous occasions. It is also dangerous as being always full of politicians, of—of course—very narrow-minded tendencies. As an instance, we may state that the governor—Roberts—declined to officially present one of our Royal Humane Society's medals to the collector of customs of Indianola, for saving the life of a British subject. The collector and the governor differing radically in politics, is the reason generally assigned, but the worthy chief magistrate may think, of course, that the British subject should have been allowed to drown; and thus not have been afforded the opportunity to write this paragraph or any other.[8]

Next morning we were off in a hired spring-waggon, over the

8. An intriguing comment but no explanation of this incident could be discovered.

proposed extension of the International and Great Northern to San Antonio. This line, when completed, will be the prettiest in the State, as the scenery is sometimes almost mountainous, and a great deal of thrifty German agriculture—cotton and Indian corn—lines the way occasionally. Of this route we present two views: one, the avenue of trees near the source of the San Marcos river; the next shows the upper waters of the Gaudalupe, a lovely forest and river scene, the shadows being perfect in the stilly depths, and the curious bulb-shaped roots—so typical of trees in South-West Texas—coming out well.

Having no chance of changing horses, we were obliged to sleep one night at San Marcos, a pretty little town, near the large spring, where the bright river it takes its name from, leaps at once suddenly into healthy and active existence. How far it may have traversed the bowels of the earth before, no one can guess. Next morning across the Gaudalupe, and through the thriving German settlement of New Braunfels. Middle-aged men born here cannot always speak English. We proceeded still through timber, and hill, and dale, but over a very dry country, to a comfortable haven, which for months we had had in view—the residence of Mr. G.W. Brackenridge, near San Antonio; and thus ended an eighty-mile very pleasant drive.

CHAPTER XVIII

San Antonio—Its Missions and later History—Its Buildings and Society—The National Bank—The Head of the River—Its Navigation by the S.A.M.A. and R. Soc.—English Settlers about San Antonio.

"English and Irish, French and Spanish,
German, Italian, Dutch, and Danish,
Crossing their veins until they vanish
In one conglomeration."

Saxe

San Antonio is a very curious, quaint, old town, established just one hundred and fifty years ago, by special authority from King Ferdinand of Spain, after whom it was first named San Fernando de Asturia; this name was supplanted by the more recent one of San Antonio, but there are no records to show when. The Jesuits were entrusted with the organization and quasi-government of the new settlement, and they at once proceeded to build the beautiful missions of Concepcion, San Juan, San Jose, and La Espada, the ruins of which are the greatest ornaments of this locality to-day.

Another mission, the Alamo, was commenced, but the wildness of the Indians, the inroads of the French, and probably the absence of any bank to lend money for the completion of this pious project, caused it to be abandoned. The Alamo, however, though it was not destined to tremble with the sonorous harmony of the great organ, and ring with the voices of choristers, was fated to be more celebrated than any of the missions, for when Texas rebelled against Mexico, the Alamo—then garrisoned by Colonel Travis, and one hundred and seventy of his men—was surrounded by the whole Mexican army on February 25, 1836.

"No surrender!" was as determinately written on the banner of Travis as it was long before on that of the old city of Derry;[1] and, after the final assault of March 6, only a woman and a child were found alive of all that were in the Alamo before the investment of it by that cruel bloodhound, General Santa Anna.

"Thermopylae had its messenger of defeat—the Alamo had none!" is the fitting inscription that commemorates the awful history.[2] Santa Anna left, however, fifteen hundred of his men dead in and around the Alamo, and was finally conquered and taken prisoner only six weeks later at San Jacinto, by General Sam Houston; a name,

Epigraph: John Godfrey Saxe, "The Proud Miss MacBride: A Legend of Gotham," *Poems of John Godfrey Saxe* (1868).

1. In April 1689, as part of a larger war between the Protestant William of Orange and the Catholic King James II, forces loyal to James besieged Derry (officially Londonderry) in northern Ireland. The Siege of Derry lasted 105 days, finally ending in late July 1689 when relief ships broke through the Jacobite barricade on the River Foyle. *Encyclopedia Britannica Online*, s.v. "Londonderry," accessed July 22, 2015, www.britannica.com/place/Londonderry-city-and-district-Northern-Ireland; see also "The Siege of Derry," *Culture of Northern Ireland*, accessed August 14, 2015, www.culturenorthernireland.org/features/heritage/siege-derry.

2. This statement, comparing the Alamo (1836) to the Battle of Thermopylae (480 B.C.), is credited to a speech written by Thomas Jefferson Green and delivered by Gen. Edward Burleson in 1841–42. Dobie, "The Alamo's Immortalization of Words," 406–10.

by the way, pronounced Heuston, and spelled in that way by all the ancestors and collateral relatives of the general, whose having left home very young, and deficiency of education, are assigned by them as the only reasons for his using an o instead of an e. The fact that the general—subsequently first governor of Texas—pronounced his name correctly, though he spelled it wrongly, bears out the statement made on the subject by his accomplished nephew, Mr. H. M. Heuston, of San Francisco, a scion of the old Tipperary stock.[3]

San Antonio, then, has many and most interesting associations. It was, so to speak, born old; for all the first and, until very recently, most of the new buildings that succeeded them, were of the mediæval Spanish style. Every nationality blends in this cosmopolitan place, and a very large Mexican element must be added to the category of races enumerated in the verse heading this chapter. Broad and shady verandahs surround most of the houses, and the San Antonio river winds in so many S-like forms through the city, that you never can tell on which side of it you are. The city ordinances and corporate notices are printed in three languages—English, German, and Spanish—and occasionally a man arrives in the Alamo-city, to whom all three are as Greek.

San Antonio is the military departmental head-quarters of Texas, which General E. O. C. Ord commands, in a manner more pleasing to the Texans whom he protects, than to the Mexicans he awes.[4]

The Mexican raids were indeed, until very recently, so serious and so persistent into Texas, that things looked very like a war with

"A neighbouring people rich in landed spoils,
But weak with ignorance and domestic broils;
A haughty nation, full of pride for what
Their fathers were, though they themselves are not;
A people fond of pageants and parade,
Replete at once with gas and gasconade,
With all the vapour of the Spanish sire,
Without one spark of the Castilian fire."[5]

About San Antonio there is an air of very great solidity: not only are the houses built of handsome cream-coloured stone, but the city institutions, banks, and houses of business are of old and good standing, and society partakes there of the same reliable, respectable type. American friendships are likely usually to prove rather fleeting and evanescent. The quick, sympathetic, mercurial temperament of the American, interests itself so kindly and warmly in you, that you feel resentment for the way it forgets you, once you leave its immediate neighbourhood,—almost more keenly than pleasure at, and gratitude for the original kindness. Of the American ladies this is particularly true; but in San Antonio, if you make friends, you make fast and firm ones of all gentlemen, and of most ladies.

Let us now leave the city, and wander up the course of the San Antonio river, to the prettiest demesne in Texas,—that of Mr. George W. Brackenridge, the president of the National Bank in San Antonio.[6] Mr. Brackenridge has been a kind and true friend of the respectable English in Texas. We believe his is the only bank in the State with direct London agents (Messrs. H. S. King, of Cornhill), but we know that he has rarely allowed English settlers to be charged anything for their bank business, and has kept many of them with their heads above water, who would but for him have long since gone under.

We now depart for the "*Head of the River,*" as Mr. Brackenridge's demesne is named.

3. H. M. Heuston was a prominent figure in northern California, partner in Heuston & Hastings, a tailor and clothing firm in San Francisco. However, the connection Townshend attempts to draw here is vague; Sam Houston was of Scots-Irish descent, his ancestry traced through northern Ireland, not Tipperary. Tinkham, *Half-Century of California Odd Fellowship*.

4. Edward Otho Cresap Ord (1818–83) commanded the Military Department of Texas with three thousand to nine thousand troops under his direction. During his tenure he supervised the construction of Fort Sam Houston and oversaw the construction and maintenance of telegraph lines. His troops suppressed cattle rustlers and hostile Indians and discovered grazing land in the trans-Pecos region as well as silver, iron, lead and copper deposits elsewhere in the state. Cutrer, "Ord, Edward Otho Cresap."

5. John Godfrey Saxe, "The Times," *Poems of John Godfrey Saxe* (1868).

6. George Washington Brackenridge (1832–1920) organized the San Antonio National Bank in 1866. "Brackenridge, George Washington."

Here Nature has not been interfered with more than can be helped. Enormous banana-trees droop over the many springs from which—Hydra-headed—the San Antonio river in a quarter of a mile gains a volume nearly equal to that of the Thames at Oxford. Live oaks and elms, Texas laurels, and wesache—that beautiful, perfumed tree—are everywhere. The fish-pond, the bath, and hydrants are the only innovations of art, except where Miss Brackenridge grafts some curious plant upon some more curious plant, and produces a still more curious plant as a result.

> "Here orange-trees with blooms and pendants shine,
> And vernal honours to their autumn join,
> Exceed their promise in the ripen'd store,
> Yet in the rising blossom promise more."[7]

This beautifully descriptive verse of Pope's is perfectly true of South Texas. In Mr. Brackenridge's demesne we have often noticed the new green leaves forcing off the old green, and, a little further South, three crops of figs on a tree at the same time—*i.e.*, ripe, half-grown, and embryotic figlets.

The turtles in this demesne, not being disturbed, are very numerous, and on any occasion dozens of them may be seen on every log in the river, and alongside of it; for these turtles not only like to bask in the sun, but they specially wish to avoid the leeches in the river: and what a lovely one it is to drift down, or pull up, in the fast light gig of Miss Brackenridge! The sub-tropical trees arch overhead, the interstices between their branches filled with brown Texan moss, or the ever-present powerful mustang vine, some stems of which we have measured five feet round. Large, handsome, grave turkey-buzzards gaze stolidly down from their lofty perches at "the society" in the boat; squirrels peep and wink wickedly at it. Now comes a rapid to be shot—a delicate piece of helmsmanship. The boughs arch low over it, and tempting flowers and mosses dangle in all directions round. "The society" are seven girls, Palinurus, and Ulysses. "Down low with your heads," commands Ulysses, "and grab not at anything; pulling one fern would deviate the ship's course, and submerge us thereby in yonder whirlpool." The rush of waters is now around the frail craft; a fair hand resolutely grasps a large fern. "May the devil!" yelled Ulysses—but

> "The rest of the tale I can't tell now,—
> Except that Ulysses got out of the row
> With the rest of his crew,—it is no matter how."[8]

"The Society." The Mutual Admiration and Reprovement Society of San Antonio, as it appeared in formal meeting, to hear the president, Miss Brackenridge's, annual address, we fortunately were able to photograph, and, we would ask, does not every reader wish he or she were a member of it? If not, then they are lost to all sense of the good and beautiful, and would be as such altogether out of place in the brilliant roll of the S.A.M.A. and R. Soc. Why, the title itself is worth any amount of foreign travel to acquire a right to, and if we were as vain as most authors, we would have printed these initials after our names on the title-page; but, truth to tell, we preferred to let our readers find out, later on in the book, how the world had honoured us. The Galveston, Harrisburg, and San Antonio Railway is the only one that as yet reaches San Antonio, and it annually brings many adventurous English gentleman to San Antonio, from whence they usually go West, or North,—not one of them settling, as far as we know, on the line of the road. Thus Captain Glyn Turquand, late of the Coldstream Guards, is ranching near Boerne, twenty miles north of here. General Davidson, late of the Indian Army, has, we believe, made an extensive poultry-raising farm a success. Mr. Maurice, late of the 1st Royals, has got a good many thousand sheep together near Fort Clark. Mr. Wm. H. Burr, late of the engineering staff of the Khedive, has done the same thing near Beeville; and north, back of Austin, there is no end to the number of young English gentlemen doing fairly well, with both sheep and cattle, on a small

7. Alexander Pope, "Cowley: The Garden," *Early Poems: Imitations of English Poets* (1736).
8. John Godfrey Saxe, "Polyphemus and Ulysses," *Poems of John Godfrey Saxe* (1868).

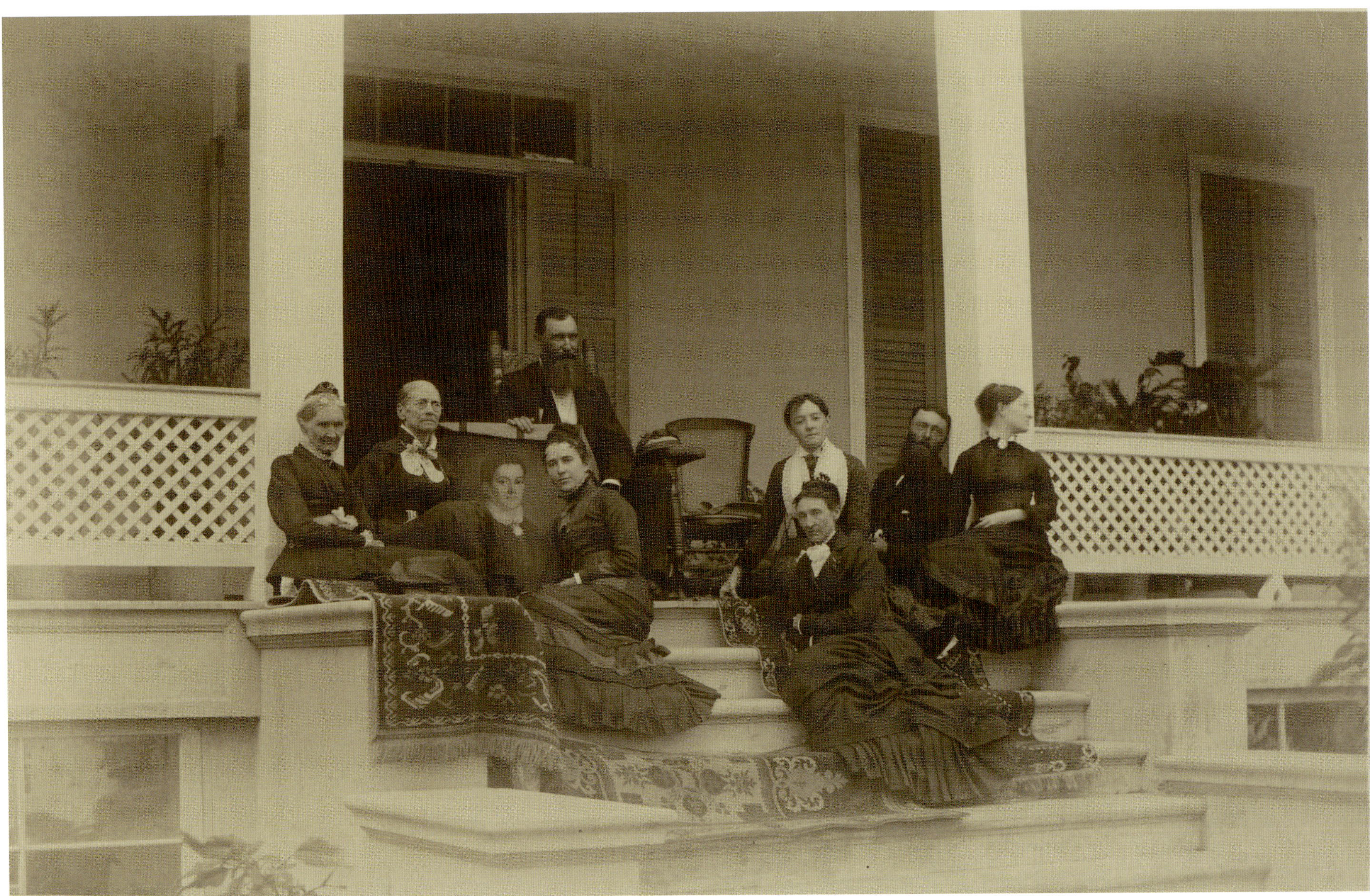

"River Head," San Antonio, Texas.
The scene is of the home of George W. Brackenridge, who is presumably depicted at the center of the group. Miss Brackenridge is one of the women shown. Townshend leans against the post at right.

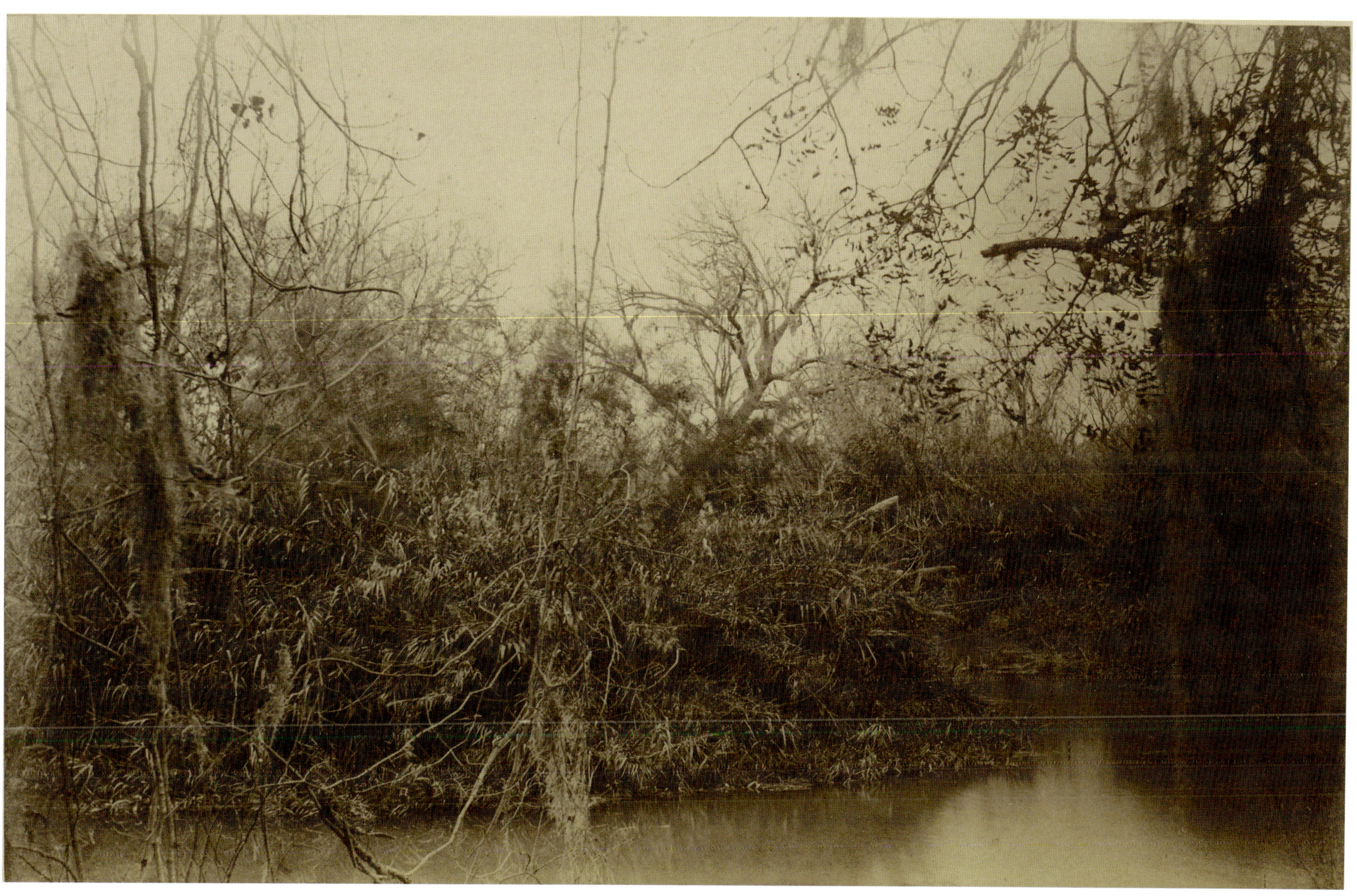

View at "River Head," San Antonio, Texas.
This view is of the same locale that was chosen for the frontispiece photograph of the book *Source of the San Antonio River, Texas.*

scale. Mr. Philip Cross is the committee on English society credentials in San Antonio, and the visitor there is foolish indeed if he does not hunt Mr. Cross up, for to him are open the very exclusive gates of the Head of the River; the unrivalled dinner-table of that eccentric, but most hospitable, Irish gentleman, Mr. John Twohig; the matinées of Mrs. H. B. Andrews, and soirées of Mrs. E. O. C. Ord. In the fulness of time, no doubt, even the magic circle of the S.A.M.A. and R. Soc. will be opened to Mr. Cross, and then his friends will have no further honour to wish him.[9]

San Antonio is one of the most agreeable places in the winter, and Mr. Hord's hotel is one of the most agreeable stopping-places in it. With the splendid new city waterworks, there is now no danger of fire, no want of a bath, and no dust; but in summer let the tourist beware of San Antonio.

"Heaven help us all in those terrific days!
The burning sun upon the earth is pelting
With his directest, fiercest, hottest rays,
And everything is melting!
E'en stoics now are in the melting mood,
And vestal cheeks are most unseemly florid;
The very zone that girts the frigid prude
Is now intensely torrid!"[10]

9. The list of British émigrés to Texas, often via colonial military service, is instructive. Of those named, John Twohig made a lasting impression on Texas history. A native of Cork, Ireland, he became a hero of the Texas Revolution and a wealthy San Antonio banker. Many such British newcomers to Texas favored sheep, lending the business legitimacy during this period. Carlson, *Texas Woollybacks*; Baker, "Twohig, John."

10. John Godfrey Saxe, "The Dog Days," *Sartain's Union Magazine of Literature and Art* 3 (July–December 1848).

CHAPTER XIX

Preparations for Bay Shooting—Railway Run to Galveston—Its Attractions—The Morgan Lines of Steamers—Our Voyage to Matagorda Bay—Shooting on Matagorda Island—At the Mouth of the Gaudalupe, and at Ayre's Dug-out—A large Bag of Game—We turn Homewards.

"From lip and cheek a chilling mist,
From life and soul a frozen rime,
By every breath seem'd softly kiss'd—
God's blessing on its radiant clime."

Saxe

Guns were, like other good things, abundant at the Head of the River. There were guns of Greener and Reilly, Silver and Clarboro, and there were Springfield rifles of diverse patterns. These were now all got into readiness. The cartridge magazines were overhauled and sorted, and many hundreds of new cartridges were loaded. The telegraph-wire to Indianola was kept going for some time in order to charter a schooner, and properly provision her for a ten days' cruise when chartered. But all things earthly come to an end, and the evening of November 29th found our preparations absolutely complete, and ourselves at the station of the Galveston, Harrisburg, and San Antonio Railway. The photograph of this terminus shows the General's staff, and Mrs. and Miss Ord on the platform; the General being in the extreme left-hand corner of the picture. The ladies, unfortunately, we left in San Antonio, but Generals Ord and Card, Major Brown, A.D.C., and Dr. Smith, principal medical officer of the department, went with us as far as Galveston. The train, being a night one, gives us an excuse for passing the very pretty scenery of the line without comment, which would be an act of inexcusable neglect, considering the courtesy of the general manager, Colonel H. B. Andrews, to us; only that we have in other publications written a good deal about it, and that we are anxious to get on to our shooting-ground. Early next morning we found ourselves in Houston, over two hundred miles East, and then taking the Galveston, Houston, and Henderson Railway, reached Galveston, over fifty miles of low coast prairie. Here, finding that the Morgan steamer to Indianola had been detained twenty-four hours, we had to inspect things in general, and found Galveston a fine, substantial city, full of enterprise and enterprising men. The Cotton Exchange is the great sight there, and next to that the Tremont Hotel. Mr. Brackenridge, however, preferred the culinary arrangements of the much smaller Girardin, and our entertainment there certainly paved the way to gout in the future.

The 1st of December saw us off the land once more, and in one of the most comfortable and scrupulously-kept steamers imaginable,—the "City of Norfolk," of the Morgan line. On board was Mr. Hutchinson, the general manager of the route, and

Epigraph: Townshend misidentifies these lines from "Melanie" in *Melanie and Other Poems* (1837) by Nathaniel Parker Willis (1806–67). Willis was an American journalist, editor, and poet. "Melanie" imitates the style of the Romantics, particularly Lord Byron. Its melancholy narrator travels to Italy where his sister falls in love with a painter who is actually her half-brother.

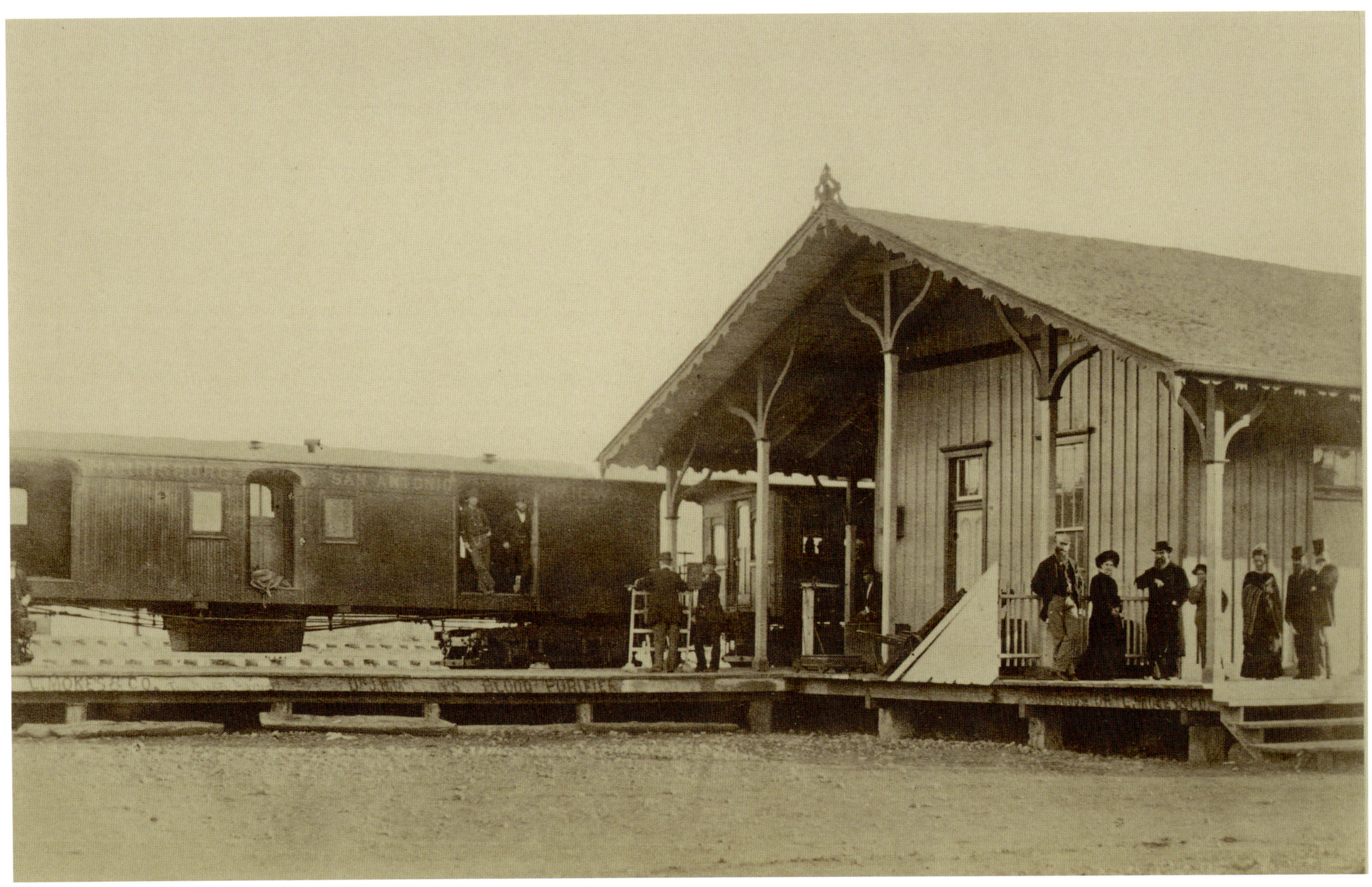

San Antonio Depôt, G. H. and S. A. R. W.

The narrative indicates that General Ord is at the left corner; others include Mrs. and Miss Ord and members of the general's staff.

it may not be out of place to remark that the Houston and Texas Central Railway is only a part of the Morgan system, of which the representatives of the late Mr. Charles Morgan are owners, and which consists of six lines of gulf or ocean steamers, four lines of railway (three in Texas and one in Louisiana), and three canals—one of twelve miles long—cut by the company for its own use.[1]

All night we ploughed the lovely waters of the Gulf of Mexico, and

"We watch'd toward the land of dreams
The fair moon draw the murmuring main;
A single thread of silver beams
Was made the monster's rippling chain."[2]

Before light we were over the bar at Pass Cavallo, and inside Matagorda Island, where our schooner was to meet us; but, as it was perfectly calm, we took for granted she had been unable to creep down from Indianola, and our rather unreasonable request to be landed at Saluria Point, on the island of Matagorda, was at once kindly granted by Captain Thiessen. The vessel was stopped, a boat launched, and we were soon on the sandy beach with our tent and baggage, waiting for day, or anything else that might turn up.

Captain Farwell, the Morgan pilot, had requested us to go to his house for breakfast, and as soon as we could see our way, we went,—shooting five ducks close to the house, and four more immediately after breakfast. Then we walked up a nearly dry lagoon towards the lighthouse. Here we had previously shot forty brace of snipe in two hours, but the continued drought of the past summer had made "the slav" as hard as a brick; very few snipe were to be seen; so, having Mrs. Farwell's waggon and pair of horses with us, we drove off to the beach, where were the sails of our craft gleaming in the morning air, and were soon skimming over the waters of Espiritu Santo Bay, on board the "Seagull," westward.

The "Seagull" appears in photographic guise in this chapter. She was nearly thirteen tons; just the sort of boat that a party of three required to make themselves comfortable in. She had, besides the captain, a crew of one, and then there were Mr. Brackenridge's cook and a servant.

All that day we sailed, and far into the night, through sandbanks and "dug-outs;" and, before light, were again on deck, ready for work at the mouth of the Gaudalupe, in San Antonio Bay. We knew generally where we were, but none of us—not even the skipper—had been there before; and so, during darkness, the lead was our only reliance. When it got light even, none of us were very certain exactly where the mouth of the Gaudalupe was; but the continued calling of myriads of wildfowl, the stridulous song of the goose, the quawk of many-toned duck voices, the pipe of all sorts of shore-birds, and the heavy beating of the wings of swan and crane, brought us to the conclusion that whatever might be the name of the place, it was a particularly good one for our purpose.

Whilst morning twilight yet faintly struggled with the stars, we started off South in the dinghy. A soft feathery mist was settled over shore and bay alike.

"By ocean bar, by woodland belt,
Our silent course a syren led;
Till dark in dawn began to melt,
Through the wild wizard work o'erhead.
And on the burden of the air
The breath of buds came faint and rare."[3]

It is true that the reader will have to scan the works both of Lord Lytton and Willis to find the foregoing, but very few should object to agreeable mixtures of any sort.

Landing, and after a short push inland, a large lake is discovered, covered with ducks, geese, and swans; all, however, out of range. These large sheets of water are not what best suits the sportsman; so we came back to breakfast, and whilst engaged in discussing it,

1. Charles Morgan expanded from steamship lines into railroads, forming Morgan's Louisiana and Texas Railroad and Steamship Company. Baughman, *Charles Morgan*.
2. Robert, Lord Lytton, "The Magic Land," *The Wanderer* (1859).
3. The first four lines are the third quatrain from Lytton's "The Magic Land." The last two lines appear in Nathaniel Parker Willis's *Loiterings of Travel*, chapter 4, in which he enthusiastically addresses his time in Italy.

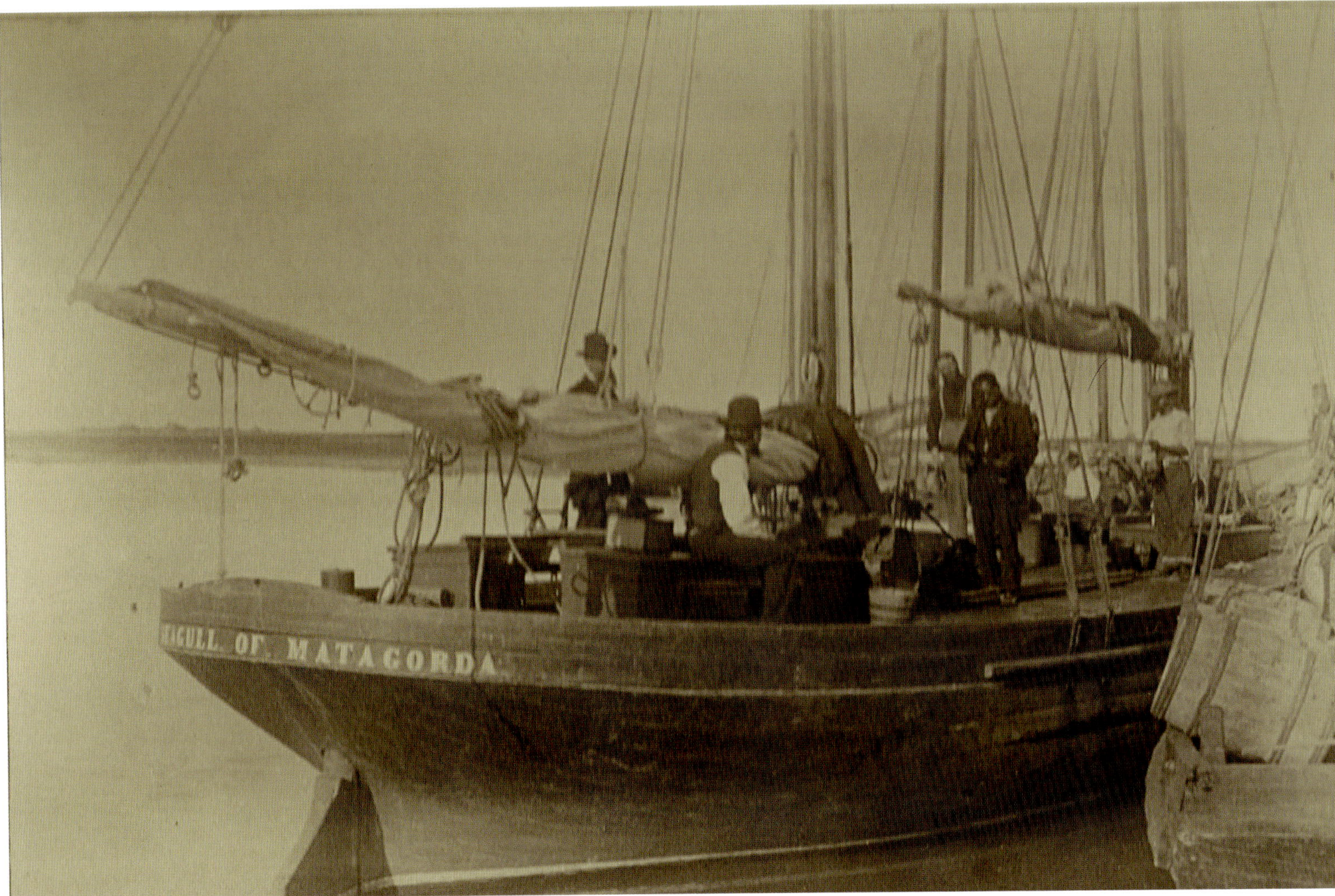

YACHT AT INDIANOLA.
The *Seagull*, shown with crew and servants, from which the travelers hunted on Matagorda Island, belonged to Brackenridge. Townshend is visible in the shot. (Courtesy Amarillo Public Library)

ordered the "Seagull" to be got under way for the opposite shore, near Long Motte, where the mammoth reeds covered all the land. Amongst these reeds we imagined, not erroneously, that game lay, and the music of our guns soon woke the echoes of this unfrequented shore. Not knowing the flight of the fowls, we were for some time unsuccessful; but twenty-five ducks graced our decks that evening, and then we knew better how to go to work next morning; on which, before breakfast, Mr. Brackenridge brought in twenty ducks to his own gun, and we had five and eight respectively. Tired of this slaughter, we sailed up the bay in the afternoon, and got with the dinghy up a narrow channel, which was overhung with dank reeds, fifteen feet high, and which opened into a lake we christened Swan Lake, because it was filled with splendid swans. We could not get near them, because the water was too shallow at the outlet of our channel; but Mr. Brackenridge shot a splendid fellow with his rifle through the neck, and thus the skin remained quite uninjured. Here we also got

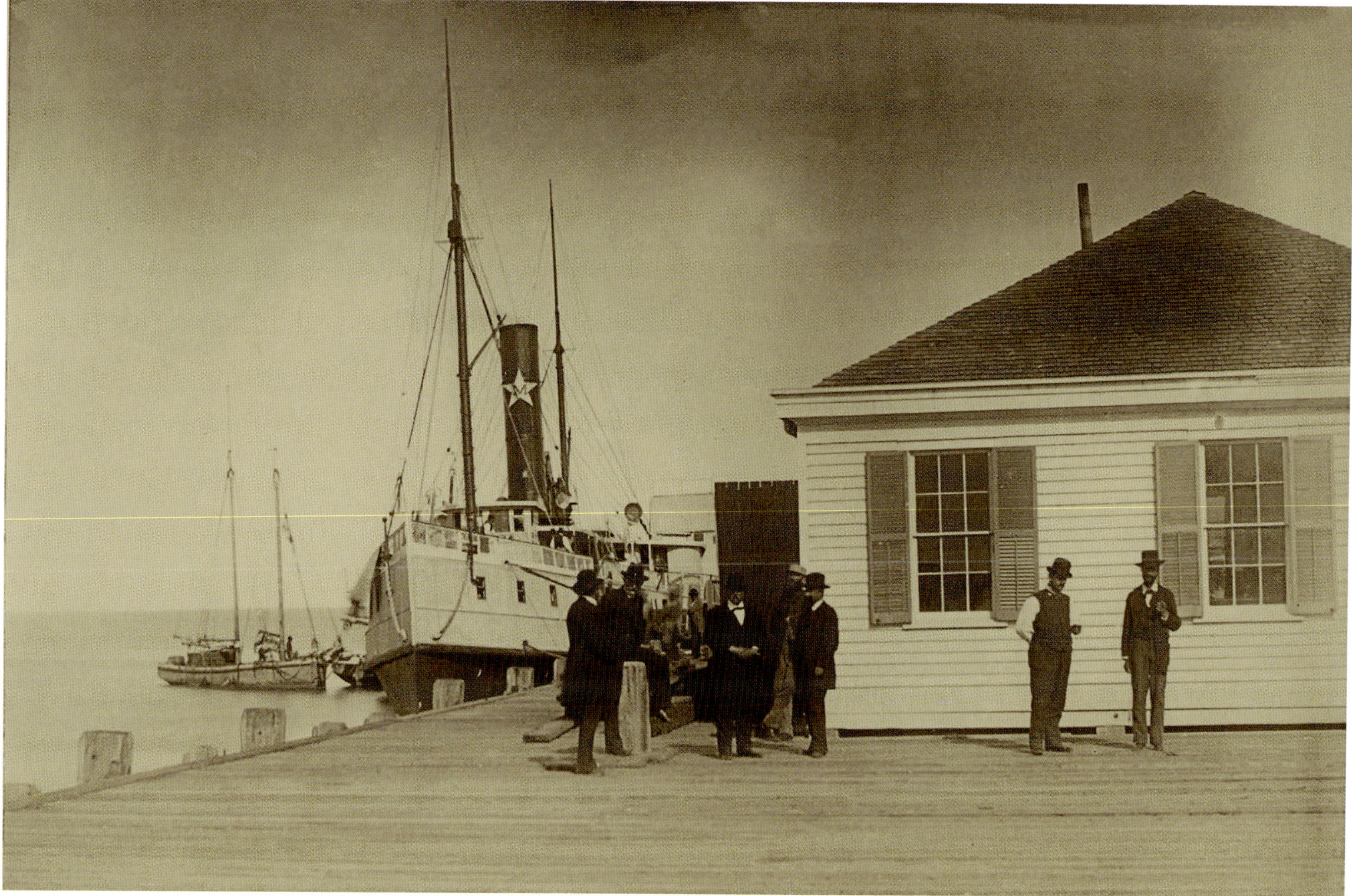

INDIANOLA PIER. [1]
Townshend appears leaning against the wall behind the party of men. The *City of Norfolk* of the Morgan steamship line is at the pier. (Courtesy Amarillo Public Library)

nine brace of delicious small snipe, and explored an alligator's trail, or path, but did not find the owner. Then we sailed for Ayre's Dugout,[4] near the entrance of Aransas Bay, and here again saw thousands of swans, geese, and ducks; but, as all the water here is in large sheets, with scarcely any cover on the margins, we fired an infinity of shots, and only bagged fifteen birds, losing the only deer we fired at, and hit. We now saw that the mouth of the Gaudalupe was clearly the place to make a bag, and returned thither, getting a few *en route* at Blackberry Island. Mr. Brackenridge's time to return home was getting near, and we wanted to send a large bag with him; therefore

4. Ayre's Dugout is a channel between the Aransas National Wildlife Refuge and Matagorda Island. The refuge provides winter habitat for more than three hundred bird species. Kleiner, "Aransas National Wildlife Refuge."

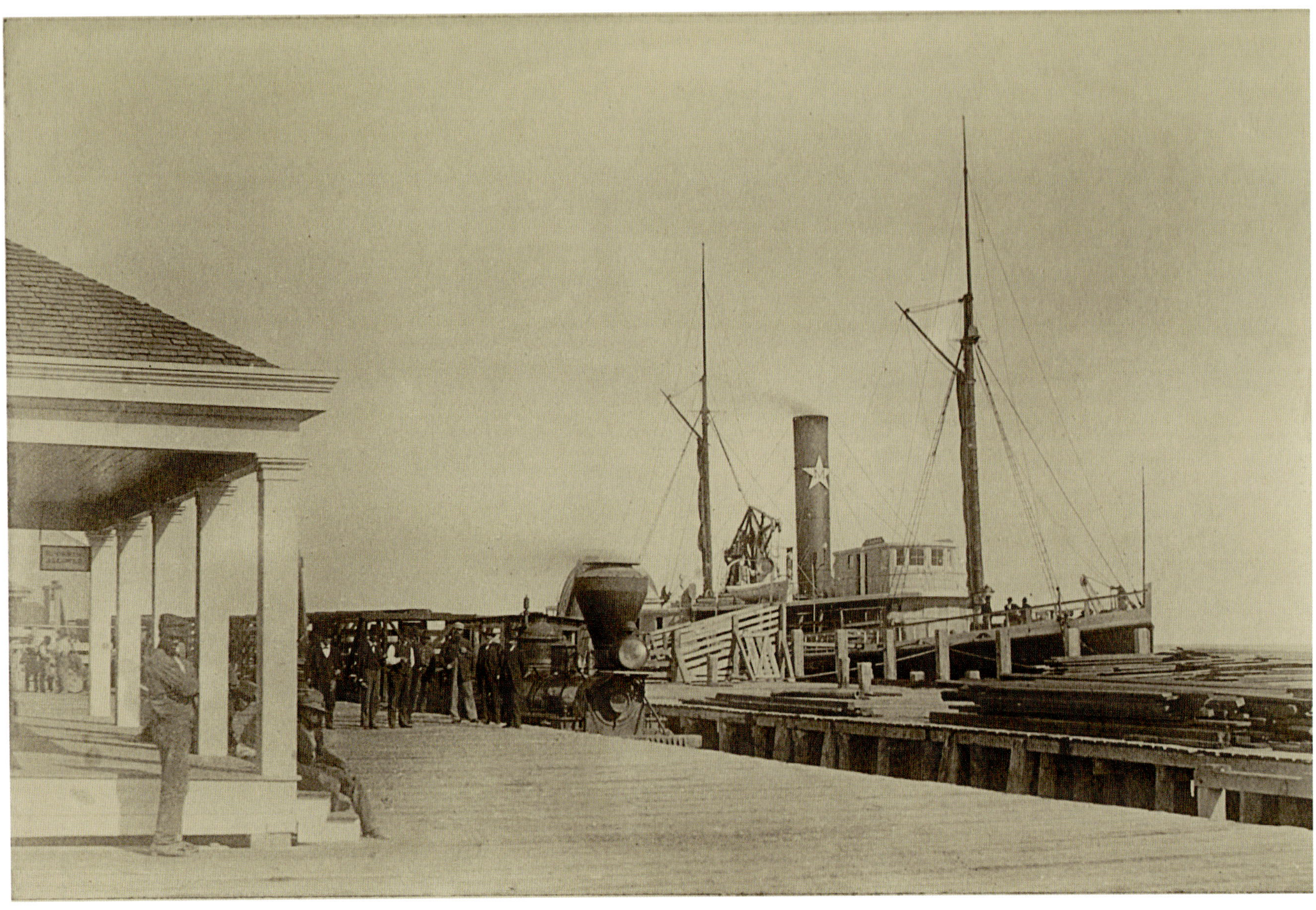

INDIANOLA PIER. [2]

Another view of the *City of Norfolk.* The letter "M" within a star is visible on the stack. (Courtesy Amarillo Public Library)

we went so systematically to work, that on the next day we shot eighty ducks, four geese, and two swans. We did this by taking stands behind a few reeds on the bay shore. The more we fired, the more the birds flew up and down, often within range, ofterner out of it; but we fired with five drachms of powder, and let fly on all occasions towards the termination of our time. We shot at least twice as many birds as we recovered, for it was usually impossible to retrieve anything in the dense tall reeds, which exhaled a warm vapour, and amongst which the mosquitos fairly revelled on the face and hands of the intruder; and, despite the splendid shooting, made him too uncomfortable to remain long in any one position, hoping in vain for some less fly-infested place.

"A man that flies before the pest,
From wind to wind my course is whirl'd;
This cursed fly stung Io first,
And drove her wild across the world!"[5]

Lord Lytton remarks; and in all parts of Texas, but more especially the south, thousands agree feelingly with him. However, bang! bang! go our good guns; Silver's anti-recoil heel-plate bearing well the repeated shocks of the five-drachm charges, but allowing the trigger-guard to back rather forcibly on our fingers. One of us gets two swans right and left; another gets two geese; now a duck flies low along the whole line, and laughs at six barrels discharged at sixty yards off. Now we take the dinghy, and rake the shore for cripples; getting, thereby, within five yards of an immense alligator asleep on the bank. In him we insert sundry shots, just behind the fore-leg, and terrible is the way he lashes the sand in his expiring agonies.

We had now to start for home. Our bag for ten days—on many of which we merely sailed or very successfully fished—amounted to two hundred and fifty-one ducks, twelve geese, five swans, a few snipe, and an alligator. With retrievers we might have brought home at least six hundred head of game; but we had more than we wanted, as after three days the birds were never eatable, and barely so in two. Let us up anchor, and say good-bye to our scene of devastation—

"Where doves in flocks the leafless trees o'ershade,
And lonely woodcocks haunt the watery glade."[6]

5. Robert, Lord Lytton, "The Fugitive," *The Wanderer* (1859). These lines appear in book 5, *In Holland*. "The Fugitive" expresses the haunted loneliness of the traveler.
6. Alexander Pope, *Windsor Forest* (1713).

CHAPTER XX

The Commencement of a Farewell—Long Motte to Indianola—Our Run Back to New York, and Embarkation on board the "City of Richmond"—Final Farewell—Life at Sea—The Moral Reform Club—A Heavy Gale—Conclusion.

"Farewell to the friends we have left with regret,
May they sometimes recall what we cannot forget:
That communion of heart and that parley of soul
Which has lengthen'd our nights and illumined our bowl."

Moore's *Variations*

To say farewell is nearly always a trying task. If you are very sorry, it is generally wise to conceal most of your grief. If you are very glad, it is imperative that your pleasure must in no way become manifest. But now we had to say farewell of all we liked, first in Texas, then more generally in the United States. We had had a great deal of varied experience in the United States, and met with nothing but unvarying kindness from one end to the other of the country, from Niagara to the Rocky Mountains, and from the Pacific slope to the Gulf of Mexico. We had met more colonels in Texas, and more honourables in Kansas, than if we had been attending for a lifetime every levée given by the Duke of Cambridge,[1] and every court held by Her Majesty.[2] We had carried out our programme to the full, and been assisted through with it as generally as though it were an Act of Congress that no obstacle should be placed in our path, and all existing ones removed from our course of 8,600 miles. And now our best friend of all we were going to say good-by to, and leave him on his sunny shores, while we ourselves have to contemplate the effect of a wintry London fog on the human constitution. Much too quickly the "Seagull" sped over the waters that separate Long Motte from Indianola; and at that town, three-fourths of which was washed away in a tornado in 1874,[3] we found the good ship "City of Norfolk" duly awaiting us; whilst one of the Morgan railways—the Gulf, Western Texas, and Pacific—had a train ready alongside the steamer to bear our kind host, Brackenridge, back to San Antonio. "Good-bye, and God bless you," is spoken. The big beam-engine turns ahead, and backward we return to Galveston

Epigraph: Thomas Moore, "To the Boston Frigate, On Leaving Halifax for England" (October 1804). The poem appears in *Epistles, Odes, and Other Poems* (1806), in which Moore recorded his observations of and prejudices against America; American reviewers were harsh. Here, Townshend manipulates and softens the original lines, though possibly unintentionally: "Farewell to the few I have left with regret, / May they sometimes recall, what I cannot forget."

1. George William Frederick Charles, 2nd Duke of Cambridge (1819–1904), inherited the dukedom from his father Aldolphus Frederick, youngest son of King George III, in 1850. He served in the Crimean War, after which he was promoted to field marshal (1862) and commander in chief (1887). *Encyclopedia Britannica Online,* s.v. "George William Frederick Charles, 2nd Duke of Cambridge," accessed July 16, 2015, www.britannica.com/biography/George-William-Frederick-Charles-2nd-Duke-of-Cambridge.

2. "Her Majesty" refers to Queen Victoria, who reigned from 1837 to 1901.

3. Indianola, Texas, was a small port town of about five thousand located on Matagorda Bay in Calhoun County, Texas. On September 15, 1875, a hurricane destroyed all but eight buildings and killed between 150 and 300 people. A second hurricane and the resulting fire completely destroyed the town on August 19, 1886. Malsch, "Indianola"; Frantz, "Indianola Hurricanes."

and to Houston; and then over the International and Great Northern, Texas Pacific, St. Louis, Iron Mountain and Southern Ohio and Mississippi, Atlantic and Great Western, and Erie railways, our course lies for twenty-three hundred miles to New York. The International runs through dense pine forests for hundreds of miles. The hundred miles over which we go on the Texas Pacific to Texarkana (half the town—the Tex—in Texas, and the other half—Arkana—in Arkansas) presents the same scenery. Along the Iron Mountain, for nearly five hundred miles, the views are diversified but not striking, until we get within a hundred miles of St. Louis, when high cultivation, and the traffic on the Mississippi appear. Undulating and fairly well-farmed country lies along our lines now into Salamanca, in south-west New York, where the romantic Erie railway picks us up; and thenceforth mountain and stream, hill and dale, river and cascade, is the highland scenery which meets the eye on both sides of this fine road for two of its four hundred miles. Then again we are in the old city of New York, and again at that excellent hotel—the Metropolitan. One of us has to return by the White Star vessel "Britannic," and the other by the Inman ship, "City of Richmond;"[4] but, though thus parting in practice, we agreed not to do so in theory, and in that way for the purposes of this record go together on the "City of Richmond." Each vessel named taking eight and a-half days to reach Queenstown, proved that there was very little difference between them, and it would be difficult to imagine the comforts of either exceeded. The "City of Richmond" is over 5,000 tons burden, or 4,623.12 register, with a nominal horse-power of 850, being really about 2,500. She is 470 ft. long, 43 ft. 5 in. beam, her depth is 34 ft., and her daily consumption of coal ninety tons on an average. She carries a crew of one hundred and fifty men, of whom forty-nine are in the engineer's department. Her superb passenger accommodation is arranged for two hundred, and fifteen hundred is the number of steerage passengers she is fitted for.

Our old ship "The Queen," of the National line, lay near us as we cast off sharp to time from New York wharf. A fog lay over the upper waters of the harbour as we slowly turned in then, but soon the air and the water brightened. "Go ahead full speed," rang the signal, and, with a measured and life-like throb, the beautiful, powerful, graceful, delicate engines responded to the call. That throb, and that speed, never for one moment varied until we ran between Forts Camden and Carlisle in the noble harbour of Queenstown,[5] eight days and a-half afterwards. After a lot of American drinks,—which are, however, probably better suited to the climate there than any of ours would be,—it was a great luxury to get hold of such old friends as Bass, Guinness, and Jameson again, and their imbibition did not in any way darken our last views of the shore of that great land, where toil is nobility; where honesty is more sought after and more appreciated than in any land on earth; where the foreigner is so welcomed, and so appreciated, that but twelve members of the United States' Senate last year were native-born Americans.[6] America! that offers so tempting a home to the brave, homeless, unfortunate, ruined, or expatriated of every country, we leave thee in the full hope of returning and shaking once again the hands of your true, sympathetic, energetic sons, and of your bright, affectionate daughters. Parnell has failed as egregiously to get you to express any sympathy

4. The White Star Line was a British shipping company best known for the *Titanic* disaster. When the S.S. *Britannic* launched in February 1874, she was the second largest ship crossing the North Atlantic. The Inman Line was one of the largest British passenger shipping companies in the North Atlantic, and one of the first to cater to emigrant passengers. The *City of Richmond* launched in February 1873 and sailed between New York and Liverpool until it was scrapped in 1896. For more information on North Atlantic ships and shipping companies, see www.norwayheritage.com.

5. From 1849 until 1922 Cobh, Ireland, was known as Queenstown in honor of Queen Victoria. Forts Camden and Carlisle are situated on opposite promontories at the entrance to Cork Harbour, the second largest natural harbor and Ireland's largest port. *Encyclopedia Britannica Online,* s.v. "Cobh (Ireland)," accessed July 22, 2015, www.britannica.com/place/Cobh; s.v. "Cork (Ireland)," accessed July 22, 2015, www.britannica.com/place/Cork-Ireland.

6. Townshend refers to the 45th Congress (March 4, 1877–March 3, 1879), in which seventy-six senators served. "45th Congress [1877–1879]," *History, Art, and Archives: United States House of Representatives*, accessed August 14, 2015, http://history.house.gov/Congressional-Overview/Profiles/45th/.

with proposed disintegration of the British Empire[7] as has your own would-be patriot—his countryman—Denis Kearney failed to get you to expel the poor Chinese,[8] or failed in convincing you

> "How lying rags for honest coin shall pass,
> And foreign gold be paid in native brass."[9]

"God save Ireland;" she produces strange politicians!

But to Ireland we are going, and going fast. "Haul the main down," the sailors sing, and

> "We view the swelling sail, flowing out before the gale,
> Full and round, without a wrinkle or a fold."[10]

The great ship bends slightly over to acknowledge this attention on the part of Captain Leitch; the wind freshens, and our speed goes up from thirteen, to fourteen, fifteen, and sixteen miles an hour. It blows a gale after a while; but the gale is after us, and though during the night the fore-topsail is blown out of the bolt-ropes, we soon have new canvas out in its stead.

"The Moral Reform Club" took on board the "City of Richmond" the place of "The Antient and Honorable Society of Whisky Corks" on board "The Queen," but the M.R.C.'s wore no uniform. They held frequent meetings in the smoking-room, and appeared rather lax in their moral reform proceedings, until one day, when they tried an elderly gentleman who had been flirting very heavily, for breach of promise of marriage, as a warning to others. This trial was conducted in the saloon in great state; two very talented Boston lawyers prosecuting and defending in regulation style. A New Zealand colonist was the principal witness, and he proved the proposal having been made in the fore-top; he having heard it from the main-topgallant cross-trees, through a telephone which was connected with the fore-top through the main-topgallant stay. The ladies were above all things pleased with this trial, and the M.R.C.'s were voted the greatest reformers, and the most moral people in the world. Nevertheless, flirting did thereafter greatly increase, and in no way whatsoever diminish.

The sun shone almost warmly as the wind veered a few points to the north, but "the blow" was by no means over.

> "Dark glance the waves beneath our feet,
> And dark the clouds on high.
> The white foam on the blacken'd tide
> Laughs as it flashes by."[11]

The good ship rolled heavily; only a portion of the hurricane-deck was dry; and a splendid sight it was to see the spindrift flying from beneath our counter, and the tops blown off the mountainous billows that cannot follow quite as fast as we run from them.

Though the "City of Richmond" rolled heavily, she did so in a stately and deliberate manner, as though she said, "I yield a good deal to you, Father Neptune, but you can't conquer me. You could certainly make it very unpleasant for me, if I didn't bow to you; so I do so as a matter of mutual concession, for I knock you about, too, a good deal." Æolus, hoarsely singing, speeds us meanwhile on our way over the angriest upreared crests of Neptune. The sea-god spits angrily but ineffectively at our port-quarter, but in our comfortable deck smoking-room, we sing:

7. Charles Stewart Parnell (1846–91) was a member of the British Parliament, an Irish nationalist, and leader of struggle for Irish Home Rule. *Encyclopedia BritannicaOnline*, s.v. Charles Stewart Parnell, accessed July 22, 2015, www.britannica.com/biography/Charles-Stewart-Parnell.

8. Denis Kearney (1847–1907) was the leader of the Workingmen's Party in California during the late 1870s. Although he emigrated from Ireland in 1868, Kearney argued against immigrant labor (specifically Chinese) claiming their willingness to work for lower pay took jobs from Americans. "Denis Kearney," *New Perspectives on the West*, 2001, www.pbs.org/weta/thewest/people/i_r/kearney.htm.

9. John Godfrey Saxe, "El Dorado," *Poems of John Godfrey Saxe* (1868).

10. Similar lines appear in the street song "Far, Far upon the Sea," published in *Curiosities of Street Literature* (London: Reeves and Turner, 1871).

11. Charlotte Pendleton, "The Water Spirit of the Saguenay," *Songs of the Year and Other Poems by "Charlton"* (1875). Pendleton's poem describes a trip down the Saguenay River, a major river of Quebec, Canada, and an encounter with the river's siren.

"I love well the darkness, I love well the sound
Of the thunder-drift howling this way o'er the ocean:
For 'tis though as in Nature my spirit had found
A trouble akin to its own fierce emotion."[12]

There is no such splendid sight in the world as a first-class ship on the open ocean in a gale of wind. Nowhere does science, in both subtlety and power, cope so directly with the most potential forces of nature, and nowhere is the result so almost triumphantly certain for science.

The sun, as we said, shone almost warmly, and the decks dry nearly as fast as they are wet by the masses of green water, as well as rainbows of spray which we dash in our onward course, right, centre, and left; some of them far out sideways, some of them caught by the wind returning to buffet the unwary deck-walker. Our wake runs like a green sea-serpent behind, up one mountain, down another, for our powerful propeller cuts too big a hole even in the Atlantic storm-wave for it to forget it all at once, and for a minute or two we leave our mark on even the billows of the "roaring forties."

A two-masted cargo-steamer we meet ploughing her way to the westward. Poor thing! hasn't she a rough time of it! We can see her tremendous plunges, and yet her power can scarcely send her at all ahead. Such is life. The powerful vessel has a favouring gale: the weak one finds everything against it.

Mr. Thomas Kinsey, the purser, and Dr. David T. Dore, the surgeon, to whom the captain in this rough weather confided his passengers and their comfort, were simply indefatigable in their exertions to make us all enjoy everything, and succeeded in every case.

A more agreeable and gentlemanly set of officers, and a better conducted crew than were on board the "City of Richmond" would be difficult to find. So in conclusion, generalizing the Schuylkill all over America, we say with Moore:

"The stranger is gone, but he will not forget,
When at home he shall talk of the toil he has known,
To tell with a sigh what endearments he met
As he stray'd by the wave of the Schuylkill alone."[13]

12. Robert, Lord Lytton, "A Night in the Fisherman's Hut," *The Poetical Works of Owen Meredith (Robert, Lord Lytton)* (1880). In these lines, the poem's speaker revels in the dark, tempestuous night.

13. Thomas Moore, "Lines, Written on Leaving Philadelphia," *Epistles, Odes, and Other Poems* (1806).

BIBLIOGRAPHY

Aldridge, Reginald. *Life on a Ranch: Ranch Notes in Kansas, Colorado, the Indian Territory, and Northern Texas*. London: Longmans, Green, 1884.

American Medical Association. *Nostrums and Quackery: Articles on the Nostrum Evil and Quackery Reprinted, with Additions and Modifications, from the Journal of the American Medical Association*. 2nd ed. Chicago: American Medical Association Press, 1912.

Anderson, H. Allen. "Cator, James Hamilton." *Handbook of Texas Online*. Published by the Texas State Historical Association. Accessed March 26, 2015. www.tshaonline.org/handbook/online/articles/fca95.

———. "Clarendon, Texas." *Handbook of Texas Online*. Published by the Texas State Historical Association. Accessed March 26, 2015 www.tshaonline.org/handbook/online/articles/hjc11.

———. "Dubbs, Emanuel." *Handbook of Texas Online*. Published by the Texas State Historical Association. Accessed January 12, 2015. www.tshaonline.org/handbook/online/articles/fdu01.

———. "Romero, Casimero." *Handbook of Texas Online*. Published by the Texas State Historical Association. Accessed March 21, 2015. www.tshaonline.org/handbook/online/articles/froaq.

———."Rowe, Alfred." *Handbook of Texas Online*. Published by the Texas State Historical Association. Accessed March 13, 2015. www.tshaonline.org/handbook/online/articles/froba.

Andreas, Alfred Theodore. *History of the State of Kansas*. Chicago: A. T. Andreas, 1883.

Athearn, Robert G. *Rebel of the Rockies: The Denver and Rio Grande Western Railroad*. New Haven, Conn.: Yale University Press, 1963.

———. *Westward the Briton*. New York: Scribner's, 1953.

Baker, Erma. "Twohig, John." *Handbook of Texas Online*. Published by the Texas State Historical Association. Accessed March 26, 2015. www.tshaonline.org/handbook/online/articles/ftw04.

Barkley, Roy R. "Blue Norther." *Handbook of Texas Online*. Published by the Texas State Historical Association. Accessed March 13, 2015. www.tshaonline.org/handbook/online/articles/ybb01.

"Barton Creek (Donley County)." *Handbook of Texas Online*. Published by the Texas State Historical Association. Accessed March 26, 2015. www.tshaonline.org/handbook/online/articles/rbb27.

"Battle Creek (Armstrong County)." *Handbook of Texas Online*. Published by the Texas State Historical Association. Accessed March 27, 2015. www.tshaonline.org/handbook/online/articles/rbb37.

Baughman, James P. *Charles Morgan and the Development of Southern Transportation*. Nashville, Tenn.: Vanderbilt University Press, 1968.

Beadle, J. H. "Arizona and New Mexico." *The Undeveloped West, or, Five Years in the Territories. . . .* Philadelphia: National Publishing, 1873. http://catalog.hathitrust.org/Record/001268776.

Bender, Steven W. *Greasers and Gringos: Latinos, Law, and the American Imagination*. New York: New York University Press, 2003.

Biographical History of Barton County, Kansas. Great Bend, Kans.: Tribune Publishing, 1912.

"Brackenridge, George Washington." *Handbook of Texas Online*. Published by the Texas State Historical Association. Accessed March 26, 2015. www.tshaonline.org/handbook/online/articles/fbr02.

Brand Book Containing the Brands of the Cherokee Strip and Southwestern Cattle-growers' Association, 1882. Medicine Lodge, Kans.: W. Proviso Bush, 1882.

Brayer, Herbert O. *William Blackmore: Early Financing of the Denver and Rio Grande Railway and Ancillary Land Companies 1871–1878*. Denver: Bradford-Robinson, 1949.

Bryant, Keith L., Jr., "Entering the Global Economy." In *The Oxford History of the American West*, edited by Clyde A. Milner, Carol A. O'Connor, and Martha A. Sandweiss, 195–235. New York: Oxford University Press, 1994.

———. *History of the Atchison, Topeka, and Santa Fe Railway*. New York: Macmillan Publishing, 1974.

Buckman, George Rex. "Ranches and Rancheros of the Far West." *Lippincott's Magazine of Popular Literature and Science*, 425–35. Philadephia: J. B. Lippincott, 1882.

Burton, Harley True. *A History of the JA Ranch*. New York: Argonaut Press, 1966.

Camp, Walter Mason. "Necrology, 1916." *Railway Review* 59 (December 30, 1916): 909.

Carlson, Paul H. *Texas Woollybacks: The Range Sheep and Goat Industry*. Austin: University of Texas Press, 1982.

Carriker, Robert C. *Fort Supply, Indian Territory: Frontier Outpost on the Plains*. Norman: University of Oklahoma Press, 1971.

Castleberry, May. Introduction to *Perpetual Mirage: Photographic Narratives of the Desert West*, 13–19. New York: Whitney Museum of American Art, 1996.

Chambers, Frank. *Hayden and His Men: A Selection of 108 Photographs by William Henry Jackson of the United States Geological and Geographical Survey of the Territorie*. Dillsburg, Penn.: Francis Paul Geoscience, 1988.

Cheeseman, Bruce S. "King, Richard." *Handbook of Texas Online*. Published by the Texas State Historical Association. Accessed March 26, 2015. www.tshaonline.org/handbook/online/articles/fki19.

Clarke, Graham. *The Photograph*. New York: Oxford University Press, 1997.

A Compendium *of Irish Biography*. 1878. Accessed July 22, 2015. www.libraryireland.com/biography/TheobaldMathew.php.

Conrad, Joseph. *Heart of Darkness*. New York: W. W. Norton, 2006.

Crawford, Mary G. "Texas Almanac." *Handbook of Texas Online*. Published by the Texas State Historical Association. Accessed January 30, 2015. www.tshaonline.org/handbook/online/articles/eft01.

Cutler, William G. *History of the State of Kansas*. Chicago: A. T. Andreas, 1883.

Cutrer, Thomas W. "Ord, Edward Otho Cresap." *Handbook of Texas Online*. Published by the Texas State Historical Association. Accessed March 26, 2015. www.tshaonline.org/handbook/online/articles/for01.

Davis, Kenneth S. *Kansas: A Bicentennial History*. New York: W. W. Norton, 1976.

Deutsch, Sarah. *No Separate Refuge: Culture, Class, and Gender on an Anglo-Hispanic Frontier in the American Southwest, 1880–1940*. New York: Oxford University Press, 1987.

Dinges, Bruce J. "Flipper, Henry Ossian." *Handbook of Texas Online*. Published by the Texas State Historical Association. Accessed January 12, 2015. www.tshaonline.org/handbook/online/articles/ff113.

———. "Rattlesnake Springs, Battle of." *Handbook of Texas Online*. Published by the Texas State Historical Association. Accessed January 12, 2015. www.tshaonline.org/handbook/online/articles/qfrpg.

Dobie, J. Frank. "The Alamo's Immortalization of Words." *Southwest Review*, Summer 1942, 406–10.

"Emigrants' Guides to Texas." *Handbook of Texas Online*. Published by the Texas State Historical Association. Accessed January 30, 2015.

www.tshaonline.org/handbook/online/articles/kve01.

Emmons, David M. *Garden in the Grasslands: Boomer Literature of the Central Great Plains*. Lincoln: University of Nebraska Press, 1971.

Epp, Melvin D. *The Petals of a Kansas Sunflower: A Mennonite Diaspora*. Eugene, Ore.: Wipf and Stock, 2012.

"Felicia Dorothea Browne Hemans." In *British Literature 1780–1830*, edited by Anne K. Mellor and Richard E. Matlak, 1179–80. Boston: Heinle and Heinle, 1996.

Flores, Dan L. *Caprock Canyonlands: Journey into the Heart of the Southern Plains*. Austin: University of Texas Press, 1990.

Frantz, Helen B. "Indianola Hurricanes." *Handbook of Texas Online*. Published by the Texas State Historical Association. Accessed March 26, 2015. www.tshaonline.org/handbook/online/articles/ydi01.

Fried, Stephen. *Appetite for America: How Visionary Businessman Fred Harvey Built a Railroad Hospitality Empire that Civilized the Wild West*. New York: Bantam, 2010.

Gaylord, Kristina. "Harvey County, Kansas." *Kansas Historical Society*. Accessed March 18, 2015. www.kshs.org/kansapedia/harvey-county-kansas/15295.

Grauer, Michael R. "Graphic Images of the JA Ranch." *Panhandle-Plains Historical Review* 75 (2002): 13–14.

Grohman, W. B. "Cattle Ranches in the Far West." *Fortnightly Review* 34 (1880): 34.

Hagan, William T. *Charles Goodnight: Father of the Texas Panhandle*. Norman: University of Oklahoma Press, 2007.

Haley, J. Evetts. *Charles Goodnight: Cowmen and Plainsmen*. Norman: University of Oklahoma Press, 1936.

Hamner, Laura. *The No Gun Man of Texas; A Century of Achievement, 1835–1929*. Amarillo, Tex.: self-published, 1935.

Harris, Sallie B. *Hide Town in the Texas Panhandle: 100 Years in Wheeler County and Panhandle of Texas*. Hereford, Tex.: Pioneer Book Publishers, 1968.

"Has Served Its Last Meal: Metropolitan Hotel Will Entertain No More Guests—History of the Famous Broadway Hostelry." *New York Times*, February 1, 1895.

Haywood, C. Robert. *Trails South: The Wagon-Road Economy in the Dodge City-Panhandle Region*. Norman: University of Oklahoma Press, 1986.

Hendrix, John. *If I Can Do It Horseback: A Cow-Country Sketchbook*. Austin: University of Texas Press, 1964.

Hooker, Anne W. "Noonan, George Henry." *Handbook of Texas Online*. Published by the Texas State Historical Association. Accessed March 27, 2015. www.tshaonline.org/handbook/online/articles/fn003.

Hunt, Alex. "Hunting Goodnight's Buffalo." *Panhandle-Plains Historical Review* 77 (2004): 1–13.

Ing, Janet Thompson. "Charles Whittingham the Younger and the Chiswick Press, 1852–59." Ph.D. dissertation, University of California, Berkeley, 1985.

Jackson, W. Turrentine. "British Interests in the Range Cattle Industry." In *When Grass Was King: Contributions to the Western Range Cattle Industry Study*, edited by Maurice Frink, 133–330. Boulder: University of Colorado Press, 1956.

Jones, Fayette Alexander. *New Mexico Mines and Minerals*. Santa Fe: New Mexican Printing Company, 1904.

Josephson, Matthew. *The Robber Barons*. Boston: Mariner Books, 1962.

Juhnke, James C. "Mob Violence and Kansas Mennonites in 1918." *Kansas Historical Quarterly*. Accessed August 13, 2015. www.kshs.org/p/kansas-historical-quarterly-mob-violence and kansas-mennonites-in-1918/13278.

Julyan, Robert. *The Place Names of New Mexico*. Albuquerque: University of New Mexico Press, 1996.

Kansas Historical Society. "C. B. Schmidt." *Kansapedia*. Accessed March 26, 2015. www.kshs.org/kansapedia/c-b-schmidt/17252.

———. "Pawnee Rock." *Kansapedia*. Accessed March 26, 2015. www.kshs.org/kansapedia/pawnee-rock/11905.

———. "Quantrill's Raids." *Kansapedia*. Last modified July 2013. www.kshs.org/kansapedia/quantrill-s-raids/18335.

Kerr, W. G. *Scottish Capital on the American Credit Frontier*. Denton, Tex.: Texas State Historical Association, 1976.

King, James L., ed. *History of Shawnee County, Kansas and Representative Citizens*. Chicago: Richmond and Arnold, 1905.

Kipling, Rudyard. "The White Man's Burden: The United States and the Philippine Islands." *McClure's Magazine* 12 (February 1899): 290–91.

Kleiner, Diana J. "Aransas National Wildlife Refuge." *Handbook of Texas Online*. Published by the Texas State Historical Association. Accessed March 25, 2015. www.tshaonline.org/handbook/online/articles/gka03.

Krahn, Cornelius N. "Sudermann, Leonard (1821–1900)." *Global Anabaptist Mennonite Encyclopedia Online*. 1959. http://gameo.org/index.php?title=Sudermann,_Leonard_(1821–1900)&oldid=96636.

Kyvig, David E. "Fort Elliott." *Handbook of Texas Online*. Published by the Texas State Historical Association. Accessed January 12, 2015. www.tshaonline.org/handbook/online/articles/qbf18.

Leach, Harry. *The Ship Captain's Medical Guide*. 2nd ed. London: Simpkin, 1868.

Leatherwood, Art. "Llano Estacado." *Handbook of Texas Online*. Published by the Texas State Historical Association. Accessed March 13, 2015. www.tshaonline.org/handbook/online/articles/ry102.

Levine, Philippa. "Anthropology, Colonialism, and Eugenics." In *The Oxford Handbook of The History of Eugenics*, edited by Alison Bashford and Philippa Levine. New York: Oxford University Press, 2010.

Mallory, P. A. "The Dodge City War." *Wild West*, June 1997. www.historynet.com/the-dodge-city-war.htm.

Malsch, Brownson. "Indianola, Texas." *Handbook of Texas Online*. Published by the Texas State Historical Association. Accessed March 26, 2015. www.tshaonline.org/handbook/online/articles/hvi11.

"McClellan Creek." *Handbook of Texas Online*. Published by the Texas State Historical Association. Accessed March 12, 2015. www.tshaonline.org/handbook/online/articles/rbm38.

Morgan, Richard. "Garrett, Alexander Charles." *Handbook of Texas Online*. Published by the Texas State Historical Association. Accessed March 03, 2015. www.tshaonline.org/handbook/online/articles/fga25.

Morris, John Miller. *El Llano Estacado: Exploration and Imagination on the High Plains of Texas and New Mexico, 1536–1860*. Denton, Tex.: Texas State Historical Association, 1997.

———. "When Corporations Rule the Llano Estacado." In *The Future of the Southern Plains*, edited by Sherry L. Smith, 44–94. Norman: University of Oklahoma Press, 2003.

"Mr. Nugent Townshend." Obituary. *London Times*, December 19, 1910, p. 13.

"The New Equitable Life Building." *New York Times*, January 22, 1875.

Newhall, Beaumont. *The History of Photography*. New York: Museum of Modern Art, 1982.

New Mexico: A Guide to the Colorful State. Complied by WWP. Albuquerque: Coronado Cuarto Centennial Commission, 1940.

"New York City: The New Hotel." *New York Daily Times*, September 2, 1852.

Odintz, Mark. "Buffalo Soldiers." *Handbook of Texas Online*. Published by the Texas State Historical Association. Accessed January 12, 2015. www.tshaonline.org/handbook/online/articles/qlb01.

Olson, Lee. *Marmalade and Whiskey: British Remittance Men in the West*. Golden, Colo.: Fulcrum Press, 1993.

O'Neil, Floyd A., ed. *The Southern Utes: A Tribal History*. Ignacio, Colo.: Southern Ute Tribe, 1973.

Orvell, Miles. *American Photography*. New York: Oxford University Press, 2003.

Otero, Miguel Antonio. *My Life on the Frontier, 1882–1897*. Vols. 1 and 2. Albuquerque: University of New Mexico Press, 1935, 1939.

Pagnamenta, Peter. *Prairie Fever: British Aristocrats in the American West 1830–1890*. New York: W. W. Norton, 2012.

Parssinen, Terry M. *Secret Passions, Secret Remedies: Narcotic Drugs in British Society, 1820–1930*. Manchester, UK: Manchester University Press, 1983.

Patterson, J. D., ed. *Western Dental Journal*. Vol. 11. Kansas City, Mo.: Pearson-Allendorph, 1897.

Payne, Darwin. *Owen Wister: Chronicler of the West, Gentleman of the East.* Lincoln: University of Nebraska Press, 1985.

Peterson, John Allen. "Lefors, Rufe." *Handbook of Texas Online.* Published by the Texas State Historical Association. Accessed March 21, 2015. www.tshaonline.org/handbook/online/articles/fle78.

"Photographic Views of Arizona and New Mexico." *Locke's National Monthly*, November 1874. http://babel.hathitrust.org/cgi/pt/search?q1=photographic%20views%20of%20arizona;id=uc1.b5218285;view=1up;seq=1;start=1;sz=10;page=search;orient=0.

Price, B. Byron. *Imagining the Open Range: Erwin E. Smith, Cowboy Photographer.* Fort Worth, Tex.: Amon Carter Museum, 1998.

———, and Wyman Meinzer. *Charles Goodnight: A Man for All Ages.* Benjamin, Tex.: Badlands Design and Production, 2012.

Rathjen, Frederick. *The Texas Panhandle Frontier.* Austin: University of Texas Press, 1973.

Riegel, Robert Edgar. *The Story of the Western Railroads: From 1852 through the Reign of the Giants.* Lincoln: University of Nebraska Press, 1964.

Roach, Joyce Gibson. "Goodnight, Mary Ann Dyer (Molly)." *Handbook of Texas Online.* Published by the Texas State Historical Association. Accessed March 26, 2015. www.tshaonline.org/handbook/online/articles/fgo35.

Salvato, Richard. "Moses Taylor Papers, 1793–1906." *New York Public Library Humanities and Social Sciences Library Manuscripts and Archives Division.* Accessed March 28, 2015. www.nypl.org/sites/default/files/archivalcollections/pdf/taylor.pdf.

Sánchez, Joseph P., Robert L. Spude, and Arthur R. Gómez. *New Mexico: A History.* Norman: University of Oklahoma Press, 2013.

Sandweiss, Martha A. "Dry Light: Photographic Books and the Arid West." In *Perpetual Mirage: Photographic Narratives of the Desert West*, 24. New York: Whitney Museum of American Art, 1996.

———. *Print the Legend: Photography and the American West.* New Haven, Conn.: Yale University Press, 2002.

Saul, Normal E. "The Migration of the Russian-Germans to Kansas." *Kansas Historical Quarterly.* Accessed March 26, 2015. www.kshs.org/p/kansas-historical-quarterly-the-migration-of-the-russian-germans-to-kansas/13242.

Schofield, Donald F. "Lee, William McDole." *Handbook of Texas Online.* Published by the Texas State Historical Association. Accessed January 9, 2015. www.tshaonline.org/handbook/online/articles/fle54.

Sheffy, L. F. "British Capital and the Cattle Business" In *A Compilation of Articles Published 1909–1936 by L. F. Sheffy*, 29. Canyon: West Texas State College, 1961.

Sosebee, Ronald E. "Mesquite." *Handbook of Texas Online.* Published by the Texas State Historical Association. Accessed March 25, 2015. www.tshaonline.org/handbook/online/articles/tpm01.

Southern Colorado. Canon City, Colo.: Binckley and Hartwell, 1879.

Speer, William S. *Encyclopedia of the New West.* Easley, S.C.: Southern Historical Press, 1978.

Spence, Clark C. *British Investments and the American Mining Frontier, 1860–1901.* Ithaca, N.Y.: Cornell University Press, 1958.

Stanley, F. *The Montezuma, New Mexico Story.* Pep, Tex.: self-published, 1963.

Stedman, Edmund Clarence, ed. *An American Anthology, 1787–1900.* Boston: Houghton Mifflin, 1900. Bartleby.com, 2001. www.bartleby.com/248/.

Strahorn, Robert Edmund. *Handbook of Wyoming and Guide to Black Hills and Big Horn Region.* Cheyenne: Western Press, 1877.

Stuart, Richard W., ed. "Winning the West: The Army in the Indian Wars." In *American Military History.* Vol. 1. Washington, D.C.: Center of Military History, United States Army, 2005. www.history.army.mil/books/AMH-V1/ch14.htm.

Thrapp, Dan L. *Encyclopedia of Frontier Biography.* Vol. 3. Lincoln: University of Nebraska Press, 1991.

Timmons, William H. Preface to *John F. Finerty Reports Porfirian Mexico 1879.* El Paso: Texas Western Press, 1974.

Tinkham, George Henry. *The Half Century of California Odd Fellowship.* Stockton, Calif.: Record Publishing, 1906.

Townshend, R. B. *An Officer of the Long Parliament and His Descendants.* London: Oxford University Press, 1892.

Townshend, Samuel Nugent. *Colorado*. London: Field, 1879.

———. "Notes from America." *The Field*. January 12, 1878, 31.

———. "Notes from America." *The Field*. October 5, 1878, 432.

U.S. Department of the Army. *Register of the Army of the United States for 1897*. Washington, D.C.: U.S. Government Printing Office, 1896.

Vaughn, W. E. *Sin, Sheep and Scotsmen: John George Adair and the Denyveagh Evictions, 1861*. Belfast: Appletree Press, 1983.

The Vermont Encyclopedia. Edited by John J. Duffy, Samuel B. Hand, and Ralph H. Orth. Lebanon, N.H.: University Press of New England, 2003.

Von Lintel, Amy M. "Camera to Crayon: A Reconsideration of Henri Rivière's Two Series on the Eiffel Tower." M.A. thesis, Southern Methodist University, 2003.

Waters, L. L. *Steel Trails to Santa Fe*. Lawrence: University of Kansas Press, 1950.

Wellman, Paul I., and Hal R. Taylor. "Callaghan Ranch." *Handbook of Texas Online*. Published by the Texas State Historical Association. Accessed March 26, 2015. www.tshaonline.org/handbook/online/articles/apc01.

Werner, George C. "Houston Belt and Magnolia Park Railway." *Handbook of Texas Online*. Published by the Texas State Historical Association. Accessed March 24, 2015. www.tshaonline.org/handbook/online/articles/eqh10.

———. "International–Great Northern Railroad." *Handbook of Texas Online*. Published by the Texas State Historical Association. Accessed March 3, 2015. www.tshaonline.org/handbook/online/articles/eqi04.

———. "Texas and Pacific Railway." *Handbook of Texas Online*. Published by the Texas State Historical Association. Accessed March 3, 2015. www.tshaonline.org/handbook/online/articles/eqt08.

White, Richard. *Railroaded: The Transcontinentals and the Making of Modern America*. New York: W. W. Norton, 2011.

Wieland, Terry. *Vintage British Shotguns*. East Peoria, Ill.: Versa Press, 2008.

Wilder, D. W. *The Annals of Kansas*. Topeka, Kans.: T. Dwight Thacher, 1886.

Wilson, H. T. *Historical Sketch of Las Vegas, New Mexico*. Chicago: Hotel World Publishing, 1880.

Wister, Owen. "Evolution of the Cow-Puncher." *Harper's New Monthly Magazine* 91 (September 1895): 603–604.

Woods, Lawrence. *British Gentlemen in the Wild West: The Era of the Intensely English Cowboy*. New York: Macmillan, 1989.

INDEX

Italic page numbers indicate photographs.